Reverentially Turning to God from Idols Devotional

By Gregory L. Madison

The Awe Factory

Reverentially Turning to God from Idols Devotional
Copyright © 2021 by Gregory L. Madison

THE AWE FACTORY
www.turningtoGodfromidols.com

All Scripture quotations, unless otherwise indicated, are taken from The ESV® Bible (The Holy Bible, English Standard Version®), copyright © 2001 by Crossway, a publishing ministry of Good News Publishers. Used by permission. All rights reserved.

All rights reserved. No part of this publication may be reproduced, stored in a retrieval system, or transmitted in any form or by any means – except for brief quotations in printed reviews, without the prior permission of the publisher.

Library of Congress Cataloging-in-Publication Data
Madison, Gregory L.

Reverentially Turning to God from Idols Devotional

ISBN: 9798391962472

*This book is dedicated to all who have contributed
to offer a simplistic solution to addiction
that is found in Christ Jesus!*

Introduction

The question of *why* is a tremendous theme that defines our actions. When others learn of our addiction, they often ask *why*. Many of us have asked ourselves the same question as addiction has become a stronghold.

Why is also an important question for those who want to develop new habits! The answer is found in three little words that are used in the *King James Bible* over twelve thousand times. Those three words are "unto the Lord." ***A love for God and an appreciation for His blessings will always be the strongest deterrent to addiction!***

We were made for God. Awe towards God is essential for becoming whole. Sobriety is not primarily for *your* satisfaction. I encourage you to turn to God from the idols of addiction because God deserves nothing less.

You may have heard that the fear of the Lord is the beginning of wisdom (Proverbs 9:10.) There is a reverential factor of addiction that must not be overlooked. Self-introspection will never take us where God wants us to be. The highest form of sobriety known to man is in Jesus Christ!

There are four basic reasons why a person decides to abstain from an addiction. (Only four, although they sometimes coincide with one another or can be expressed in other words.)

1. To better your life
2. To avoid the consequences
3. To better the lives of those around you
4. Out of reverence for God (which includes being in awe of Him.)

Where is also an important question! Where do you find the answers that will help you to understand and overcome addiction? Where do you find something that will replace self-centered activities that deny God and others of the person that God created you to be?

Perhaps, like me, you have searched for answers to addictions for years. It is a joy and a delight for me to share the answers that I once sought. My research discovered that you won't find any substantial Bible-based literature specifically written about addictions that were published before the late 1990s.

One thing that I have found is that As bread addresses and attacks the physical hunger, the Word of God addresses and attacks the spiritual hunger that some of us try to fill with an addiction. There are only four ways to handle addiction.

1. Suicide   (sudden death)
2. Continuance   (uncertain death)
3. Non-biblical   (dead to God)

4. Biblically-based   (some are more complete)

This devotional is based on the book *Turning to God from Idols: A Biblical Approach to Addictions*. It was my first book and it took 17 years to publish. Since then, I published about 20 more books. This devotional is designed to walk you through the process of giving your awe to God while turning from the awe of addiction.

The writing of *Turning to God from Idols* began around 1995. While I was in the men's Bible program in Kansas City I was asked by a pastor to begin a support group at our church after I had been off drugs for 6 months. We were both in agreement that the group was to be bible-based.

The pastor brought me some literature that was an adaptation of the 12 steps of *Alcoholics Anonymous* with the Scriptures thrown in. When I told the pastor that I was not comfortable with the literature, he told me to do what I thought would be best.

I kept an open mind concerning the literature and prayed to God while meditating on each of the scriptures that were in the writing. When I read the passages, I noticed that the theme of idolatry commonly surfaced. I quickly constructed an outline of my findings and drew up a draft of what the support group would look like. Before we had a chance to begin the support group, I started using crack again.

After living on the street for a while, I asked to be admitted to *Opportunity Farm* away from the city. Once on the farm, I was led by God in a more intense study of the outline that I had constructed for the support group in Kansas City. The leading passage that I chose to describe the process of breaking free of addiction through Christ is found in 1 Thessalonians 1:9.

> For they themselves shew of us what manner of entering in we had unto you, and how ye turned to God from idols to serve the living and true God. *KJV*

Though we each had work assignments at *Opportunity Farm*, I spent all my free time writing and studying. It was at this time that God began to show me that the issue of reverence for God is a huge part of sobriety/abstinence. I was amazed over how God had allowed me to construct an outline on reverence years before I even thought about using drugs.

I remained at *Opportunity Farm* for about five months until the first draft was done and went back home to Cleveland, Ohio. The work was originally titled *Idolatry Assassination*. Shortly after returning to Cleveland, I started using crack again. My next opportunity to seriously pursue my writing began in 1999 while at another Christian facility.

For the next ten years, my life was so unstable that I never had the opportunity to do any serious work on *Turning to God from Idols*. To be honest, I wasn't even interested most of the time because I had become more immersed in drug use than ever. Yet, God was very gracious towards me in allowing me to discover some of the finest writing that has ever been written on addictions.

I became familiar with *Addictions: A Banquet in the Grave* by Dr. Edward T. Welch within this period. I was so delighted that Dr. Welch's writing mirrors my own that I cried in thanks to God that He had honored my prayer of bringing others with a sounder approach to addictions. I read *Addictions: A Banquet in the Grave* no less than six times.

My next revision for *Turning to God from Idols* took place in 2012 after a year of sobriety and moving to the city of Memphis, Tennessee from Cleveland, Ohio. I finally published *Turning to God from idols* in 2018. When I began to publish, I made a vow to my readers similar to the one the Apostle Paul made to the Christians at Ephesus.

And how I kept back nothing that was profitable unto you.
Acts 20:20a

January 1

20/20 Vision

For I delivered to you as of first importance what I also received: that Christ died for our sins in accordance with the Scriptures, that He was buried, that He was raised on the third day in accordance with the Scriptures. 1 Corinthians 15:3-4

In 2020, my goal was to maintain a 20/20 vision. But, I now see that a 20/20 vision is necessary at all times (especially in our treatment of addiction.) If you are reading this, you have lived to join God on the first day of a new year. He has been here all along. He dwells in eternity.

The Apostle Paul describes what is of first importance for the new year and the years after. What is first is given precedence. And, first establishes order. What is first often determines what is to follow. What we designate as first is what we set our sights on (vision.)

For as long as I live, one of the first things my step-father taught me proves to be true. What he said was that "you can tell a lot about a person by asking them what they think of Jesus." How we see Jesus determines how we deal with addictions. Jesus has given us all we need to have a vital life with God.

First often indicates a beginning. All our problems began in the *Garden of Eden* when we inherited sin. Sin is the only thing that can separate you from God. A disease cannot separate you from God (that's just one of the reasons that I do not believe addiction to be a disease.)

What we call first is often given priority. Our verses indicate that the first thing that Paul discussed with the Corinthians was the most important. "First aid" can be used to describe Paul's concern as well as how we handle addictions. But, it takes more than just a Band-Aid to treat addictions (it takes the blood of Christ.)

The vision shared in First Corinthians 15:3-4 applied to addiction is so tremendous that I can only list a few (without references or comments.) All of these are necessary for understanding and conquering addiction.

1. A statement from God
2. Proof of how much God loves you
3. Proof of how much God hates sin
4. Reveals the extent that God has gone to in providing the means of fellowship with Himself
5. Exhibits the power of Christ
6. Shows how Jesus was tempted as we are yet without sin
7. It explains how Jesus alone conquered sin and death

January 2

Looking out for number one!

And they sing the song of Moses, the servant of God, and the song of the Lamb, saying, "Great and amazing are your deeds, O Lord God the Almighty! Just and true are your ways, O King of the nations! Who will not fear, O Lord, and glorify your name? Revelation 15:3-4a

As you begin the new year, you want to make sure that you look out for number one! This is the philosophy of a Christ-centered approach to addiction as well as a secular approach to addiction. The only difference is who we choose as our number one. No one can argue that addictions are self-seeking. Some methods of handling addiction are like adding more water to a flood.

As we expose and dispose of addictions, we must do so in a manner that is *biblically* correct to give unto God the glory that is due to His name and to establish a formula that would be our greatest good. The root of addiction is when *we* prescribe what is good outside of God and His Word.

> "There once was in man a true happiness of which now remain to him only the mark and empty trace, which he in vain tries to fill from all his surroundings, seeking from things absent the help he does not obtain in things present. But these are all inadequate because the infinite abyss can only be filled by an infinite and immutable object, that is to say, only by God Himself." –*Pensees*, Pascal

What's so great about addiction? There must be something that leads people back to them time and again despite the consequences. Have you ever considered the amount of praise, glory, honor, sacrifice, awe, and trust that are given to addictions?

Along with the dominion that we give to addictions, these contribute to and define worship. The old English word for worship was "worthship." It meant that we express the worth of whatever or whoever we worship. In the course of your reading, I will offer many definitions for addiction.

> "Arising out of our alienation from the Living God, addiction is bondage to the rule of a substance, activity, or state of mind, which then becomes the center of life, defending itself from the truth so that even bad consequences don't bring repentance, and leading to further estrangement from God's kingdom." -*Addictions a Banquet in the Grave*, Edward T. Welch

Are you looking out for number one?

In the beginning

In the beginning, God created the heavens and the earth. The earth was without form and void, and darkness was over the face of the deep. Genesis 1:1-2a

In the beginning God (*Elohim*) created [by forming from nothing] the heavens and the earth. The earth was formless and void *or* a waste and emptiness, and darkness was upon the face of the deep *Amplified Version*

Genesis 1:2 describes the peril of addiction. Some commentators say that before the creation there was only chaos. Addictions are not only formless, void, wasteful, and empty, but dark; they are chaotic as well. God is not a God of confusion.

For God is not a God of confusion but of peace. 1 Corinthians 14:33

Are you an orderly person? God is! Jesus was the most orderly, trustworthy person that ever lived on this earth! How many of us live a life that is out of order? Addiction is a worship disorder! There must be some order in the way that we combat addictions!

"Addictions are ultimately a disorder of worship. Will we worship ourselves and our own desires or will we worship the true God?" - *Addictions a Banquet in the Grave*, Edward T. Welch

One of the goals of reverence is pleasing God. In *Turning to God from Idols*, I said that this can be summed up with the words "unto the Lord." Jesus sought to please the Father above all else. ***Your reverence for God will determine where you look for the answers to addiction and how hard you search!***

My son, if you receive my words and treasure up my commandments with you, making your ear attentive to wisdom and inclining your heart to understanding; yes, if you call out for insight and raise your voice for understanding, if you seek it like silver and search for it as for hidden treasures, then you will understand the fear of the LORD and find the knowledge of God. Proverbs 2:1-5

Why not get your order from above?

January 4

Let me be clear!

Seeing then that we have such hope, we use great plainness of speech. 2 Corinthians 3:12 KJV

"Let me be clear," is a phrase that began to surface along with President Joe Biden's presidential campaign in 2020. Just as Biden's clarity helped to win his presidential election, the Word of God can win our hearts to God's rule. The superiority of the Scriptures to address the darkness of addictions is evident when we look at the relevancy of 2 Peter 1:19.

We have also a more <u>sure</u> word of prophecy; whereunto ye do well that ye take heed, as unto a light that shineth in a dark place, until the day dawn, and the day star arise in your hearts. 2 Peter 2:19 KJV

According to *Strong's Bible Dictionary,* the Greek word that Peter uses that is interpreted as "sure" in the *King James Version* means "stable, firm, of force, steadfast, and trusty." Not only do we find these qualities in the Word of God, but these are the qualities that we find in the Person of God.

While I do not fully embrace the philosophies of *Alcoholics Anonymous,* I agree, as they, that alcohol is "cunning, baffling, and powerful." In answer, "the testimony of the Lord is sure, making wise the simple" (Psalms 19:7b).

To think of God as the kind of God that has created us but does not give us the instructions that we need to survive, and even prosper and be at peace, is an irreverent and distorted view of God. Here is yet another question for us to consider! *Is God worthy of being heard?* Who would dare say no?

In *Addictions: A Banquet in the Grave,* Edward T. Welch asks his readers, "Do you have a good grasp on the wealth of biblical material that speaks precisely to the modern problems of addictions? Can you go through any book in scripture, even if it doesn't mention alcohol, food, or sex, and see how it speaks to addictions?"

Using the Word of God to expose and dispose of addiction is an act of worship. When we share the Word of God to confront addiction, we see God as worthy of being heard. **Worship** was originally spelled "worthship" and it means to express worth. The fear of the Lord cannot leave us indifferent to the Word of God; when we fear him, we sense the infinite weightiness of His Word.

Feel the weight of His Word!
It infinitely outweighs addiction!

January 5

Choose!

Now therefore fear the LORD and serve him in sincerity and in faithfulness. Put away the gods that your fathers served beyond the River and in Egypt, and serve the LORD. And if it is evil in your eyes to serve the LORD, choose this day whom you will serve, whether the gods your fathers served in the region beyond the River, or the gods of the Amorites in whose land you dwell. But as for me and my house, we will serve the LORD. Joshua 24:14-15

Irreverence for God leads only to calamity and confusion. Without God, there is no order or direction. When we choose to ignore, slight, and despise the Lord we are placing ourselves in a precarious situation. **A refusal to revere God is both irrational and insane**.

Not only that but there are also degrees or amounts of reverence each program or individual decides. I cannot overemphasize the relevance of reverence. Addiction is just one of the ways that we choose to reject Christ (who is personified as wisdom, while addictions are foolish.)

Early in my drug addiction, I would often find myself indulging unexpectedly and wondering afterward how I had fallen into such a state. It was after a few years that my indulgences were not so unexpected and rather intentional.

I had become wholehearted in my drug use. To be wholehearted is to be committed. Our wholeheartedness functions much like the cruise control of an automobile. It is our heart that drives us to where we choose.

> "The mind as it reasons, discerns and judges; the emotions as they like or dislike; the conscience as it determines and warns; and the will as it chooses or refuses—are all together called the heart."
> -Puritan John Owen

Our priorities are indicative of our sanity! You can be free of whatever addiction has bothered you and still not be sane. The soundest approach to addiction is to first bridge the gap between us and God.

The ultimate answer to addiction is to choose God over everything else. We come to our senses as we choose what is of the greatest value. Can you name anything of greater value than being in one accord with God? The biggest question that you must answer concerning addiction is whether God is worthy of your soul.

> For what does it profit a man to gain the whole world and forfeit his soul? Mark 8:36

January 6

Start with the heart!

For where your treasure is, there your heart your wishes, your desires; that on which your life centers will be also. Matthew 6:21 *Amplified Version*

Despite all of the scientific studies and theories, addiction always has been and ever will be an issue of the heart. That's why the chapters to my workbook *Addictions Tugging* are all related to the heart.

Have you ever had a heart attack? As quiet as it is kept, every one of us has! *If you have ever been tempted and/or overcome by anything that has tried to pull you from God (or at least what is decent and honorable), then you have had a heart attack.*

The titles of the chapter in *Addictions Tugging* are *The heart of the matter, Where your treasure is ..., A heart condition, Heart failure, An empty heart, A stony heart, A divided heart, and A conditioned heart.* In the days to come, we will discuss each of these, but for now, I want you to know that God desires to change our hearts.

I will give them a heart to know that I am the LORD, and they shall be my people and I will be their God, for they shall return to me with their whole heart. Jeremiah 24:7

2 Corinthians 5:17 says that if anyone is in Christ they are a new creation. God is ever reaching out to us all to make us new. It goes beyond what some call recovery because God wants to make us into what we weren't before, give us things that we have never had, take us places that we have never been, and show us things that we have never seen.

God doesn't want you to be normal. God wants you to be different! He wants you to be like Himself. In a word- unselfish. Who would argue that addiction is a selfish practice? *Your degree of sobriety reflects how much you are like Christ.* And the amazing thing is that God wants this more than you ever could because He wants your fellowship!

"Love is beautiful, but it is also terrible—terrible in its determination to allow nothing blemished or unworthy to remain in the beloved." -*Hinds' Feet on High Places,* Hannah Hurnard

What is the condition of your heart? What controls your heart? Are you ready for God to renew and strengthen your heart?

January 7

What's in your heart?

The LORD said to him, "What is that in your hand?" Exodus 4:2

What is in our hearts is often in our hands. Addictions are an example. God has allowed us to embrace the Word of God to combat the addictions that not only wage war against our souls but give Him great displeasure. The Word of God conditions your heart, soul, and mind with every reason to love God more and more fully.

There is no need for anyone to go outside of the Word of God for answers to addiction. If the Word of God had nothing to say about addictions then God would not have created us! The Scriptures have more to say about addiction than most people realize.

Every program has its benefits. Some are more relevant than others. If you don't address the spiritual issues of addiction (from the very start) then you will always lack the level of sobriety that is necessary for becoming whole.

> All scripture is given by inspiration of God, and is **profitable** for doctrine, for reproof, for correction, for instruction in righteousness: That the man of God may be perfect, thoroughly furnished unto all good works. 2 Timothy 3:16-17 *KJV*

The Word of God reasons with us. Through the aid of the Holy Spirit convictions are formed. Conviction is defined as **a settled persuasion**, the state of being **convinced**. The Word of God reveals the Living Word of God to us (that's Christ.) The Word of God purifies our hearts so that we can be changed more into the image of Christ.

Sobriety in Christ is the highest form of sobriety known to man. *There has never been anyone as sane and sober as Jesus (nor will there ever be.)* That's why John 3:36 says, "Whoever believes in the Son has eternal life; whoever does not obey the Son shall not see life, but the wrath of God remains on him."

There was never anyone as intimate with the Father as Jesus. God wants that for you as well. *The reason that God created us is so that we could have the highest degree of intimacy/fellowship with Him, radiating His image and likeness and thereby becoming a blessing to others in whatever way He chooses.*

The only answer to addiction approved by God is for Him to make us more like Christ! Every other method is self-righteous.

January 8

Before the Lord

Search me, O God, and know my heart: try me, and know my thoughts: And see if there be any wicked way in me, and lead me in the way everlasting. Psalms 139:23-24 *KJV*

You'll never reach the level of sobriety that God wants for you unless you are searched by God. Unfortunately, many settle for less. What does this say about us? Is this not an indication of our apathy toward God? I have heard it said that apathy is the opposite of love, rather than hatred.

I love the way that the illustration of houses can be used to typify our relationship with God! The type of sobriety that God desires is that He is allowed to enter your entire house with a search warrant and remove every bit of dirt and debris, remodel, and renovate as He chooses, and restore what has been stolen, broken, forfeited, or lost and rule forevermore.

> "Yet another element of reverencing which is contained in all that has been mentioned is that the fear of the Lord is before the Lord. Can you think of anything more sobering, more serious than to go before the Lord? To be in the presence of God can be frightening, but it can also be comforting. To stand before God with a clear conscious is a matter of great strength. Going before the Lord requires transparency that is impossible apart from sincerity." -*The Fear of the Almighty,* Madison

To stand before God with a clear conscience is one of the greatest practices for conquering addictions. I cannot overemphasize that intimacy with God is one of the major themes of *Turning to God from Idols*. Have you called upon Him to cleanse you of your sins? Don't fool yourself, <u>apart from the blood of Christ you don't even have a connection with God!</u>

To stand in agreement with God gives us strength and confidence that we will not find elsewhere. But, most of all, God desires your presence before Him. He longs to bless you beyond your imagination!

A.N. Martin says that the main ingredients of reverencing God are "correct concepts of the character of God, a widespread sense of the presence of God, and a constant awareness of our obligations to God." If you investigate addictions, you will find a deficiency in each ingredient.

For the eyes of the LORD run to and fro throughout the whole earth, to show Himself strong on behalf of those whose heart is loyal to Him. 2 Chronicles 16:9 *NKJV*

January 9

Reverential Reasoning

> Be not wise in your own eyes; fear the LORD, and turn away from evil. Proverbs 3:7

Just as sure as you have been created in the image of God, you are capable of reasoning. God has been reasoning with Man from the beginning of creation. Just look at the first three chapters of Genesis! The Scriptures tell us how God reasoned with Israel during Isaiah's time.

> Come now, and let us <u>reason</u> together, saith the Lord.
> Isaiah 1:18a *KJV*

Many other passages refer to reasoning as well as understanding. Your reasoning is essential to <u>sobriety</u>. Active addictions is sometimes labeled as insanity. Does insanity reason? Cool reasoning is just one of the definitions of sobriety.

In a biblical sense, the word sober means to be discreet, watchful, of a sound mind, humble, and disciplined. Sobriety compels you to think about what *really* matters. It can be said that Jesus Christ was and always will be the sanest person that ever lives. Perhaps, this is why He said to seek first the kingdom of God and His righteousness, and all of our other needs would be met (Matthew 6:33).

500 years before Jesus was even born the prophet Isaiah said, "The Spirit of the LORD will rest on Him- the Spirit of wisdom and of understanding, the Spirit of counsel and of power, the Spirit of knowledge and of the fear of the LORD- and He will delight in the fear of the LORD" (Isaiah 11:2-3a).

This is just what every addict needs! In an article that is titled *The Distinguishing Feature of Christian Counseling*, Dr. Wayne A. Mack expresses the change that describes true sobriety. Just as you were made for God, He wants to remake you in Christ!

> "Christ-centered counseling involves understanding the nature and courses of our human difficulties, understanding the ways we are unlike Christ in our values, aspirations, desires, thoughts, feelings, choices, attitudes, actions, and responses. Resolving those sin-related difficulties includes being redeemed and justified through Christ, receiving God's forgiveness through Christ, and acquiring from Christ the enabling power to replace unChristlike (sinful) patterns of life with Christlike, godly ones." -*The Distinguishing Feature of Christian Counseling*, Dr. Wayne A. Mack

January 10

Are you serious?

> And as if it had been a light thing for him to walk in the sins of Jeroboam the son of Nebat, he took for his wife Jezebel the daughter of Ethbaal king of the Sidonians, and went and served Baal and worshiped him. 1 Kings 16:31

If you don't think that the Bible speaks plainly about addiction then think about the implications of 1 Kings 16:31! Addiction is to be taken seriously. Dr. Tony Evans said that reverencing God means that we take Him seriously. One of the definitions for sobriety is to be serious.

Asking God to search you is serious business. A search warrant is a legal document authorizing a police officer or other official to enter and search premises. God has every right to search our hearts, as our Creator and Sustainer! But how sobering is God's search! It requires that we go before the Lord.

The search that God issues is indispensable to the elimination of the idols of addictions. God wants to free us of everything that is not of Himself because it will enslave and corrupt us, as well as damage our relationship with Himself and others. The love of Christ compels us to seriously consider the invitation that God has made to all.

> "And taking your life as a whole, with all your innumerable choices, all your life long you are slowly turning this central thing either into a heavenly creature or into a hellish creature: either into a creature that is in harmony with God, and with other creatures, and with itself, or else into one that is in a state of war and hatred with God, and with its fellow-creatures, and with itself." -*Mere Christianity*, C. S. Lewis

> For you have not come to what may be touched, a blazing fire and darkness and gloom and a tempest and the sound of a trumpet and a voice whose words made the hearers beg that no further messages be spoken to them. ... See that you do not refuse him who is speaking. For if they did not escape when they refused him who warned them on earth, much less will we escape if we reject him who warns from heaven. ...Therefore let us be grateful for receiving a kingdom that cannot be shaken, and thus let us offer to God acceptable worship, with reverence and awe, for our God is a consuming fire. Hebrews 12:18-19, 25, 28-29

Sobriety in its simplicity is not letting anything come between you and God!

Abide in Christ- abiding in truth

> So Jesus said to the Jews who had believed him, "If you abide in my word, you are truly my disciples, and you will know the truth, and the truth will set you free." John 8:31-32

A divided heart is deceived. Deception can only be dispelled through discernment. But before discernment, repentance is needed for the addict and/or those who are outside of Christ. When was the last time that you went to a meeting for addictions and heard about repentance?

Repentance is a word that is connected with God. It is a more accurate and concise explanation of the phenomenon of turning to God from the idols of addiction and turning to Christ than *recovery*. You won't hear anything about repentance in an environment that wants little or no God.

> "Dozens of people go to Him to be cured of some one particular sin which they are ashamed of (like masturbation or physical cowardice) or which is obviously spoiling daily life (like bad temper or drunkenness.) Well, He will cure it all right: but He will not stop there. That may be all you asked; but if once you call Him in, He will give you the full treatment." -C.S. Lewis

Abiding in Christ gives you the mind of Christ. You are thereby under the influence of Christ. Being baptized into Christ removes the deformity that we have before God from birth and gives us the power of the Spirit to conquer our dysfunction.

> John answered them all, "I baptize you with water. But one who is more powerful than I will come, the straps of whose sandals I am not worthy to untie. He will baptize you with the Holy Spirit and fire." Luke 3:16

A friend once explained how being baptized not only means to be immersed, but it means "to be brought under the power of." As an example, he mentioned how when you immerse a cloth into a pool of red dye, the cloth is brought under the power of the red dye.

One of the Hebrew words for an idol is a lie. If I am under the influence of an addiction, I am under the power of a lie. Outside of God, there is no sanity. Addictions are just one expression of insanity. Addictions go beyond our understanding without the truth of God unmasking their deception.

It is impossible for someone who is abiding in Christ to relapse!

January 12

Reason, repent, rejoice!

> ... our gospel came to you not only in word, but also in power and in the Holy Spirit and with full conviction. ... And you became imitators of us and of the Lord, for you received the word in much affliction, with the joy of the Holy Spirit, ... For they themselves report concerning us the kind of reception we had among you, and how you turned to God from idols to serve the living and true God, and to wait for his Son from heaven, whom he raised from the dead, Jesus who delivers us from the wrath to come. 1 Thessalonians 1:5a, 6, 9-10

Turning to God from idols is a simple process for dealing with addictions biblically. But, as the saying goes, it is "easier said than done." Reasoning, repentance, and rejoicing are all that are necessary for you to live a life that is pleasing to God. These three phases are strengthened by reverence for God.

A Biblical approach to addictions, in its simplest form, is a proclamation of Jesus Christ being worthy of the throne of your life above all else because of the blood that He shed on the cross and the fact that He is KING OF KINGS AND LORD OF LORDS. In my opinion, the most ingenious approach to addictions is to start by viewing them as idols

> "Ever since the fall of man in the Garden of Eden man has listened to his desires more than his reasoning. When God created man, the reason, the emotion, and the will all worked in perfect harmony. Reason led way in the understanding of God's will, the will consented to God's will, and the emotions delighted in doing it. But with the entrance of sin into man's soul, these three faculties began to work at cross purposes to one another and to God." -Puritan Thomas Manton

Reason, repentance, and rejoicing are found in every program that deals with addictions, in one form or another (although it may be expressed in other words.) The *degrees* of reason, repentance, and rejoicing are different for each program as well.

It is in reasoning with God, ourselves, and others that we can see that addictions are but worthless idols. They are only given power when we imagine them to be greater than God. Reasoning gives us the basis for turning from addictions, repentance is the response to our reasoning, and rejoicing comes from having unity with God.

Good, better, best, never let it rest. Til your good is better, and your better is best -St. Jerome

January 13

Thinking soberly

> For by the grace given to me I say to everyone among you not to think of himself more highly than he ought to think, but to think with sober judgment, each according to the measure of faith that God has assigned. Romans 12:3

There are degrees of sobriety, just as there are degrees of sanity and godliness. Your degree of sobriety is related to how you see God. Addictions are empowered by a low estimation of God and self-elevation. Addictions are fueled by the fallacy that I am wiser than God.

No matter what someone thinks about the origin of addiction, everyone agrees that addictions are focused on one individual. This is one of the aspects that prove the idolatry of addiction.

> "We usually do not think of pride as an idol. And yet the inclination to place one's self in the place of God is endemic to human nature. All human beings have the natural inclination to think a lot more about themselves than they think about God. It is, therefore, true that human beings in practice think and act as if they themselves are more important than God. Thus, if thinking and acting are valid indicators, human beings attribute more worth to themselves than to God." –*Idolatry and the Hardening of the Heart*, Edward P. Meadors

Meadors goes on to say that "repentance thus occurs out of an awareness that one's true value and worth is only discovered in a peaceful and honest relationship with one's Creator and not from servitude to one's own creation—whether material or mental." Once again, we see the issue of reverence as a significant factor in our transformation. Because with every addiction we place ourselves above God.

Humility is the frame of mind a man possesses who is fully aware of his nothingness apart from God and his sinfulness that would eternally separate him from God were not God willing to rescue him. Humility starts with being born again. We need the nature of Christ (as He was more humble than anyone.)

> "The quality of our sobriety insists on God's rights. The question of whether God has the right to rule our lives comes with every temptation. When we insist on our 'so-called' rule, we are irreverently attempting to cheat God of what is His." -*Why Not Get High!*, Gregory L. Madison

January 14

Priorities

> One thing have I asked of the LORD, that will I seek after: that I may dwell in the house of the LORD all the days of my life, to gaze upon the beauty of the LORD and to inquire in his temple.
> Psalm 27:4

Awe determines our priorities. ***How we view God determines whether we turn from idols.*** We do not gravitate to people and things that we do not find attractive in some form or fashion. I remember meeting a woman with a skin disease that most would view as unattractive and yet her baby boy saw her as the most beautiful woman in the world. It was the love of that mother that gave the boy such joy and glee.

The love of God is unimaginably more attractive than a mother's love. I am living proof that, despite our ugliness, God loves us. Calvary is the *greatest* proof! 1 John 4:10 says "In this is love, not that we have loved God but that He loved us and sent His Son to be the propitiation for our sins."

Looking for life in an idol is beneath you. A god is distinguished by its rule or dominion. If it has power over you, then it is 'above' you. If it controls you it is your god! The cause of addiction lies within its definition (idolatry.) The attractiveness that these idols pretend to offer is alluring outside of the influence of God.

> "This is the essence of temptation…We will meditate on truth, inflaming our desires for God; or we will meditate upon lies, inflaming our desires for things that will become idolatrous replacements for Him." -*Changed Into His Image,* Jim Berg

All the science in the world cannot solve the problems that we have with addictions. While you may turn from one idolatrous addiction, unless you turn to the true and living God, then you will seek another idol that may be more socially acceptable and/or less costly.

Addictions reveal our priorities. Repentance insists on the proper priorities while restoring order and manageability. In *My Beloved Addiction*, Jeff Mullins says, "When you become a follower of Jesus, you have a new life, and that includes a new outlook, new purposes, and new priorities. The new purposes in life become the basis for new behaviors."

I challenge anyone to give me an answer that explains addiction more clearly and plainly than idolatry and a solution that is more relevant than reverencing God!

Understanding

> There is none that understandeth, There is none that seeketh after God. Romans 3:11 *KJV*

Understanding brings unity. Erroneous thought could be one of the leading causes of addiction. Ever since the Fall of Man, our thinking has been deficient. And even at his best, man cannot attain the infinitude of God's understanding.

> Seek the LORD while he may be found; call upon him while he is near; let the wicked forsake his way, and the unrighteous man his thoughts; let him return to the LORD, that he may have compassion on him, and to our God, for he will abundantly pardon. For my thoughts are not your thoughts, neither are your ways my ways, declares the LORD. For as the heavens are higher than the earth, so are my ways higher than your ways and my thoughts than your thoughts. Isaiah 55:6-9

> "We who have been in the habit of putting our trust in an addiction, need to develop and maintain faith in God. Faith comes by hearing and hearing by the Word of God (Romans 10:17). As quiet as it is kept (though some may deny it) addicts have a small view of God. Addicts have trouble seeing how good God is. Addicts don't understand how merciful and forgiving God is. Addicts have trouble believing that God has all power. It is because of this deficiency of faith that people lean upon their *own* understanding and put their trust in idolatrous addictions." –*Bible Verses Addictions,* Madison (intro. to each volume)

In Proverbs 2:10-11, Solomon said: "When wisdom enters your heart, and knowledge is pleasant to your soul, discretion will preserve you; **understanding** will keep you." Ignorance harbors pride leading to a hard heart and estrangement from God as well as others.

Ignorance keeps us from understanding the nature of addictions, God, and ourselves. Whenever you turn to addiction, you are leaning on your own understanding. ***To lean on your own understanding could be the most basic definition of insanity.*** All of your pride must be exchanged for the humility of Christ. As Christ has the spirit of understanding, He shares it with His own (Isaiah 11:2).

> Be not as the horse, or as the mule, which have no <u>understanding</u>: whose mouth must be held in with bit and bridle. Psalm 32:9a *KJV*

January 16

Beyond Understanding

Not unto us, O Lord, not unto us, but unto Thy name give glory, for Thy mercy, and for Thy truth's sake. Wherefore should the heathen say, Where is now their God? But our God is in the heavens: He hath done whatsoever He hath pleased. Their idols are silver and gold, the work of men's hands. They have mouths, but they speak not: eyes have they, but they see not: They have ears, but they hear not: noses have they, but they smell not: They have hands, but they handle not: feet have they, but they walk not: neither speak they through their throat. They that make them are like unto them; so is every one that trusteth in them. O Israel, trust thou in the Lord: He is their help and their shield. Psalms 115:1-9 *KJV*

Addictions go beyond our understanding without the truth of God unmasking their deception.

The issue of addiction can be very complicated. The reason behind this is that you are dealing with something foreign. The element of addiction is an instrument of the devil. Dealing with an addiction can be difficult because the devil is a liar and a deceiver. Gaining understanding from God is essential to your sobriety.

Cool Hand Luke is a 1967 American prison drama film directed by Stuart Rosenberg, starring Paul Newman and featuring George Kennedy in an Oscar-winning performance. Newman stars in the title role as Luke, a prisoner in a Florida prison camp who refuses to submit to the system. The most famous line in the movie is where the warden says to Luke, "What we have here is failure to communicate."

> The natural person does not accept the things of the Spirit of God, for they are folly to him, and he is not able to understand them because they are spiritually discerned. 1 Corinthians 2:14

Because Adam disobeyed God, sin entered the world. "Thus, our reason [or understanding] was darkened (Ephesians 4:18), our desires were entangled (Ephesians 2:3), and our wills perverted (John 5:40). With the new birth, our reason is again enlightened, our affections and desires redirected, and our wills subdued. Yet, it doesn't happen all of a sudden; it's something we grow into" (Jerry Bridges).

> They are darkened in their understanding and separated from the life of God because of the ignorance that is in them due to the hardening of their hearts. Ephesians 4:18

January 17

The voice of addiction

> And Balak said to Balaam, "Did I not send to you to call you? Why did you not come to me? Am I not able to honor you?" Numbers 22:37

The voice of Balak is like the voice of addiction. **Balak is demanding answers from Balaam as addiction demands attention.** Balak is persistent. Yet, he has no right to Balaam's allegiance. He is an ungodly man who has devised an ungodly plan against the people of God as those who sell and promote some of the addictions that our society embraces.

Balak's first two questions to Balaam in Numbers 22:37 reveals his arrogance. Arrogance and pride go hand-in-hand. Just as Balak thought that he could control Balaam, you may think that you are in control when pursuing addictions. Balaam answers Balak with a question.

> Balaam said to Balak, "Behold, I have come to you! Have I now any power of my own to speak anything? The word that God puts in my mouth, that must I speak." Numbers 22:38

I love to read how *behold* is used in Scripture because it often is drawing our attention to God. While our society is faced with the treachery of addiction, you need to recognize the power and authority of the Lord Jesus Christ. Balak is also like those who devise schemes against addiction that exclude Christ. John the Baptist introduced Jesus while using the word *behold*!

> The next day he saw Jesus coming toward him, and said, "Behold, the Lamb of God, who takes away the sin of the world!" John 1:29

Balaam's answer to Balak is much like the answer that you can use when addiction tries to control you. Balaam was telling Balak that his focus was aimed toward God. Balaam said that he honored the Word of God as you must do when confronted with the demands of addiction.

Balak was as irreverent as Pharaoh when he asked Moses, "who is the Lord that I should obey Him?" (Exodus 5:2) Neither Balak nor Pharaoh had reverence for God. Your determination to live by the Word of God is based on the reverence that you have for God. Every program that promises freedom from addiction is measured by it's reverence.

The truth of the matter is that many programs are just as self-seeking as active addiction. It's the reason that so many chase other addictions that cause less damage so long as they are not seeking God..

January 18

Why I get high!

> Because you have said, "We have made a covenant with death, and with Sheol we have an agreement, when the overwhelming whip passes through it will not come to us, for we have made lies our refuge, and in falsehood we have taken shelter." Isaiah 28:15

What gets you high? What do you get a kick out of? What turns you on? What are the things that give you great pleasure? Is there anything in your life that you are so thrilled about that you would risk your life for it? What are the things that you are willing to defend?

In his booklet *Just One More*, Dr. Edward T. Welch offers a list of *perceived* (or at best temporary) assets. He says that "even with all the associated misery, people drink because on some level drinking does something for them." Dr. Welch says, "their drinking is purposeful." It may allow a brief opportunity to:

- Forget
- Punish
- Cure self-consciousness and timidity
- Avoid pain
- Fill holes in one's image
- Manage emotions
- Prove to yourself that you can do what you want
- Keep loneliness at bay

Why did I get high? I got high because I have faith in my addiction! Can you trust an addiction? Does it do just what you ask? A more relevant question would be if you do just what the addiction asks! One of the characteristics that we look for in objects and individuals is faithfulness (or reliability.) Reliability is also a characteristic of worship.

Along with euphoria, addictive habits bring a sense of comfort. Just how important is that comfort? The sacrifices that are made for addictions are an indication of how important our comfort is. The irony is that whatever comfort we think we have in an addiction, in the long run, they cause trouble and *discomfort*.

I got high because I was looking for satisfaction. At what point do you turn to addiction while seeking satisfaction? What does your dissatisfaction say about your relationship with God?

> Thus says the LORD: "What wrong did your fathers find in me that they went far from me, and went after worthlessness, and became worthless?" Jeremiah 2:5

January 19

I love me some me!

> But understand this, that in the last days there will come times of difficulty. For people will be lovers of self, lovers of money, proud, arrogant, abusive, disobedient to their parents, ungrateful, unholy, heartless, unappeasable, slanderous, without self-control, brutal, not loving good, treacherous, reckless, swollen with conceit, lovers of pleasure rather than lovers of God.
> 2 Timothy 3:1-4

I got high because I love myself to death! While many believe that addictions express self-hatred, I see addiction as being an expression of self-love. Do you think that people indulge so that they can experience the negative consequences of addictions? No. They wish that they could have an addiction without negative consequences.

People don't participate in addiction to experience negative consequences. (Even people who are addicted to harming themselves think that it is going to make them feel good.) It is no mystery that addictions are selfish. Every "fix" is for me (nobody else.)

We have no problem loving ourselves. We *do* have a problem loving God and others! We love ourselves to death! That's why many people become suicidal while under the influence of an addiction. If they cannot find a way to continue feeding their addiction and still function normally, or if they are unhappy about the consequences of the addiction and cannot see a way out, then *out of self-love*, they contemplate suicide.

There is nothing wrong with self-love. But loving yourself at the expense of others demotes their God-given value and is a reflection of what you think of God. Everyone is born with a natural love for themselves. *Loving God and loving others as God does is supernatural.*

> But the fruit of the Spirit is love, joy, peace, patience, kindness, goodness, faithfulness, gentleness, self-control; against such things there is no law. And those who belong to Christ Jesus have crucified the flesh with its passions and desires. Galatians 5:22-24

If you love God then the Scriptures say that you will naturally love others. What prevents you from loving others is your love for the world. One of the qualities of love is an interest in who or what you love.

Your life is a gift from God.
What you do with your life is a gift to Him.

January 20

Praise and worship

> You shall fear the Lord your God; you shall serve Him, and to Him you shall hold fast, and take oaths in His name. He is your praise, and He is your God, who has done for you these great and awesome things which your eyes have seen.
> Deuteronomy 10:20-21

What you praise is often in your thoughts and conversation. You have good thoughts and you speak well of whoever or whatever you praise. During my years of drug treatment, I would often hear people being told to be careful not to glorify their addiction (while sharing their experiences.)

What you praise influences you. Praise is indicative of what is important to you. For instance, Food is important to me. I think about it. I speak well of it. If I am not careful, it becomes my praise.

I like to eat. Eating is such a big thing for me that when I started getting bigger, my dad said that if I continued to eat as much as I did, I would have to learn to cook and buy the food myself. My cooking career began in fear of not getting all that I wanted to eat.

I once heard someone say that whatever you fear is your God. That which you fear influences you, just as that which is your praise. One of the dynamics of an addiction is to be under its influence.

True sobriety does not exist without praise to God. For if sobriety is equal to sanity, then we do not have sound minds by withholding from God the praise that He is due.

There are at least five ways that you worship:

1. Through making sacrifices
2. Allowing something to dominate or control
3. Give honor/glorify, praise
4. To exhibit trust
5. Possessing and expressing awe

Praise is in your soul. There is no doubt that we all value our souls. The soul is the will, emotions, and consciousness. Your soul becomes damaged whenever you put anything before God.

Praise originates from within and can be verbally expressed. Praise is a valuable combatant against addiction in many ways. Initially, praise unto God counteracts the praise that you give to yourself in deserving the honor that you wish to bestow upon yourself by partaking in whatever it is that God has forbidden.

January 21

Attraction

He had no beauty or majesty to attract us to him, nothing in his appearance that we should desire him. He was despised and rejected by mankind, a man of suffering, and familiar with pain Like one from whom people hide their faces he was despised, and we held him in low esteem. Isaiah 53:2b-3 *NIV*

"In God, you come up against something which is in every respect immeasurably superior to yourself. Unless you know God as that—and, therefore, know yourself as nothing in comparison—you do not know God at all." -*Mere Christianity,* C.S. Lewis

I was very much attracted to Herbert Lockyer's book *All the Messianic Prophecies of the Bible* in my sobriety curriculum. According to Isaiah, Jesus would not be very attractive to us (on the surface). Addictions sure do look good on the surface! Now, where does that sound familiar?

When the woman saw that the fruit of the tree was good for food and pleasing to the eye, and also desirable for gaining wisdom, she took some and ate it. Genesis 3:6a *NIV*

Since I don't think that there is anything wrong with an occasional bag of potato chips for me, I went and purchased a bag yesterday. I could not help but notice the beautiful wrapper that the chips were sold in. It looked as though Christmas had come again!
And then, I remembered how I did some soul-searching years ago while attempting to put an end to my cigarette smoking. I thought about how nicely the cigarettes were packaged, and it was like giving myself a present every day.
On the contrary, Jesus said that if any man would come after Him, he is to deny himself daily, take up his cross and follow Him (Luke 9:23). *A sober look at Jesus gives you a sober look at addictions.*

"The greatest way to overcome addictions is with a greater desire. Addictions are a problem of passion. The problem is not with the passion itself. The problem is with the object our passion calls us to pursue. So why does our passion cause us to run to an idol? Because we believe that idol is most attractive. The power to change is available in Christ, yet we don't go there because the pleasure of the idol seems more desirous than Christ. However, if we can see Jesus Christ as more satisfying - which He is, we will never pursue another idol again in our lives." -Randy Smith

January 22

The aroma

> Then Jesus declared, "I am the bread of life. Whoever comes to me will never go hungry, and whoever believes in me will never be thirsty." John 6:35

Just the other day, as I was talking with a man about a bakery that was being demolished, he began reminiscing over his past delight of smelling freshly baked bread while the bakery was in operation. ***Addictions stink in the nostrils of God.*** As the Bread of Life, Jesus is fully appetizing.

Have you ever heard someone say something just doesn't smell right when they are about to engage in a certain matter? So long as our senses are in order, addictions don't smell right. Addictions can easily dull our senses. I am reminded of two illustrations that apply to this.

1. If you place a frog in a pot of water that is room temperature and put the pot on the stove, gradually heating the water until it boils, the frog will boil to death before noticing the change of temperature. **We are all vulnerable to sin in this same fashion.**

2. It is said that when Eskimos want to kill a wolf that has been eating the seals that the Eskimos want for themselves, the Eskimos prey on the wolf's senses. Knowing how bloodthirsty the wolf is, the Eskimos plant a sharp knife in the ice coated with the seal's blood and wait for the wolf to come to lick the blade so that the wolf cuts his tongue. The wolf becomes so frantic over the taste of blood that he does not even realize that he is licking his own blood after a while and eventually bleeds to death. This is how we are with addictions.

Death is one thing that both illustrations have in common. Indulging in addictions leads to death (whether physical death, spiritual death, the death of a relationship, or our senses going dead...) The smell of death is not hard to miss. Not only that, the smell of death spreads. So, it is with Christ also! Jesus gives a distinguishable aroma (just like the aroma of the bread at the bakery.) And not only that, Jesus spreads that same aroma to His followers.

> But thanks be to God, who always leads us as captives in Christ's triumphal procession and uses us to spread the aroma of the knowledge of him everywhere. For we are to God the pleasing aroma of Christ among those who are being saved and those who are perishing. To the one we are an aroma that brings death; to the other, an aroma that brings life. And who is equal to such a task? 2 Corinthians 2:14-16

Captivated

Call to me and I will answer you, and will tell you great and hidden things that you have not known.

Call unto me, and I will answer thee, and show thee great and mighty things, which thou knowest not. Jeremiah 33:3 *KJV*

Once upon a time, I was as mesmerized by drugs as the idol worshippers who opposed Elijah. What I found was that I did not have all the answers and the answers that I was looking for were not found in addiction. The answers that addictions gave were the same as the answers that God told Israel that they would find when chasing after idols.

And they took the bull that was given them, and they prepared it and called upon the name of Baal from morning until noon, saying, "O Baal, answer us!" But there was no voice, and no one answered. And they limped around the altar that they had made. ... And they cried aloud and cut themselves after their custom with swords and lances, until the blood gushed out upon them. And as midday passed, they raved on until the time of the offering of the oblation, but there was no voice. No one answered; no one paid attention.
1 Kings 18:26, 28-29

The Lord will send on you curses, confusion, and frustration in all that you undertake to do, until you are destroyed and perish quickly on account of the evil of your deeds, because you have forsaken Me. ... so that you are driven mad by the sights that your eyes see. Deuteronomy 28:20, 34

One of the things that I asked God for, as He gave me the strength and the wisdom to overcome my drug addiction through the matchless power of Christ, was excitement. My prayer went something like this: "Lord God, You know that I find a lot of excitement in my drug use, and yet I desire to love You with all my heart. And so, dear God, would you please take that excitement from me or replace it with another excitement."

God has honored my prayer by sometimes giving me more excitement than I can handle as we labor together. One of the greatest compliments that my wife has ever paid is when she told me that I was the most exciting man that she had ever met. I attribute this to how God keeps His promise that if we call on Him, He will answer us and show us great and mighty things. Things that conquer addictions.! Things that make us whole...

January 24

What did you come to see?

> As they went away, Jesus began to speak to the crowds concerning John: "What did you go out into the wilderness to see? A reed shaken by the wind?" Matthew 11:7

While living in Memphis, Tennessee, my wife and I saved and worked for 7 years to have the opportunity to help the Lord to rescue people from the power of addiction in Atlanta, Georgia. One of my most memorable trips from Memphis was just before the 2019 *Super Bowl*.

While on my way back to the bus station to get back to Memphis, I overheard a young black male ask an older white man if he was "that coach." When the man confirmed that he was and another young man asked for a "selfie", I decided that I would offer the man a copy of the first edition of *Turning to God from Idols: A Biblical Approach to Addiction*.

To make a long story short; the man was Urban Meyer. Urban Frank Meyer was recognized as one of the best coaches at *The Ohio State University*. It was also interesting that Meyer's wife was a drug rehabilitation nurse. I could certainly see the hand of God in this encounter. But it was not the greatest thing that I witnessed on my trip.

It was the evening before the *Super Bowl* and I was headed back to Memphis because I could only book a room for the Friday before the *Super Bowl*. I was in Atlanta so that I could attend *Trinity Community Ministries'* graduation ceremony.

Trinity House - Big Bethel Program provides transitional housing and rehabilitation services. The program helps restore hope by providing support services leading back to employment, income, and long-termed sobriety.

As I was leaving Atlanta that night, I thought about how I could have been numbered with all the guests who were visiting to witness the *Super Bowl*. I also thought of what an honor it was to meet the great Urban Meyer. And then I thought about how I had the greatest honor of watching God transform the lives of the graduates just as He did mine!

> And not only the creation, but we ourselves, who have the firstfruits of the Spirit, groan inwardly as we wait eagerly for adoption as sons, the redemption of our bodies. Romans 8:23

My greatest delight is no longer in drugs,
but it is in seeing Jesus at work!

January 25

Truth for life

You study the Scriptures diligently because you think that in them you have eternal life. These are the very Scriptures that testify about Me. John 5:39 NIV

You pore over the Scriptures because you presume that by them you possess eternal life. These are the very words that testify about Me. *Berean Study Bible*

You diligently search the Scriptures because you think to have eternal life in them, and these are they bearing witness concerning Me. *Berean Literal Bible*

Where would we be without truth? Suppose you could not distinguish if a car was speeding towards you and that you would have to wait for it to pass so that you would not become fatally injured. I could use endless examples of how important truth is to our survival. Truth for life is a simple expression that describes the life there is in Christ to combat the lies of addiction.

For years, I was confused concerning what is erroneously known as "the disease concept." It took years of discernment while being exposed to the Word of God and the impressions of the Spirit of God before I became convinced that addiction is not a disease. Just for the record, the ***Alcoholics Anonymous book never said that alcoholism is a disease. It went as far as to say that it is like a disease***.

Unfortunately, the masses have been confused over this issue. I see it as a direct result of people forsaking and rejecting the Word of God to define life. Addictions are a part of life and if we do not look to the Author of life for answers, by the Spirit of Truth, we are looking for answers from the Father of lies.

We are all born with a love for sin. We are tempted by sin in many ways. Who would argue that addictions are not tempting? Are people tempted by diseases? Allow me the liberty of using what sounds like *Narcotics Anonymous'* reading "Who is an addict?" to describe a sinner!

"Who is a sinner? Most of us do not have to twice about this question. We know! Our whole life and thinking were centered on sin in one form or another.- the thoughts, the attitudes, and the actions aimed towards sinning more and more. We lived to sin and sinned to live. Very simply. A sinner is a man or woman whose life is controlled by sin." -*Addiction: A Tug of War*, Gregory L. Madison

January 26

Correction

All Scripture is breathed out by God and profitable for teaching, for reproof, **for correction**, and for training in righteousness.
2 Timothy 3:16

Can you name anyone outside of Christ that has never been wrong? That's just one reason why He is called Wonderful Counselor (Isaiah 9:6). Yet, I don't think that anyone likes being wrong! I remember talking with my youngest uncle for about two hours on the validity of Christ. After all his excuses for rejecting Christ, his final words were, "There's nothing wrong with being wrong!" On the contrary, being wrong can be costly!

Arthur Fonzarelli, better known as "Fonzie" or "The Fonz", was played by Henry Winkler for the television show *Happy Days*. Fonzie thinks he is never wrong and, consequently, has trouble admitting so. He attempts to say he was wrong in one episode but can only get as far as an *r* with an unidentifiable vowel.

Years ago, I heard a friend who suggested that the thorn in the flesh that Paul was referring to in 2 Corinthians 12:7 may have been an addiction. One of the problems with my friend's theory is that Paul was speaking of something that was physical, while addictions begin on a spiritual level (as we exhibit worship towards an addiction over God.)

Like many others, my friend was duped into believing addictions to be a disease! Such erroneous thinking has cost us! Many a soul has gone to hell because they never owned up to the sinfulness of addictions and the need for God's forgiveness.

It has been said that we are our own worst enemies. A long time ago, I discovered this to be true as I considered how we overrated ourselves. Many of us consider ourselves to be so good that we don't need repentance, we need healing. I believe that there are, many who do not have a deep understanding of sin..

> "Sin disposes the *sovereignty* of God as much as yeah it lies. It will not that the King of kings should be on the throne, and govern this world which he has made." -*The Sinfulness of Sin*, Ralph Venning

> "Those who are inwardly taught of God discover there is abundantly more of evil in their defiled natures and sinful actions than ever they realized before. There is as great and real a difference between that general notion which the natural man has of sin and that experiential and intuitional knowledge of it which is possessed by the Divinely quickened soul as there is between the mere picture of a lion and being confronted by a living lion as it meets us roaring in the way." -A. W. Pink

January 27

The power of Christ to discern

> Then came the disciples to Jesus apart, and said, Why could not we cast him out? And Jesus said unto them, Because of your unbelief: for verily I say unto you, If ye have faith as a grain of mustard seed, ye shall say unto this mountain, Remove hence to yonder place; and it shall remove; and nothing shall be impossible unto you. Howbeit this kind goeth not out but by prayer and fasting. Matthew 17:19-21 *KJV*

I once had the privilege of being incarcerated for sixty days while my attention was aimed toward Christ. It was a blessing to be able to see things clearly during that time and to minister to other inmates. My incarceration was initiated by a warrant that had been issued years before. I decided to surrender so that I could benefit from some of the benefits that the V.A. would not render so long as I had a warrant.

While jailhouse food can initiate forced fast, I fasted voluntarily in my worship of God. I joked with my cellmates over food advertisements. I would playfully moan and groan over the food advertisements as though lusting after sex. We learn through fasting. Fasting teaches discernment.

Through fasting, you learn very early whether you are hungry because you have a <u>lust</u> for food or if you are hungry because of your <u>need</u> for food. Through fasting, you can learn to discern what is physical from what is spiritual.

I do not believe that anyone is born addicted to anything but sin (except for children who are exposed to drugs in the womb.) And we will all be sinners until the day we die (if the Lord does not return first.) We choose to become addicted to various substances and/or activities. We are, also, free to choose between relinquishing our addiction through the power of God. And so, we do not have to remain addicts for the rest of our lives.

Not until recently, have people begun to address the true spiritual aspects of addictions to the idols that they are. I know this for a fact because, in all my years of fighting an addiction to crack, I did not find anything of this nature until the early 2000s. Perhaps, we didn't want the answers that God has had for us all along. Many still do not want those answers!

To label addictions as idolatry is based on the discernment that is found in the Word of God. To yield ourselves completely to God gives us discernment. Fasting is a means of yielding ourselves completely to God. In God there is truth. Here's an easy question for you! If something is not true, then what is it? If we are not bonded and connected to the Author of Truth, we associate ourselves with the Father of lies.

January 28

What matters most

> But seek first the kingdom of God and His righteousness, and all these things will be added to you. Matthew 6:33

Matthew 6:3 is starkly related to the entries for January 25 and 27. As January 27th's entry refers to the importance of spiritual issues over physical issues and January 25th's entry deals with truth that is found in the kingdom of God, so they all give adequate answers to addiction.

Vision calls our attention. Jesus is explaining to His disciples where their attention should first be directed. Attention can be elevated to concern. But our concern can also be further advanced to worry or anxiety. And so, the things that are given our attention determine our sanity. And, of course, sanity is greatly related to sobriety.

At the risk of someone taking the passage out of context, I need to mention that Jesus is explaining that as His disciples concern themselves first with the kingdom of God and His righteousness, then their basic needs would be met. Unfortunately, while under the influence of greed, many take this to mean that God will give you *anything* that you want by being concerned about His kingdom and His righteousness. In other words, many addictions are yet socially acceptable which leads people to change the meaning of the passage. (Just a side-note)

If you care to read the passage, it extends from vv. 25-34. The principle behind the passage is of grave importance in our treatment of addictions. It is the most outstanding principle, which I stand upon until my dying day (though rarely mentioned in most cases.) The principle that I am referring to is the reverential factor.

It is our reverence for God that proves what we are most concerned about. Not only that, our reverence for God can be measured by degrees (just as our sobriety.) Pastor Albert Martin says the three essential elements for reverencing God are a view of His majesty or greatness, an awareness of His presence, and a sense of obligation to God.

In a subtitle from *The Fear of the Almighty* labeled "Comprehensive impiety," I stated that "where no genuine reverence for God exists, then God is belittled, not very highly commended, and alternately cursed. Reverencing God involves love, praise, and adoration. Irreverence involves disapproval, insult, and indifference." I also commented that we must develop and maintain **a predisposed reverential attitude**.

Learning to love God is the soberest thing that we do. In a sermon on fearing God, I heard a Christian counselor say that his job was to lead people into loving God more. Is there anything more important? While you may put other things above loving God, you will not find anything as fulfilling. It is what you were created for!

January 29

Fixation

You keep him in perfect peace whose mind is stayed on you, because he trusts in you. Isaiah 26:3

"Insatiable wanting machines, designed to desire," is how Jason Silva, public speaker, and filmmaker, describes humans in one of his videos. An article titled *Yearning Machines: Every Human is an Addict*, says, "Our bodies yearn to hold on to something; a safe line, a fixation of some sort. Human beings become dependent on a certain object and when that's not moderated, it becomes an addiction. Addiction is not only limited to alcohol, drugs, and food. It branches out to behaviors, social media, fixation on success, shopping... It's our responsibility to recognize that cycle and then break it."

What is the best definition that you can contrive for addiction? *Psychology Today* once described addiction as "a condition in which a person engages in the use of a substance or in a behavior for which the rewarding effects provide a compelling incentive to repeatedly pursue the behavior despite detrimental consequences." The *Merriam-Webster Dictionary* says that addiction is "to devote or surrender (oneself) to something habitually or excessively." Do we not yearn for what we are devoted to?

"Addiction results… from the motivated repetition of the same thoughts and behaviors until they become habitual." -*The Biology of Desire: Why Addiction is Not a Disease*, Marc Lewis

According to *etymonline.com*, "the root word addict comes from the Latin word addictus (past tense addicere), which means 'to devote, sacrifice, **sell out**, betray or abandon.' In the Roman law, an addict was a person that became enslaved through a court ruling." *Dictionary.com* defines addiction as "the state of being compulsively committed to a habit or practice or to something that is psychologically or physically habit-forming, as narcotics, to such an extent that its cessation causes severe trauma."

Commitment and devotion may be used to describe addiction as well as our relationship with God. Right from the beginning, I want to let you in on a little secret that took me years to discover with certainty and clarity. *Addiction is not a disease! Addiction is something that we devote ourselves to. For years I struggled with the idea that addiction could be a disease.* Quite frankly, I am appalled that many seek to find answers to addictions through science while dismissing the clear and distinct answers that are given in the Word of God.

Are you fixed? That's your focus!

January 30

Are you blind?

Open my eyes, that I may behold wondrous things out of Your law.
Psalms 119:18

Blindness is perhaps the leading cause of addiction. The blindness of addiction is that you cannot see the goodness of God (along with His reasoning.) The blindness of addictions is that you cannot see how offensive it is to God.

The blindness of addictions is that you cannot see how your time, energy, and resources would be better spent on others. *While physical blindness may not always be preventable or treatable, spiritual blindness can always be prevented or treated!* Blindness is often the description of those who are captivated by sin. The Apostle Paul explained the details of spiritual blindness to the Ephesians, as well as to you and me.

Now this I say and testify in the Lord, that you must no longer walk as the Gentiles do, in the futility of their minds. They are darkened in their understanding, alienated from the life of God because of the ignorance that is in them, due to their hardness of heart.
Ephesians 4:17-18

Everyone knows that the cure for blindness is vision. The psalmist cried to God for vision when he asked God to open his eyes. Who would argue that we need the vision to be victorious over addictions? One of the "wondrous things" that we behold from God's Word is the formula for conquering sin.

What a wondrous thing it would be, also, to behold a grandmaster chess player. Though I haven't had the opportunity to witness a grandmaster at work, I am told that they have a such great vision that they can play multiple opponents while the chessboard is positioned in another room. Many say that a grandmaster can visualize ten moves ahead. One expert chess player boasts of being able to visualize 15 or 20 moves ahead.

The vision that the Lord provides regarding addictions can be like that of a grandmaster playing chess. Though chess is one of my favorite sports, I will freely admit that I am far from being a grandmaster. It is easier for me to admit that I don't always know the next move in chess than to admit that I don't always know the move in life. At times I forget that the best move is to take off the crown and give the Lord the command that He deserves.

I recognize that discouragement can often cloud our vision when we do not recognize the praise that God is worthy of. The greatest manifestation of God is seen at the cross of Calvary! What a delight it is to know that our soul may be secure for eternity through the sacrificial payment of our sins that would otherwise damn us!

Purity

How can a young man keep his way pure? By guarding it according to Your Word. Psalms 119:9

While purity is rarely mentioned in today's world, it always will be a concern for God. Although purity is not typically discussed in a meeting concerning addictions, it bears significance just the same. And while purity is rarely discussed, it is yet sought by many.

We like to think of ourselves as pure and clean (even if it is by our own standards.) What matters is being pure in the eyes of God! This, of course, begins from within. Jesus emphasized the importance of inward purity on multiple occasions. At times, he was very adamant about inward purity.

Blessed are the pure in heart, for they shall see God. Matthew 5:8

Woe to you, scribes and Pharisees, hypocrites! For you clean the outside of the cup and the plate, but inside they are full of greed and self-indulgence. Matthew 23:25

Most of the time, when people discuss purity, they are referring to sexual purity. And while God desires and commands us to be sexually pure, our purity extends to every area of our lives. This is why Proverbs 4:23 says to "guard your heart, for out of it are the issues of life" (*KJV*).

After you have been washed in the blood of Christ, God continues to cleanse you through the "washing of the water of the Word" (Ephesians 5:26). Most of us who want to be free of addiction want lasting sobriety- we want to remain abstinent for the remainder of our lives. The psalmist gives the formula for keeping our way pure through the sobriety that is offered in the Word of God.

Being clean takes on a whole new aspect in spiritual terms. The word clean refers to being free of dirt, impurities, stains, or defilement. It is, also, defined as being free from foreign matter, pollution, or infection, free from wrongdoing, honorable, morally pure, and virtuous.

We use the word "clean" in association with abstinence from drugs by having "clean" urine when tested for drug use (no detection of drug use.) Being clean in a spiritual sense involves moral purity, a proper standing before God, and the absence of guile. To be spiritually pure means more than just being clean from drugs.

Would you say that God always has good sense? On the other hand, we do not. Furthermore, our thoughts are not always clean. If we rely upon God's thoughts rather than our own, the result will be purity.

February 1

The origin of addiction

Moreover, by them is your servant warned; in keeping them there is great reward. Psalm 19:11

Biblical Quotes that Expose Addiction contains seven features. The origin nature, depravity, disappointment, deceit, insanity, and devastation of addiction as explained by the Word of God are necessary for all who want freedom and those who are concerned about those who struggle.

There has been a lot of confusion about the origin of addiction outside of the realm of God. It is when we search the Scriptures that everything becomes clear. You need to know the true origin of addictions so that you can devise the best plan of escape from "fleshly lusts that wage war against your souls" (1 Peter 2:11).

"The whole Bible is written as a full-scale assault on idolatry."
-Ligon Duncan, President of *Reformed Theological Seminary*

"Idolatry isn't just one of many sins; Rather it's the one great sin that all others come from. So if you start scratching at whatever struggle you're dealing with, eventually you'll find that underneath it is a false god. Until that god is dethroned, and the Lord God takes his rightful place, you will not have victory. Idolatry isn't *an* issue; it is *the* issue. All roads lead to the dusty, overlooked concept of false gods. Deal with life on the glossy outer layers, and you might never see it; scratch a little beneath the surface, and you begin to see that it's always there, under some other coat of paint. There are a hundred million different symptoms, but the issue is always idolatry." -*gods at war,* Kyle Idleman

In Christ, we get a full view of addictions because the nature of Christ is at war with the nature of addictions (mainly selfishness.) All that addiction is, Christ is not! The nature of addiction is rebellious and hostile toward God. Its nature is first and foremost an insult to God.

The nature of addiction is, perhaps, more severe than we anticipated. While addiction can lead to confusion, it becomes simple when it is evaluated through the lens of Scripture. For instance; lust is a strong component of addiction. The Scripture gives us much insight into lust.

The nature of addiction is two-fold. Addictions think of God as small, but on the contrary, they are futile (or useless.) Most people are only concerned over how addictions leave them dissatisfied with no regard for God's satisfaction. The full nature of addiction must be understood if we are to devise a complete and godly plan for its destruction.

February 2

The nature of addiction

The natural person does not accept the things of the Spirit of God, for they are folly to him, and he is not able to understand them because they are spiritually discerned. 1 Corinthians 2:14

The best way for us to meet with an opponent is to know their tactics and strengths. The nature of addictions can only be seen in Scripture well enough to humble us in our reverence to God and to seek divine intervention in our daily pursuit of godliness.

As quiet as it is kept, **addictions are a natural response to the things of the world that capture our attention by appealing to our senses.** In an article titled *Union with Christ: the Ground of Sanctification* Michael P.V. Barrett said: "natural reasoning always perverts the truth." If the nature of man's problem is misdiagnosed, a faulty prescription is sure to follow. Supernatural power breaks the chains of addiction.

"God has endued the soul with two principal faculties: The one, that by which it is capable of perception and speculation, or by which it discerns and judges of things, which is called the *understanding*. The other, that by which the soul is some way inclined with respect to the things it views or considers: or it is the faculty by which the soul beholds things—not as an indifferent unaffected spectator, but—either liking or disliking, pleased or displeased, approving or rejecting. This faculty is called by various names; it is sometimes called *inclination;* and as respects the actions determined and governed by it, the *will;* and the *mind*, with regard to the exercises of this faculty, is often called the heart" - *Treatise Concerning the Religious Affections,* Jonathan Edwards

"One of the most common portrayal of the human condition, and one which captures both the in-control and out-of-control experiences of addictions, is the theme of idolatry. ...the true nature of all addictions is that we have chosen to go outside the boundaries of the kingdom of God and look for blessing in the land of idols. In turning to idols, we are saying that we desire something in creation more than we desire the Creator." -*Addictions a Banquet in the Grave*, Edward T. Welch

Deceit is within the nature of addictions. The only way we can discern the truth is through Jesus Christ. Jesus said to those who believed in Him, "If you continue in My word, then you are My disciples indeed and you shall know the truth, and the truth will make you free" (John 8:32). It is only through an abiding relationship with Jesus Christ that we are free of deceit.

February 3

The depravity of addiction

> And this is the judgment, that the Light has come into the world, and people loved the darkness rather than the Light; for their deeds were evil. For everyone who does evil hates the Light, and does not come to the Light, so that his deeds will not be exposed." John 3:19-20

Depravity is defined by *The Oxford Dictionary* as "the quality or state of being corrupt, evil, or perverted." Depravity is best described as the distorted image of Man that we inherited after the Fall of Man.

Depravity is expressed as the dysfunction in our relationship with God, others, and all of creation. Depravity is a deformity of the soul that causes us to respond to God, others, and the creation in a way that is both irreverent towards God and nonbeneficial to ourselves and others.

Depravity begins with a perverted mind. Hence the correlation to insanity and deceit. Depravity increases without the exposure of light that the Word of God gives to Mankind. That's why all the formulas for resolving addiction that exclude the Lord Jesus Christ are not able to make anybody whole nor please God. (While many programs talk about God, the irony of excluding Christ proves their hypocrisy.)

Anyone can become addicted to one thing or another. It is within the nature of man to sin. John Calvin said, "the human heart is an idol factory." Given the right circumstances, any of us could become guilty of some of the most detestable acts of sins. Dr. Bob Jones Sr. used to put it this way: "Any sin that any sinner ever committed, every sinner under proper provocation could commit."

Depravity is closely related to deception. Man enters depravity and remains by deception. We cannot claim to be victims because, at one point or another, we all have a choice to turn from our wicked ways and choose wisdom. We may become engulfed in addictions after turning from the truth that God has revealed.

Depravity further proves that addictions originate from within. Depravity shows us that the spiritual nature of addiction must be attended to for us to be on the same page as God, to achieve the satisfaction that we desire apart from addiction, and to love others as we do ourselves.

> Because they hated knowledge and did not choose the fear of the Lord, would have none of my counsel and despised all my reproof, therefore they shall eat the fruit of their way, and have their fill of their own devices. Proverbs 1:29-31

> "His environment, circumstances, hormones, health, and genetics will never account for the level of wickedness that a man's heart can generate on its own." -Jim Berg

February 4

The disappointment of addictions

Why do you spend your money for that which is not bread, and your labor for that which does not satisfy? Listen diligently to me, and eat what is good, and delight yourselves in rich food. Isaiah 55:2

Depravity always produces disappointment. Why? Because as Augustine said, "our hearts are restless until they rest in you." The peace of God is the result of having peace *with* God. Becoming a new creation in Christ gives us a nature that can commune with God and find satisfaction in Him. If you are not satisfied with God, you will never be satisfied with anything!

> "My brethren, the reason why you have not got contentment in the things of the world is not because you have not got enough of them-that is not the reason-but the reason is, because they are not things proportionate to that immortal soul of yours that is capable of God himself." –*The Rare Jewel of Christian Contentment*, Jeremiah Burroughs

It is the nature of addiction to wanting more and more. It is inevitable that as soon as we fuel the fire of our addictions before they are consumed, we hunger and thirst for more if we do not find something greater. Unfortunately, our disappointment may be erroneously interrupted as a need for more addiction with no restrictions.

The disappointment of addiction has two causes. The first is our depravity and the second is the nature of addiction. Simply stated, we are too dysfunctional to be satisfied and addictions are too deficient to give us what we truly long for. Disappointment is caused by the deception of addiction. To deny the disappointment of addiction and continued to believe that there is a satisfaction to be found is insane.

Not only is our addiction limited in supply, but its effect is also limited. This often causes people to seek other addictions. People are lured into more potent drugs or more perverted practices when the effect of one addiction doesn't seem to be enough. One of the greatest deceptions of addictions is that we will get enough to completely satisfy our being (either presently or in the future.)

For some, the answer to the disappointment, unfortunately, is to look to some other addiction. It is also unfortunate that the reason why some abstain from addiction is that they know that they will never be able to gain a supply of their addiction to satisfy rather than abstaining out of reverence to God.

The disappointment of addiction begins with the fixation on an image that addiction is supposed to fulfill. In our imagination, we lack the vision to see that addictions cannot provide what they promise and that God can do so either directly and/or indirectly.

February 5

The deceit of addiction

All who fashion idols are nothing, and the things they delight in do not profit. ... He feeds on ashes; a deluded heart has led him astray, and he cannot deliver himself or say, "Is there not a lie in my right hand?" Isaiah 44:9a, 20

I encourage you to read Isaiah 44:9-20 as it is titled in some bibles as *The Folly of Idolatry*. The disappointment of addiction is found in the deceitful nature of addiction. Addictions never deliver what they promise. Deceit and depravity go hand in hand as well. This means that addiction distorts the image that we are created to embrace and portray.

The deceit of addiction is undeniable. Anyone who knows the least about addiction knows how people try to deceitfully rationalize and minimize addiction. Most of us know how people try to cover up their addictions. When you lie about the severity of addiction it spoils your sobriety. Deceit causes dysfunction.

"All sin is extremely deceptive. It allows the person to feel as though he is in control, but this is merely an illusion. In reality, sin slowly and subtly, but surely, begins to master the person's heart. The more it is indulged, the more its perspectives shroud the person's thinking." –*At the Altar of Sexual Idolatry*, Steve Gallagher

Error, deceit, and falsehood are by no means foreign to addictions! Addictions are born of error, propagated through deceit, and exhibited by falsehood. If an error is the root of addiction, then deceit is the sap and falsehood is its fruit. Every addiction can be traced to erroneous thinking.

Truth is indispensable because we need things that we can rely on. No matter how depraved someone is, they are seeking what they believe to be true. No one likes to be fooled. I often tell people that the average con man does not tell you that they are about to trick you (nor does Satan.)

It is often said that if a person knew the misery that addiction would cause in their lives, they would not have started. The problem is that Satan tells us things that are untrue about God, ourselves, and addiction.

With a fallen nature or a carnal heart, we are attracted to the lies of the devil just as a magnet to a piece of steel. Pride leads the way to falsehood. And since pride is a spiritual issue, there are no scientific solutions. It is not even in the same league!

We do not wrestle against flesh and blood, but against the rulers, against the authorities, against the cosmic powers over this present darkness, against the spiritual forces of evil in the heavenly places. Ephesians 6:12

February 6

The insanity of addiction

> This is an evil in everything that is done under the sun, that there is one fate for everyone. Furthermore, the hearts of the sons of mankind are full of evil, and insanity is in their hearts throughout their lives. Afterward *they go* to the dead. NASB

The *Oxford Dictionary* defines insanity as "the state of being seriously ill; madness." Insanity is also defined as extreme foolishness or irrationality. Insanity is related to depravity. It is a condition of the mind that is either not fully developed and/or has a deformity.

Insanity and deceit are closely related since insanity not only denies what is true, it manufactures lies. Insanity is the derivative of deceit. Insanity also has an irreverent disposition in rejecting the revealed truth of God whether in a plain and natural sense or in the supernatural revelation that is found in God's Word.

The insanity of addiction causes us to be unreasonable. Pride is associated with insanity in that we are unwilling to admit that we are unable to find the answers to life that we need on our own. And then, in the stubbornness of our hearts, we cleave to an idol rather than to God.

The major deceits of addiction are that there is something that can replace God and you can control whatever you have chosen. It is widely accepted that insanity is a mental disorder, but the idolatry of addiction helps us to understand that insanity is a spiritual/worship disorder first.

Most people define the insanity of addiction by the disappointment that it gives but there is much more involved. Awe and insanity are intricately connected. Some say that insanity is to do the same thing and expect different results. But the origin of insanity is a thinking disorder.

Insanity is a lack of understanding. To be without understanding is dysfunctional. Insanity is measured on various levels. Some are saner than others. Depraved minds are dysfunctional to various degrees. The insanity of addiction is a severe dysfunction that is largely related to our reverence or irreverence for God. Addiction is an insane attempt to dethrone God.

> "Whatever weakens your reason, impairs the tenderness of your conscience, obscures your sense of God, or takes off your relish of spiritual things; in short, whatever increases the strength and authority of your body over your mind; that thing is sin to you, however innocent it may be in itself." –Susanna Wesley

No one will be completely sane until they are fully conformed to the image of Christ. As Jesus was more human than anyone who ever lived, He is saner than any other human. John Carlson says, "We don't work on sobriety, but a New Creation – then sobriety naturally follows!"

February 7

The devastation of addiction

But what fruit were you getting at that time from the things of which you are now ashamed? For the end of those things is death.
Romans 6:21

The devastation of addiction can be seen on many levels. The personal devastation of addiction affects the condition of our minds, bodies, and souls. Spouse and child neglect and abuse represent the domestic devastation of addiction. Financial devastation occurs as addiction interferes with our work performance as well as bills that are neglected.

Addictions bring limitations. Addictions are based on lies and all lies cause limitations. If you tell a lie, you must live and speak within the confines of that lie or live by the truth. Addictions can restrict your time, energy, and resources to what will please you and you alone. One of the lies of addiction is that no one matters but you.

Addiction is not concerned with pleasing God or others. Addictions destroy your options by laying claim to your time, your thoughts, your skills and abilities, and your finances, for the sake of the addiction rather than anything else. The severity of irreverence found in addiction is more extensive and far-reaching than we could imagine.

It is widely known that most crimes involve drug and alcohol abuse. The greatest devastation of addiction is that the image of God that we were all created with is destroyed. This is where all the devastation of addiction begins.

"In the garden that day, a great and destructive exchange took place—not first an exchange of obedience for disobedience but awe of God for awe of self. ... Made God seem small. Once awe of God is lost, the loss of a heart to obey isn't far off." –*Awe: Why It Matters for Everything We Think, Say, and Do,* Paul Tripp

The greatest devastation is for God to lose His place in our hearts. From there, we lose our place as creatures with the honor of being created in the image of God. The spiritual devastation of addictions begins with deprivation and ends in damnation. Without the redemption of Christ, we remain outside the boundaries of God's care and protection leading to a taste of what hell will be (absent of the goodness of God.)

Society is devastated by addiction. Crime, accidents, insurance costs, and neglected and abused children, spouses, and elderly citizens are associated with addiction. Addictions not only hinder the advancement of our communities but they create erosion. Addiction is responsible for poverty, stagnation, demotion, and unemployability. Addictions of every kind drain us, our families, and our nations of our resources.

February 8

The greatest horror

> But when they came to the threshing floor of Nacon, Uzzah reached out toward the ark of God and took hold of it, for the oxen nearly upset it. And the anger of the Lord burned against Uzzah, and God struck him down there for his irreverence; and he died there by the ark of God. 2 Samuel 6:6-7 *NASB*

Do you like horror movies? After several years of marriage, I was surprised to find out that my wife's parents would not allow her to watch horror movies as a child. I probably don't have to tell you the horrors of addiction.

Mankind provokes God to anger through his sinful actions toward Him and others. Yes, God is a loving and caring God, but He is also a God of judgment, and one day God's anger toward mankind's rejection of His Son Jesus and their walking contrary to the commandments of His Word will bring His wrath upon mankind.

> "One cannot proclaim a true theory of society unless he sees the heinousness of sin and its relation to all social ills and disorder. No man can be a successful New Testament evangelist publishing the Gospel as 'the power of God unto salvation to every one that believeth', unless he has an adequate conception of the enormity of sin. Nor can a man hold a consistent theory of ethics or live up to the highest standard of morality, unless he is gripped with a keen sense of sin's seductive nature." -*The Fundamentals*, vol. 3, Williams, Charles

One of the atrocities of today is how many programs only emphasize how addictions affect individuals and their associates (family, acquaintances, and society.) Most programs never discuss how God is affected. The greatest horror of addiction and the love and justice of God is described by the Prophet Isaiah and the Apostle Peter.

> As many were astonished at you— his appearance was so marred, beyond human semblance, and his form beyond that of the children of mankind. Isaiah 52:14

> For Christ also suffered once for sins, the righteous for the unrighteous, that he might bring us to God, being put to death in the flesh but made alive in the spirit. 1 Peter 3:1

> "Not once are we told that God is 'provoked to love.' ... His anger requires provocation; his mercy is pent up, ready to gush forth. ... Yahweh needs no provoking to love, only to anger." -*Gentle and Lowly*, Dane Ortlund

February 9

The coin toss

Thus says the LORD: "What wrong did your fathers find in me that they went far from me, and went after worthlessness, and became worthless?" Jeremiah 2:5

Have you ever heard that there are two sides to every coin? The same is true of addictions. Have you ever had someone toss a coin and say "Heads I win, tails you lose?" That's how addictions operate!

The idolatry of addiction, reveals its two sides. You either discuss how insulting addictions are to God or you discuss their uselessness. Unfortunately, people usually think more about the futility of addictions rather than how insulting they are to God.

    a. Addictions are a form of idol worship.
    b. Addictions are a wasteful thing/they are futile.

An idol is something of human manufacture, which people have substituted for the true and living God- anything that stands between us and God or something we substitute for God. Worship was originally spelled "worthship" and it means to acknowledge the worth of the object worshipped.

There are at least five ways that we worship:

1. Through making sacrifices
2. Allowing something to dominate or control
3. Give honor/glorify, praise
4. To exhibit trust
5. Possessing and expressing awe

The very nature of idolatry is <u>impractical</u>. The *New Unger's Bible Dictionary* says an idol is "an empty thing, rendered elsewhere 'trouble,' 'iniquity,' 'vanity,' 'wickedness,' etc. The primary idea of the root word seems to be emptiness, nothingness, as a breath or a vapor. The Hebrew word for idol (awen) denotes a vain, false, wicked thing and expresses at once the essential nature of idols and the consequences of their worth."

I cannot overemphasize the importance of seeing addictions as idols, and therefore irreverent towards God. These are the spiritual implications of addictions. This is what determines the focus of every program. A program for conquering addiction is either focused on giving pleasure to the individual that is bound to addiction or giving God pleasure. What most people don't realize is that when God is pleased, we will be pleased as well!

February 10

Partaking

Because it is written, Be ye holy; for I am holy. 1 Peter 1:16 *KJV*

G.K. Beale's book *We Become What We Worship* adequately describes the relationship that we have with both God and idols. The most gracious invitation was given by God to all mankind. We are not just invited to be free of addictions. God wants us to be like Him.

To be holy, simply means to be set apart. Another definition of holy is to be pure. God (Himself) makes this possible for us through the blood of Christ and the direction that is found in His Word.

One of the questions that people ask while striving to overcome addiction is how to become normal. Yet being normal is not what God desires. God doesn't want you to be normal. God wants you to be different! He wants you to be like Himself. In a word- unselfish.

Who would argue that addiction is a selfish practice? Your degree of sobriety reflects how much you are like Christ. The question is whether we are growing more in the image of Christ. This is what true sobriety looks like. Much of what people call sobriety or "recovery" today is just as self-serving as other addictions.

> "Make no mistake about it. If you are God's child, He has placed within you a desire for Himself. If your only desires in life are for yourself and for relief from your problems, and you experience no desire whatsoever for a relationship with God, your first step needs to be a very careful examination of whether or not you even belong to Him" –*Changed into His Image*, Jim Berg

Are not addictions something that we partake in? Could not addictions be best fought as people become more like Christ? This is what the Scriptures refer to as being a partaker of the divine nature (2 Peter 1:4). If God were thoroughly pleased with Jesus, why shouldn't we want to be a partaker of the divine nature? If being a partaker of the divine nature provides us with the greatest intimacy with God that is possible, why would we deny God of ourselves?

A few years ago, I misplaced my favorite t-shirt. The message on the t-shirt gave the requirement of becoming a partaker of the divine nature. The t-shirt had a picture of a cross with the words "Try this on for size!" Becoming a partaker of the divine nature requires us to take up our cross and follow Jesus (Luke 9:23).

To partake of the divine nature is an association. Becoming associated with Christ begins as you recognize and confess that it was you that Jesus represented on the Cross. By placing your faith in Him, you become united in His death and His resurrection. This is essential because it is not of this world.

February 11

I hate recovery!

I appeal to you therefore, brothers, by the mercies of God, to present your bodies as a living sacrifice, holy and acceptable to God, which is your spiritual worship. Do not be conformed to this world, but be transformed by the renewal of your mind, that by testing you may discern what is the will of God, what is good and acceptable and perfect. Romans 12:1-2

Recovery is a word that should never be used to describe how God eliminates addiction. *Recovery* may be what some are after, but God is after much more. ***I don't want to recover any of my past. I believe that God has so much better.*** If I recover, then I will be right back to where I was. Where I was before led me to addiction.

In all fairness, I realize that people mean well when referring to recovery. I believe that it was taken out of context from *Alcoholics Anonymous* by those who had once lived a sound and prosperous life before drinking and were seeking to recover. That does not apply to us all!

Before AA, *recovery* was not used to describe overcoming addiction. The Bible has always used other words that are more adequately accurate. Words like transformed and sanctification describe how people become more like Christ. One of the questions that nobody ever asks is whether the writers of *Alcoholics Anonymous* knew more about the Bible or addiction than you, myself, or others who express their thoughts on addiction.

"Recovery is the buzzword in secular addiction counseling. Recovery means 'to regain or to recapture one's old self.' For physical healing, 'recovery' is a good word for it implies an improvement in one's condition. For spiritual healing, however, we find a better word in the Bible. Scripture teaches that God desires more for us than 'recovery' or that we recapture our old self because even when we 'recover our old self, we are left with just that—our old self. God desires a total transformation or conversion.)" -*CrossTalking*, Mark Shaw

Transformation and growth more accurately describe the process of overcoming addictions through Christ. To transform is to change the nature, condition, function, disposition, heart, character, etc.; to convert. To recover is to bring back to a previous condition or state. When is the last time that you saw something that grows recover anything? When a plant grows, it gets new leaves. It doesn't recover anything!

February 12

Transformation

And we all, with unveiled face, beholding the glory of the Lord, are being transformed into the same image from one degree of glory to another. For this comes from the Lord who is the Spirit.
2 Corinthians 3:18

You must have an accurate view of God to be changed into the image that we originally had during Creation. In *We Become What We Worship*, G.K. Beale accurately explains that you take on the characteristics of what you worship. ***The only method of disposing of addiction that is acceptable to God is your willingness for Him to make you more like Christ.***

Becoming more like Christ comes through allowing the written Word of God to reveal the Living Word of God (Christ.) True and complete sobriety that is acceptable to God is in total agreement with the Word of God. One of the definitions of sobriety has to do with the soundness of the mind.

Does God have a sound mind? Of course! It is as you agree with the thoughts of God's mind, as they are expressed in His Word, that you develop the soundness of mind that leads you into godly decisions (such as abstaining from addiction out of reverence towards God.)

When you have the mind of Christ, you are led to an unselfish life that is opposed to self-serving addiction. ***God wants you to be different!*** He wants you to be like Himself. In a word- unselfish. John MacArthur said "If you want to be Christ's disciple, you must refuse to associate any longer with the person you are! You are sick of your sinful self and want nothing to do with you anymore."

I no longer use the word *recovery* to describe what God wants to do in the lives of those who are addicted. Recovery indicates that you are regaining something. The word of God says that *"if any man is in Christ, he is a new creation. Old things have passed away, all things have become new"* (2 Corinthians 5:17). And so, in Christ, we are not seeking to recover *anything*.

It can be said that the Apostle Paul used the illustration of a caterpillar becoming a butterfly in Romans 12:2 to describe the transforming power of God. It says to *"be not conformed to this world but be transformed by the renewing of your mind."* If God wanted us to *recover* then that would only mean that we become the same caterpillar. ***We insult God by saying that He can do nothing more than make us into what we were before.*** The Word of God says to be <u>transformed</u> not *recovered*.

The Son of God became the Son of Man so that the sons of men could become the sons of God!

February 13

To be or not to be

Ye therefore, beloved, seeing ye know these things before, beware lest ye also, being led away with the error of the wicked, fall from your own stedfastness. 2 Peter 3:17 *KJV*

Wickedness takes on many forms. **Rejecting Christ is the worst habit there is.** Jesus said, "Unless your righteousness exceeds the righteousness of the scribes and Pharisees, you will not enter the kingdom of heaven" (Matthew 5:20). We can't rely on our *own* righteousness. The righteousness of Christ saves us from the wrath of God and equips us to live a life that is pleasing to God.

For He (God) hath made Him who knew no sin (Christ) to be sin for us, that we might be the righteousness of God in Him.
2 Corinthians 5:21 *KJV*

Part One of *Addiction: A Tug of War* describes the issue of addiction as spiritual. Part Two is about how the world has taken over the methods that people have chosen to deal with addiction. Spiritual matters are too important for inadequate answers. Spiritual matters are of the Spirit.

Jesus said that His word is spirit and life (John 6:63). Apart from a connection with Christ, we are prone to offer inaccurate information about addiction. Apart from Christ, we must question the authority of those who present theories on addiction.

John Owen said, "an unsaved, unregenerate unbeliever might do something that looks like killing sin, but the thing he's done can never be acceptable to God." The main reason is that outside of Christ we are not concerned with the glory of God being manifested in and through us. Jay Adams said, "In all counseling change is a matter of greater or lesser love toward Him."

"Much change that is offered today in counseling—even in the Name of Christ—is sub-Christian. Aimed at little more than making counselees happier, it neglects the basic reason why a believer must change to please God. As if God's glory were of secondary importance, His Name's sake is omitted from the picture, out of deference to better health or a more smoothly running marriage. Such considerations, not wrong in themselves, are quite wrong when they are not subordinated to the greater purpose of pleasing and honoring God." -*How to Help People Change*, Jay Adams

February 14

The relevance of reverence

> Now all has been heard; here is the conclusion of the matter: Fear God and keep His commandments, for this is the whole duty of man. Ecclesiastes 12: 13 *KJV*

Is there anything more relevant to addiction than reverence? *I challenge anyone to give me an answer that explains addiction more clear and plain than idolatry and a solution that is more relevant than reverencing God!* Reverencing God has been the secret to sobriety since the beginning of time. According to A.N. Martin, the very nature of reverence gives a personal awareness of God's presence, creates a sense of obligation to God, and gives us an understanding of His greatness.

> "Reverence for God is an essential element, primary to the success of mankind. **Without any reverence for God, there is only chaos, confusion, disorder, and injustice.** Those who would forsake God's holy reverence are abandoning an indispensable characteristic. It is as though they are searching for the formula of life, but the major ingredient of 'integrity' is left out. The consequences of irreverence are serious and grave; this is the very thing that tears at the foundation of a nation." -*The Forgotten Fear*, Pastor A. N. Martin

The fear of the Lord (or reverence for God) is an acknowledgment of His presence, His love, His grandeur, His wisdom, and His ownership. *Vine's Expository Dictionary of Biblical Words* says that reverence is "the recognition of the power and position of an individual and render Him proper respect."

Pastor Tony Evans said that to reverence God means that you take God seriously. Irreverence leaves you vulnerable to the deception of addictions because in rejecting God you reject the truth. <u>Entire nations have been destroyed because of their irreverence for God</u>. Untold lives have been ruined because of this same hideous disposition.

> Why do the nations rage and the peoples plot in vain? The kings of the earth set themselves, and the rulers take counsel together, against the LORD and against his Anointed, saying, "Let us burst their bonds apart and cast away their cords from us." He who sits in the heavens laughs; the Lord holds them in derision. Psalm 2:1-4

February 15

The insanity of irreverence!

Great and marvelous are Your deeds, Lord God Almighty. Just and true are Your ways, King of the nations. Who will not fear You, Lord, and bring glory to Your name? Revelation 15:3 *NIV*

Revelation 15:3 reveals the root of insanity. Insanity and denial are closely related to irreverence. And just like reverence, denial, sanity, insanity, and sobriety can all be measured. They are all measured by how our thoughts line up with God's thoughts. Revelation 15:3 almost implies that those who don't revere God are crazy.

Denial is the refusal to admit the truth or to call something true that is not. Insanity is filled with lies as well. Denial and insanity are so closely related that they are hard to separate. One of the marks of insanity is to be unreasonable. Yes, insanity can be defined as doing the same thing and expecting different results, but it gets much deeper than that!

By my estimation, insanity is very closely related to irreverence for God. **Insanity is the rejection of the truth while manufacturing false perceptions.** Have you ever been insane or encountered someone in this state? When someone is insane there is a lack of communication. The insanity of irreverence is a lack of communication. At a conference on fearing God, a speaker was quoted as stating that "Christian counseling is nothing more than convincing people to fear God."

> Now, therefore, thus says the Lord of hosts: Consider your ways. You have sown much, and harvested little. You eat, but you never have enough; you drink, but you never have your fill. You clothe yourselves, but no one is warm. And he who earns wages does so to put them into a bag with holes. Haggai 1:5-6

Part of the process of overcoming addictions is to consider your ways. When you do this, with the aid of the Holy Spirit, then you will understand how much you need the truth that is found in the Word of God to combat the lies that you have embraced.

> "You wrong God in His way of wisdom, because in sin you profess God's ways are not ways of wisdom, but you know better to provide for yourself than in the way God has set before you. How you cast folly on the ways of God and set your shallow way and heart before God's, as if you could provide for yourself and your own good more wisely than God has set you in a way to do." -*The Evil of Evils*, Jeremiah Burroughs

February 16

Christ, the Cornerstone

> When I saw Him, I fell at His feet as though dead. But He laid His right hand on me, saying, "Fear not, I am the first and the last, and the living one. I died, and behold I am alive forevermore, and I have the keys of Death and Hades." Revelation 1:17-18

Unless Jesus is first then we do not have the foundation that true sobriety requires. One of the names that Jesus is given as an indication of His supremacy is the *Chief Cornerstone. Vocabulary.com* says "a cornerstone is literally a stone at the corner of a building. It's an important stone, so it also means 'the basic part of something.'"

> "In every stone building, one stone is crucial. It is laid first, and it is to ensure that the building is square and stable. It is the rock upon which the weight of the entire structure rests. It is the cornerstone. Scripture describes Jesus as the 'Chief Cornerstone' of our faith."
> –*Jesus the Chief Cornerstone of our faith,* Debra Draper, The Woodland News

So, you might ask, "what does this have to do with sobriety?" While there are many ways that I can explain this, I will try to be as simple as possible. Too many programs give us a complex explanation of addictions. That is why I had to abandon what has become a traditional approach to addictions and seek after <u>the original approach</u> that comes directly from the Scriptures.

I often explain the "awe factor" of addictions just as John was in awe of Christ in the passage above. The root of every addiction is the awe that we attribute. Awe is what either draws us to God or leads us away from Him.

Could the cornerstone of worship be its awe? Pastor Paul Tripp states that [awe wrongness] "is the root and source of every evil thing that we think, desire, choose, say, and do. It is the reason for all our personal, relational, and societal dysfunction."

Jesus came to set things in order as the cornerstone of a building. John said that he saw Jesus. Is not vision based on sight? Sobriety requires vision. When John saw Jesus, it was so sobering that he fell at His feet as though dead. And the sobriety that John experienced led to piety. ***Sobriety that is not based on piety and reverence, is not sobriety at all.***

> For it stands in Scripture: "Behold, I am laying in Zion a stone, a cornerstone chosen and precious, and whoever believes in him will not be put to shame." 1 Peter 2:6

February 17

The heart of the matter

For Ezra had **set his heart** to study the Law of the LORD, and to do it and to teach his statutes and rules in Israel. Ezra 7:10

For Ezra had **prepared his heart** to seek the law of the LORD, and to do it, and to teach in Israel statutes and judgments. *KJV*

Writing about addiction comes from my heart because I was severely affected by drug addiction for 23 intermittent years. I will never forget looking for scriptural answers. I attribute my sobriety to both the written Word of God and the Living Word of God. I have dedicated my life to sharing the clarity of what the Word of God says about addiction.

The biggest reason that addiction touches my heart is that it disgraces God. I think about how the heart of God is touched by the atrocities of addiction. *God is more grieved over addiction than any of us can or ever will be!* The fact that He sent Jesus to pay the price for our irreverently idolatrous addictions is proof!

I think about how God is ignored whenever we seek joy, comfort, and contentment outside of Him. I think of how we seek answers to our problems (including a resolution to addiction) outside of Him.

Can anyone argue that addiction does not involve our hearts? The heart of the matter is the heart of the matter! Do we not yearn for the object of our addiction? Doesn't yearning start with the heart?

Puritan John Owen said, "the mind as it reasons, discerns and judges; the emotions as they like or dislike; the conscience as it determines and warns; and the will as it chooses or refuses—are all together called *the heart*." The *Strong's Bible Dictionary* defines the heart as the "seat of appetites, determination of will, and the seat of emotions and passions."

Many have sought to define the origin of addiction apart from the Scriptures and have cheated the masses of the most accurate description of addiction and the joy of knowing Christ intimately as opposed to devoting our attention to ourselves.

One thing that we can all agree on is that we love our addictions. Whoever or whatever we love holds our attention. Preoccupation is another word that can be used to express love. Preoccupation is defined by the *Collins Dictionary* as *"a state of mind in which you think about something so much that you do not consider other things to be important."*

The heart of the matter is not just my heart or yours. The heart of the matter is the heart of God! The heart of the matter is for us to become friends with God with the highest degree of reverence that defines the highest degree of sanity that is only found in Christ.

February 18

Where your heart is, there will be your treasure also

> Thus saith the LORD, Stand ye in the ways, and see, and ask for the old paths, where is the good way, and walk therein, and ye shall find rest for your souls. But they said, We will not walk therein.
> Jeremiah 6:16 *KJV*

Quality sobriety is built on an ongoing love for God! Our lives are not complete without a love for God and others. If you are in the body of Christ, you were made for this! It is your relationship with Christ that gives your life meaning and purpose. Within that relationship, He leads you to bring others the joy and freedom that you have in Him.

> "Our love, however, is easily misdirected. Its object tends to become the creation rather than the Creator; it loses sight of the eternal for the temporal; it focuses on the self, often to the exclusion of God and others. We become idolaters, focusing a part or all of our love elsewhere. We are 'love breakers' more than 'law breakers.'" -*Baker's Evangelical Dictionary of Biblical Theology*

It is no wonder that we can define addictions as idols! Some of the definitions found in *Strong's Dictionary of the Bible* for love in the Old Testament are "to desire, to breathe after, to delight in, and to be intimate with." The insanity of addiction causes us to be unreasonable.

Pride is associated with insanity in that we are unwilling to admit that we are unable to find the answers to life that we need on our own. And then, in the stubbornness of our hearts, we cleave to an idol rather than cleaving to God. Insanity is a lack of understanding.

> "Let us beware lest we in our pride accept the erroneous notion that idolatry consists only in kneeling before visible objects of adoration, and that civilized people are therefore free from it. The essence of idolatry is the entertainment of thoughts about God that are unworthy of Him. The idolater simply imagines things about God and acts as if they were true." -*The Knowledge of God,* Tozer

Black Lives Matter (BLM) is an international movement that began in 2013. It wasn't long before the phrase, "people matter" or "all people matter" was chanted. But what if we treated addictions with the thought that God matters?

And reverence not only determines how you treat God, but how you treat others as well. When you are devoted to addiction, then you live a self-absorbed life.

February 19

A heart condition

The heart is deceitful above all things, and desperately sick; who can understand it? Jeremiah 17:9

He who trusts his own heart is a fool. Proverbs 28:26 *NKJV*

Spiritual health is most important. Spiritual disorders have been proven to cause addiction. Most people do not realize the relevance of worship and addiction. And yet, it is a basic explanation of how addiction tugs at our attention.

One of the characteristics of worship is a preoccupation. Again, **preoccupation** is defined by *Collins Dictionary* as ***"a state of mind in which you think about something so much that you do not consider other things to be important."*** Since our hearts and our minds go together, we can accurately call addiction a heart condition.

In his *95 Theses for Pure Reformation*, Mike Cleveland says that "the one trapped in sexual idolatry does not see God properly, therefore he does not perceive spiritual truth accurately." Cleveland uses the phrase "hypnotic power" in stating, "It is as if they have found some secret power, all without depending on God."

The origin of addiction is fully discovered as the process of addiction grows into a devotion to addiction that comes from its dominance or control. Dependence completes the circle. It is probably at this stage that the addiction becomes less attractive, but it doesn't matter once it has become the choice of how we fulfill our desires.

> "Addiction involves craving for something intensely, loss of control over its use, and continuing involvement with it despite adverse consequences. Addiction changes the brain, first by subverting the way it registers pleasure and then by corrupting other normal drives such as learning and motivation. Although breaking an addiction is tough, it can be done. The word 'addiction' is derived from a Latin term for 'enslaved by' or 'bound to.' Anyone who has struggled to overcome an addiction—or has tried to help someone else to do so—understands why. Addiction exerts a long and powerful influence on the brain that manifests in three distinct ways: craving for the object of addiction, loss of control over its use, and continuing involvement with it despite adverse consequences." -*How Addiction Hijacks the Brain,* A Harvard Health article

February 20

Heart failure

> Then the lust, when it hath conceived, beareth sin: and the sin, when it is full-grown, bringeth forth death. James 4:15 *KJV*

How fascinating is addiction? Addiction can capture your attention to various degrees. The same can be said about the Word of God. Just as partaking of addiction becomes a way of life, so may we develop a life of partaking of the truth of God through His Word.

I am a firm believer in exchanging addiction for something better. While the world, the flesh, and the devil call us to practice things that are not of God, the Word of God instructs us in things that are not only pleasing to God but pleasant to our souls as well.

> Sow a thought, reap an action,
> Sow an action, reap a pattern,
> Sow a pattern, reap a habit,
> Sow a habit, reap a *lifestyle,
> Sow a lifestyle, reap a destiny
> *some quotes use the word character

"To become an ADDICT, the guilt the conscience produces is ignored, stifled, silenced, and eventually restrained. The addict learns to become comfortable, either ignoring the guilt his conscience produces or the conscious becomes ineffective in producing guilt, or both. In some instances, the addict's conscience may be restrained to tell the addict that his addiction is good." -*My Beloved Addiction*, Jeff Mullins

Addiction is progressive. John Owen said, "either you kill sin or sin will be killing you." Sin creates a divided heart that often produces divided reverence. This is the reason why many start to hate themselves.

But it is a perverted hatred because it is a love for themselves that they want the best for themselves but because of the poor choices that they make, they hate themselves. It's not that they wish the worst for themselves. They want the best, but they hate themselves for the person that they are becoming.

If sin is the greatest enemy to man, pride is the vessel through which it travels. Jim Berg said, "in our wickedness, we believe that God is the biggest evil we could encounter and that it is our resistance to Him that keeps life from charging headlong into misery!"

February 21

An empty heart

> I have seen all the things that are done under the sun; all of them are meaningless, a chasing after the wind. Ecclesiastes 1:14

An empty heart will either seek the Lord or some other god. Saint Augustine was famous for stating that our hearts are restless until they find their rest in God. We were made for God and when we turn to other sources of comfort that are not of God then we not only betray God but we betray ourselves and others.

This is the condition of your heart from birth. Without Christ, you continue in this state from one depth of emptiness to another and become vulnerable to addictions that pull at your devotion. The whole meaning and goal in life for the natural man is to please himself!

> "There once was in man a true happiness of which now remain to him only the mark and empty trace, which he in vain tries to fill from all his surroundings, seeking from things absent the help he does not obtain in things present. But these are all inadequate because the infinite abyss can only be filled by an infinite and immutable object, that is to say, only by God Himself." –Pascal, *Pensees*

In his booklet *Just One More,* Dr. Edward T. Welch offers a list of perceived (or at best temporary) assets of addiction. He says that "even with all the associated misery, people drink because on some level drinking does something for them." With each experience we decide the value of what we taste, touch, hear, smell, and feel. This is what I refer to as an acquired desire.

> "Men are in a restless pursuit after satisfaction in earthly things. They will exhaust themselves in the deceitful delights of sin, and, finding them all to be vanity and emptiness, they will become very perplexed and disappointed. But they will continue their fruitless search. Though wearied, they still stagger forward under the influence of spiritual madness, and though there is no result to be reached except that of everlasting disappointment, yet they press forward. They have no forethought for their eternal state; the present hour absorbs them. They turn to another and another of earth's broken cisterns, hoping to find water where not a drop was ever discovered yet." -*Spurgeon*

February 22

A stony heart

But Jeshurun grew fat, and kicked; you grew fat, stout, and sleek; then he forsook God who made him and scoffed at the Rock of his salvation. They stirred him to jealousy with strange gods; with abominations they provoked him to anger. They sacrificed to demons that were no gods, to gods they had never known, to new gods that had come recently, whom your fathers had never dreaded. You were unmindful of the Rock that bore you, and you forgot the God who gave you birth. Deuteronomy 32:15-18

A stony heart and a divided heart resemble one another in some respects. Neither is fully committed to God. There's an old story about a pastor asking one of the members what the difference between ignorance and apathy is. When the church member said, "I don't know and I don't care," the pastor replied, "You're right!"

A stony heart is ignorant to the things of God (and perhaps doesn't care either.) A divided heart just doesn't care. A divided heart is deceived. Deception can only be dispelled through discernment. But before discernment, repentance is needed for the addict and/or those who are outside of Christ.

When was the last time that you went to a meeting for addictions and heard about repentance? **Repentance** is a word that is connected with God. It is a more accurate and concise explanation of the phenomenon of turning to God from the idols of addiction and turning to Christ than *recovery*. You won't hear anything about repentance in an environment that wants little or no God.

The heart of every addiction is that it holds out on God. And at the same time, when we seek to overcome an addiction, we are tempted to hold back from God as much as *we* can. Having the mind of Christ is essential to overcoming addiction. Jesus was the most brilliant man that ever lived.

The people were amazed at His words! When He was still a child *"all who heard him were amazed at his understanding and his answers"* in the Temple (Luke 2:47). Someone said that no one ever spoke like Christ (John 7:46). You will never fully resolve our issues with addiction without being fully committed to Christ.

Addictions discredit God. Addiction tells you that God is not to be trusted, He doesn't love you all that much, He doesn't know what He is talking about, and you don't have to answer to Him (and many other lies, if you were to think about it). Some more lies that are behind addictions are that you know what is best, you are not all that bad, and you can handle it (and again, many, many lies.)

February 23

A divided heart

And Elijah came near to all the people and said, "How long will you go limping between two different opinions? If the LORD is God, follow him; but if Baal, then follow him." And the people did not answer him a word. 1 Kings 18:21

The soundest approach to addiction is to first bridge the gap between us and God. **The ultimate answer to addiction is to choose God over everything else.** You come to your senses as you choose what is of the greatest value. Can you name anything of greater value than being in one accord with God? **Both the addictions that we invent and the way that they are dealt with apart from Christ reveal how man rebels against God.**

"Now then, little man, for a short time fly from your business; hide yourself for a moment from your turbulent thoughts. Break off now your troublesome cares, and think less of your laborious occupations. Make a little time for God, and rest for a while in Him. Enter into the chamber of your mind, shut out everything but God and whatever helps you to seek Him, and, when you have shut the door, seek Him. Speak now, O my whole heart, speak now to God: 'I seek Thy face; Thy face, Lord, do I desire.'" -*Proslogion*, Anselm

Who's on the throne? That's the question that determines the fate of a nation. Who's on the throne also determines the quality of your sobriety as well. As the second Psalm reveals the magnificence of Christ, so should you! You were created to reflect the image of God. **I challenge anyone to tell me how addictions reflect the image of God!** God is love. But addictions are purely self-seeking. Jesus was the most *selfless* person that ever lived.

The idolatry of addiction seeks self-worship. The natural inclination to worship ourselves originates in our thoughts and is manifest in our actions. We don't need anyone to teach us how to love ourselves.

Even when someone wants to commit suicide it is because they love themselves so much that they do not want to go on living the life that they possess (since they don't think that there is anything better for them, they choose not to go on.)

Teach me your way, LORD, that I may rely on your faithfulness; give me an undivided heart, that I may fear your name.
Psalm 86:11 *NIV*

February 24

A conditioned heart

For those whom he foreknew he also predestined to be conformed to the image of his Son, in order that he might be the firstborn among many brothers. Romans 8:29

A relationship with Christ is needed to confront addictions in a way that honors God. To reject Christ is not only an insult to God but it is disastrous to ourselves and others. Acts 4:12 says that "there is no other name given among men whereby we must be saved."

The way that addictions are addressed by leaders and individuals is a reflection of what they think of Jesus and whether they have become associated with Him (as well as the *degree* of association.)

To be reasonable is a mark of maturity. If man has been created in the image of God, and the image was lost in the Fall, one of the means that God restores that image is by making us more reasonable! As Christians become more reasonable, they become more conformable to the image of Christ.

One of the most horrendous characteristics of addiction is its savagery. Addiction starts as a pawn and as it is allowed to move across the board of our lives into more spaces then it has the potential of becoming a power-ruling piece as in the game of chess. Addictions often resort to uncivilized, nonproductive behavior. Addictions are typified as unreasonable. Jeremiah Burroughs said, "Certainly our contentment does not consist in getting the thing we desire, but in God's fashioning our spirits to our condition."

> "What a hopeless task if we had to do the work! Nature never can overcome nature, not even with the help of grace. Self can never cast out self, even in the regenerate man." -*Humility,* Andrew Murray

Physical conditioning will change the shape and size of your muscles. Physical conditioning can make you stronger. Spiritual conditioning will change the shape, size, and strength of your heart. A small heart has no room for God. A weak heart will not hold on to Him. A foolish heart doesn't value God. And a dark and dirty heart can not commune with Him. Spiritual conditioning, known as sanctification, is described in 2 Corinthians 7:1.

> Since we have these promises, beloved, let us cleanse ourselves from every defilement of body and spirit, bringing holiness to completion in the fear of God. 2 Corinthians 7:1

February 25

Abiding in Christ

Abide in me, and I in you. As the branch cannot bear fruit by itself, unless it abides in the vine, neither can you, unless you abide in me. I am the vine; you are the branches. Whoever abides in me and I in him, he it is that bears much fruit, for apart from me you can do nothing. John 15:4-5

It is impossible for anyone to relapse while abiding in Christ. Jesus explained the importance of abiding in Him in John 15. I like to call it perpetual reverence. Perpetual reverence gives us the consistency that is needed to form the integrity of a godly life.

One of the things that we learn from abiding in Christ is that there is more to life than remaining free of addiction. Jesus calls you to be fruitful as opposed to the destructive life of addiction. In addition, only abiding in Christ satisfies the long of the soul that you seek in addiction.

> "Tis only abiding that can really satisfy the thirsty soul, and give to drink of the rivers of pleasure that are at his right hand. Was it the weary longing to be made free from the bondage of sin, to become pure and holy, and so to find rest, the rest of God for the soul? this too can only be realized as you abide in Him,--only abiding in Jesus, gives rest in Him." -*Abide in Christ*, Andrew Murray

Abiding in Christ goes hand in hand with sanctification. Sanctification means being set apart. It's the same principle that the Apostle Paul shared in Galatians 6:14 stating, "far be it from me to boast except in the cross of our Lord Jesus Christ, by which the world has been crucified to me, and I to the world."

One of the soberest issues relating to addiction that you will seldom hear is how Jesus will see you when he returns. Ironically, this is probably the most important issue surrounding addiction. In my 23 years of jumping back and forth to addiction, God would remind me of the relevancy of Christ's return through a passage.

> And now, little children, abide in him, so that when he appears we may have confidence and not shrink from him in shame at his coming. 1 John 2:28

Quality sobriety is built and maintained by such a desire to see Christ that we abide in Him. We want to see Jesus so much that we allow Him to live through us! We want to see Jesus so much that we long for others to see Him as well.

February 26

Thy Word is a lamp unto my feet

> Your word is a lamp to my feet and a light to my path.
> Psalm 119:105

When Jesus came, a quotation from Isaiah 9:2 came to life. The people dwelling in darkness have seen a great light (Matthew 4:16). The same is true for all who turn from addiction to Christ. Both the written Word and the Living Word of God give us light.

Abiding in Christ involves walking in the light of His Word. Psalm 119 explains how valuable the Word of God is. It could be called the ABCs of the Bible because virtually every verse reveals something about God's Word. It may also be called the ABCs of the Bible because every stanza is represented by a Hebrew alphabet. Do you know the ABCs of addictions? Learn the Scriptures and you will know all about addictions.

> So Jesus said to the Jews who had believed Him, "If you abide in My word, you are truly My disciples, and you will know the truth, and the truth will set you free." John 8:31-32 *NIV*

Cherish the light! Once while traveling, I found myself in a dilapidated neighborhood at night. I booked a place while not knowing anything about the neighborhood. I could tell it was a rough neighborhood because of the people on the streets buying and selling drugs and from the look of the houses.

I was a little nervous about finding the place I was to lodge in because it was clear to all that I was not from there (my suitcase was a dead giveaway.) I would have been more comfortable if it were light. We live in a dark world. God has provided the light of His Word so that you can see where He wants you to be. If you fail to look to the Word of God for the answers to addiction:

a.   You are saying that God doesn't know enough- He's a fool
b.   You are saying that God doesn't care enough- He is evil and can't be trusted
c.   You are saying that God doesn't have enough power- He is weak and sorry
d.   You are saying that you don't care what God has to say- You've got all the answers
e.   You are saying that you don't mind taking a chance of being deceived
f.   You are saying that God doesn't have the right to tell you what to do

February 27

The severity of the affliction of addiction

I am severely afflicted; give me life, O Lord, according to Your Word! Psalms 119:107 *NIV*

Addictions can be called afflictions. While afflictions are often thought of as illnesses, their definition is much broader. I do not believe that addiction is an illness or disease (people don't practice diseases.) Afflictions cover more than illnesses. An affliction can be defined by disposition, distress, trouble, and adversity.

I can relate to the psalmist's severe affliction as I experienced severe affliction throughout the years of my drug use. Anybody who has been chronically addicted has probably been through various phases. During one phase of my life, I decided that I would not ever stop smoking crack.

The severity of addictions occurs in stages. While the stages of addiction are usually listed as **experimentation, regular use, high-risk use, and dependency**, I prefer explaining the stages of addiction differently. My definition of the stages of addiction involves five phases.

1. Acquaintance
2. Attention
3. Acknowledgment
4. Affection
5. Allegiance

One of the readings from *Alcoholics Anonymous* refers to alcoholism as "conning, baffling, and powerful." Psalms 19:7b says, "the testimony of the Lord is sure, making wise the simple." Just as the psalmist asked God to give him life when faced with severe affliction, you must look to the Word of God for answers to the severity of addictions.

If Your sobriety is not based on the principles of God, then you are living by your own standards. *You* determine what's right and what's wrong. Who's to say that you might not change your mind about whether it's right to engage in addiction? What's to keep you from doing *other* things that are not in your best interest or the interest of others (as well as displeasing to God?) You, in effect, design your own program. At best, you will possess a *form* of godliness.

"The Bible embodies all of the knowledge man needs to fill the longing of his soul and solve all of his problems" -Billy Graham

February 28

Carest Thou not that we perish?

> If Your law had not been my delight, I would have perished in my affliction. Psalms 119:92

Millions of lives lay in the balance while addictions are in rule. We find ourselves to be just as powerless as the disciples of Christ when confronted with a raging sea while tossed about by the addictions of the day.

> And there arose a great storm of wind, and the waves beat into the ship, so that it was now full. And He was in the hinder part of the ship, asleep on a pillow: and they awake Him, and say unto Him, Master, carest Thou not that we perish? And He arose, and rebuked the wind, and said unto the sea, Peace, be still. And the wind ceased, and there was a great calm. And He said unto them, Why are ye so fearful? How is it that ye have no faith? And they feared exceedingly, and said one to another, What manner of Man is this, that even the wind and the sea obey Him? Mark 4:38

God doesn't want us to perish. The most well-known verse from the Bible tells us that "God so loved the world that He gave His only begotten Son, that whosoever believeth in Him **shall not perish** but have everlasting life" (John 3:16 *KJV*). God is most concerned about individuals who are perishing as well as families, neighborhoods, countries and the entire world. He is longing for us to seek the reconciliation that is available to us in Christ.

The psalmist said that he would have perished if the law of the Lord were not his delight. Christ is the fulfillment of the law. Without Him, we are "dead men walking." You don't just wait to be condemned without Christ- you are already condemned without Him.

The psalmist found delightful answers from the Word of God. The ultimate answers to addictions are found by delighting and abiding in the living Word of God (Christ is the living Word.)

The Word of God discloses and eradicates the deception and error on which addictions are rooted. Three basic areas of deceit that give addictions their strength are; the misinformation that they give concerning God, concerning ourselves, and the addiction (itself.) Addictions deceive you into thinking that they can bring fulfillment, they are harmless (or at least don't cause much harm), and you could never be under their control. The Word of God teaches us differently.

Proverbs 29:18 says, "where there is no vision, the people perish." Only the Word of God has the complete vision necessary for people to avoid perishing from addiction.

March 1

Trained

Blessed are those whose way is blameless, who walk in the law of the Lord! Psalms 119:1

Blessed are those whose lives have integrity, those who follow the teachings of the LORD. *God's Worded Translation*

It is said that walking is good exercise. I would have to say that it depends on where you are walking. If you are walking in the direction of a cliff, it would not be a good exercise to continue walking in the same direction. Walking is often used in Scripture to describe the way that we live. I am fascinated by all the implications behind walking and living.

Walking can also be defined as a practice. The most distinguishable thing about a walk is the direction it leads. It has been said that we are either walking toward God or walking away from Him.

A walk eventually accumulates distance. Just start walking, and before you know it, you have traveled a distance. That's how addictions get you into trouble. But, for all that it's worth- your walk is a daily walk. **"Sin will take you farther than you want to go, keep you longer than you want to stay, and cost you more than you want to pay."**

Many argue that the Scriptures don't say anything about addictions. I beg to differ. The world wants to free us of our guilt by saying that sin does not exist rather than looking to Jesus. The Scriptures clearly state that some things are godly and others are ungodly. Addictions are ungodly.

No one is born walking. In the same manner, when you are born-again, you must learn to walk as you mature. Hebrews 5:14 says that those who have a mature walk with the Lord "have their powers of discernment trained by constant practice to distinguish good from evil."

Have nothing to do with irreverent, silly myths. Rather **train yourself for godliness**; for while bodily training is of some value, godliness is of value in every way, as it holds promise for the present life and also for the life to come. 1 Timothy 4:7-8 *(The KJV uses the word "exercise" rather than train)*

As you are trained to walk, it becomes almost natural. Training well describes the process that God wants to perform in our war against addictions.

He trains my hands for war, so that my arms can bend a bow of bronze. Psalms 18:34

March 2

Craving

My soul is consumed with longing for Your rules at all times.
Psalms 119:20

It is no mystery that an addiction is something that is intensely longed for. The psalmist so longed for the rules (judgments, *KJV*) of God that his soul was consumed with his longing. **Craving** can be used as a synonym for *longing*. You acquire a taste for the things that you crave.

You have the capability of craving what is good and acceptable to God and what is evil and displeasing to God. The choice is yours. How we acquire a taste for reverencing God more and more while longing for His Word relates to my experiences with my dad.

My mother was a single parent until she met my stepfather. Our relationship was rocky at first, but by the time he died, we had become the best of friends. A week before my dad died, I was blessed with a precious memory. I asked him one morning if he remembered the day that we met. He said, "Why don't you remind me?" And so, I proceeded.

"You and my mom had met and decided to get married and it was time for us two to meet. I remember how you prepared some squash on our first encounter. When you asked me how I liked the squash, I was saying, that I could take it or leave it."

Then I said, "After you married my mother, you would ask me what I thought of Jesus. My attitude was the same as the squash, I thought that I could take Him or leave Him." Then I told him, "Now, thanks to you, Dad, I love squash and I really, really love Jesus."

As the Bread of Life, the Word of God provides nourishment for our souls that can not be found elsewhere. Psalms 1:2 refers to those whose delight is in the law of the Lord. There are promises of enjoyment and fulfillment by reverentially following the leadings of God. Proverbs 2:10 says "Knowledge will be pleasant to your soul."

> "True godliness lies very much in desires. As we are not what we shall be, so also we are not what we would be. The desires of gracious men after holiness are intense, they cause a wear of heart, a straining of the mind, till it feels ready to snap with the heavenly pull. A high value of the Lord's commandment leads to a pressing desire to know and to do it, and this so weighs upon the soul that it is ready to break in pieces under the crush of its own longings. What a blessing it is when all our desires are after the things of God. We may well long for such longings." -Spurgeon

March 3

Conditioned cravings

My eyes long for Your salvation and for the fulfillment of Your righteous promise. Psalms 119:123

How's your appetite? What is it that you long for? Does not longing describe addiction? You could say that the psalmist was addicted to the salvation of the Lord and the fulfillment of His promise.

Because some addictions are not in God's safety zone, addictions are given a bad name. Whether addiction is good or evil, it rules our lives. The interesting thing about addiction is that we don't just consume it, but addictions consume us!

Blessed are those who hunger and thirst for righteousness, for they shall be satisfied. Matthew 5:6

We eat and drink our thoughts just as we do food. The phrase "garbage in-garbage out" used by the computer world describes our thinking as well. Whatever we put into our minds affects our actions. And not only do our cravings condition us, but we condition our cravings.

A good man out of the good treasure of his heart brings forth good things, and an evil man out of the evil treasure brings forth evil things. Matthew 12:35 *NKJV*

In 1927, Ivan Pavlov experimented with his dog on psychological training—specifically, condition stimuli and response. He found that when he rang a bell each time before he fed his dog, the dog no longer salivated in response to the food, but to the bell.

I still remember the days of my drug use when the time would draw near to get my next fix and how my body would respond. By the same token, as I grow in the knowledge of Christ, I associate every situation with my relationship with Him (producing a longing.) One of my most often cherished quotes comes from Edward T. Welch.

"Imagine having drug cravings subdued by the joy of knowing and obeying Christ. Imagine having temptations lose their allure because there is more pleasure in walking humbly with our God. Imagine waking up and strategizing how to please the God who loves you rather than where you will get your next drink." - *Addictions: A Banquet in the Grave,* Edward T. Welch

March 4

Stuck like Chuck

I cling to Your testimonies, O Lord; let me not be put to shame!
Psalms 119:31

"Stuck like Chuck" used to be a rhyme I would often hear during my drug use to describe someone who had allowed a drug to completely control them. The *New International Version* of Jonah 2:8 gives an accurate description of the devastation of addictions.

Those who cling to worthless idols turn away from God's love for them. Jonah 2:8 *NIV*

Jesus stated that "No one can serve two masters, for either he will hate the one and love the other, or he will be devoted to the one and despise the other" (Matthew 6:24). So what is it to "cling to the testimonies" of the Lord? The *King James Version* uses the word "stuck." The definitions given by *Strong's Bible Dictionary* for the Hebrew word are:

"to cling, stick, stay close, cleave, keep close, stick to, stick with, follow closely, join to, overtake, and catch"

One of the characteristics of an addiction is the uncertainty they deliver. A lot of disappointment is experienced while seeking satisfaction from an addiction. The cry of the psalmist was not to be put to shame. Think of the shame that relates to addictions!
Alcoholics Anonymous accurately describes alcoholism as "cunning, baffling, and powerful." How adequate it is to look to the Word of the Lord to address addictions when we are told that "the testimony of the Lord is sure, making wise the simple" (Psalm 19:7).
The psalmist said that he stuck to the testimonies of the Lord. As he stuck to the Word of God, he received the nourishment that his soul could not find elsewhere. We could describe the Word of God as soul food. Jesus also said that those who hunger and thirst after righteousness will be filled (Matthew 5:6). Addictions are elusive.

"When something good becomes a god, the pleasure it brings dies in the process. Pleasure has this unique trait: the more intensely you chase it, the less likely you are to catch it. Philosophers call this the 'hedonistic paradox.' The idea is that pleasure, pursued for its own sake, evaporates before our eyes." -*gods at War*, Kyle Idleman

March 5

Imagine your passion!

Hot indignation seizes me because of the wicked, who forsake Your law. Your statutes have been my songs in the house of my sojourning. Psalms 119:53-54

Passion is a characteristic that we all possess. It is the passion that we have for the perceived assets of a substance or behavior that makes it an addiction. The *Google* dictionary defines passion as a "strong and barely controllable emotion." *Merriam-Webster* offers an array of definitions for passion.

- the state or capacity of being acted on by external agents or forces
- intense, driving, or overmastering feeling or conviction
- a strong liking or desire for or devotion to some activity, object, or concept
- an object of desire or deep interest

The passion held by the psalmist seemed to move from one extreme to the next. He moves from the hot indignation of anger to the joy of song over the Word of God. Are we not driven from one extreme to the other by our addictions?

We angrily argue and defend our addictions on the one hand, and on the other, we sing the praise of their "glorious attributes." Yet the psalmist's passion was governed by self-control (unlike addictions.) The fact that our passion can be turned towards the things of the world or to the things of God is seen in the Scriptures.

Do not love the world or the things in the world. If anyone loves the world, the love of the Father is not in him. For all that is in the world—the desires of the flesh and the desires of the eyes and pride of life—is not from the Father but is from the world. And the world is passing away along with its desires, but whoever does the will of God abides forever. 1 John 2:15-17

Many cannot believe that the passion that they have for an addiction can be replaced by a passion for the things of Christ! I am a living witness. I can tell you one story after another of the joy and excitement of my adventures with Christ!

The greatest pleasure that I now treasure is the glory of God!

March 6

What's in a name?

> I remember Your name in the night, O Lord, and keep Your law. This blessing has fallen to me, that I have kept Your precepts.
> Psalms 119:55-56

"What's in a name?" is a question that I have heard since I was young. As I encounter various situations, I have learned the value of a name more and more. Your battle against addictions is highly dependent on the name that is above all other names. That name is Jesus!

> And there is salvation in no one else, for there is no other name under heaven given among men by which we must be saved.
> Acts 4:12

> The name of the LORD is a strong tower; the righteous man runs into it and is safe. Proverbs 18:10

Ten years ago, I borrowed a book from a homeless shelter library that proved to be instrumental to the foundation of my sobriety. After gathering a year of sobriety, I purchased the book and have read it no less than five times. The title of the book is *All the Divine Names and Titles of the Bible* by Herbert Lockyer.

On reverencing the name of the Lord, Lockyer quotes George MacDonald that, "name of the Lord God should be a precious jewel in the cabinet of our heart, to be taken out only at great times, and with loving care." Lockyer says, "we would go further and say that all the names used of the Three in One should be taken out at *all* times, not merely as precious jewels to admire, but as treasure to use for our constant spiritual enrichment."

We use names as a source of identity. God has an identity that is so tremendous that the names that we have for Him are not enough to describe His magnificence. A name invokes our trust. Think of the products that we buy and how the name of the brand draws us.

God has a reputation for fixing things. Jonah professed the reputation of God. God is the same today as He was during the days of Jonah. It is we who need to change!

> for I knew that you are a gracious God and merciful, slow to anger and abounding in steadfast love, and relenting from disaster.
> Jonah 4:2b

March 7

What's good? (part 1)

You are good and do good; teach me Your statutes. Psalms 119:68

There is not a person alive who does not want what they perceive to be good. The problem comes when you prescribe what is good outside of God and His Word. As quiet as it is kept, this is the root and origin of addictions. Rather than proclaiming that God is good, as the psalmist, when clinging to the idols of addictions, we are calling God evil, insufficient, and limited (usually non-verbally.)

> Woe to those who call evil good and good evil, who put darkness for light and light for darkness, who put bitter for sweet and sweet for bitter! Isaiah 5:20

Good is often used in Scripture. The Hebrew word used most often for good also means to be pleasant or agreeable. That doesn't sound like an addiction to me! Some of the other words that describe the Hebrew words for *good* as defined by *Strong's Bible Dictionary* draw an interesting contrast to addictions as well.

> "Beautiful, best, better, bountiful, cheerful, at ease, fair, joyful, kindly, kindness, loving, precious, prosperity, sweet, wealth, welfare, and well-favored."

The word "good" occurs 720 times in the Scriptures. God was the first to call something good. Of the six times that good is used in Psalms 119, four of those uses occur in verses 66-71. Verse 72 not only speaks of what is good, but it also gives what is better. There seems to be an order in the use of the word *good*.

> Teach me good judgment and knowledge, for I believe in your commandments. Psalms 119:66

> You are good and do good; teach me your statutes. Psalms 119:68

> It is good for me that I was afflicted, that I might learn your statutes. Psalms 119:71

> The law of your mouth is better to me than thousands of gold and silver pieces. Psalms 119:72

March 8

What's good? (part 2)

> The insolent smear me with lies, but with my whole heart I keep Your precepts; their heart is unfeeling like fat, but I delight in your law. Psalms 119:69-70

Evil is as clearly revealed, just as the goodness of God. If only it were easy for us to see the evil of addictions. Many say that addictions are not a problem of morality. They say that addictions are strictly physiological.

Just as Psalms 119:69-70 mentions two hearts, we may respond to the allurements of the world in two manners. We may have a heart that is sensitive to God or an unfeeling heart. The heart that is referred to is not our physical heart. The Scriptures more often refer to our souls as our hearts.

We have proven ourselves as fallible in distinguishing good from evil since the *Garden of Eden.* Since then we have only changed for the worse. Outside of the redemption that is in Christ, we are doomed. Had Adam and Eve believed the Word that God had spoken all would be well.

> So when the woman saw that the tree was good for food, and that it was a delight to the eyes, and that the tree was to be desired to make one wise, she took of its fruit and ate, and she also gave some to her husband who was with her, and he ate. Genesis 3:8

Because of the decision made by Adam and Eve, they begot offspring such as the insolent who smeared David with lies. The devil uses lies to keep us bound to addictions. As the Lord Jesus said that the truth will make us free, so it is that we need the Word of Truth to distinguish good from evil and grow in our maturity as children of God after being born again.

> for everyone who lives on milk is unskilled in the word of righteousness, since he is a child. But solid food is for the mature, for those who have their powers of discernment trained by constant practice to distinguish good from evil. Hebrews 5:13-14

> "Their heart is as fat as grease. They delight in fatness, but I delight in Thee. Their hearts, through sensual indulgence, have grown insensible, coarse, and grovelling; but Thou hast saved me from such a fate through Thy chastening hand. Proud men grow fat through carnal luxuries, and this makes them prouder still. They riot in their prosperity, and fill their hearts therewith till they become insensible, effeminate, and self indulgent." –*The Treasury of David,* Spurgeon

March 9

What's good? (part 3)

It is good for me that I was afflicted, that I might learn Your statutes. Psalms 119:71

I can remember dad telling me that he had learned to appreciate the *Muscular Dystrophy* he was afflicted with. He told me very candidly that if he did not suffer from an affliction he did not know if he would have as much of an interest in the things of God.

Troubles can be defined as afflictions as well. Trouble is something that you cannot escape. Job said that "man is born unto trouble." (Job 5:7) No addiction can keep you from trouble or eliminate trouble once it occurs. (If anything, addictions add to your troubles.) Someone once told me that life has enough problems without adding any more.

Afflictions come in many forms. Illness is usually associated with affliction. Pain is an affliction. No matter the affliction, it stands as a trial. It doesn't necessarily mean that you have transgressed; it does mean that you need special guidance. The psalmist considered this to be a good thing.

I once spoke with someone who helped me to distinguish the value of our trials better. He said that **our temptations have an appeal but cause harm; while our trials are disdained yet most beneficial**. But, whether we suffer from trials or temptations, each is an opportunity for us to become more intimate with God.

> "God says, 'Here is one, if he could be rid of this lust I should never hear of him more; let him wrestle with this, or he is lost.' Astonishing! God ordains to leave a lust with me till I become the sort of warrior who will still seek his aid when this victory is won. God knows when we can bear the triumphs of his grace." -*The Mortification of Sin*, John Owen

While afflictions can draw us closer to God, addictions never do. The highest levels of reverence we can express for God were exemplified through Christ. The goal of every program for addictions should be to be more Christlike.

> In the days of his flesh, Jesus offered up prayers and supplications, with loud cries and tears, to him who was able to save him from death, and he was heard because of his reverence. Although he was a son, he learned obedience through what he suffered. And being made perfect, he became the source of eternal salvation to all who obey him. Hebrews 5:7-9

March 10

What's good (part 4)

> The law of Your mouth is better to me than thousands of gold and silver pieces. Psalms 119:72

What's your favorite book in the Bible? My favorite book is Hebrews. I love the way that the book of Hebrews covers the annals of time. Another feature of Hebrews that is mentioned by scholars is how the word "better" is often used. The Psalms said that the law of the Lord was better to him than thousands of gold and silver pieces. Better is far from being a description of addictions.

I can remember how strange it sounded in elementary school to classify things as good, better, and best. (Some people still say that this or that was **gooder**.) For the last few days, we have been discussing how "good" is used in Psalm 119. We have been able to discern the following points:

1. Everyone is seeking what they think to be good
2. We make our own evaluations
3. Discerning good and evil requires spiritual maturity
4. God is good
5. Addictions *claim* to be good
6. Addictions accuse God of evil
7. An affliction is an evil that is used by God for good
8. The best of everything is in Christ

I doubt if you can find anyone to argue over the wealth of God. God owns everything. We could never imagine the wealth that God possesses. Among the wonderful wealth that God possesses is the knowledge that is found in Christ. Grace and truth come through Christ (John 1:17). Grace is of great value (more than silver or gold.)

The abundance of God's grace is found in Christ. Without God's grace, we would be left with no forgiveness. Apart from forgiveness, we have no fellowship with God. Jesus Christ is the best that God has to offer! An acronym for grace is God's riches at Christ's expense.

> "I cannot better compare the folly of those men and women who think they will get contentment by musing about other circumstances than to the way of children: perhaps they have climbed a hill and look a good way off and see another hill, and they think if they were on the top of that, they would be able to touch the clouds with their fingers; but when they are on the top of that hill, alas, they are as far from the clouds as they were before." -*The Rare Jewel of Christian Contentment*, Jeremiah Burroughs

March 11

What's good (part 5)

The law of Your mouth is better to me than thousands of gold and silver pieces. Psalms 119:72

For about thirty-four years, I have been exposed to all kinds of methods of dealing with addictions. In 1995, I began writing about addictions from out of the Scriptures. I started publishing my writing in 2018 after seven years of sobriety.

Among the programs that address addictions, some are good, others are better, and one is best. The more Christ-centered a program is the better. Time will not allow me to elaborate (I will just list a few reasons.)

1. Without Christ, there is no remission of sin
2. We need the wisdom that is found in Christ to conquer addictions
3. We need the power that is in Christ to conquer addictions
4. Through Christ, we have the Holy Spirit

I learned to cook at an early age. Over the years, I have learned to appreciate the value of sharing my cooking with others. I take great care in the preparation of a special meal. I consider it an insult for someone to reject a dining invitation. I strive to give my guests my very best.

How much more is it an insult if we reject what God has given to us in Christ to conquer addictions? God went through much preparation in the presentation of His Son. "Good, better, best. Never let it rest. 'Til your good is better and your better is best" is a quotation from St. Jerome.

> Long ago, at many times and in many ways, God spoke to our fathers by the prophets, but in these last days He has spoken to us by His Son, whom He appointed the Heir of all things, through whom also He created the world. Hebrews 1:1-2

Proverbs 10:22 says, "The blessing of the LORD makes rich, and he adds no sorrow with it." Have you traded the wealth of God's Word and His fellowship for worthless idols? God wants so much more for you!

> "Do not sell yourself short by believing the lies of Satan and worldly wisdom that merely want you to 'stay clean and sober' while on this earth with no hope for eternal life. God wants you to have a higher goal of worshiping Him alone because when you succeed in that goal, you will receive both heaven and earth." -*The Heart of Addiction,* Mark E. Shaw

March 12

Consider your ways! (part 1)

> When I think on my ways, I turn my feet to Your testimonies; I hasten and do not delay to keep Your commandments.
> Psalms 119:59-60

Immediately after reading Psalm 119:59, I thought of how God told Israel to consider their ways through Haggai. The word *consider* occurs four times in the book of Haggai. One is found in Haggai 1:5

> Now, therefore, thus says the Lord of hosts: Consider your ways. You have sown much, and harvested little. You eat, but you never have enough; you drink, but you never have your fill. You clothe yourselves, but no one is warm. And he who earns wages does so to put them into a bag with holes. Haggai 1:5-6.

Part of the process of overcoming addictions is to consider our ways. When we do this, with the aid of the Holy Spirit, then we understand how much we need the truth that is found in the Word of God to combat the lies that we have embraced. This is precisely what Israel did in response to the Word of God that came through Haggai.

In reading the first chapter of Haggai, we discover that Israel was addicted to her houses. They had made idols of their houses. They put their houses above God. This is the nature of every addiction. It's no mystery because as John Calvin said "the human heart is an idol factory."

1. They are given more attention than God.
2. They are lifted higher than God.
3. More of our resources are given to them.
4. Our fellowship with God is broken by them.

The people of Israel had a greater concern for *their* houses than the house of God. They had given their houses priority over God. Addictions reveal your priorities. You learn what is important as you consider your ways. Jesus said that there are but two ways available.

> Enter by the narrow gate. For the gate is wide and the way is easy that leads to destruction, and those who enter by it are many. For the gate is narrow and the way is hard that leads to life, and those who find it are few. Matthew 7:13

March 13

Consider your ways! (part 2)

When I think on my ways, I turn my feet to Your testimonies; I hasten and do not delay to keep Your commandments.
Psalms 119:59-60

A way is governed and defined by action. These actions can be categorized as either futile and fruitful, reverent or insulting. That is the sum of every action. These are the two issues that confront us when addressing addictions. We either discuss how insulting addictions are to God or we discuss their uselessness.

While the latter is more important the remainder of our discussion will center on the issue of futility. Haggai draws Israel's attention to how futile their actions were and how they had insulted God.

1. Harvested little
2. Never full
3. Not warm enough
4. Lost wages

Unfortunately, people usually think more about the futility of addictions rather than how insulting they are to God. Many have only left addictions that cause trouble because they cannot finance their supply. Addictions are built on lust. And if the lust is not destroyed, God has still been rejected.

> "Lust can be unreasonable. As quiet as it is kept; there is no one as reasonable as God. One of the greatest errors that addictions feed off is accusing God of being unreasonable (when, in fact, we are the ones who are unreasonable.)" -*Turning to God from Idols: A Biblical Approach to Addictions,* Gregory L. Madison

Amazingly, Israel's response to disposing of their addiction is the same that we need. I cannot understand why the issue of reverencing God is rarely mentioned while addressing addictions. Is this not the root of the matter?

The only two sources that I know that discuss reverencing God and addictions are *Turning to God from Idols* and *Addictions: A Banquet in the Grave.* Born of reverence are at least two elements that Israel displayed in breaking the chains of addiction.

1. A hunger for the Word of God.
2. A desire to please God.

March 14

Consider your ways! (part 3)

> When I think on my ways, I turn my feet to Your testimonies; I hasten and do not delay to keep Your commandments.
> Psalms 119:59-60

Addictions quickly capture your affection because they usually appeal to the pleasure center of your brain. Once the addiction captures your affection, they gain your **allegiance**. God wants your full attention. He deserves it! Just like Israel, you show reverence for God by allowing Him to have your full attention.

> Then Zerubbabel the son of Shealtiel, and Joshua the son of Jehozadak, the high priest, with all the remnant of the people, obeyed the voice of the Lord their God, and the words of Haggai the prophet, as the Lord their God had sent him. And the people feared the Lord. Haggai 1:12

> "When God delivers you from addiction, get as far away from that behavior and lifestyle as you can. Prisoners don't continue to hang around the prison after they're released." -*From an unknown source*

> "God has endued the soul with two principal faculties: The one, that by which it is capable of perception and speculation, or by which it discerns and judges of things, which is called the *understanding*. The other, that by which the soul is some way inclined with respect to the things it views or considers: or it is the faculty by which the soul beholds things—not as an indifferent unaffected spectator, but—either liking or disliking, pleased or displeased, approving or rejecting. This faculty is called by various names; it is sometimes called *inclination;* and as respects the actions determined and governed by it, the *will;* and the *mind*, with regard to the exercises of this faculty, is often called the heart" -*Treatise Concerning the Religious Affections,* Jonathan Edwards

> One reason why redemption is imperative is so that our yearning for what is not of God may desist! 1 Peter 1:23 refers to it as being "born again, not of perishable seed, but of imperishable, through the living and enduring word of God.

> "At the root, then, all idolatry is human rejection of the Goodness of God and the finality of God's authority." -*We Become What We Worship,* G.K. Beale

March 15

Counteraction

At midnight I rise to praise You, because of Your righteous rules.
Psalms 119:62

One of the greatest spiritual methods of combating addictions is counteraction. When the follower in Christ is told to put off the old man, he is further instructed to put on the new man (Ephesians 4:22-24; Colossians 3:10). And as far back as Ezekiel 11:19 and Jeremiah 31:33 God said that He would give His people a new heart to replace their old heart.

It is out of our hearts that we develop affection or passion. In Psalm 119:53-54, we discussed how God gives us the ability to counteract addictions through a change in our affections and having a passion for the things of God rather than the things of the world. Passion produces praise.

One of the ways that we can prove that addictions are idols is by considering how worship is expressed. Worship involves relinquishing control or dominion, making sacrifices, evoking trust, giving praise, glory, honor, and a state of awe.

> "The power of music unto the Lord in our war against addictions is truly amazing! I began to discover this on a personal level in the mid-'90s while living on the streets. There was a couple who would play gospel music every week while serving a meal. To this very day, I, also, look for the opportunity to play gospel music in places where free meals are being served. I believe that every Bible-based support group should provide gospel music as well. First and foremost, I think that when we immerse ourselves in gospel music, then God recognizes that we mean business. With music, we gain affirmation, we are motivated toward change, and we receive encouragement. Music has the potential of relieving stress and easing sorrow. As we meditate on the words of various selections, we are given the ability to express our faith, our praise, our gratitude, and our love toward God. And then, most importantly, God can speak to us through such music!" -*Turning to God from Idols*, Gregory L. Madison

In 2011, I began to exercise several times a week to counteract the process of aging. Through exercising your mind in praise, your mind becomes stronger. While physical exercise counteracts weak bodies; the exercise of praise counteracts weak minds. My physical exercise will never make me younger, nor will it make me completely new. The practice of praise towards God makes you completely new and frees you from the bounds of addictions.

March 16

Evidence demands a verdict (part 1)

The earth, O Lord, is full of Your steadfast love; teach me Your statutes! Psalms 119:64

Would you judge God? I have borrowed a title from an excellently detailed composition of the validities of the Bible by Josh McDowell to explain how the evidence of God's love leads us to love Him in return. *A love for God and an appreciation for His blessings will ever remain the highest and strongest deterrent against addictions.*

If there are people who are willing to lay down their lives for Christ out of their love for God, certainly there are those who would lay down their addictions out of a love for God. Even though Napoleon Bonaparte was not known as a follower of Christ, he recognized how others considered Christ to be worthy of their lives.

"I know men and I tell you that Jesus Christ is no mere man. Between Him and every other person in the world there is no possible term of comparison. Alexander, Caesar, Charlemagne, and I have founded empires. But on what did we rest the creations of our genius? Upon force. Jesus Christ founded His empire upon love; and at this hour millions of men would die for Him." - Napoleon Bonaparte

He died for all, that those who live should no longer live for themselves but for Him who died for them and was raised again.
2 Corinthians 5:15

For years upon years, I asked myself whether I would be willing to die for Christ, until one day the Lord gave me the answer. He told me that presently, in the United States, the question is not whether I would be willing to die for Him, but whether I would be willing to live for Him every day.

The greatest evidence of God's love is the gift of His Son. Perhaps the most well-known verse in the Bible is about how God loves us so much that He sent His only begotten Son (John 3:16). As I said: A love for God and an appreciation for His blessings will ever remain the highest and strongest deterrent against addictions.

The evidence is before you and the verdict is your life.

March 17

Evidence demands a verdict (part 2)

> The earth, O Lord, is full of Your steadfast love; teach me Your statutes! Psalms 119:64

The joy of being taught by God is like nothing else. Being taught by God is necessary for your redemption. One reason why redemption is imperative is so that our yearning for what is not of God may desist!

The Apostle Paul had a tremendous understanding of God's love. It was because of this understanding that he did not consider his life to be "dear to himself" (Acts 20:24). He said that the reason that he shared the message of the cross was that "the love of Christ constrains us" (2 Corinthians 5:14). Does not the love of Christ constrain us against addictions?

> "'Be good' and 'Do right' are fine messages, but when they stand alone they have more in common with the boy scouts handbook than scripture. Remember that in the Bible, 'This is who God is and what He has done' always precedes 'this is what you must do'. Action follows our knowledge of God and trust in Him. It is as if God has said to us. 'Now that you have seen who I am, you will want to love me in return. This is how you can love me.' And then God teaches us how to love Him." -Addiction: A Banquet in the Grave, Edward T. Welch

According to the *Strong's Dictionary* of the Bible, the Greek word used for constrain in 2 Corinthians 5:14 means "to be taken with." It reminds me of a phrase used in 1 Corinthians 12:2 which describes the effect that addictions have on us.

> Ye know that ye were Gentiles, carried away unto these dumb idols, even as ye were led. 1 Corinthians 12:2 *KJV*

If our verdict is based on the evidence that has been presented. We gratefully submit to God just as David did when he asked God to teach him in response to God's steadfast love. This is a principle that has been 'practically' ignored in our discussion of addictions today. As we learn more about God's worthiness, as we are more and more attracted to Him as a result of spending time with Him, then we are less and less moved by other things. Paul had to grow to this point, as we must also.

> We love because he first loved us. 1 John 4:19

March 18

I think that I'll stay!

You have dealt well with Your servant, O Lord, according to Your Word. Teach me knowledge and good judgment, for I trust Your commands. Psalms 119:65-66

My Aunt Jean was my favorite of all my mother's aunts. While my mother had no sisters, she had enough aunts of her own for me to claim. I used to love to visit Aunt Jean to meet the children she fostered.

During one of my visits, my Aunt Jean explained how the new boy was at first a little hesitant about staying. She said that the boy asked if she had any cookies. "Yes", she said. The boy asked if she had soda pop. "Yes", she said. The boy asked if she had ice cream, hot dogs, and a list of other items. "Yes", was her reply to them all. My aunt was relieved by the boy's announcement, "I think I'll stay!"

David asked God to teach him knowledge and good judgment after He saw how well God had dealt with him. Don't we need good judgment and knowledge to keep us from falling for addictions? Most certainly! You can trust God for the direction you need as David—and as much as my Aunt Jean's foster child trusted her for potato chips, ice cream, candy, soda pop, hot dogs, macaroni and cheese ...

> "If a man has a great investment in a voyage, he aims at such an end as may be worth his investment. So when God above all things lays out His wisdom, power, mercy, goodness, and faithfulness, and sets at work all His counsels to be laid out upon such a business as to get man to attain to His last end, then, certainly, man's end and happiness must be worth it all. And it must be a glorious thing God intends for the children of men, to make them happy, when the great counsels of God, and the ways of God's wisdom and power, are so about this business of bringing man to happiness." –*The Evil of Evils*, Jeremiah Burroughs

By the same token, it takes *time* to learn the things that God wants to teach you. You must be willing to stay long enough to receive the things that God has for you. While I do not condone individuals abstaining from addictions just for rewards, you must also recognize and enjoy the fruit of your labors. It is most important that you abstain in honor of His Majesty. And, it is equally important that you recognize that a life of sobriety is not always "cookies and candy."

March 19

The Great Shepherd (part 1)

> Before I was afflicted I went astray, but now I keep Your Word.
> Psalms 119:67

In verse 64, I briefly discussed how the love of Christ constrains (from 2 Corinthians 5:14, the Greek word being "to be taken with.") I also discussed how the Corinthians were carried away or led by idols, just as we may be by addictions. We are all led toward God or away from Him.

Just the other day, the Lord helped me get through a moment of excruciating pain by allowing me to divert my attention. As my attention was diverted, my focus was intensified upon matters of more importance at the time. As the staff of a shepherd, afflictions are of great use to God in our development.

As much as we hate to admit it, God must often get our attention as we are distracted or led astray as the psalmist honestly admits. There was a time in my life when addictions got most of my attention (perhaps an understatement.) The pain that I experienced, just the other day, really got my attention as well. The difference is that God used the pain that I experienced to sharpen my focus on things of greater importance.

Psalms 23 depicts the Lord as the great Shepherd that He is. Shepherds are responsible for leading their sheep. As sheep are inclined to go astray, a good shepherd knows how to keep them safe by getting their attention. Whether we have succumbed to addiction or not, we have all been guilty of going astray.

> All we like sheep have gone astray; we have turned—every one—to his own way. Isaiah 53:6a

> "A carnal heart has no contentment but from what he sees before him in this world, but a godly heart has contentment from what he sees laid up for him in the highest heavens." -*The Rare Jewel of Christian Contentment*, Jeremiah Burroughs

The safest place in the world is in the Word of God as it gives you faith in the God of all power and might that loves you far beyond what you could imagine and can do far more than addictions.

> Little children (believers, dear ones), guard yourselves from idols—[false teachings, moral compromises, and anything that would take God's place in your heart]. 1 John 5:21 Amplified Version

March 20

The Great Shepherd (part 2)

Before I was afflicted I went astray, but now I keep Your Word.
Psalms 119:67

In a book titled *A Shepherd Looks at Psalm 23*, Phillip Keller refers to the Word of God as the rod of a shepherd. Keller explains how the Lord uses affliction to discipline us, thereby getting our attention and leading us on a safe and useful path. Keller's word on the staff of the Shepherd is just as useful (since we haven't enough space in this discussion, you'll have to secure a copy for yourself.)

> "Just as for the sheep of David's day, there was comfort and consolation in seeing the rod in the shepherd's skillful hands, so in our day there is great assurance in our own hearts as we contemplate the power, veracity and potent authority vested in God's Word. For, in fact, the Scriptures are His rod. They are the extension of His mind and will and intentions to mortal man. Living as we do in an era when numerous confused voices and strange philosophies are presented to people it is reassuring to the child of God to turn to the Word of God and know it to be his Shepherd's hand of authority ... By it we are kept from confusion and chaos. There is a second dimension in which the rod is used by a shepherd for the welfare of his sheep- namely that of discipline. If anything, the club is used for this purpose more than any other. I could never get over how often, and with what accuracy, the African herders would hurl their knobkerries at some recalcitrant beast that misbehaved. If the shepherd saw a sheep wandering away from its own, approaching poisonous weeds, or getting too close to danger of one sort or another, the club would go whistling the air to send the wayward animal scurrying back to the bunch." -Phillip Keller

Hebrews 12 explains that as the most loving Father, God uses discipline in our lives so that we can share in the greatest gift there is (it comes along with accepting Jesus as our Savior.) **The greatest gift, which everyone longs for, (whether they care to admit it or not) is to be "partakers of His holiness" (Hebrew 12:10).**

Any program dealing with addictions that is devoid of this principle is not Biblical and does not meet God's standards. Besides the element of discipline making us all that God wants us to be, it is ironically where we find comfort. Addictions pretend to offer comfort. David said that he found comfort in the Shepherd's rod and staff (Psalm 23:4).

March 21

Danger (part 1)

I hold my life in my hand continually, but I do not forget Your law.
Psalms 119:109

"My soul is continually in my hand. He lived in the midst of danger. He had to be always fighting for existence -- hiding in caves, or contending in battles. This is a very uncomfortable and trying state of affairs, and men are apt to think any expedient justifiable by which they can end such a condition: but David did not turn aside to find safety in sin, for he says, Yet do I not forget thy law.' -*The Treasury of David,* Spurgeon

The issues of life are to be met with faith. As Romans 10:17 says, "faith comes from hearing, and hearing through the Word of Christ" so it is that we learn to rely upon God rather than the idols of addictions. While we may not be confronted with the same dangers as David, we live in dangerous times as well.

The dangers that David faced threatened his life. The dangers that addictions present threaten your soul (and perhaps your life.) We have a warning in 1 Peter 2:11 to "abstain from the passions of the flesh, which wage war against your soul."

Unfortunately, we don't always view addictions as a threat. While speaking with someone about their addiction to alcohol recently, I mentioned how most people don't turn from addiction if it doesn't seem to cause them harm. Quite often, we cannot see the harm of addictions on the surface.

The marks of addiction

- It is a form of idolatry   Poor use of energy
- Waste of time   Wasted money
- Endangers your health   Endangers your safety
- Endangers the safety of others   Non-productive
- Tears relationships apart   Bad example to others
- Improper use of God's creation   Supports those who supply others with harmful sources of addiction
- Reinforces a false sense of security
- A stumbling block to others   It gives a bad testimony

While the consequences of addiction should not be overlooked, the greater reason for forsaking the addiction is loving God.

March 22

Danger (part 2)

> The wicked have laid a snare for me, but I do not stray from Your precepts. Psalms 119:110

Who or what is your greatest enemy? Is it the devil? Is it the wicked people? Or, is it society or even yourself? Is not the greatest enemy to man whatever lures or separates him from God? The world is bent on convincing us that addiction is a disease rather than sin. Do diseases separate us from God? Sin alone is what separates us from God. Christ alone offers restoration.

> For I am sure that neither death nor life, nor angels nor rulers, nor things present nor things to come, nor powers, nor height, nor depth, nor anything else in all creation, will be able to separate us from the love of God in Christ Jesus our Lord. Romans 8:38-39

If sin is the greatest enemy to man, pride is the vessel through which it travels. I often tell people that if God wants us to have something no one can keep us from getting it but us. We tend to be our worst enemies. It is no mystery that Satan is an enemy of man. The name itself is defined as an adversary. His greatest weapon is deception. And just as the psalmist, we can avoid the snares of the wicked (Satan included) by not straying from the Word of God.

> "If you want to catch a monkey, you have to trap it. Here's how A farmer or hunter will take a gourd, or they'll cut a small hole into a termite mound if they're in Africa. The small hole they cut will be just big enough for the monkey to fit their hand through. Inside the gourd or the jar, they'll put nuts or sweets, something the monkey craves. Then they wait. Sooner or later a monkey will come by and smell the nuts, and they'll want it. They'll put their hand through the hole, grab a fistful of nuts, and then they'll try to pull their hand back out. But they can't. The hole is small enough to put their empty hand through, but not big enough for a hand clutching a fistful of nuts. They're stuck. Now, at this point, the monkey should realize, 'Hey, I'm stuck, drop the nuts.' But they don't. They want the nuts. They don't want to surrender the nuts. So they pull and pull and pull, refusing to drop the nuts, and the hunter or farmer comes up behind and snatches them. If they just surrendered what they were holding on to, they could have been free. But because they refused to surrender, they lost their ultimate freedom." -https://www.patheos.com/blogs/newwineskins/how-do-you-catch-a-monkey-the-trap-we-humans-fall-for/

March 23

The protection of God

> I have done what is just and right; do not leave me to my oppressors. Give Your servant a pledge of good; let not the insolent oppress me. Psalms 119:121-122

> "This was a great thing for an Eastern ruler to say at any time, for these despots mostly cared more far gain than justice. Some of them altogether neglected their duty, and would not even do judgment at all, preferring their pleasures to their duties; and many more of them sold their judgments to the highest bidders by taking bribes, or regarding the persons of men." -*The Treasury of David,* Spurgeon

We often hear the psalmist asking God for protection as he followed God's Word. When dealing with addiction, we need God's protection. This is especially true when we are tempted to give in to the lure of addiction after remaining abstinent for a while. It is most comforting to know that God longs to protect us.

We can be sure of God's protection so long as our goal is to give God glory (not to just remain abstinent.) The psalmist was seeking God's protection from oppression. While the psalmist faced *people* who oppress, addiction is a *power* that oppresses.

> Finally, my brethren, be strong in the Lord, and in the power of His might. Put on the whole armour of God, that ye may be able to stand against the wiles of the devil. For we wrestle not against flesh and blood, but against principalities, against powers, against the rulers of the darkness of this world, against spiritual wickedness in high places. Ephesians 6:10-12 *KJV*

For us to receive the protection that we need from God against addictions, we must walk in the light. God makes a distinction between light and darkness. Walking in the light is imperative to having fellowship with God. True fellowship with God begins with the light that is in Christ.

Through Christ, we are not only protected from the judgment of God over addictions but we are also protected from the dark deceit of addiction that would lure us from the safety of God's protection. Far too often, people are only concerned about getting rid of an addiction that is causing them trouble, rather than whatever is giving *God* trouble.

God is not merely troubled over addiction, but He is troubled over anything that stands in the way of you becoming more like His Son!

March 24

Sheltered

You are my hiding place and my shield; I hope in Your Word.
Psalms 119:114

Have you ever needed shelter? Whether you realize it or not, we are born in need of shelter. The physical and spiritual elements that surround us threaten our existence. God has offered us the greatest shelter against addictions within Himself.

While growing up in the city of Cleveland, Ohio, the greatest rainstorm that I remember was when I had to seek shelter under a large tree just a few blocks from home because the rain was so intense. After moving to the city of Memphis, I discovered even more intense rain. It always reminded me of the rain in Florida.

Once upon a time, my addiction to crack was so intense that I decided that I would never stop smoking. Then I thought that it would be best to go to Florida where I could indulge in what is considered the best cocaine in all the nation. I was amazed to discover how intense the rain was there. I used to tell people that I felt like the whole ocean had rolled upon us. I was even more astonished by the storm that my addiction had caused.

Have you ever been caught in a hurricane? A hurricane is a sobering environment. If you have ever been engulfed by an addiction, you have been caught in a hurricane! Addictions not only bring the darkness of a storm, but they also envelop you and cause grave danger.

But, the irony of an addiction is that we think that they offer some sort of shelter. That's just how intense the storm of addiction is. This storm of addiction gets down to your very soul. It is the truth that is found in God's Word that shelters us from the lies of the devil (from which addictions originate.)

One way that you can shelter yourself from a rainstorm is by moving to an area where they are not likely to occur. The problem with an addiction is that the storm is in your soul. Yet, God is available to you wherever you go as well.

We don't have to get trapped in the storms of addiction. But if we are, we can always find refuge in Jesus. As quiet as it is kept, we all live a sheltered life. It is either found in the shelter of sin or the shelter of God.

In *Mere Christianity*, C.S. Lewis said "bad people, in one sense, know very little about badness — they have lived a sheltered life by always giving in. We never find out the strength of the evil impulse inside us until we try to fight it: and Christ, because He was the only man who never yielded to temptation, is also the only man who knows to the full what temptation means. "

March 25

The judgment of God (part 1)

All the wicked of the earth You discard like dross, therefore I love Your testimonies. My flesh trembles for fear of You, and I am afraid of Your judgments. Psalms 119:119-120

Are we allowed to speak of the judgment of God while discussing addictions? Probably not in some circles! But, if we are truly seeking sobriety, then the judgment of God cannot be sidestepped or overlooked. As God is sure to judge idolatry, He judges addiction (a form of idolatry.) While writing *Turning to God from Idols,* I was led by God to construct an outline of Scriptures about idolatry.

- Warnings against idolatry
- Judgment against idolatry
- Futility and deceit of idolatry
- Examples of idolatry
- Repentance: turning from idolatry

Here are a few of the passages about God's judgment of idolatry:

But if your heart turns away so that you do not hear, and are drawn away, and worship other gods and serve them, I announce to you today that you shall surely perish; you shall not prolong your days in the land which you cross over the Jordan to go in and possess. I call heaven and earth as witnesses today against you, that I have set before you life and death, blessing and cursing; therefore choose life, that both you and your descendants may live. Deuteronomy 30:17-19 *NIV*

For the Lord of hosts, who planted you, has pronounced doom against you for the evil of the house of Israel and of the house of Judah, which they have done against themselves to provoke Me to anger in offering incense to Baal. Jeremiah 11:17 *NIV*

Equal rights have been the theme of the United States for more than one hundred years. Does God have rights? Do the rights of God include permission to judge? Does He need our permission to judge? What happens when we take the judgment of God lightly? Again, reverencing God means that we take Him seriously. Perhaps, the severest judgment would be for God to just let us go on with our addiction (which never truly satisfies and leads us to Hell.)

March 26

The judgment of God (part 2)

> All the wicked of the earth You discard like dross, therefore I love Your testimonies. My flesh trembles for fear of You, and I am afraid of Your judgments. Psalms 119:119-120

Addiction is just one of the ways that we choose to reject Christ (who is personified wisdom, while addictions are foolish.) Addictions judge God as being unjust and unreasonable. To deny that God judges addictions is to deny Him ownership.

The fear of the Lord will ever remain a dominating power against addiction (though seldom mentioned.) One author defines the fear of the Lord as "the controlling awesome awareness of God's power and righteous judgment, wholesome dread of displeasing Him."

God offers forgiveness in Christ. Do we not need forgiveness to escape judgment? The judgment of God is real. If we ignore the judgment of God, the level of our sobriety is shallow!

> Whoever believes in the Son has eternal life; whoever does not obey the Son shall not see life, but the wrath of God remains on him. John 3:36

The wrath of God is an expression that signifies the intensity of the judgment of God because of His anger. The severity of God's judgment can be seen in the consequences of our actions. You can trust God to judge (whether directly or indirectly.)

The judgment that Israel received as a result of her idolatry is like the consequences of addiction. We often see the severity of God's judgment as Israel was judged for their idolatry in Scripture. Yet, the judgment of God is not without warning. The judgment of God has led many to change.

The most severe judgment that God will ever issue was laid upon His Son. The severity of the judgment was based on how Jesus was stripped of all His glory. Before being sent to earth and being judged for our sins, He reflected the glory of God with perfect for all eternity.

The glory that *we* possess is founded on our reflection of God (as we were created in His image.) The judgment that was passed down by Adam is that we would no longer bear the image of God. As quiet as it is kept, outside of Christ, we bear the image of Satan (children of wrath, Ephesians 2:3.)

One of the aspects of God's judgment is where God decides who belongs to Him and who does not. Jesus described this as separating the wheat from the tares. My initial study on tares indicates that they are poisonous.

March 27

The judgment of God (part 3)

All the wicked of the earth You discard like dross, therefore I love Your testimonies. My flesh trembles for fear of You, and I am afraid of Your judgments. Psalms 119:119-120

Who wants to be known as wicked? Probably few! Even wicked people try to justify themselves as being good. Our last discussion ended by stating that tares are poisonous. The tares in Jesus' parable symbolize the wicked. By the judgment of God, the wicked are banished from His sight! The psalmist took delight in this aspect of God's judgment (therefore I love Your testimonies.)

The judgment of God can be both delightful and unpleasant. How was the fear that the psalmist had of God's judgment unpleasant? The psalmist knew what was written in Deuteronomy concerning the judgment of God that was promised should Israel have turned away from God. The similarities between God's judgment on Israel's irreverent idolatry and the consequences of addiction are astounding! See if you can recognize the resemblance!

    1. Cursed in the city   2. Cursed in the country   3. Basket cursed
    4. Kneading trough cursed   5. Cursed when you come in
    6. Cursed when you go out   7. Confusion   8. Sudden ruin
    9. Affliction   10. Madness   11. Confusion of mind
    12. Robbed, no rescuer   13. Violated   14. Slavery, captivity
    15. You will be a byword   16. Demotion, humiliation
    17. Curses will pursue and overtake you   18. Hunger
    19. Thirst   20. Dire poverty

All of these have been drawn from Deuteronomy 28. Clearly, the judgment of God upon our irreverence demands a curse. Who wants to be cursed? Some would rather pretend that the judgment of God does not exist or that we do not deserve His judgment than be cursed! There is, however, a third alternative that we will discuss in our conclusion to this series.

The list that was drawn from Deuteronomy 28 is only a sample of the innumerable passages that are listed in Scripture. The consequences of deserting God lead to instability both individually and nationally. As I have stated on several occasions- addictions are a matter of national security. If there is one thing that we learn from the judgments of God; it is that God is not to be trifled with!

March 28

The judgment of God (final)

> All the wicked of the earth You discard like dross, therefore I love Your testimonies. My flesh trembles for fear of You, and I am afraid of Your judgments. Psalms 119:119-120

I began this series by establishing that God has every right to judge. Next, I had you consider the severity of God's judgment. God's reason and methods of judging were the themes of my last entry. In this final entry, we will contemplate true judgment and mercy.

Wherever there is judgment, I believe that there are two initial questions that we all ask. The first question is whether the judgment is true. We often have a hard time determining what is true. One thing that I love about God is that He shows us the truth through the person of the Holy Spirit.

The Holy Spirit is also referred to as the Spirit of Truth. We desperately need Him to cut through the deception of addictions. Deception is a way of life with addictions. You can get used to false judgment. The true judgment of God can be relieving (so long as you embrace it.) While embracing the judgment of God, you embrace the truth!

The second question that we ask concerning judgment is that of mercy. Wherever guilt is determined, there is a cry for mercy. Those who have no guilt have no reason to cry for mercy. In a book titled *Manhood Restored: How the Gospel Makes Men Whole*, Eric Mason says that we have four options in our dealings with sin.

> Option #1: You can deny that it is sin and accept it as normal behavior.
> Option #2: You can attempt to excuse it or justify it.
> Option #3: You can hate it and suffer under the guilt of it.
> Option #4: You can repent and be cleansed from it.

> There are those who are clean in their own eyes but are not washed of their filth. Proverbs 30:12

God is a merciful Judge. If you want mercy from a judge, you must first declare yourself guilty. It has been said that the one who represents himself in court is a fool. With Jesus as your representative before God, you receive mercy. Jesus paid the price for your irreverence.

Am I guilty of seeking addiction over God? Yes. Am I guilty of stealing the things that God wants me to use to bless others? Yes. Am I guilty of following Satan? Yes. Perhaps, the greatest miracle that Jesus ever performed is making me *not guilty*!

March 29

You are what you eat!

Oh how I love Your law! It is my meditation all the day. Your commandment makes me wiser than my enemies, for it is ever with me. I have more understanding than all my teachers, for Your testimonies are my meditation. Psalms 119:97-99

When I was just a boy, I remember the phrase, "You are what you eat" being repeated by many. "You are what you eat" means that it is important to eat good food to be healthy and fit. This is especially true for those of us who have abused our bodies with various addictions.

> "Every cell in your body has a shelf life – a stomach cell lives about a day or two, a skin cell about a month, and a red blood cell about four months. So each and every day, your body is busy making new cells to replace those that have expired. And how healthy those new cells are is directly determined by how well you've been eating. A diet filled with highly processed food that's low on nutrients doesn't give your body much to work with. I always say it's like constructing a house with cardboard and tape instead of bricks and mortar. But a clean, nutrient-rich, whole foods eating plan can help you build cells to work better, and are less susceptible to premature aging and disease." -*cynthiasass.com*

While the saying "you are what you eat" is true on a physical level, it also has mental and spiritual implications. Meditation has to do with thinking. For some of us, meditation is a healthy addiction.

One of the ways that God allows us to break the chains of addictions and to live a healthy life is by giving us new thoughts just as our bodies need new cells to function properly. Joy is directly connected with what we think.

Joy is something that you need to keep from returning to addiction. Nehemiah 8: says "the joy of the Lord is your strength." Some say that the predominant theme of the letter that the Apostle Paul wrote to the Philippians is joy.

> Finally, brothers, whatever is true, whatever is honorable, whatever is just, whatever is pure, whatever is lovely, whatever is commendable, if there is any excellence, if there is anything worthy of praise, think about these things. Philippians 4:8

Most of the time, we all choose what we eat.
Choose joy for your spiritual diet!

March 30

Double-minded

I hate the double-minded, but I love Your law. Psalms 119:113

While the *King James Version* of the Bible translates the phrase "vain thoughts", the *English Standard Version* reads "double-minded." Addictions are derived from vain thoughts and double-mindedness. The lexicon to the *Strong Concordance* gives us a better understanding of the Hebrew word that is used in Psalms 119 for vain thoughts or double-minded.

> "ambivalent, divided, half-hearted divided, i.e. a person of a divided mind, who, being destitute of firm faith and persuasion as to divine things, is driven hither and thither, a doubter, a sceptic."

Would you not agree that this is an accurate description of the addict? So ambivalent was I during my years of drug addiction that while I said that I was saved, my dad would sometimes lovingly state, "I don't know what you are!" I was so divided that even if I tried to remain abstinent, I had a hard time getting my mind off drugs.

I was so half-hearted that I would not commit myself to fellowshipping with others who professed Christ or reading the Word of God regularly. Being as double-minded as I was, I fit the description given by James.

> If any of you lacks wisdom, let him ask God, who gives generously to all without reproach, and it will be given him. But let him ask in faith, with no doubting, for the one who doubts is like a wave of the sea that is driven and tossed by the wind. For that person must not suppose that he will receive anything from the Lord; he is a double-minded man, unstable in all his ways. James 1:5-8

James is speaking of our need for wisdom and our need for faith. Faith and wisdom are essential in your struggle with addictions. There is much to be said about how the wisdom of God leads you from addictions as well. An entire book would not exhaust this theme.

I can never overemphasize how the fear of the Lord is the most valuable theme in your treatment of addictions. The fear of the Lord is the beginning of wisdom. If addictions are foolish, they cannot be labeled as a disease. As the Living Word of God, Christ is the wisdom of God (1 Corinthians 1:24). Wisdom is also found in the written Word of God.

> The testimony of the Lord is sure, making wise the simple.
> Psalms 19:7b

March 31

Selective memory

I will delight in Your statutes; I will not forget Your Word.
Psalms 119:16

The psalmist said he would remember God's Word. Remembrance is essential to our relationship with God and remaining abstinent from addictions. One of the funny things about addiction is that it can have such an appeal that we may only remember the "good times." Some people call this "selective memory."

God wants you to select His Word to be etched upon your memory. The Israelites who wanted to go back to Egypt are examples of how addictions can cause "selective memory." When it comes to addictions, we may be inclined to forget the enslavement we suffered as the Israelites did.

Lust is what causes us to have "selective memory." Concerning the Israelites who desired to return to Egypt 1 Corinthians 10:6 tells us "These things were our examples, to the intent we should not lust after evil things, as they also lusted."

We remember the fish we ate in Egypt that cost nothing, the cucumbers, the melons, the leeks, the onions, and the garlic.
Numbers 11:5

One of the books that God has used in my life to convince me of the importance of having the "selective memory" that God desires is Jerry Bridges' book *The Discipline of Grace*. Bridges' main message is that we should "preach the gospel to ourselves every day." It reminds you of the power that is available in Christ and the love that God has for you.

From the Word of God, you find the wisdom to overcome the temptations of addictions through the power of Christ. The Word of God brings you to your senses. From 1 Corinthians 10, we see how the example of the Israelites who desired to go back to Egypt continues to speak.

Now these things happened to them as an example, but they were written down for our instruction, on whom the end of the ages has come. Therefore, let anyone who thinks that he stands take heed lest he fall. No temptation has overtaken you that is not common to man. God is faithful, and he will not let you be tempted beyond your ability, but with the temptation he will also provide the way of escape, that you may be able to endure it. 1 Corinthians 10:11-13

April 1

Failure to communicate

Make me understand the way of Your precepts, and I will meditate on Your wondrous works. Psalms 119:27

Cool Hand Luke is a 1967 American prison drama film directed by Stuart Rosenberg, starring Paul Newman and featuring George Kennedy in an Oscar-winning performance. Newman stars in the title role as Luke, a prisoner in a Florida prison camp who refuses to submit to the system. The most famous line in the movie is where the warden says to Luke, "What we've got here is failure to communicate."

Addictions are fueled and produced by a lack of communication or understanding with God. Just as Luke remained imprisoned for lack of understanding, we remain enslaved to addictions without understanding from God. As I stated in *Turning to God from Idols* the first step to dealing with an addiction in every program (Christian or otherwise) is reasoning. Reasoning involves understanding.

The understanding that we need to face the issues of life does not come from within. A well-known Proverbs tells us not to lean on our own understanding, but rather trust in the Lord with all our heart (Proverbs 3:5). Romans 3:11 reports that in our natural state, "no one understands, no one seeks God." *Turning to God from Idols* also contains an outline of understanding in Appendix A.

- God's understanding
- Our lack of understanding
- Understanding being sought
- The source of understanding
- The results of understanding

Until I draw my last breath, I insist that true and lasting sobriety is based on our reverence for God. While writing *The Fear of the Almighty*, I discovered that reverence begins as God gives us understanding which it is based on His Word, as with the Israelites in the wilderness.

Specially the day that thou stoodest before the LORD thy God in Horeb, when the LORD said unto me, Gather me the people together, and I will make them hear My Words, that they may learn to fear Me all the days that they shall live upon the earth, and that they may teach their children. Deuteronomy 4:10

His understanding is unsearchable. Isaiah 40:28c

April 2

Promises

I will keep Your statutes; do not utterly forsake me! Psalms 119:8

Within this short verse, we could dwell upon many different aspects. Among these are the themes of commitment, the presence of God, dependence, protection, and fear (to say the least.) I want you to consider the promise that the psalmist makes.

Throughout Psalms 119, you will notice the words "I will" on many occasions. David says "I will" eleven times in this psalm to God. Over and over, he is making a promise. Promises say a lot about relationships. Promises are solemnly sober. And, promises are often broken where addictions are given precedence.

We value the importance of our relationships based on promises. Think about the vows that are expressed when we engage in matrimony! Promises bind us to others. David was expressing his desire to be bound to God with a promise.

David's promise is his allegiance to God. We value the allegiance we have to God and others based on how well we keep our promises. Unfortunately, children often feel unloved over broken promises. When promises are kept it provides a level of security that is needed for children to become adults.

Promises are a major issue with addictions. Domestic relationships are strained over broken promises. Jobs are at risk when promises are not fulfilled. Many of the promises that bind us are based on the roles that we serve. Some of the promises that we must make are spoken; others are *unspoken.*

If only we were like God in keeping our promises. I often say that "consistency leads to stability." Promises that are fulfilled are indicative of consistency. Stable lives and relationships are built on consistency.

Everyone wants someone that they can rely on (even God.) Jesus is someone we can always count on. He proved his allegiance by not turning back when faced with the assignment of paying the price for our sins. **The most important thing about a biblical approach to addiction is how God wants to make us more like Jesus.** It is in Christ that we have the power to fulfill the promises to which we are bound.

According to *Wikipedia, I Promise School* is a public elementary school in Akron, Ohio opened in 2018, supported by *The Lebron James Family Foundation,* and specifically aimed at at-risk children. God has an I Promise School for His at-risk children that are susceptible to addictions. The curriculum is His Word!

April 3

A long obedience in the same direction

> You have commanded Your precepts to be kept diligently. Oh that my ways may be steadfast in keeping Your statutes!
> Psalms 119:4-5

While commenting on promises yesterday, I mentioned stability. Psalms 119:5 speaks of steadfastness. Diligence and steadfastness are at least two words that describe the long-term sobriety that God is longing for you to have.

A remark concerning Eugene Peterson's book titled *A Long Obedience in the Same Direction* is that "as a society, we are still obsessed with the immediate; new technologies have only intensified our quest for the quick fix. But Peterson's time-tested prescription for discipleship remains the same—a long obedience in the same direction."

Jesus said, "The truth will set you free" (John 8:32). However, the truth is not often easily obtained. As quiet as it's kept, much of what we do is seek after truth. Our very senses are trained to distinguish whether what we see or hear is true. We are becoming disciplined from birth the discern truth in the physical world.

It is in knowing the truth about the spiritual world that you find freedom from addictions. Truth is what God uses to separate you from the evils of the world that come from the Father of Lies and our deceitful hearts. ***Sanctification*** is a big word for being separate or set apart. To be disciplined by Christ is to be set apart from lies. Jesus said, "**If you abide in My word, you are truly My disciples**, and you will know the truth, and the truth will set you free" (John 8:31b-32).

Truth comes with a price. Someone once said that the salvation that God provides through Christ's blood doesn't cost us, the sanctification that God wants for us does. Discovering and embracing truth requires diligence and steadfastness. As Peterson says, it is "a long journey in the same direction."

Do you know of anyone who wants to go in the wrong direction? Wherever we are headed, we want to be sure that we are going the right way. One of the funny things about addictions is that they make promises of peace and well-being that can only be found in Christ. And so, if you pursue an addiction to find fulfillment, you are headed in the wrong direction.

How many people ask you to tell them a pack of lies? Who do you know who loves to be lied to? Just look in the mirror! Every one of us tells lies and loves to be lied to in various degrees.

We will be that way in various degrees until we see the Lord Jesus (He alone is the Truth.) Some of the lies that we believe are not as extreme as others. The lies of addiction are severe. They are idolatrous and if we deny God of ourselves then we deny ourselves of God.

April 4

Hold on to your valuables!

> Teach me, O Lord, the way of Your statutes; and I will keep it to the end. Give me understanding, that I may keep Your law and observe it with my whole heart. Psalms 119:33-34

When was the last time you used a four-lettered word? Hopefully, you have eliminated the four-lettered words that are displeasing to God from your vocabulary. ***Keep*** is a four-lettered word used in Psalms 119 that you need to keep (no pun intended.)

I never noticed until now that the word ***keep*** is used 22 times in Psalms 119. (It must be important; it must be of value.) Do you not keep the things that you find to be valuable and useful? What does the psalmist say that he will keep? Every single time, he says that he will keep the Word of God!

Your sobriety is indicative of the value that you have for God's Word. That's because sobriety must be based on truth and the truth is found in the Word of God. This is not the typical approach to addiction that has been chosen. But, if we have reverence for God then we have a desire for His Word.

During my years of drug addiction, I often experienced homelessness. Just as when I climbed mountains in Colorado, I had to decide what things were valuable and useful and the things that were worthless, useless, and too heavy to carry.

Addictions are a heavy burden. They weaken our souls every step of the way. The Word of God is heavy too. But the irony is that the Word of God strengthens your soul.

The Hebrew word that is used in Psalms 119:33-34 not only means to keep, but to guard and watch over. What is it that you value most? I'll bet you'll keep it! That's why I kept going back to my drug addiction. To be frank- I valued my addiction over the Word of God.

And it gets worse because if you have no value for God's Word, that means that you don't value *Him*. Worship is another word for value. That's why the value that is placed on addiction is idol worship. Thank God for showing us the value of His Word. Now it is up to us to guard and embrace it!

Ironically, what you keep is also indicative of what you give to God. Sobriety can be looked at as what we give to God. While writing this entry, I have been counseling a friend who has tried to fix things apart from a structured environment that will give him a foundation to grow. His commitment to a long-term program is going to be a chance to give more to God and to keep what God wants him to have.

April 5

Truth's Options

> And take not the word of truth utterly out of my mouth, for my hope is in Your rules. I will keep Your law continually, forever and ever, and I shall walk in a wide place, for I have sought Your precepts. Psalms 119:43-45

The psalmist sought to abide in the truth of God's Word. He rallied in the freedom of a wide place that results from living by God's Word. Contrary to popular belief, the Word of God gives freedom rather than restrictions. It has been said the Bible will lead you from sin or sin will lead you from the Bible.

> For the grace of God has appeared, bringing salvation for all people, training us to renounce ungodliness and worldly passions, and to live self-controlled, upright, and godly lives in the present age. Titus 2:11-12

When you are trained at something it gives you the freedom to do some things that you could not do otherwise. Think of the way that some athletes train! While they are constricted to certain activities, (such as a strict diet), they have the freedom of doing things they could not do unless they were trained. Titus 2:11-12 tells us that the grace of God trains just as the psalmist was trained by the Word of God.

Addictions bring limitations. Addictions are based on lies and all lies cause limitations. If you tell a lie, you must live and speak within the confines of that lie or live by the truth. Truth offers freedom. Addictions can restrict your time, energy, and resources to what will please *you and you alone*. But, quite often they don't offer the satisfaction that you seek.

Addictions destroy your options by capturing your time, thoughts, skills, abilities, and finances, for the sake of the addiction rather than anything else. One example is the way that many addictions are so costly that they render people homeless. There is no option, no freedom, and the wide place that is offered is the whole outdoors.

Sometimes I think of the sacrifices that are made for the sake of technology. I wonder how far we would be if the goal of every life were to seek all the pleasures of the world as much as possible rather than sacrifice time in study and experimentation for the advancement of society. A related discussion is that ***the civilized world rests upon the godliness that reverencing God produces.*** It is because of godliness that we show concern for others (a characteristic that will always be foreign to addictions.)

April 6

The buck stops here!

Forever, O Lord, Your Word is firmly fixed in the heavens. Your faithfulness endures to all generations; You have established the earth, and it stands fast. Psalms 119:89-90

Forever. Firmly fixed. Faithfulness. Endures. Established. Stands fast. These are words of certainty. Addictions are not. In the first place, since addictions originate in our hearts, there is uncertainty. Jeremiah 17:9-10 declares that "the heart is deceitful" and that only the Lord knows and searches the heart with accuracy. Who would argue that deceit is uncertain in its ways?

Secondly, addictions are uncertain because of their brevity. Just like everything else that has been created, the objects of our addictions do not last. You run out of drugs and must get more. The car that you worship and have make your obsession begins to rust. Or the content of your pornography needs to be more graphic or intense to produce arousal. Addictions cannot be trusted.

Thirdly, the consequences of addictions are uncertain as well. Addiction welcomes health issues, financial problems, and domestic strain with spiritual and emotional immaturity. The effects that addictions have on society are just as devastatingly uncertain. It would be nearly impossible for us to calculate how much different our lives would be without the addictions that we have allowed to infiltrate our communities. No one knows how much money is being spent on addictions that could be better used.

I was honored to witness the graduation ceremony for one of my brothers in Christ who completed a long-term residency in a Bible-based program that addresses addictions. I admired his speech, as he told his daughter that the addictions that plagued their family for generations would end with him. The reason that he spoke with such certainty is that he began to trust in God's Word.

Sobriety is not merely defined as being free of a toxin, it is the ability to make sound decisions. At some point in your life, you must be convinced that the supply of your addictions is not forever. You must understand that addictions are not firmly fixed (with positive results.)

You must stop believing that addictions are faithful. As you discover how God possesses the qualities that you need for an abundant life then the deceptions of addictions are nullified. The Word of God gives you the confidence that you need to face any and every circumstance.

And I am sure of this, that he who began a good work in you will bring it to completion at the day of Jesus Christ. Philippians 1:6

April 7

His design is divine

> Forever, O Lord, Your Word is firmly fixed in the heavens. Your faithfulness endures to all generations; You have established the earth, and it stands fast. By Your appointment they stand this day, for all things are Your servants. Psalms 119:89-91

Perhaps, the greatest problem with addictions (from which all our other problems stem) is our discord with God. It is by being in one accord with God that we discover the mind of God, which includes His will for our lives and how we were made for His glory. This has nothing to do with addictions. Addictions invoke self-absorption.

It has been said that all of the creation freely submits to the will of God except man. This is what the psalmist meant when he said, "By Your appointment they stand this day, for all things are Your servants." Many other Bible verses refer to the command or sovereignty of God.

> "Both great things and small pay homage to the Lord. No atom escapes His rule, no world avoids His government. Shall we wish to be free of the Lord's sway and become lords unto ourselves? If we were so, we should be dreadful exceptions to a law which secures the well being of the universe." -Spurgeon

I can remember how graciously God would intervene in my life while I was in pursuit of drugs creating diversions and difficulties. Though I begrudged those moments, as they often delayed or prevented my drug use, I now see them as evidence of God's love. There were times when my bank accounts were not accessible, I would wind up in jail, encounter people who hindered my activities, or some other situation preventing me from doing as I pleased (if only for a moment.)

In addictions, I insanely sought to fashion the world to my liking. I would govern the universe to meet my desires were it possible. By the same token, since I left my drug addiction while seeking to glorify God, God arranges things to suit His purposes. I would be amiss not to mention that He often designs things to occur that bring more delight than I could ever find in addictions.

I am not saying that you will get everything that you want by seeking to do God's will. The main issue is that we become in accord with God. By being in accord with God you will see how every situation (whether painful or pleasant) is to your advantage as well as others in your life. My dad once taught me that in Christ, things only get better. I have also learned that when God is in charge, you always win (even when it appears that you have lost.)

April 8

In His image (part 1)

> Your hands have made and fashioned me; give me understanding that I may learn Your commandments. Psalms 119:73

Of all the blessings that were bestowed, the greatest blessing was for man to be created in the image of God (Genesis 1:27). The psalmist realized this while stating that God had made and fashioned him. He further realized how he was created in God's image by asking for understanding.

As we reflect the image of God, we reflect His character. We are kind as He while reflecting His image. We are faithful and loving as He while reflecting His image. These are not properties that belong to addictions. Addictions are grounded in selfishness. Addictions cause us to be unreliable. Addictions do not bear nor reflect the image of God.

We must be in sync with God to overcome addictions to the degree that we reflect His image. Here is the wisdom that is better known as understanding. For addictions to be dealt with there must be reasoning. The stock of reasoning is understanding.

Only in Christ are we able to reach the level of understanding that God requires. Currently, I have 672 pages of *Bible Verses Addictions* notes. **Understanding** is mentioned 158 times in my notes. In Psalms 119:27 I listed the outline of understanding from *Turning to God from Idols*. I will list some of the references today and continue tomorrow (from the *King James Version* of the Bible.)

1. God's

> Great *is* our Lord, and of great power: His **understanding** *is* infinite. Psalms 147:5

> Hast thou not known? hast thou not heard, that the everlasting God, the LORD, the Creator of the ends of the earth, fainteth not, neither is weary? there is no searching of His **understanding**. Isaiah 40:28

> And the spirit of the LORD shall rest upon Him, the spirit of wisdom and **understanding,** the spirit of counsel and might, the spirit of knowledge and of the fear of the LORD; And shall make Him of quick **understanding** in the fear of the LORD: and He shall not judge after the sight of His eyes, neither reprove after the hearing of His ears: Isaiah 11:2-3

April 9

In His image (part 2)

2. Lacking

And none considereth in his heart, neither *is there* knowledge nor **understanding** to say, I have burned part of it in the fire; yea, also I have baked bread upon the coals thereof; I have roasted flesh, and eaten *it*: and shall I make the residue thereof an abomination? shall I fall down to the stock of a tree? Isaiah 44:19

Having the **understanding** darkened, being alienated from the life of God through the ignorance that is in them, because of the blindness of their heart: Ephesians 4:18

3. Sought after

I *am* Thy servant; give me **understanding,** that I may know Thy testimonies. Psalms 119:125

Wisdom *is* the principal thing; *therefore* get wisdom: and with all thy getting get **understanding**. Proverbs 4:7

4. Source

And unto man He said, Behold, the fear of the Lord, that *is* wisdom; and to depart from evil *is* **understanding.** Job 28:28

Through Thy precepts I get **understanding:** therefore I hate every false way. Psalms 119:104

5. Results

A wise *man* will hear, and will increase learning; and a man of **understanding** shall attain unto wise counsels. Proverbs 1:5

The eyes of your **understanding** being enlightened; that ye may know what is the hope of His calling, and what the riches of the glory of His inheritance in the saints. Ephesians 1:18

Another part of being created in the image of God is your fruitfulness. God has created you for a purpose. As you gain the understanding that He gives, you begin to realize this more and more.

April 10

Sobriety made simple

> I understand more than the aged, for I keep Your precepts. I hold back my feet from every evil way, in order to keep Your Word. I do not turn aside from Your rules, for You have taught me. How sweet are Your Words to my taste, sweeter than honey to my mouth! Through Your precepts I get understanding; therefore I hate every false way. Psalms 119:100-104

The psalmist expresses his obedience to God. Each of the phrases is an accurate description of what it means to abstain from an addiction. Let's look at each of the phrases that describe the psalmist's obedience followed by a shorter list describing the process that produces loving obedience.

1. I keep Your precepts
2. I hold back my feet from every evil way
3. To keep Your Word
4. I do not turn aside from Your rules
5. I hate every false way

True and complete sobriety that is acceptable to God is in total accordance with the Word of God. One of the definitions of sobriety is soundness of mind. Does God have a sound mind? Of course! It is as you agree with the thoughts of God's mind, as they are expressed in His Word, that you develop the soundness of mind that leads you into godly decisions (such as abstaining from addiction out of reverence towards God.)

The process that God uses for sobriety is simple. While the process may be described in many other ways, Psalms 119:100-104 gives us the vital steps. Sobriety in its simplest terms contains three elements.

1. Understanding (mentioned twice)
2. Taught by God
3. Enjoyment (How sweet are your words)

The psalmist's obedience to God was first taught by God (giving him understanding) and then enjoyed (as the Word of God was sweet to him.) Though there are multiple programs with various formulas to combat addictions, the best of them could probably all be summarized with the two elements that I just mentioned. In all the years that I have been exposed to lists that confront addictions, I have found that the best of them involve comprehending the thoughts of God leading to a pleasurable experience (even more pleasurable than the addiction.)

April 11

Fed up

My soul fainteth for Thy salvation: but I hope in Thy Word. Mine eyes fail for Thy Word, saying, "When wilt Thou comfort me?" Psalm 119:81-82 *KJV*

Our reading is titled "Fed up" because of the *King James Version* of the chosen passage of Scripture. Whereas the word "long" is used in the two verses out of the *English Standard Version,* the *King James Version* offers "fainteth" and "fail" instead. The *King James Version* seems more intense. The Hebrew word is **kalah**. It means to consume, cease, finish, complete, spent, or to be at an end.

How often do the events of our lives seem to consume us? Addictions have this effect. It is then that our hearts and souls grow faint! We seem to be "at our wit's end." After reading Psalms 119:81-82 the words of Christ came to mind as He told His followers how to react to the pressures that preclude His return.

> And there will be signs in sun and moon and stars, and on the earth distress of nations in perplexity because of the roaring of the sea and the waves, people fainting with fear and with foreboding of what is coming on the world. ... And then they will see the Son of Man coming in a cloud with power and great glory. Now when these things begin to take place, straighten up and raise your heads, because your redemption is drawing near. But watch yourselves lest your hearts be weighed down with dissipation and drunkenness and cares of this life, and that day come upon you suddenly like a trap. Luke 21:25-28, 34

Just as the psalmist relied on the fulfillment of God's Word for strength, Jesus advised His followers to do the same. Jesus encourages His followers to consider His return. This is an important element when conquering addictions.

> "What are the benefits of meditating on the return of Christ? There are several. First, it reminds us that there is a deadline. The battle with sin is hard, but it will someday be over...A third benefit of meditating on the grace to come is that it reveals our true destiny... Reckless self-indulgence and bondage to sinful passions are simply not what God intended for human beings. Such behavior has much more in common with a dog than it does with God's design for us."
> -*Addictions: A Banquet in the Grave,* Edward T. Welch

April 12

The pilgrim

I am a sojourner on the earth; hide not Your commandments from me! Psalms 119:19

"How's the pilgrim?", was the question my favorite uncle would ask my dad concerning me. Pilgrim is another word for sojourner (the *King James Version* uses the word "stranger.") How I wish that I had lived up to the title my uncle gave me sooner, rather than being absorbed by 23 intermittent years of crack addiction.

A stranger or a sojourner is unfamiliar with his surroundings. Addictions start with familiarity. It is by becoming a stranger to this world that we are set free of addictions. The force behind that strength is the fear of the Lord. A few select verses from 1 Peter are supportive:

> And if you call on Him as Father who judges impartially according to each one's deeds, conduct yourselves with fear throughout the time of your exile. 1 Peter 1:17

> Beloved, I urge you as sojourners and exiles to abstain from the passions of the flesh, which wage war against your soul.
> 1 Peter 2:11

Our participation in addictions begins long before we engage in their use. It first begins as we allow what is foreign to God into our spirits. This is why the psalmist asked God to not hide His commandments from him.

We live in an evil, confusing world. Without reverence for God, we are only left with calamity and confusion. The psalmist knew that, as a sojourner, he would not be able to navigate his way through this world without God's instructions. It is no wonder that the acronym some have chosen for the word ***Bible*** is "Basic instructions before leaving earth."

As Israel was a stranger to other nations, God commanded them not to inquire about the gods of the other nations. The Lord said to "take care that you be not ensnared to follow them, ... and that you do not inquire about their gods, saying, 'How did these nations serve their gods? —that I also may do the same'" (Deuteronomy 12:30).

> "Those who would forsake God's holy reverence are abandoning an indispensable characteristic. It is as though they are searching for the formula of life, but the major ingredient of 'integrity' is left out." -*The Forgotten Fear*, A.N. Martin

April 13

The flow

> I will run in the way of Your commandments when You enlarge my heart! Psalms 119:32

It is because I used to be a crack addict that I know of the dangers that it has upon our hearts. Cocaine is a very strong stimulant that causes the heart to speed up. It also causes all the blood vessels to constrict or tighten. This combination stresses the heart that is trying to pump blood through the constricted arteries and veins.

The effect of repeated use of cocaine is an enlarged heart that is less able to pump blood efficiently. While an enlarged heart can kill physically, a spiritually enlarged heart will save your life and rescue you from addictions. A spiritually enlarged heart makes room for the Spirit of God and the things that He wants to have precedence.

When the psalmist said that he would run in the way of God's commandments it means that he would run from anything contrary to God's will. Since addictions are clearly against the will of God, then to run in the way of His commandments would mean to forsake our addictions.

Proverbs warn us to keep our hearts "with all diligence." It says that "out of it are the issues of life" (Proverbs 4:23). But, what does it mean to have an enlarged heart in a spiritual sense?

> "When thou shalt enlarge my heart. Yes, the heart is the master; the feet soon run when the heart is free and energetic. Let the affections be aroused and eagerly set on divine things, and our actions will be full of force, swiftness, and delight. God must work in us first, and then we shall will and do according to His good pleasure. He must change the heart, unite the heart, encourage the heart, strengthen the heart, and enlarge the heart…" -*The Treasury of David,* C.H. Spurgeon

Unless our heart is spiritually enlarged, we are not open to God's flow! The translation that I am using is the *English Standard Version*. While referring to an enlarged heart, other translations speak of "a broader understanding, better insight, and a heart that is willing." All of these are necessary for breaking the chains of addictions around our hearts.

While a heart that is enlarged physically is not open to flowing blood when a heart is spiritually enlarged it is not open to the flow of sin.

April 14

Let's be reasonable!

> Let Your steadfast love comfort me according to Your promise to your servant. Let Your mercy come to me, that I may live; for Your law is my delight. Let the insolent be put to shame, because they have wronged me with falsehood; as for me, I will meditate on Your precepts. Let those who fear You turn to me, that they may know Your testimonies. Psalms 119:76-79

The element of reason will always be a factor so long as God addresses addictions. Once your response to God's reasoning begins to build, then you start to see how God thinks. You need this to mature. As you begin to see how God thinks, then your requests to God become closer to His will. From there, you build confidence and assurance each time you go to God in prayer.

> And this is the confidence that we have toward Him, that if we ask anything according to His will He hears us. And if we know that He hears us in whatever we ask, we know that we have the requests that we have asked of Him. 1 John 5:14-15

One of the common denominators of verses 76-79 of Psalms 119 is also found in verses 41, 169, 170, 173, and 175. Each of the verses begins by asking God to let something occur. Time will not allow us to explore, but with each request, the psalmist gives a reason why God should grant him his request.

As quiet as it is kept; there is no one as reasonable as God. One of the greatest errors that addictions feed off is accusing God of being unreasonable (when, in fact, *we* are the ones who are unreasonable.)

To be reasonable is a mark of maturity. If Man has been created in the image of God, and the image was lost in the Fall, one of the means of redemption is when God restores that image by making us more reasonable! As you become more reasonable, you become more conformable to the image of Christ.

One of the most horrendous characteristics of addiction is its savagery. Addictions often resort to uncivilized, nonproductive behavior. Addictions are typified as unreasonable. As I said before, insanity will not be reasoned with.

Before my marriage, I remember a couple in an apartment next to mine argued so loudly that I could hear them. Since I had given myself to God, my dwelling was marked with harmony. One day, I knocked on their door and said that I could hear them argue from my apartment though there was no one there but me and God "and *we* don't argue anymore."

April 15

Solidarity (part 1)

> I am a companion of all who fear You, of those who keep Your precepts. Psalms 119:63

It appears that God has placed a deep appreciation for the solidarity of every believer of Christ in me from the day that I was born again until now. One thing that I rely on is that I can go anywhere in the world and immediately connect with another believer in Christ as though we have known each other from birth (so long as we both are yielded to the Spirit of God.)

It is our reverence for God that joins us. There are only two types of people in this world - those who reverence God and those who do not. Those who reverence God have a godly perspective (to one degree or another.) Two types of people are under the influence of addiction. Those who have no reverence for God at all; and those who don't revere Him enough.

Those who do not revere God enough need the help of those who do. Though it is rarely mentioned, reverencing God is the ultimate solution to addictions because "the fear of the Lord is the beginning of wisdom" (Proverbs 9:10). I have gained the ability to explain addictions concisely from the Scriptures. I have greatly benefited from the help of mature, godly people.

> "You can learn to follow Jesus by following the example of someone who is following Jesus, regardless of whether that person has been an addict or not. Only someone who is following Jesus can teach you to follow Jesus. The person who knows God and the truth of God is able to understand the addict's problem and God's solution without ever having been an addict. The follower of God knows about sin, slavery to sin, the deceptiveness of sin, and the idolatry of sin because he also is a sinner." -*My Beloved Addiction*, Jeff Mullins

I also have an appreciation for the people that I fellowship with by reading their writing. Just as with my interaction with others on a personal level, when I read the writing of others, we become united in thought (as our thoughts are those that give glory and honor to God, God joins the fellowship as well.)

> Not forsaking the assembling of ourselves together, as the manner of some is; but exhorting one another: and so much the more, as ye see the day approaching. Hebrews 10:25

April 16

Solidarity (part 2)

> I am a companion of all who fear You, of those who keep Your precepts. Psalms 119:63

The Word of God creates the strongest unity there is. The bonds of addiction are no match for the Church as expressed in both the Old Testament and the New Testament.

> Two are better than one; because they have a good reward for their labour. For if they fall, the one will lift up his fellow: but woe to him that is alone when he falleth; for he hath not another to help him up. Again, if two lie together, then they have heat: but how can one be warm alone? And if one prevail against him, two shall withstand him; and a threefold cord is not quickly broken. Ecclesiastes 4:9-12 *KJV*

> On this rock I will build my church, and the gates of hell shall not prevail against it. Matthew 16:18b

It is a known fact that when we engage in addictions, we draw the companionship of others (directly or indirectly.) Since addictions are against the will of God, they are foolish. We are not only fools for choosing idols over God but we are fools for rejecting the people that God wants us to fellowship with and keeping company with fools.

> Whoever walks with the wise becomes wise, but the companion of fools will suffer harm. Proverbs 13:20

> The eye cannot say to the hand, "I have no need of you," nor again the head to the feet, "I have no need of you." 1 Corinthians 12:21

Fellowship is a commitment. It requires devotion. Just as Hebrews 10:25 from yesterday's reading explains "the manner of some." Other translations of Hebrews 10:25 refer to the "habit" of others.

> "The level of devotion and commitment to God a person needs to have to be saved is similar to the level of devotion and commitment an addict has to his addiction. ... The addict though understands what it means to be exclusively and wholeheartedly committed to something. He knows what it means to sacrifice everything for something of exceedingly great value. It is this level of devotion Jesus requires of His followers." -*My Beloved Addiction*, Jeff Mullins

April 17

Half-minded vs. wholehearted

With my whole heart I cry; answer me, O Lord! I will keep Your statutes. Psalms 110:145

It matters not whether you are Christian, Hindu, Muslim, man or woman, child or baby, straight or gay ...It doesn't matter if you are Black or white, yellow, American, Persian, Puerto Rican, or European ... Whoever or whatever you are, you give your heart to something!

One of the most basic descriptions of addiction is defined as a heart that is committed. We are often perplexed as we approach our assault on addictions with half a mind. Yet, as we pursue addictions, we do so with a whole heart.

If you are attempting to break free of addiction, what good does half a mind do? Half a mind is enough to get you in a whole lot of trouble! Addictions don't want half of your mind! Nor does God want just a piece of your heart! God is worthy of our whole being. That's why some people don't want to admit God's existence. Deep inside, they know that if there is a God, then He deserves everything. Addictions withhold from God.

To illustrate the importance of giving your whole heart to God rather than having half a mind, think of your mind as an unprotected city. It is no mystery that your actions are decided by your mind. For God to protect your mind from evil, He needs your whole heart. A mind that has been given to addiction is like a city that has been torn down.."

- Engage the battle- separate from the object of your affection
- Turn to Christ and commit yourself to keep turning to Christ
- Surround yourself with wise counselors- be a part of a church
- Speak honestly- uncover the more subtle lies
- Commit yourself to thinking God's thoughts about addictions and wise living
- Engage the battle to the lower level of the imagination
- Delight in the fear of the Lord

Addictions: A Banquet in the Grave "The Process of Change", Edward T. Welch

So we built the wall. And all the wall was joined together to half its height, for **the people had a mind to work**. Nehemiah 4:6

So we rebuilt the wall till all of it reached half its height, for the **people worked with all their heart.** *NIV*

April 18

Vigor

I call to you; save me, that I may observe Your testimonies. I rise before dawn and cry for help; I hope in Your words. My eyes are awake before the watches of the night, that I may meditate on Your promise. Psalms 119:146-148

Vigor is a word that can be used to describe Psalms 119:146-148. The call of the psalmist was vigorous. The hope of the psalmist was vigorous. And, the *meditation* of the psalmist was vigorous.

Vigor is marked by intensity. Vigor is a measurement of strength. Vigor defines our lives. We are vigorous about the things we consider serious. Vigor is also a word that may be used to describe addictions. How vigorous are addictions? How vigorous, indeed!

> "Addiction involves craving for something intensely, loss of control over its use, and continuing involvement with it despite adverse consequences. Addiction changes the brain, first by subverting the way it registers pleasure and then by corrupting other normal drives such as learning and motivation. Although breaking an addiction is tough, it can be done. The word 'addiction' is derived from a Latin term for 'enslaved by' or 'bound to.' Anyone who has struggled to overcome an addiction—or has tried to help someone else to do so—understands why. Addiction exerts a long and powerful influence on the brain that manifests in three distinct ways: craving for the object of addiction, loss of control over its use, and continuing involvement with it despite adverse consequences."
> -*How Addiction Hijacks the Brain,* A Harvard Health article

We take addictions seriously! Just as the psalmist called to the Lord, you may call out to addictions. As the psalmist hoped in the Lord, you may place your hope in addictions. And, we may meditate on addictions as the psalmist meditated on the Lord.

The intensity of addiction can only be combatted with a force that is greater than itself. Vigor, again, demonstrates how serious we are. Serious is one of the definitions for sobriety. You can't get any more serious than Jesus. Until my dying day, I insist that "the highest form of sobriety known unto mankind is found in Jesus Christ."

Does your assault upon addictions involve Jesus Christ? Is the intensity of your craving met by the power that is in Christ? There is no power greater than the power found in Christ.

April 19

The hand of the Lord (part 1)

Let Your hand be ready to help me, for I have chosen Your precepts. Psalms 119:173

On January 8th, I talked about how sober it is to be before the Lord. At one point in my life, had to recant my statement of being before the Lord as being most sober while commenting that the Word of the Lord provides the highest degree of sobriety. Early in my sobriety, I was led by God to research some of the most serious themes found in Scripture.

- The Word of the Lord (came)
- Before the Lord
- The Name of the Lord
- The Presence of the Lord
- The eye of the Lord
- Unto the Lord

The hand of the Lord is another important theme. The hand of the Lord is not to be overlooked in our discussion on addictions! In *Turning to God from Idols* I stated that "being before the Lord can be either comforting or disturbing." This applies to the hand of the Lord as well. I once stated that "if the hand of the Lord is not upon you, then the hand of the Lord is against you." The book of Hebrews presents a very serious look at the hand of the Lord.

It is a fearful thing to fall into the hands of the living God. Hebrews 10:31

Time will not allow me to list a great number of passages that refer to the hand of the Lord. If you wish to study this awesome theme on your own, I found a great listing at https://www.openbible.info/topics/hand_of_god I leave you with several references while praying that God will show you the significance of addictions. More references are listed in tomorrow's reading.

Humble yourselves, therefore, under the mighty hand of God so that at the proper time He may exalt you. 1 Peter 5:6

My Father, who has given them to Me, is greater than all, and no one is able to snatch them out of the Father's hand. John 10:29

April 20

The hand of the Lord (part 2)

Let Your hand be ready to help me, for I have chosen Your precepts. Psalms 119:173

Yesterday, I started sharing how significant the hand of the Lord is to your life. Psalms 104:27 declares how all of creation waits on God to "give them their meat in due season *(KJV)*. Here are some other references to the hand of the Lord in Scripture:

But Zion said, "The Lord has forsaken me; my Lord has forgotten me." "Can a woman forget her nursing child, that she should have no compassion on the son of her womb? Even these may forget, yet I will not forget you. Behold, I have engraved you on the palms of My hands; your walls are continually before Me. Isaiah 49:14-16

I took courage, for the hand of the LORD my God was on me. Ezra 7:28b

The hand of our God is for good on all who seek Him, and the power of His wrath is against all who forsake Him. Ezra 8:22

The Word of the Lord came to Ezekiel the priest, the son of Buzi, in the land of the Chaldeans by the Chebar canal, and the hand of the Lord was upon him there. Ezekiel 1:3

Fear not, for I am with you; be not dismayed, for I am your God; I will strengthen you, I will help you, I will uphold you with My righteous right hand. Isaiah 41:10

"O house of Israel, can I not do with you as this potter has done?" declares the Lord. Behold, like the clay in the potter's hand, so are you in My hand, O house of Israel. Jeremiah 18:6

So long as we are not touched by the hand of God, we will never reach the level of sobriety that gives God glory. In the hand of the Lord are His strength and authority. The hand of the Lord can be gentle or stern. The dexterity of His fingers is ingenious.

The magnificence of the work of His hands is masterful. We should ever desire to be in His hand; under His hand; with His hand upon us; His hand working through us; an instrument of His hand; as we cry for His helping hand! And yet, we should seek His face above His hand!

April 21

Lost and found

I have gone astray like a lost sheep; seek Your servant, for I do not forget Your commandments. Psalms 119:176

Have you ever been lost? If not, I can tell you that being lost can be scary. My first recollection of being lost was on my very first Halloween outing (when I was about 4 years old.) I got separated from my relatives and wound up wandering into a convenience store for answers.

The answer that I got was to just sit there and wait to see if my family showed up. Are you lost as you "trick and treat" after addictions? To wait on the Lord for answers is the best solution.

Getting lost that Halloween turned into a pleasant experience as the customers at the store gave me Halloween gifts while I waited to see if my relatives would show. Getting lost was not so bad so long as I had people looking after me. Yet, I thought about how they could not replace my family and that there would come a time when the store would close.

Needless to say, my relatives came after a while. It was guaranteed because of the love that they had for me. I did not doubt that they would show up. Addiction doesn't offer any guarantees. And after you start burning bridges, it gets worse.

One of the deceits of addiction is the promise of a treat while you are being tricked into forfeiting relationships (just as I had been separated from my loved ones that Halloween.) One of the advantages we have is that God places people in our path that can direct us when we are lost and provide safety and comfort until we are found.

Why would you look at addictions as a treat? Addictions are monstrous! Addictions have ruined millions. They reek with the smell of death.

Have you ever had someone looking for you? Maybe you drifted away from the family as I did during my first Halloween experience. Maybe your drifting was not as pleasant as mine.

Though I was only 4 years old, I knew that being lost was not supposed to be that fun. God is looking for you. He wants to give you more joy and fulfillment than you ever thought possible. Christ is the Good Shepherd. As the Good Shepherd, Christ is willing and able to seek those who have gone astray and lead them safely to the presence of the Father.

"Our minds are mental greenhouses where unlawful thoughts, once planted, are nurtured and watered before being transplanted into the real world of unlawful actions… These actions are savored in the mind long before they are enjoyed in reality. The thought life, then, is our first line of defense in the battle of self-control."
-Jerry Bridges

April 22

Much help

> Where no counsel is, the people fall: but in the multitude of counselors there is safety. Proverbs 11:14

Years ago, I began to discover some of the most vital resources for overcoming addiction. When I started publishing in 2018, I vowed that I would seek to give my readers the best there is for overcoming addiction. You can find a list of resources on my Facebook group *Quality Christian Resources on Addiction*.

God also wants us to have the greatest there is for combatting addiction. I often ask people if they think that the founders of Alcoholics Anonymous knew everything there is to know about addiction. Proverbs 2:1-4 explains the importance of finding the best help that you can.

> My son, if you accept my words and store up my commands within you, turning your ear to wisdom and applying your heart to understanding, and if you call out for insight and cry aloud for understanding, and if you look for it as for silver and search for it as for hidden treasure, then you will understand the fear of the LORD and find the knowledge of God. Proverbs 2:1-4

We have been *really* blessed with some tremendous Bible-based resources on addictions. There was a time when I would search bookstores and libraries for resources (during my struggle with crack.) God is not a stingy Commander-in-Chief who orders His army to go forth against a mighty force with just a puny arsenal. Nor is He a Provider who sends His servants out to feed the masses with just a smidgen of food.

1. God is not limited
2. The whole counsel of God — Acts 20:27
3. That which is profitable — Acts 20:20
4. Out of love for others
5. An appreciation of the body of Christ — 1 Cor. 12:21
6. Equipping ourselves and others to be more effective

> And he gave the apostles, the prophets, the evangelists, the shepherds and teachers, to equip the saints for the work of ministry, for building up the body of Christ, until we all attain to the unity of the faith and of the knowledge of the Son of God, to mature manhood, to the measure of the stature of the fullness of Christ. Ephesians 4:11-13

April 23 (handwritten)

What is repentance?

For if we have been united with Him in a death like His, we shall certainly be united with Him in a resurrection like His. Romans 6:5

I have repented from giving my awe to the idols of addiction and began reverencing God. The intensity of your reverence affects your repentance. In short, to repent is to turn away from sin and toward Christ.

Placing your faith in God's Word (His point of view) as well as the recognition of Who God is leads you to repentance. Romans 2:4 says that the goodness of God leads to repentance. The change in overcoming addiction has been given many labels. Some of these terms are more accurate than others. Not only that, everyone decides on the degree of changes they will make.

Recovery Sobriety Restoration Healing Set free Maturity Growth Holiness Sanctified Deliverance Reconciliation Being saved Revival Transformation Being made whole
(I prefer the words repentance, transformation, and sanctification.)

True sobriety can be defined as agreeing with God. There is no agreement with God until our sin has been dealt with through the blood of Christ. And so, for the process of sobriety to begin, we must be born again, saved, and united with Christ

Without repentance, there is not much communication between us and God!

Repentance begins with a change of mind, as the Spirit of God shows us, convinces us of the truth about sin, and points us to Christ. As God gives us the ability to reason and the capacity to understand, then, we can form convictions over addictions. Contrary to what I once believed; a **conviction is not the same as condemnation** (although, convictions lead to condemnation *without* repentance.)

The title of *Turning to God from Idols* comes from 1 Thessalonians 1:9 where it was said that the believers had "turned to God from idols to serve the true and living God." How is it that the believers of Thessalonica were led to repent by turning to God from idols? Verse five says "because our gospel came to you not simply with words but also with power, with the Holy Spirit and **deep conviction**."

April 24

Strong repentance (part 1)

> For godly grief produces a repentance that leads to salvation without regret, whereas worldly grief produces death. For see what earnestness this godly grief has produced in you, but also what eagerness to clear yourselves, what indignation, what fear, what longing, what zeal, what punishment! At every point you have proved yourselves innocent in the matter. 2 Corinthians 7:10-11

A simple explanation of turning to God from the idols of addiction is repentance which is built on reverence, followed by reason, and leads to rejoicing. Repentance is commanded to all by God (Acts 20:21). Repentance goes hand in hand with faith in Christ.

From Acts 26:20, we learn that our deeds prove our repentance. Repentance is to be fueled by earnestness and zeal. Change of focus, desires, interests, importance, direction, thoughts, habits thus patterns... Repentance requires vision.

In *Idolatry and the Hardening of the Heart,* Edward P. Meadors said, "Repentance thus occurs out of an awareness that one's true value and worth is only discovered in a peaceful and honest relationship with one's Creator and not from servitude to one's own creation—whether material or mental."

Since the opposite of a hard heart is a broken heart then for us to thoroughly repent from idolatry, we must have a broken heart. Humility is the frame of mind a man possesses who is fully aware of his nothingness apart from God and his sinfulness that would eternally separate him from God were not God willing to rescue him.

> "Such a conviction requires a turning away from self, and dependence on God and His grace. Perhaps there's no simpler definition of repentance than the life process of turning away from self and toward our Father. This kind of faith requires believing that our Creator is authoring a masterpiece tapestry of all our realities beyond the mere landscape of what we can see and feel. When we're committed to knowing, loving, and trusting God beyond our circumstances, then we begin movement in a different direction. We realize our selfish agendas of feeling safe, comfortable, and happy all the time are not priorities from God's perspective. He's committed to a much deeper, much more radical love of our souls. Our transformation into Christlikeness (sanctification) takes precedence over our comfort and convenience." -*A Repentant Heart*, Dudley J. Delffs

April 25

Strong repentance (part 2)

> For godly grief produces a repentance that leads to salvation without regret, whereas worldly grief produces death. For see what earnestness this godly grief has produced in you, but also what eagerness to clear yourselves, what indignation, what fear, what longing, what zeal, what punishment! At every point you have proved yourselves innocent in the matter. 2 Corinthians 7:10-11

I used a picture in the study guide for *Turning to God from Idols* with roads that overlap but do not all take you to where you want to be. It's an illustration of how many programs for addictions overlap, but they do not all take you where God wants you to be.

A lot of programs deal with different aspects of addiction (psychological, medical, spiritual...) The most important aspect of addiction is the spiritual aspect. If you don't address the spiritual issues of addiction (from the very start) then you will always lack the level of sobriety that is necessary for becoming whole.

Change and repentance are synonymous. Repentance calls for a change of interest as well as your attention redirected. Repentance allows you to love God and love others as God would have you to.

> "Much change that is offered today in counseling—even in the Name of Christ—is sub-Christian. Aimed at little more than making counselees happier, it neglects the basic reason why a believer must change to please God. As if God's glory were of secondary importance, His Name's sake is omitted from the picture, out of deference to better health or a more smoothly running marriage. Such considerations, not wrong in themselves, are quite wrong when they are not subordinated to the greater purpose of pleasing and honoring God." -*How to Help People Change*, Jay Adams

Discernment gives power to repentance! To have faith in Christ means that you can have the same ability to discern what is pleasing to God as Jesus. Any type of sobriety outside of faith in Christ is but a facade.

Discernment protects us from the lies of deceit. The *Amplified Bible* says, "The beginning of wisdom is: Get [skillful and godly] wisdom [it is preeminent]! And with all your acquiring, get understanding [actively seek spiritual **discernment**, mature comprehension, and logical interpretation]" (Proverbs 4:7). No one can understand addictions more accurately than someone who is rightly related to God! "The secret of the LORD is with them that fear him; and he will shew them his covenant" (Psalms 25:14 *KJV*).

April 26

Strong repentance (part 3)

> For godly grief produces a repentance that leads to salvation without regret, whereas worldly grief produces death. For see what earnestness this godly grief has produced in you, but also what eagerness to clear yourselves, what indignation, what fear, what longing, what zeal, what punishment! At every point you have proved yourselves innocent in the matter. 2 Corinthians 7:10-11

Repentance is to turn from self and to follow Christ. It occurs in stages after you become born again. Many do not realize that change does not often occur at once. While I don't condone people holding on to things that hinder their relationship with God, I have come to understand that it takes time for people to change.

> "There is a Christian myth that change is an event rather than a process; that it is more like a light switch that is turned on than a battle that must be engaged. For some reason, we tend to think-wrongly-that immediate liberation from the slavery of addiction is more glamorous than the gradual process of taking a little bit of land at a time." -*Addictions: A Banquet in the Grave,* Welch

On the other hand, change requires intensity. Just as Jesus said that if anyone would follow Him they must deny themselves and take up their cross daily (Luke 9:23). Now, that's more intense than addiction! In a most worth reading called *Hard to Believe,* John MacArthur, states that the original Greek word for "deny" means "to refuse to associate with."

> "The thought is that if you want to be Christ's disciple, and receive forgiveness and eternal life, you must refuse to associate any longer with the person you are! You are sick of your sinful self and want nothing to do with you anymore." -John MacArthur

> "Let the wicked forsake his way, and the unrighteous man his thoughts: and let him return unto the Lord, and He will have mercy upon him; and to our God, for He will abundantly pardon. For My thoughts are not your thoughts, neither are your ways My ways, saith the Lord. For as the heavens are higher than the earth, so are My ways higher than your ways, and My thoughts than your thoughts." Isaiah 55:7-9

Repentance is a reflection of what you think of God!

April 27

Looking for you

> So when they saw Him, they were amazed; and His mother said to Him, "Son, why have You done this to us? Look, Your father and I have sought You anxiously." And He said to them, "Why did you seek Me? Did you not know that I must be about My Father's business?" Luke 2:48-49

One of the funniest stories that I have ever heard was when my dad's mother visited Cleveland, Ohio from Memphis, Tennessee. She used to call my dad Skip and when she arrived in Cleveland, she called the in-laws asking for my dad. The brother-in-law, Jimmy, didn't know her and became apprehensive when she asked to speak to her son Skip.

"Is Skip there?" she said. "Yeah, he's here," said Jimmy. When she asked if she could talk to him, Jimmy said, "Yeah, you can talk to him, but I don't know if he will answer." When she said that she was his mother, Jimmy hung up the phone. She was longing for her son and this stranger was standing in the way. After calling back, she found out that the family's dog was named Skip also.

The whole idea behind repentance is that God is looking for you. Others are looking for you as well. Addictions deprive God and others of you. I learned a valuable lesson in 1989 at a drug treatment center that made an impact to this day. A counselor helped me to see that while I thought that I had never stolen from my parents, I was stealing the son that my parents longed for. As quiet as it is kept, God wants you to have a life of sobriety more than _you_ ever could.

> "Much-Afraid trembled and looked at him shamefacedly, 'I don't think—I want hinds' feet, if it means I have to go on a path like that,' she said slowly and painfully. The Shepherd was a very surprising person. Instead of looking either disappointed or disapproving, he actually laughed again. 'Oh, yes you do,' he said cheerfully. 'I know you better than you know yourself, Much-Afraid. You want it very much indeed, and I promise you these hinds' feet.'" -*Hinds Feet on High Places*, Hannah Hunard

What are your deepest longings? Do they include the purposes that God has for your life? One of the things that drew me from addiction was how when I died, I would not be recognized as the man that God created me to be no more than Skip the dog bore the resemblance to my dad.

> And not only the creation, but we ourselves, who have the firstfruits of the Spirit, groan inwardly as we wait eagerly for adoption as sons, the redemption of our bodies. Romans 8:23

April 28

Refreshing repentance

And now, brothers, I know that you acted in ignorance, as did also your rulers. But what God foretold by the mouth of all the prophets, that his Christ would suffer, he thus fulfilled. Repent therefore, and turn back, that your sins may be blotted out, that times of refreshing may come from the presence of the Lord, and that he may send the Christ appointed for you, Jesus. Acts 3:17-20

Repentance goes beyond recovery. True repentance is not just a change of behavior but a change of heart as well. Recovering what you were will never make you into the person that God wants you to be. While recovery leaves us with the possibility of *excluding* God, repentance has always referred to moving *toward* God.

A.N. Martin said that one of the ingredients of reverence is an awareness of the obligation that we have to God. No one likes to be in debt. And when the debt that we have to God is lifted through the payment that Christ made for our sins it is a relief. We find more relief as we turn from anything that is not of God. I've always said that a clear conscience goes a long way.

What greater joy could there be than to be at peace with God? But, not only that, through repentance, you don't have to suffer the immediate consequences of addiction. While it is true that you may suffer some of the consequences that resulted from addiction, you won't have to worry about the direct dangers. For instance, some drugs are known to kill you right away; but then they could always cause permanent damage that may kill you years later even if you stop using them.

The greatest thing about repentance is the joy that God experiences. While you may only be concerned about your satisfaction in pursuit of addiction or turning from it, are you ever concerned about God's satisfaction? Luke 15:10 says "there is joy before the angels of God over one sinner who repents." The joy that God gets from our repentance is like the joy that the father had for the prodigal in Luke 15:11-32.

> "Suppose someone skilled in navigation sees a picture drawn like a navigator would draw. He takes delight in it because there is something of himself in it; but now suppose he has a child, and he puts skill into him, and he sees him work as he works and discourse about naval affairs as he himself would do. This is wonderfully delightful to him. So when God sees the same life in His creature that is in Himself, that he works and wills as He does, this takes the very heart of God, and this shows the excellency of grace."
> -*The Evil of Evils*, Jeremiah Burroughs

April 29

Rescuing Awe

> Stand in awe, and sin not: commune with your own heart upon your bed, and be still. Selah. Psalms 4:4 *KJV*

Do you know what is sure to rescue people from the idols of addiction? I recently watched how the new *Black Panther* character in *Wakanda Forever* emerged by consuming a serum. Someone who witnessed the power of the serum asked, "Can I get some of that?" We should be so filled with the Spirit that others ask, "Can I get some of that!"

While some translations of Psalms 4:4 offer certain aspects, I like the *King James* and the *American Standard Version* translations because it reminds me of my dad. Only those versions refer to the significance of awe and standing.

The love that my dad had for God was his most distinguishing characteristic. Everyone was amazed at how he remained contagiously joyful despite his inability to stand for the last 20 years of his life because of *Muscular Dystrophy*. And yet, he stood in awe. It was as though his affliction had little effect on his disposition. Or perhaps, it had a greater effect on his reverence for God.

While other translations of Psalms 4:4 refer to trembling and pondering, these are only a portion of what I call the awe factor. Standing indicates the stability that other translations do not convey.

My dad was standing on the solid rock of Christ as he taught me that you can tell a lot about a person by asking them what they think of Christ. The way that we address addiction says a lot about what we think of Christ as well.

Years ago, I began to learn more about the significance of awe and addiction. I learned that awe is both the gateway to addiction and the way out. Somehow, I began to internalize my dad's disposition as a lifestyle.

The most valuably challenging legacy that my dad left me was to stand in awe of God for the rest of my days. My dad was an awe-factory. My website says that an awe-factory is someone who is so in awe of God that nothing external matters except to bring others into awe of God as well.

Do you want to know what rescued me from the clutches of addiction? Do you think that it was because I was sick and tired of being sick and tired? No. It was the awe of the Almighty that I saw in my dad and the Word of God through the Spirit of God. Where do *you* stand?

> For the creation waits with eager longing for the revealing of the sons of God. Romans 8:19

April 30

Yearning and repentance

> Indeed, I count everything as loss because of the surpassing worth of knowing Christ Jesus my Lord. For his sake I have suffered the loss of all things and count them as rubbish, in order that I may gain Christ ... that I may know him and the power of his resurrection, and may share his sufferings, becoming like him in his death. Philippians 3:8, 10

Healthy yearning starts with repentance. As quiet as it's kept, we are all in need of repentance for the rest of our lives because even after we are united with God through Christ, we still must grow into the likeness of Christ more and more. Repentance allows us to love God and love others as God would have us to. Unhealthy yearning *breeds* selfishness.

It is no mystery that unhealthy yearning can take control of our lives. I remember the facetious response from a stranger as my wife and I announced our engagement. "Say goodbye to your life", he said. It doesn't take long for an addiction to take over someone's life. And believe me, it's no honeymoon!

How do you reverse your life once you are overcome by addiction? What is the degree of reversal you are looking for? Is this not related to the awe that you give God rather than addictions?

Reverence is another word for awe. I could never overemphasize how reverence is a key issue to healthy yearning and the destruction of every idolatrous addiction that competes with God. The degree of your repentance corresponds to the degree of awe that you have for God!

I had to agree with the stranger who told me to say goodbye to my life. As I said 'goodbye' to my old life, I was saying 'hello' to a new and improved life. By the same token, no one's life is complete without a healthy yearning that starts with a loving, reverential relationship with Christ. **A complete reversal from addictions is not mere abstinence; for the most accurate definition of addiction is idolatry. An addiction captures our attention more than God.**

> "To save us completely Christ must reverse the bent of our nature. He must plant a new principle within us so that our subsequent conduct will spring out of a desire to promote the honor of God and the good of our fellow man." -*The Knowledge of the Holy*, A.W. Tozer

Whereas unhealthy yearning is based on *deficiency*, healthy yearning is *sufficient*. The discontentment of dreadful yearning proves it to be empty. Healthy yearning is fulfilling.

May 1

Just reverence

But you, you are to be feared! Who can stand before you when once your anger is roused? From the heavens you uttered judgment; the earth feared and was still, when God arose to establish judgment, to save all the humble of the earth. Selah Psalms 76:7-9

In the introduction to every copy of *Quality Sobriety,* I explain how the fear of the Lord has two sides to it. The emphasis of my series is mainly on how the fear of the Lord is one of honor, love, respect, and amazement or awe. I also said that the fear of the Lord can be frightful, terrifying, and maybe dreadful.

"Is it right to be afraid of God? Yes, if you have biblical grounds to be afraid of Him. Was it right for Adam to be afraid? Of course, it was. He had sinned against God. He had willfully and wickedly disobeyed the explicit command of God." -*The Forgotten Fear,* A.N. Martin

Some people say that there is no justice in the world. They say that justice means "just us." "Just us" could mean that the only people who are treated fairly are the ruling class. But real justice is not just us but rather just Him (God.)

We have all heard that God is good, and some of us believe that He is with all of our hearts. **Addictions ever question the goodness of God.** God is so good that anything that is not of Him is subject to condemnation. That includes ourselves!

If anyone deserves justice; then God does. Judgment is God claiming what is rightfully His. The methods that He uses can be disturbing. His anger is righteous, just, and holy. It is something that we don't always understand. Addictions accuse God of being unjust!

Enduringword.com says, "Our respect and reverence for God goes beyond admiration of His greatness. It is also connected to our knowledge of His righteousness, His power, and His authority as Judge. We understand that God is the best friend and the worst enemy."

At the core of addiction is fear. We turn to addiction for fear of loneliness, boredom, painful memories, physical pain, or more. Rather than looking to God for the answers to our fear we allow addictions to take God's place. Psalms 76 assures Israel that she need not fear anyone but God.

And do not fear those who kill the body but cannot kill the soul. Rather fear him who can destroy both soul and body in hell. Matthew 10:28

May 2

The first sign of reverence (part 1)

> Abraham said, "I did it because I thought, There is no fear of God at all in this place, and they will kill me because of my wife." Genesis 20:11

In this first reference to reverencing God, there are numerous explanations concerning addictions. The first explanation lies in Abraham's motives for lying. The second explanation concerning addictions has to do with why Abraham <u>perceived</u> that he would be killed.

The motives of our abstinence must be pure for us to become truly sober. The highest motive for abstaining from addictions is reverencing God. The fear of God causes us to recognize good and evil. And the fear of the Lord provides the wisdom that we desperately need to govern our lives. *You are either free from God and limited by sin or you are limited by God and free from sin.*

So why did Abraham lie? Abraham's lie--as all lies, began with a thought. Abraham lied because his thoughts were erroneous. Addictions originate from erroneous thoughts. **We don't just stumble into addictions; we think our way into them.** Abraham's thinking underestimated God.

You might say that Abraham's thinking was irreverent toward God. Abraham did not understand that God was great enough to protect Him (even *if* the people of the land he was visiting had no fear of God.) **Just as Abraham, addictions deny the adequacy of God.**

Our thinking either honors God or degrades Him. God's method of sobriety involves renewing our minds. Just as we are given opportunities to reverence God in our trials and temptations, so Abraham was tested. In this instance, he failed the test. When he trusted God enough to offer his son, then Abraham passed the test of reverencing God (Genesis 22:12).

> "The Bible asks the question, who will be king? The one true God or worthless idols? ... They started moving towards idols very gradually by rubbing shoulders with the foreigner. They found they weren't so bad so they moved closer. They began to see that their gods made some promises that were very appealing: rain and fertility in particular. Maybe, they thought, they could worship both God and idols, and in so doing get what they wanted. But the promises by the other gods were false promises. Gradually, these foreign gods demanded and received worship, and the children of Israel started walking in the dark." -*Addictions a Banquet in the Grave*, Edward T. Welch

May 3

The first sign of reverence (part 2)

> Abraham said, "I did it because I thought, There is no fear of God at all in this place, and they will kill me because of my wife." Genesis 20:11

Abraham thought that he would be killed if there were no fear of God in the place where he was. The fear of the Lord determines the disposition of every individual as well as every nation.

Notice how **it was a well-known fact, very early in history, that the fear of God determines how we treat one another!** One of the main characteristics of reverence is that it is civil. Addictions are not. Addictions unchecked become barbaric.

There would be no civilization without reverence for God. As I have said on many occasions, "If you can't trust a God-fearing person, who can you trust?" Proverbs 14:2 says that a God-fearing person's walk is upright. When we refer to reverence as being civil, we not only mean that it is fair or just but benevolent and kind as well.

When Abraham said that he thought that he would be killed because of his wife, it reveals to us that addictions have been around since ancient days. (Look deep enough into the account of the *Garden of Eden* and you will see the fountain from which all addictions flow!) Abraham's testimony reveals that some were so addicted to women that they would kill for them. Addiction can cause the best of us to become inhuman.

Freedom from addiction requires conviction. Animals have no conviction. They don't need any conviction to reverence God. Man is the only creation of God that does not freely submit to God apart from conviction. The fear of the Lord creates the love and understanding that destroys a corrupt mentality leading to idolatry in all its forms.

Abraham said that he thought that there was no fear of God "at all" where he was residing. The fear of the Lord can be measured. Your reverence is based upon how much you are in awe of God, how you allow God to control you, how you sacrifice to Him, how you place your trust in Him, and how you give Him glory. **Addictions are not in awe of God, they do not allow Him control, make no sacrifices to Him, have no trust in God, and do not glorify Him.**

Spiritual growth demands that you grow in your reverence. *The degree of your sobriety is determined by your reverence.* Just as there are degrees of reverence for God, there are degrees in which you agree to be used by God. There are, also, degrees or levels of sobriety and degrees of joy. True joy cannot exist without the fear of the Lord. Joy is the crown of reverence.

May 4

Progressing reverence (part 1)

> He said, "Do not lay your hand on the boy or do anything to him, for now I know that you fear God, seeing you have not withheld your son, your only son, from me." Genesis 22:12

Are we not all seeking progress? Even while pursuing addictions we are seeking what we *perceive* as progress. The progress of Abraham is noted in Genesis 22:12. Abraham's reverence was recognized by God.

Does God recognize *your* reverence? It is an honor for God to recognize our reverence. Does not the highest honor come from God? ***The simplest solution to addictions is to strive after living a life that is pleasing to God.*** While the world may never recognize your piety, the most important thing is how you look in the sight of God.

> Let the words of my mouth and the meditation of my heart be acceptable in your sight, O Lord, my rock and my redeemer. Psalms 19:14

"Now I know that you fear God" indicates that Abram did not always fear God. This was demonstrated by the times that he dishonored God by lying to protect himself rather than recognizing that God was willing and able to protect Him (Genesis 12:13; 20:2). Abraham wanted to be comfortable. How often have we turned to addiction for comfort? God told Abraham that he would make him a great nation (Genesis 12:2-3).

Abraham began as a stranger to God. Now there finally seemed to be a clear understanding between God and Abraham. You might say that Abraham had matured in his faith. How important it is for those who struggle with addictions to mature in their faith! What is commonly referred to as recovery should be called maturity! (Recovery is an inaccurate term because you can't recover something that you don't have.)

You cannot mature without practicing reverence. Abram had come from a land of false gods. The world is full of any false god that suits your liking. Just like Abraham, we are all born strangers to God. **Before you make addictions gods, you make the true and living God a small god.** Addictions prove how estranged we are from God.

> "Arising out of our alienation from the Living God, addiction is bondage to the rule of a substance, activity, or state of mind, which then becomes the center of life, defending itself from the truth, and leading to further estrangement from God's kingdom."-Edward T. Welch

May 5

Progressing reverence (part 2)

> He said, "Do not lay your hand on the boy or do anything to him, for now I know that you fear God, seeing you have not withheld your son, your only son, from me." Genesis 22:12

You can read in the Scriptures about all the encounters that Abraham had with God until the sacrifice of Isaac. Think of your encounters with God (or lack of encounters!) As you are exposed to God, you will either embrace Him or become hostile. **The bottom line is that you either strive to please God or please yourself.**

Progression is based on conversion and transformation. Conversion occurs when you first turn to Jesus. Transformation occurs for the rest of your life. Transformation describes the change that is needed to break the chains of addiction.

As with Abraham, change does not always happen at once. **The process of becoming less attached to the things of the world and more to God is called sanctification.** Your sanctification relies on your conversation with God. Sanctification, sobriety, and sanity are all related. Who in their right mind would choose anything over God?

It is an irony that the word "repentance" is rarely discussed in group meetings concerning addictions. Without the revelation that God brings in His conversation with us, there are no grounds for reverence (because God does not appear to be all that great.) Without reverence, there is no repentance. Without repentance, no regeneration, no reconciliation with God, no redemption of our souls, no restoration of our condition, no revival, and no times of refreshing.

Quality of sobriety that is based on what God has said. (Otherwise, we are in a state of confusion.) Likewise, the quality of your sobriety is based on the quality of reverence you possess. Jesus said that he came so that we might have life and have it more abundantly (John 10:10).

If the quality of our lives depends on the quality of our reverence, then the quality of our reverence relies on our relationship with Christ. Two things are necessary for a changed life. One is to be born again and the other is to abide in Christ. With these two, you are made complete (not just sober.) Abiding in Christ supplies the progress that is necessary for a fruitful life. And to have the mind of Christ is to be sober!

> His divine power has granted to us all things that pertain to life and godliness, through the knowledge of him who called us to his own glory and excellence. 2 Peter 1:3

May 6

Progressing reverence (part 3)

> He said, "Do not lay your hand on the boy or do anything to him, for now I know that you fear God, seeing you have not withheld your son, your only son, from me." Genesis 22:12

Earlier in Genesis 20, God reasoned with Abimelech. God spoke to him in a dream concerning Abraham. Abimelech had a desire to please God and his life was spared because of God's rebuke. Abraham's reverence for God led him to obey the Word of God (saving his life.) If you want a life that is pleasing to God, then you must follow *the Word of God*.

> I will instruct you and teach you in the way you should go; I will counsel you with my eye upon you. Be not like a horse or a mule, without understanding, which must be curbed with bit and bridle, or it will not stay near you. Psalms 32:8-9

Let's go back to Abraham's conversation with God! Beginning with Genesis 12, we see how God initiated a conversation with Abraham, just as He wishes to do with us all. Abraham responded to God by leaving an idolatrous environment that had no regard for the true and living God.

Abraham separated himself from those who had no concern for God just as Noah separated himself (Genesis 6). While turning from addiction, you must distance yourself from others who are still engulfed in addiction. There are people that you must not associate with (at least not so closely, in some cases not at all.)

Abraham did not prove his allegiance to God at once. As we look at the life of Abraham, we see how God conversed with Him for years. At times Abraham honored God, and at other times he did not. Abraham had no stability. He was inconsistent.

Many of us long for consistent sobriety! Consistency leads to stability. Reverencing God is a practice. There was a time when God changed Abram's name to Abraham. But Abraham was still not ready to give God his all. We all have heard of people that God has freed from addiction all at once. That does not happen with everyone.

> "There is a Christian myth that change is an event rather than a process; that it is more like a light switch that is turned on than a battle that must be engaged. For some reason, we tend to think-wrongly-that immediate liberation from the slavery of addiction is more glamorous than the gradual process of taking a little bit of land at a time." -*Addictions: A Banquet in the Grave,* Welch

May 7

Progressing reverence (part 4)

> He said, "Do not lay your hand on the boy or do anything to him, for now I know that you fear God, seeing you have not withheld your son, your only son, from me." Genesis 22:12

Yesterday, I mentioned how God had started a conversation with Abraham years before Abraham was willing to offer Isaac as a sacrifice. Abraham's conversation with God continues with Abraham's response to God. As the saying goes— "Action speaks louder than words."

At last, Abraham's reverence had grown in placing God before everything. Abraham was different. A simple definition of being holy is to be different. 2 Corinthians 7:1 describes the process that we must experience to enjoy the sobriety that comes from God by becoming more like Christ, while 2 Corinthians 7:10b describes fake sobriety.

> My friends, God has made us these promises. So we should stay away from everything that keeps our bodies and spirits from being clean. We should honor God and try to be completely like him.
> 2 Corinthians 7:1 Contemporary English Version

> Therefore, since we have these promises, dear friends, let us purify ourselves from everything that contaminates body and spirit, perfecting holiness out of reverence for God. NIV

> For godly grief produces a repentance that leads to salvation without regret, whereas **worldly grief produces death**.
> 2 Corinthians 7:10b

Reverence is proof of our devotion. Abraham's reverence proves that reverence leads to action. *Turning to God from Idols* suggest three reverential actions to counteract addictions. Abstinence, fasting, and communing with God, and others are acts of repentance.

To revere God is to trust Him. **It is impossible to revere God without sacrifice.** As recorded in Scripture, Abraham had made his sacrifice to God a way of life. God had earlier told Abraham (in Genesis 21:12) that his son Isaac would be the key to the future.

For Abraham, Isaac was at the very center of both his own heart and of God's promise. He loved Isaac very much as a father and Isaac was the fulfillment of God's promises to him. God was asking Abraham to trust Him with everything – his son and God's promise.

May 8

Progressing reverence (part 5)

He said, "Do not lay your hand on the boy or do anything to him, for now I know that you fear God, seeing you have not withheld your son, your only son, from me." Genesis 22:12

Our reverence for God must go beyond our understanding. Addiction involves leaning on our *own* understanding. As with Abraham regarding Isaac, God tells us to let go of our addictions (which may be just as dear.) We must ask ourselves how much is the fear of the Lord worth.

If we would measure the value of our reverence it must at least cost us the things that we would treasure beside.

Sacrificing Isaac was a sacrifice that went beyond any other sacrifice that Abraham had made. Perhaps, sacrificing addiction goes beyond any other sacrifice you could make to God. An author of one of my sources on addictions speaks as though Abraham had made an idol of Isaac as we do with addictions.

The Scriptures speak of sacrifices that are made unto the Lord as being a sweet savor. How sweet are the sacrifices that are made to the idols of addictions? Every time we reject a temptation, we make a sacrifice. Jesus knows what it is like to be tempted far beyond what we can imagine. The sacrifices that Jesus made go beyond any of our own.

Sacrifice requires that you deny yourself. Self-denial must be a priority in the lives of us who desire to glorify God and bear His image. Addiction is contrary to self-denial and is much less concerned about glorifying God and bearing His image. **Anything that you withhold from God, you place above God.** With addiction, you also deny yourself of being taught by God.

How often you sacrifice for what you cherish; whatever you think is worthy of your sacrifice! The sacrifices that are made for addictions prove them as idols because one of the main expressions of worship is sacrifice. Romans 12:1 says that God wants His people to be living sacrifices. An old joke says that the problem with a living sacrifice is that it keeps trying to jump off the altar. Abraham did not withhold his only son. God did not withhold His Son from us. Are you withholding anything from God?

Is God worthy of your all? The pivoting point of quality sobriety is your delight in the Lord and delight in the fear of the Lord. The question is whether you delight in Him greater than all else. There are degrees of delight just as there are degrees of sanity and insanity, joy and misery, reverence, and irreverence, as well as degrees of sobriety. When in awe of God, you delight in Him.

May 9

A new song (part 1)

He put a new song in my mouth, a song of praise to our God. Many will see and fear, and put their trust in the LORD Psalms 40:3

Psalms 40 is loved by many because they can relate to the first two verses where David said that he waited patiently for the Lord and that God drew him up from the pit of destruction, out of the miry bog, and set his feet upon a rock, making his steps secure.

I am eternally grateful that God has drawn me from the pit and destruction of addiction. As a result, God has removed the taste of addiction and put a song of praise in my mouth unto Him. You will always have a taste for one addiction or another so long as God is not your praise!

New is said to be one of the most appealing words in advertising. What's new is often best! Do you want the best to combat addiction? Many will say "yes" while not realizing that the best comes at a price. It has been said that salvation is free but sanctification will cost you everything.

What if your war on addiction could be fought with your praise to God? After all, addictions are objects of praise. Why couldn't we devote our praise to God alone? We praise what we value. Unfortunately, one of the lures of addiction deceives us into thinking that addictions are valuable.

It has been over twenty years since the Lord made it clear to me that addictions are idols. One of the ways that we worship God and idols is through praise. *Addictions are an object of praise in the heart and on the lips of every idol worshipper.*

It is to the degree that we give God the praise that He deserves that we become free of our addictions. There is also an unbreakable relationship between *reverencing* God and praising Him.

Praise towards God breaks the bonds of addictions because it is an expression of reverence. While our praise to God is not *primarily* a weapon to conquer addictions, it is most effective. Jesus said that "No one can serve two masters, for either he will hate the one and love the other, or he will be devoted to the one and despise the other" (Luke 6:24). Just like addiction, reverence is marked with devotion.

A word that is closely related to praise is *delight*. Who doesn't praise what they delight in? When you see something as true and beautiful and valuable, you savor it. That is, you treasure it. You cherish and admire and prize it.

In *Desiring God*, John Piper says "We praise what we enjoy because the delight is incomplete until it is expressed in praise. If we were not allowed to speak of what we value and celebrate what we love and praise what we admire, our joy would not be."

May 10

A new song (part 2)

> He put a new song in my mouth, a song of praise to our God. Many will see and fear, and put their trust in the LORD Psalms 40:3

Karleen Elizabeth Okoh, a *Facebook* friend, says, "When we praise God, we take our eyes off ourselves. Addictions, anger, and resentments are just some of the things that flee when we take our eyes off of self and worship/praise the One who our hearts were made for!"

The song of addiction begins in our hearts. It's a sad song. It is heard on the lips of everyone who happily advertises the quality of dope that one drug dealer has over another. The song of addiction is the frustration that comes with the pornographic scene that doesn't satisfy. This is the nature of addiction. It can never do what God alone can.

Just as God gave David a new song, He can give you one also. God is not into recovery, He wants to make all things new. God desires regeneration, not recovery. Recovery is old. Contrary to its popularity, recovery is a word that should never be used when referring to overcoming addiction.

God wants to take you places that you have never been to and show you things that you have never seen!

The song that the Lord gives you is one of joy and satisfaction. ***There is not a song that compares to the one that God gives.*** Peter referred to it as *"joy unspeakable and full of glory"* (1 Peter 1:8, *KJV*). The new song speaks of the redemption that took place on Calvary. It speaks of how God has created the opportunity for us to have fellowship with Him though we were shaped in iniquity. A new song comes from a new man.

> Therefore, if anyone is in Christ, he is a new creation. The old has passed away; behold, the new has come. 2 Corinthians 5:17

John Piper says that "God is most glorified in us when we are most satisfied in Him. The joy of experiencing the power of God's grace defeating selfishness is an insatiable addiction." The new song that comes from God not only comes from the new life of a new man but it is new every day.

We need to be renewed and revived daily so that we might enjoy the Lord and become more like Him. George Muller said, "the first great and primary business to which I ought to attend every day is have my soul happy in the Lord."

May 11

A new song (part 3)

He put a new song in my mouth, a song of praise to our God. Many will see and fear, and put their trust in the LORD Psalms 40:3

A new song is filled with life. Addictions lead to stagnation and death (whether mental, spiritual, social, or physical.) A new song is an awareness of God that is progressive. A new song stimulates our being. *A new song is found in satisfaction. There is no satisfaction to be found in addiction.*

"To keep up the freshness of worship is a great thing, and in private it is indispensable. Let us not present old worn out praise, but put life, and soul, and heart, into every song, since we have new mercies every day, and see new beauties in the work and word of our Lord." -*Spurgeon*

A new song prevents relapse and adds to our growth and intimacy with the Lord. Years ago, I learned the value of Gospel music for overcoming addiction. I highly recommend that everyone serious about overcoming addiction and every group that wants to help people to turn from addiction use music that would speak directly to the issues of addiction.

Nehemiah 8:10 says that "the joy of the Lord is your strength." Psalms 33:3 is another verse that encourages us to "sing unto the Lord a new song." You were made for praising God and without it you are incomplete!

The glory of God is my greatest delight. Ephesians 1:6 says that believers in Christ are chosen *"to the praise of His glorious grace." There is more at stake than most people realize in our war on addiction. The glory of God is at stake.* If God is not glorified in this world then we are headed to destruction. If Man does not seek the glory of God, he seeks his own glory. And with every man for himself, we are left with barbarism.

But you are a chosen race, a royal priesthood, a holy nation, a people for his own possession, that you may proclaim the excellencies of him who called you out of darkness into his marvelous light. 1 Peter 2:9

The new song that God has for you is an expression of joy. Joy is an indispensable element of singing and praise in our elimination of addiction. The third phase of *Turning to God from Idols* is rejoicing. Joy is refreshing. It allows us to maintain our faith while rescuing us from the agonies of addiction. Most of all, joy expresses the delight that God is worthy of.

May 12

Considerable praise (part 1)

> Oh sing to the LORD a new song; sing to the LORD, all the earth! Sing to the LORD, bless his name; tell of his salvation from day to day. Declare his glory among the nations, his marvelous works among all the peoples! For great is the LORD, and greatly to be praised; he is to be feared above all gods. Psalms 96:1-4

Psalms 96 begins by invoking the reader to sing a new song. This is just the thing for an addict. The song that you sing of the glories of addiction must be changed to a song of the majesty of God. From Psalms 40:3, I emphasized the relationship between singing, sobriety, and reverence. What you sing reveals your frame of mind (sometimes known as sobriety.)

> He put a new song in my mouth, a song of praise to our God. Many will see and fear, and put their trust in the LORD. Psalms 40:3

I also mentioned how our singing praise to God combats addiction. Singing is a sign of devotion. We express delight and satisfaction in song. Psalms 96:1-4 says to focus on God, addiction tells you to focus on yourself.

Among the programs that offer help in overcoming addiction, some focus on individuals more than on Christ. This is a subtle tactic of the devil to keep people bonded and not as useful to God. This is the same old song of addiction in disguise.

People often trade an addiction that is causing discomfort for one that does less financial or domestic damage. A few days ago, I said, "You will always have a taste for one addiction or another so long as God is not your praise."

I believe that the new song of Psalms 96:1 is part of what verse nine calls the splendor of holiness (the *KJV* calls it the beauty of holiness.) What is holy is what is right and befitting. A song unto the Lord declares that He is worthy of recognition. It is wrong to withhold from God the praise that God deserves.

Addictions tell us that God is lacking. Praise exalts the sufficiency of God. Praise recognizes Who God is and what He does. Addictions keep you blind. To praise God is to concur with God. Addiction does not concur with God's plans for your life.

Praise comes from your heart as well as your lips. Singing comes from our hearts and our lips too. The Scriptures make it plain that we all must have a new heart to be in sync with God. Your heart determines your walk and your walk is accompanied by praise as you grow into the person that God wants you to be (which includes being free of addictions.)

May 13

Considerable praise (part 2)

Oh sing to the LORD a new song; sing to the LORD, all the earth! Sing to the LORD, bless his name; tell of his salvation from day to day. Declare his glory among the nations, his marvelous works among all the peoples! For great is the LORD, and greatly to be praised; he is to be feared above all gods. Psalms 96:1-4

Passion and awe produce praise. When in awe of addictions, you say to the object of your addiction "Who is like you?" In Exodus 15:11, Moses is telling God that He is holy. To be holy means to be different. What we see in addiction is natural, but what we see in God is supernatural.

Another definition of *holy* is to be set apart. God wants you to become more and more set apart; more like Him and less like yourself. **Reducing God is one of the most horrific traits of addiction**! It reduces *us* as well!

We sanctify the Lord in our praise. The Old Testament word "sanctify," when used in a general sense means to consecrate, dedicate, consider holy, or separate. In a specific sense, the word means to set apart, devote, consecrate, regard, or treat as sacred or hallow. The New Testament word means to render or acknowledge or to be venerable or hallow.

Another way that we can describe what it is to sanctify the Lord is by making Him special or giving Him a special place in our hearts. Someone has said, "We live in a time when people fill their lives, their time, and their priorities with little more than trivialities."

To sanctify the Lord means that we make a distinction between He and all else. While the phrase "sanctify the Lord" can only be found twice in Scripture, it is greatly significant for overcoming addiction.

Sanctify the Lord of hosts Himself; and let Him be your fear, and let Him be your dread. Isaiah 8:13

But sanctify the Lord God in your hearts: and be ready always to give an answer to every man that asketh you a reason of the hope that is in you with meekness and fear. 1 Peter 3:15 *KJV*

That which we praise is often in our thoughts and conversation. We have good thoughts about what we praise. We speak well of that which we praise. That which we boast about, that which we positively talk about much, and that which we embrace, we praise.

Funk and Wagnalls Standard Desk Dictionary defines praise as "an expression of approval and commendation." The satisfaction that you find in God accompanies your reverence for Him.

May 14

Reverential Quest

That I may know him and the power of his resurrection, and may share his sufferings, becoming like him in his death ... Not that I have already obtained this or am already perfect, but I press on to make it my own, because Christ Jesus has made me his own. Brothers, I do not consider that I have made it my own. But one thing I do: forgetting what lies behind and straining forward to what lies ahead, I press on toward the goal for the prize of the upward call of God in Christ Jesus. Philippians 3:10, 12-14

Philippians 3:10-14 describe a reverential quest! It may also be referred to as *The Road to Zion*. The *Road to Zion* reflects the mission of a Christian approach to addiction. It first expresses the need for salvation through Christ and then to follow the steps of Christ. *The Road to Zion* endeavors to lead people from their awe of addiction into reverential awe of God.

I long for you to have a 20/20 vision! A reverential quest will bless you with the vision to see God as greater than anything else because reverence produces purity. Jesus said the pure in heart would see God (Matthew 5:8).

The alternative is to gaze upon the world while we need vision to comfort us. No addiction has ever been contrived by Man that can comfort us like the vision that is provided by God through His Word.

The vision of God produces awe. When we are in awe of God, we pass it on to others. **The mission that God has given every one of us is to acquire and develop a stronger and higher reverence for Himself for all eternity!**

We're all on a mission. A journey or a quest. Unfortunately, our mission does not always line up with the mission that God has for us. A reverential quest defines our sobering mission. You are either on a reverential quest or a mission that is hell bound!

Your expressions are a part of what you do. Your direction is an expression as well. A reverential quest reveals what you value and who you are. An example is Jonah when asked who he was. Jonah answered, "I am a Hebrew, and I fear the LORD, the God of heaven, who made the sea and the dry land." You are identified by your reverence or *irreverence*.

Just as when you go on a trip, you check and recheck your bearings; you ask for directions; you enlist aid from maps and guides--there are many questions to be asked concerning reverence. What does it mean to reverence God? What do we look for? What are the implications and effects? Why is it important? The Scriptures provide the map and Jesus is our guide as we travel through this world onto the next while seeking quality sobriety.

May 15

What's this awe about? (part 1)

The Almighty—we cannot find him; he is great in power; justice and abundant righteousness he will not violate. Therefore men fear him; he does not regard any who are wise in their own conceit.
Job 37:23-24

Is anybody in awe? I think that we all are in awe! The real question is what we are in awe of. Though seldom mentioned, awe is the component that most often rules and governs our lives, our homes, our neighborhoods, our nation, our world, and ultimately our destiny.

Awe can build or destroy. Awe is related to reverence. Awe is related to sanity as well as insanity. You can be so in awe of something outside of God that it can drive you crazy. The awe that you possess may be a distortion.

A disproportionate view can be either disturbing, disillusioning, or perverting. Disillusionment can be called the opposite of the truth. Disillusionment is one of the sources of addictions. John Piper said, "Disillusionment often follows naïve admiration." Only awe of God can give us the right mind. A sober mind begins with our perspective. To be in awe of anything more than God is to think of it as greater than God.

I remember witnessing a child's christening as one of the gifts was a cross-eyed bear. The minister said that the bear was to remind the parents to teach the child to always look at everything through the eyes of the Cross that Jesus bore and to teach the child that they would have a cross to bear themselves. The awe that is found at the Cross of Christ is the highest level of sobriety.

What is awe? Awe involves wonder, amazement, astonishment, and admiration. Awe can sometimes be filled with fear or dread. We become afraid of the things that we see as overpowering, overwhelming, and grand. One of the distinctions of the awe of God is that it is desirable (while dreadful awe is often undesirable.)

Awe can attract or repel. No one in their right mind is attracted to dreadful awe. The awe that is found in God attracts us. Though there may be other entities that attract us, they are not the same as the awe of God. The awe that God gives is initiated in response to the love that He has shown in sending His Son as a ransom for our sins. Awe of anything else pales in comparison (and has been known to rob people of the joy that is in Christ.)

I think that we are motivated by fear, worry, dread, and anxiety much more than we realize. The decisions we make and the actions we take are motivated more often to avoid what we fear rather than by courage. Awe produces the courage that we need to live soberly, righteously, and godly.

May 16

What's this awe about? (part 2)

The Almighty—we cannot find him; he is great in power; justice and abundant righteousness he will not violate. Therefore men fear him; he does not regard any who are wise in their own conceit. Job 37:23-24

The Almighty is beyond our reach and exalted in power; in his justice and great righteousness, he does not oppress. Therefore, people revere him, for does he not have regard for all the wise in heart? *NIV*

What's the matter with God? That's the underlying question in Job! There is either something wrong with Job or there is something wrong with God. That's the same issue that you face with addiction. Either God changes or you do! The way that you deal with an addiction reveals what you think of God. There are <u>only</u> four answers to addiction!

1. Suicide (ungodly and sudden death)
2. Continue the addiction (ungodly and unsudden death)
3. Non-biblical means (ungodly, permissible with no guarantees)
4. Biblical (some are more accurate and Christ-centered than others)

The accuracy of the revelation of God affects God's reputation as well as our understanding of God, ourselves, and the world we live in (including how we judge addictions.) The first thing we need to understand about God is that He is beyond our understanding.

"There are four things which, unless we are well-instructed in and know, we will know nothing to any purpose. The things which we must know are God, sin, Christ, and eternity." -*The Evil of Evils*, Jeremiah Burroughs

"In God, you come up against something which is in every respect immeasurably superior to yourself. Unless you know God as that—and, therefore, know yourself as nothing in comparison—you do not know God at all." -*Mere Christianity,* C.S. Lewis

By His grace, He gives us the understanding that we need. It is in our irreverence that we desire to go beyond those boundaries. **Man has an insane desire to discover the answer to everything outside the knowledge of God.** Reverence not only begins with self-denial but perhaps the highest reverence is displayed by self-denial. Self-denial is essential to repentance.

May 17

What's this awe about? (part 3)

The Almighty—we cannot find him; he is great in power; justice and abundant righteousness he will not violate. Therefore men fear him; he does not regard any who are wise in their own conceit. Job 37:23-24

Years ago I heard that the usual greeting in a certain Christian community was for one member to ask the other if they were still broken. So long as we think that we are not broken and we don't need mending then we do not need God.

Jesus said, *"Those who are well have no need of a physician, but those who are sick. I came not to call the righteous, but sinners"* (Mark 2:17). God rebuked Israel for trying to make *themselves* into what they wanted and, in essence, telling Him that He didn't know what He was doing.

Woe to him who strives with him who formed him, a pot among earthen pots! Does the clay say to him who forms it, "What are you making?" or "Your work has no handles?" Isaiah 45:9

Now, therefore, say to the men of Judah and the inhabitants of Jerusalem: "Thus says the LORD, Behold, I am shaping disaster against you and devising a plan against you. Return, every one from his evil way, and amend your ways and your deeds." But they say, "That is in vain! We will follow our own plans, and will every one act according to the stubbornness of his evil heart." Jeremiah 18:11-12

I remember a younger brother in Christ confiding in me years ago as he was distraught over his co-workers' questions about things that are unanswered in the Bible. Immediately, I recognized this was their answer to sin. They thought that if they could discredit the Bible then that would discredit God, and then they would not have to be bothered with sin.

The theme of reason is unleashed time and again in our pursuit of quality sobriety that is rooted in reverence. Addictions accuse God of being unreasonable. Out of his reverence, Job patiently waited to hear what God had to say and he refused to accuse God of evil.

When you think about it, we put God on trial over and over throughout our entire life. There are so many questions that we ask both verbally and nonverbally concerning God. Is God worth knowing and can God be trusted are two of the major questions we ask from the start over and over again! To exclude God or change the image that He has revealed to us is irreverent.

May 18

What's this awe about? (part 4)

> The Almighty—we cannot find him; he is great in power; justice and abundant righteousness he will not violate. Therefore men fear him; he does not regard any who are wise in their own conceit.
> Job 37:23-24

The book of Job reads like a court case. Must God go on trial or is it *we* who need to be examined? As I said, we put God on trial over and over throughout our entire life. On several occasions, I have read Christian authors say that we will be getting rid of our misconceptions of God for the rest of our lives.

> Hear the word of the LORD, O children of Israel, for the LORD has a controversy with the inhabitants of the land. There is no faithfulness or steadfast love, and no knowledge of God in the land.
> Hosea 4:1

God never gets a fair trial because He doesn't belong in the courtroom unless He is allowed to be the Judge or the lawyer! Every trial requires accurate information. Here we are, with limited information, putting the Judge of all the earth on trial while defending addictions!

People need an adequate description of God to follow Him. One of the deficiencies of a non-Christian group is that they don't offer an adequate description of God. God will always seem different as we mature. C. S. Lewis made a profound illustration of this in *The Narnia Chronicles*. Those who have grown in Christ can teach others how magnificent He is in comparison to shameful, petty addictions.

> "'Aslan' said Lucy 'you're bigger'. 'That is because you are older, little one' answered he. 'Not because you are?' 'I am not. But every year you grow, you will find me bigger.'" -*Prince Caspian*, C.S. Lewis

There is no better answer to addictions than God. God cannot be fully understood but He has graciously provided us with a connection with Himself in Christ. An inaccurate understanding of Him will affect the level of your sobriety and the destiny of your soul. One of the thoughts that led to my long-termed sobriety and will ever be a source of strength and comfort is that *God is and ever will be eternally greater than I could ever imagine.* Elihu says, "The Almighty—we cannot find Him out."

May 19

What's this awe about? (part 5)

> The Almighty—we cannot find him; he is great in power; justice and abundant righteousness he will not violate. Therefore men fear him; he does not regard any who are wise in their own conceit.
> Job 37:23-24

The book of Hebrews is my favorite book of the Bible. It was written to early Christians who had begun to wonder if they were on the right path as you may wonder while seeking the highest quality of sobriety. Hebrews starts by informing the readers how God revealed Himself in the past and how He has revealed Himself in these last days.

> Long ago, at many times and in many ways, God spoke to our fathers by the prophets, but in these last days he has spoken to us by his Son, whom he appointed the heir of all things, through whom also he created the world. He is the radiance of the glory of God and the exact imprint of his nature, and he upholds the universe by the word of his power. After making purification for sins, he sat down at the right hand of the Majesty on high, having become as much superior to angels as the name he has inherited is more excellent than theirs. Hebrews 1:1-4

Sometimes I am amazed by how different it was for me to clean on a professional level and how people clean around the house (I was a professional custodian for seven years.) While most of us have been cleaning since we were children, professional cleaning is different.

Addiction is a part of life. We all know something about life, but when you deal with life as Jesus does, it is infinitely greater than someone doing housecleaning compared to someone cleaning a state office or a large department store. A failure to understand addictions as Christ does makes us as unequipped as the average person cleaning on a professional level.

Last year, I started writing a book from Hebrews that is aimed towards relapse prevention called *Lest We Drift*. Ask any shipmate whether drifting is enjoyable! Drifting relinquishes control. There is no security or stability found in drifting. God does not want you to drift through life.

Apart from the Word of God, you do not have a complete picture of God. You're drifting. If you ignore the Word of God you are not seeking the true and living God. This is the very reason why there are so many that turn to false gods. What else is left?

And so, it's awe for One and one for awe as you embark on a life of sobriety that involves remaining free of anything that would obscure your awe for God. Quality sobriety!

May 20

Whose are you?

> And Joshua said to them, "Who are you? And where do you come from?" Joshua 9:8

Joshua 9:8 is asking two questions that are relevant to addiction. Joshua asked the Hivites their identity and origin because just like addictions and your responses to Christ, they determine your values and practices.

As a leader of Israel, Joshua was concerned about their safety. He knew that if the Hivites were not identified with the God of Israel then there would be no peace between them. The Scriptures give us a picture of the identity of those who follow the true and living God in both the Old and New Testaments. Jonah and Colossians are just two examples.

> Then they said to him, "Tell us on whose account this evil has come upon us. What is your occupation? And where do you come from? What is your country? And of what people are you?" And he said to them, "I am a Hebrew, and I fear the LORD, the God of heaven, Who made the sea and the dry land." Jonah 1:8-9

> If then you have been raised with Christ, seek the things that are above, where Christ is, seated at the right hand of God. Set your minds on things that are above, not on things that are on earth. For you have died, and your life is hidden with Christ in God. Colossians 3:1-3

What you think of Christ makes a huge difference in the way that you look at addiction. According to the Scriptures, if you are without Christ, then you are without God and hopeless (Ephesians 2:12). It has been said that we are products of our environment. Christ reminds us of where we come from and where we are going.

We all come from Adam. Because of this, we are all born in sin. You must recognize the atrocity of sin against God to look to Christ for forgiveness. There are no other means of forgiveness except Christ. Your identity with Christ determines where you are going.

> And there is salvation in no one else, for there is no other name under heaven given among men by which we must be saved.
> Acts 4:12

Just as the identity and origin of the Hivites were important to Joshua, they are important to God. You are either *for* God or against Him. There is no middle ground.

May 21

Great delight (part 1)

Praise the LORD! Blessed is the man who fears the LORD, who greatly delights in his commandments! Psalms 112:1

In the February 25th entry, I mentioned how the quality of your sobriety is related to perpetual reverence. Closely related to perpetual reverence is the delight that you find in the Lord. Just as the delight of an addiction maintains your devotion, so it is with your delight in the Lord.

To delight in something or someone is to treasure, hold dear, and take pleasure in. In most cases, we love what we delight in. *Strong's Bible Dictionary* also says "the love of a thing is to take pleasure in the thing, prize it above other things, be unwilling to abandon it or do without it."

It is no wonder that we can define addictions as idols! Some of the definitions found in *Strong's Dictionary of the Bible* for love in the Old Testament are "to desire, to breathe after, to delight in, and to be intimate with."

> "Our love, however, is easily misdirected. Its object tends to become the creation rather than the Creator; it loses sight of the eternal for the temporal; it focuses on the self, often to the exclusion of God and others. We become idolaters, focusing a part or all of our love elsewhere. We are 'love breakers' more than 'law breakers.'" -*Baker's Evangelical Dictionary of Biblical Theology*

While love is one of the attributes of delight, joy is another. We need the joy of the Lord to remain sober because being truly sober involves the mind of Christ. Without the mind of Christ, our evaluation is warped. Jesus puts everything into perspective. Isaiah 11:3 says, *"And his <u>delight</u> shall be in the fear of the LORD. He shall not judge by what his eyes see, or decide disputes by what his ears hear,"* (whereas in addiction we make decisions based on our senses.)

You rejoice in what you value. Just think of the value that is placed on addictions! People give up their very lives over addictions! Delight and misery stand in opposition. Have you experienced the misery of addiction?

Many years ago, while attending an *Alcoholics Anonymous* meeting, I listened to a speaker who had such broken English that I thought that I heard him say that he was 'merciful' during the many times that he had stopped drinking and so he would go back to drinking time and time again.

Over and over, the speaker said that he was 'very merciful' when he stopped drinking. Towards the end of his speech, I finally realized that the speaker had been telling us that he had been '<u>miserable</u>' during those times of abstinence (without true fellowship with God.)

May 22

Great delight (part 2)

Praise the LORD! Blessed is the man who fears the LORD, who greatly delights in his commandments! Psalms 112:1

Psalm 112:1 mentions *great* delight! George Muller is credited for saying, "our first duty as Christians is to get ourselves happy in God." Nehemiah 8:10 says **"the joy of the Lord is your strength."**
Matthew 2:10 tells of the wise men who "*rejoiced with **exceeding** great joy*" when they saw the star that would lead them to Christ (*KJV*). Thrill and delight are something that we seek in addictions. Wise men find this and more in seeking Christ.

> "That delighteth greatly in his commandments. The man not only studies the divine precepts and endeavours to observe them, but rejoices to do so: holiness is his happiness, devotion is his delight, truth is his treasure. He rejoices in the precepts of godliness, yea, and delights greatly in them. We have known hypocrites rejoice in the doctrines, but never in the commandments. Ungodly men may in some measure obey the commandments out of fear, but only a gracious man will observe them with delight. Cheerful obedience is the only acceptable obedience; he who obeys reluctantly is disobedient at heart, but he who takes pleasure in the command is truly loyal" -Spurgeon

Psalms 112:1 describes those who fear the Lord as blessed. There is contentment for those who reverence God. Contentment is a necessity for those who want a life that is free of addiction. Jesus promises contentment for those who follow Him. In Matthew 11:28-29, Jesus promises rest to those who follow Him. In *Addiction: A Tug of War*, I said that **one reason why redemption is imperative is so that our yearning for what is not of God may desist!**
The blessedness of those who fear the Lord is also a reward. There are at least forty-two references in the Scriptures that specifically promise a reward for our reverence. Everyone wants prosperity for their faithfulness to God. Prosperity is a popular theme that is often misunderstood.

> "If your desire conforms to God's will, He will look upon your request with favor and allow it to come to pass. Christians are not to dictate to God, but to petition (make requests of) Him. In Prosperity Theology, people have become the rulers, and God has become the servant. In the Bible, God is sovereign over the entire universe, and His people are His servants." -*Prosperity Gospel, www.hopefortheheart*

May 23

Reverential repentance (part 1)

> So I said, "The thing that you are doing is not good. Ought you not to walk in the fear of our God to prevent the taunts of the nations our enemies?" Nehemiah 5:9

The most prevailing topic in Nehemiah 5:9 relating to both reverence and addictions is repentance. Some of the other topics in Nehemiah 5:9 that relate to reverence and addiction are the revelation of God, our response to God, restoration, and revival.

Many years ago, God began to show me how essential reverence is. While I was publishing *The Fear of the Almighty*, I began to learn more about howimportant our reverence is during a revival service. Revivals are aimed at bringing life back into people who have regressed in their relationship with God.

I learned that as God reveals things about Himself (as well as ourselves) there is a rebuke from God over the things that displease Him. We are, then, given the opportunity to respond with reverence. I learned that there can be no revival without reverence. For us to move forward, our reverence must contain remorse.

If we respond to God reverentially then we are reconciled to God. Restoration follows reconciliation. After our restoration, we become revived. Finally, once we have become revived then God continues our transformation through the process of sanctification by His Holy Spirit. And so, there is the process of regression to restoration and on to sanctification.

1. Revelation
2. Rebuke
3. Response
4. Reverence
5. Remorse
6. Restoration
7. Revival
8. Transformation
9. Sanctification

Lack of repentance can be very dangerous. The alternative to repentance is to perish according to 2 Peter 3:9. It is through 2 Timothy 2:24-26 that we learn gentle instruction leads to repentance, repentance is a thing that is granted by God, repentance leads to a knowledge of the truth, through repentance people come to their senses, and that it is through repentance that people escape the trap of the devil.

May 24

Reverential repentance (part 2)

> So I said, "The thing that you are doing is not good. Ought you not to walk in the fear of our God to prevent the taunts of the nations our enemies?" Nehemiah 5:9

The reason that Nehemiah confronted the Israelites is that they had regressed in their relationship with God. That's why the walls of Jerusalem had been torndown. Anytime you regress in your relationship with God your defense against sin and foolishness is broken like the walls of Jerusalem.

Recovery was the word originally used by *Alcoholics Anonymous* to describe how somebody who once led a normal life could be restored. ***It is not an accurate term for someone who has never known a life without addiction. There is nothing to recover.***

Relapse is the word that we use for those who regress from sobriety back to active addiction. Regression begins the day that we are born and will continue without God's intervention and a reverential response from us. Relapse is just another phase of the bigger picture.

We don't need an addiction to prove we're ungodly. And as quiet as it is kept we suffer from more addictions than we care to admit. Only by being born-again and made more like Christ can we overcome the things that separate us from God.

> "Killing sin then is not the immediate job an unsaved, unregenerated person is called to do. God has called him instead first to conversion- the conversion of the whole person- not just the killing of this or that specific sin or evil desire. You would laugh if you saw someone trying to erect a tall building without first pouring a foundation- especially if you saw him try to do it a thousand times and saw his tower collapse every single time without him ever wondering why. It's like that with unbelievers. Whatever ground they gain against sin today, they'll lose again tomorrow. It's a sad cycle repeated over and over again. But they never ask themselves why this happens or what they need to do differently." -*The Mortification of Sin*, John Owen

Sin is to be repented of. We cannot repent from a disease. The only thing that can separate us from God is sin. For many years in my struggle with addiction, I wondered whether addiction was a disease. *A disease cannot separate you from God, only sin separates us from God!*

May 25

Reverential repentance (part 3)

> So I said, "The thing that you are doing is not good. Ought you not to walk in the fear of our God to prevent the taunts of the nations our enemies?" Nehemiah 5:9

As God reveals how great He is, He also reveals the horrors of addictions and our frailties. ***The Word of God has more to say about addictions than you could ever imagine.*** Unfortunately, many do not respond to what the Word of God says about addictions as agreeably as Israel did when Nehemiah exposed their impiety. ***If we do not look to the Word of God for answers to addictions and rely upon other sources alone, we are acting irreverently towards God.***

> "Al Wolters taught that in the biblical view of things, ***the main problem in life is sin, and the only solution is God and his grace. The alternative to this view is to identify something besides sin as the main problem with the world and something besides God as the main remedy***. That demonizes something that is not completely bad, and makes an idol out of something that cannot be the ultimate goal." –*Desiring God*, John Piper

A deeper study of the Word of God discloses and eradicates the deception and error onwhich addictions are rooted. Three basic areas of deceit that give addictions their strength are; the misinformation that they give concerning God, concerning ourselves, and the addiction (itself.)

The written Word of God gives us the most accurate description there is of God. **The most vivid description of God is found in the living Word of God (Jesus Christ, *also described in the written Word of God*.)** Addictions discredit God. Addiction tells us that God is not to be trusted, He doesn't love us all that much, He doesn't know what He is talking about, and we don't have to answer to Him.

The lies that are behind addictions concerning ourselves are that we know what is best, we are not all that bad, and we can handle it (and again, many, many lies.)Addictions deceive us into thinking that they can fulfil our lives, they are harmless (or at least don't cause much harm), and we could never be under their control.

Faith in God's Word (His point of view), as well as the recognition of Who God is, leads us to repentance. Romans 2:4 states that the goodness of God leads to repentance. ***Repentance begins with a change of mind, as the Spirit of God reveals to us the truth about sin, and points us to Christ.***

May 26

Reverential repentance (part 4)

> So I said, "The thing that you are doing is not good. Ought you not to walk in the fear of our God to prevent the taunts of the nations our enemies?" Nehemiah 5:9

Repentance is a major concern for those who wish to overcome addiction. *Turning to God from Idols: A Biblical Approach to Addictions* emphasizes that almost every program that offers freedom from addiction is comprised of just three basic principles.

Those principles are reasoning, **repentance**, and rejoicing. Reasoning leads to repentance. The Apostle Paul led many to Christ through reasoning. God reasoned with Israel. And Jesus reasoned as well.

> And Paul went in, as was his custom, and on three Sabbath days he **reasoned** with them from the Scriptures. Acts 17:2

> Come now, let us **reason** together, says the Lord: though your sins are like scarlet, they shall be as white as snow; though they are red like crimson, they shall become like wool. Isaiah 1:18

> And now, O inhabitants of Jerusalem and men of Judah, judge between me and my vineyard. What more was there to do for my vineyard, that I have not done in it? When I looked for it to yield grapes, why did it yield wild grapes? Isaiah 5:3-4

> Hear the word of the Lord, O children of Israel, for the Lord has a controversy with the inhabitants of the land. There is no faithfulness or steadfast love, and no knowledge of God in the land. Hosea 4:1

> O Jerusalem, Jerusalem, the city that kills the prophets and stones those who are sent to it! How often would I have gathered your children together as a hen gathers her brood under her wings, and you were not willing. Luke 13:34

When referring to Christ, the officers answered, "No man ever spoke like this Man!" (John 7:46). Jesus was persuasive. Persuasion is another word for reasoning. Reason produces order. A life that is ruined by addiction needs order. Counselors reason with their clients. I heard a Christian counselor say that his job was to convince people to reverence God.

May 27

Reverential repentance (part 5)

> So I said, "The thing that you are doing is not good. Ought you not to walk in the fear of our God to prevent the taunts of the nations our enemies?" Nehemiah 5:9

Repentance is an act of self-denial. It is to surrender to the kingdom of God, relinquish your power, and stop seeking glory for yourself. The need for repentance can be expressed in so many ways. The change in overcoming addiction has been given many labels. Some of these terms are more accurate than others. Not only that, *everyone decides on the degree of changes they will make. This is what determines the quality of our sobriety.*

> Recovery   Sobriety   Restoration Healing   Set free   Maturity   Growth Holiness   Sanctified   Deliverance   Reconciliation   Being saved Revival   Transformation   Being made whole   Turning to God from idols   **(I prefer the words repentance, transformation, and sanctification.)**

> "Paul does not prescribe some long, convoluted series of therapy steps. He says, 'You got yourself into this mess by obeying your flesh and denying God, and the only way out is to start denying the flesh and obeying God.'" –*Changed Into His Image,* Jim Berg

Repentance determines our intimacy with the Almighty. This is because one of the components of repentance is confession. To confess to God means to say the same thing that God is saying about a matter. Repentance sets us apart from the world. Repentance is a by-product of reverence leading to godliness. Repentance creates the right priorities while restoring order and manageability.

Repentance provides us with transformation. The transformation makes us as human as Jesus is (though He was also God, a mystery.) One of the most valuable lessons that I learned in a class on the doctrine of Christ is that ***Jesus was more human than anyone that has ever lived.***

The truth of the matter is that addictions cause us to think and behave like animals. The fact that addictions cause us to think and behave like animals can be seen on so many levels. Animals tend to be unreasonable- addictions cause us to be unreasonable.

> I will instruct you and teach you in the way you should go; I will counsel you with my eye upon you. **Be not like a horse or a mule, without understanding,** which must be curbed with bit and bridle, or it will not stay near you. Psalms 32:8-9

May 28

Reverential repentance (part 6)

> So I said, "The thing that you are doing is not good. Ought you not to walk in the fear of our God to prevent the taunts of the nations our enemies?" Nehemiah 5:9

Revelation 3:18-19 teaches us that repentance is the result of counsel from the Wonderful Counselor (JesusChrist.) We, also, learn that repentance produces spiritual health and wealth and that rebuke and chastisement bring about repentance. In his wonderfulbook titled, *How to Help People Change*, Jay Adams stated, **"In all counseling change is a matter of greater or lesser love toward Him."**

I have heard it said that apathy is the opposite of love. Apathy is a lack of concern. Apathy diverts our attention and assassinates our interests. Repentance brings a change of interest as well as *redirects* our attention. **Repentance allows us to love God and love others as God would have us to.** In this, we experience the joy of repentance.

> "Rejoicing and repentance must go together. Repentance without rejoicing will lead to despair. Rejoicing without repentance is shallow and will only provide passing inspiration instead of deep change. Indeed, it is when we rejoice over Jesus's sacrificial love for us most fully that, paradoxically, we are most truly convicted of our sin. **When we repent out of fear of consequences, we are not really sorry for the sin, but for ourselves… In fear-based repentance, we don't learn to hate the sin for itself, and it doesn't lose its attractive power. We learn only to refrain from it for our own sake…** Fear-based repentance makes us hate ourselves. Joy-based repentance makes us hate the sin." –*Counterfeit gods,* Tim Keller

The continuation of repentance is promoted in Scripture. There will never come a time in our lives when there is no room for improvement, no need for change, some way that we can reverence God deeper and stronger and become more like Christ. That's why quality sobriety goes beyond being abstinent. **One of the most common mistakes is for us to disregard other things that are displeasing to God simply because they have not caused us trouble.**

> "There's a great mistake in the world in the matter of trouble for sin. They think repentance or mourning for sin is but one act, that if once they have been troubled for sin they need never be troubled anymore. It is a dangerous mistake, for we need to know that true sorrow for sin, true repentance, is a continual act that must abide all our lives." -*The Evils of Evils*, Jeremiah Burroughs

May 29

The nature of repentance

A. Leads to salvation (safety, salvaging your life) 2 Corinthians 7:10
B. Leaves no regret
C. Earnestness
D. Eagerness
E. Longing
F. Concern
G. Readiness to see justice done
H. Produces fruit Matthew 3:8
I. Produces spiritual health and wealth Revelation 3:19
J. Based on truth (a response to the truth) John 8:32
K. Assurance of truth comes before repentance Acts 2:36-38
L. Gives direction
M. Individual and personal
N. Involves confession
O. Intimacy with God
P. Honesty
Q. Commanded to all by God Acts 20:21
R. Repentance goes hand in hand with faith in Christ
S. Summoned by God's spokesmen
T. Offers promises
U. Repentance is a serious matter (thus, it is sobering)
V. Turning from ignorance to God Acts 3:17-20
W. The Lord God takes joy in repentance Luke 15:7, 10, 24
X. Necessary for forgiveness from God Acts 2:38
Y. God commands all people everywhere to repent Acts 17:30
Z. Our deeds prove our repentance Acts 26:20
AA. Beyond knowledge (it is an experience with Christ)
BB. The Holy Spirit tells us to repent 1 John 2:27-29
CC. Repentance places us in the right position before God Luke 5:8
DD. Repentance <u>determines</u> our intimacy with the Almighty 2 Corinthians 6:18-7:1
EE. Allows us to separate from the world
FF. Leads to sanctification
GG. It is a by-product of reverence
HH. Repentance is godly
II. Leads to purity
JJ. Creates priorities
KK. Restores order and manageability
LL. Repentance is granted by God 2 Timothy 2:2

May 30

Transformation

To put off your old self, which belongs to your former manner of life and is corrupt through deceitful desires, and to be renewed in the spirit of your minds, and to put on the new self, created after the likeness of God in true righteousness and holiness.
Ephesians 4:22-24 *NIV*

Transformation describes the change that is needed to break the chains of addiction. To be transformed is to be changed. Change does not always happen at once. That's why you must wait on the Lord! While it is true that we can make some external changes, *internal* changes come from Him.

In addition, there are degrees of change. The changes that are of Christ go beyond what some offer. The main issue is not how pleased I am, but how pleased *God* is, and to please God we must do things His way with the proper motives. Jay Adams explained the difference in his book, *How to Help People Change*.

> "Change affected by non-Christian counselors is not neutral either. In one way or another, it dishonors God, either by adopting attitudes or actions contrary to His will or by outwardly, hypocritically confirming to His law without a changed heart (a form of godliness that denies the power thereof.)" -*How to Help People Change, Jay Adams*

When I think of biblical change, I am reminded of how the poor of Biblical days rarely got a change of clothing and how they discarded the old clothing and embraced the new. This is an illustration of how Ephesians 4:22-24 exhorts the believer in Christ. Romans 13:14 says to *"clothe yourselves with the Lord Jesus Christ, and do not think about how to gratify the desires of the flesh"*

Sanctification is the process of becoming less attached to the things of the world and more to God. Our sanctification begins with the new birth. Sanctification, sobriety, and sanity are all related. Who in their right mind would choose anything over God?

Unfortunately, God must prove Himself to us through multiple encounters! As He does, over time, we start to choose Him more frequently and fervently. Colossians 3:1-3 describes a person who is no longer addicted as having risen with Christ, their mind [affection, *KJV*] is set on things above, not on things of the earth, who died with Christ, and their life is hidden with Christ in God.

May 31

The handwriting on the wall (part 1)

This is the interpretation of the matter: Mene, God has numbered the days of your kingdom and brought it to an end; Tekel, you have been weighed in the balances and found wanting; Peres, your kingdom is divided and given to the Medes and Persians.
Daniel 5:26-28

Daniel may as well have been writing to the addicts of today. I hope that you are as amazed as I am over the relevancy of Scripture for exposing and disposing of addiction. King Belshazzar's experiences were very similar to those of addicts today.

1. God has numbered the days of your kingdom and brought it to an end.
2. You have been weighed in the balance and found wanting.
3. Your kingdom is divided and given to the Medes and Persians

There are at least 3 things that apply to addicts in this context.

1. Sooner or later addicts find that they are not in control (unfortunately, some don't find out until they die.)
2. Addictions are futile.
3. Loss is eminent with addictions.

Pharaoh was warned just as King Belshazzar and anyone who turns to addiction. Pharaoh's subjects asked, "Do you not yet understand that Egypt is ruined? (Exodus 10:7). This was the question that Pharaoh's servants asked him after the eighth plague that was released upon Egypt by the hand of God. Are there no signs of how addiction ruins your life? Is it not foolish to ignore the proverbial handwriting on the wall?

Insanity opposes reality!

Addiction doesn't go without warning. It doesn't take most of us long to notice the negative effects of addiction. It can seem as though there is no way out. The old saying is that trouble is easy to get into and hard to get out of. Only the grace of God can pull you through.

June 1

The handwriting on the wall (part 2)

> This is the interpretation of the matter: Mene, God has numbered the days of your kingdom and brought it to an end; Tekel, you have been weighed in the balances and found wanting; Peres, your kingdom is divided and given to the Medes and Persians.
> Daniel 5:26-28

Yearning after addictions is a warning sign. Innumerable Bible verses relate to yearning. The awe-factor of idolatry brazenly associates yearning with worship. We see this association vividly displayed in the worship of Baal during the days of Elijah. The same frenzied devotion is seen with the worshippers of Artemis in the Apostle Paul's travels. They all yearned for their gods with intensity.

> And they took the bull that was given them, and they prepared it and called upon the name of Baal from morning until noon, saying, "O Baal, answer us!" But there was no voice, and no one answered. And they limped around the altar that they had made. And at noon Elijah mocked them, saying, "Cry aloud, for he is a god. Either he is musing, or he is relieving himself, or he is on a journey, or perhaps he is asleep and must be awakened." And they cried aloud and cut themselves after their custom with swords and lances, until the blood gushed out upon them. And as midday passed, they raved on until the time of the offering of the oblation, but there was no voice. No one answered; no one paid attention. 1 Kings 18:26-28

The raving of the prophets of Baal reminded me of an experience I was not proud of during my childhood. Since my mother was single until I was nine years old, she arranged for me to stay with her aunt and uncle during the week as she worked. When I was nine, my mother married a man who became my best friend by the time he died.

My new dad did all he could to help me adjust to living with him and my mother full-time. They got married in late June and in early July a conflict arose as I began to rant and rave over my desire to go with my aunt's family to an amusement park that I had grown very fond of as a yearly event while living with them.

My yearning was so strong that the night before and half of the rest of the day of the event I chanted, "I want to go to Chippewa Lake, I want to go to Chippewa Lake!" I was as passionately committed to Chippewa Lake as the prophets of Baal and the worshippers of Artemis.

June 2

The handwriting on the wall (part 3)

And there is danger not only that this trade of ours may come into disrepute but also that the temple of the great goddess Artemis may be counted as nothing, and that she may even be deposed from her magnificence, she whom all Asia and the world worship. When they heard this they were enraged and were crying out, "Great is Artemis of the Ephesians!" So the city was filled with the confusion.... for about two hours they all cried out with one voice, "Great is Artemis of the Ephesians!" Acts 19:27-29a, 34b

"What is an idol? It is anything more important to you than God, anything that absorbs your heart and imagination more than God, anything you seek to give you what only God can give. A counterfeit god is anything so central and essential to your life that, should you lose it, your life would feel hardly worth living. An idol has such a controlling position in your heart that you can spend most of your passion and energy, your emotional and financial resources, on it without a second thought... An idol is whatever you look at and say, in your heart of hearts, 'If I have that, then I'll feel my life has meaning, then I'll know I have value, then I'll feel significant and secure.'" -*Counterfeit gods*, Tim Keller

What do you passionately yearn for? Yearning is in our nature. You have been yearning since the day that you were born (perhaps even before birth, you have yearned.) We sometimes yearn unknowingly. And we yearn for good or for evil for all eternity. Since I believe that our soul is eternal, I believe that our yearning continues after our body is deceased.

One reason why redemption is imperative is so that our yearning for what is not of God may desist. One of the agonies of Hell is an everlasting thirst that only God can quench. But Hell is absent of God. Everyone in Hell decided on earth that they did not want God. So, what else is left?

Hell and destruction are never full; so the eyes of man are never satisfied. Proverbs 27:20

Because you have said, "We have made a covenant with death, and with Sheol we have an agreement, when the overwhelming whip passes through it will not come to us, for we have made lies our refuge, and in falsehood we have taken shelter" Isaiah 28:15

"If we find ourselves with a desire that nothing in this world can satisfy, the most probable explanation is that we were made for another world." -C.S. Lewis

Check your motives at the door

> He who loves father or mother more than Me is not worthy of Me. And he who loves son or daughter more than Me is not worthy of Me. And he who does not take his cross and follow after Me is not worthy of Me. He who finds his life will lose it, and he who loses his life for My sake will find it. Matthew 10:37-39

What is your main reason for not drinking and/or drugging? Is it because it was ruining your life? Or, was it because you recognized it as being wrong in the sight of God? I'm not saying that we should not be concerned about other areas, but if we do not abstain out of reverence for God, then our motives will be less than pure. It's a question of what we value.

Do you value God or do you value family, possessions, or, reputation more? These have the same possibility of capturing your attention more than God that addictions have. First, God is worthy of your undivided attention. Second, only the fear of the Lord can give you the wisdom that you need to confront addiction the way that God wants you to.

> For the weapons of our warfare are not of the flesh but have divine power to destroy strongholds. We destroy arguments and every lofty opinion raised against the knowledge of God, and take every thought captive to obey Christ. 2 Corinthians 10:4-5

The most indescribably amazing moment in history is when God gave Himself entirely to us while abiding with us and laying Himself before us open and bare as a sacrifice for our sins. The question ever remains of how much of myself will I give to God.

My favorite t-shirt will always be one with a picture of the cross with the caption "Try this on for size!" It's a perfect fit for us all! If you wear this every day, you will be what God wants you to be!

The most glorious result of giving ourselves to God is that the image that was lost in the *Garden of Eden* is restored and we once more bear the image of God. This is the only time that I find the use of the word **recovery** as biblically accurate. In bearing the image of God, we are granted the highest level of communion with Him and are fit for the greatest use. Abstaining from addiction because of reverence means that God is worthy of the life that He calls you to.

> "As idols separate us from God, we become less like God and less human as well. We can either portray the nature and image of God through healthy yearning or the nature and image of the Devil through *unhealthy* yearning." *–The Highest Yearning*, Madison

June 4

Choose sides! (part 1)

> But sanctify the Lord God in your hearts, and always be ready to give a defense to everyone who asks you a reason for the hope that is in you, with meekness and fear 1 Peter 3:15

Do you remember playing *Tug of War* as a child? Do you remember how carefully you sized up your opponents? Do you remember carefully choosing your team? You knew that your team could not win unless your members were strong and healthy.

We all chose sides with those who were capable of moving their opponents. We must have capable individuals to fight against the addictions that are destroying lives. Addiction is first and foremost a spiritual problem. Why would you place your trust in what a spiritually blind person has to say about spiritual matters? ***There are various aspects of addiction that many are blind to and have not been touched on.***

The way that addiction has been viewed has changed dramatically over the last hundred years. The change can be easily explained with a story that you may have heard when you were a child. Remember the story of the blind men who each had a different description of an elephant when they touched it?

> "The parable of the blind men and an elephant originated in the ancient Indian subcontinent from where it has been widely diffused. It is a story of a group of blind men who have never come across an elephant before and who learn and imagine what the elephant is like by touching it. Each blind man feels a different part of the elephant's body, but only one part, such as the side or the tusk. They then describe the elephant based on their limited experience and their descriptions of the elephant are different from each other. In some versions, they come to suspect that the other person is dishonest and they come to blows. ***The moral of the parable is that humans have a tendency to claim absolute truth based on their limited, subjective experience as they ignore other people's limited, subjective experiences which may be equally true.***" -*Wikipedia*

The Scriptures describe everyone that is outside of Christ as spiritually blind (Ephesians 2:1). Why would you place your trust in what a spiritually blind person has to say about spiritual matters? For one thing, salvation is not a concern for the world. They make it seem as though people can have an intimate relationship with God outside of Christ.

June 5

Choose sides! (part 2)

> But sanctify the Lord God in your hearts, and always be ready to give a defense to everyone who asks you a reason for the hope that is in you, with meekness and fear. 1 Peter 3:15

It is no mystery that the world's view of addiction is self-centered rather than Christ-centered. For example, instead of the first step of A.A. admitting we are powerless, perhaps we should admit that we are not like Christ. The difference is that when we say that we are powerless, we are stating that we are not satisfied with ourselves.

But when we admit that we are not like Christ, we are stating that *God* is not satisfied with us. This is the root of our problems. This would allow everyone the priority of being made right with God and starting a new life in Christ. Without Jesus we do not have a complete view of God nor can we be friends with Him.

Salvation is not an issue for many. This is an insult to Calvary as well as unscriptural. It is not godly nor loving to lead people away from Christ. In many 12-step groups, it is forbidden to even speak of Christ. Billy Graham said, "Our society strives to avoid any possibility of offending anyone except God."

You may ask if there is any truth in non-biblical programs. The falsities of many programs have damaged many lives by prolonging their addiction. Most programs have failed to rescue people from hell through Christ and don't care about people living selfish lives (in some cases even more than before their primary addiction.)

Addiction is so complex that only the divine can sort through the confusion and deception. The world is erroneous in its assessment of addiction as well as its treatment. It uses inaccurate, misleading phrases and dwells on self-introspection to the point of self-worship.

> "One cannot proclaim a true theory of society unless he sees the heinousness of sin and its relation to all social ills and disorder. No man can be a successful New Testament evangelist publishing the Gospel as 'the power of God unto salvation to every one that believeth', unless he has an adequate conception of the enormity of sin. Nor can a man hold a consistent theory of ethics or live up to the highest standard of morality, unless he is gripped with a keen sense of sin's seductive nature." -*The Fundamentals*, vol. 3, Charles Williams

I'm not saying that everyone who attends secular meetings is without Christ. I _am_ saying that everyone without Christ is without God.

June 6

Choose sides! (part 3)

For what does it profit a man to gain the whole world and forfeit his soul? Mark 8:36

The biggest question you have to face is whether you can face God. If this is not settled at the beginning of your quest for sobriety, you will have a weak foundation. If you do not begin your sobriety in one accord with God, then you don't have the safety that is found in escaping Hell. But, hell is not an issue with people who exclude Christ from their answer to addiction.

I once read that "A.A. can not get you to heaven but it can keep you sober long enough to find out how to get there." An old saying claims that "everybody wants to get to heaven but nobody wants to die." It is equally true that many want to go to heaven but they are not looking for God. Likewise, many say that they are perfectly sane outside a relationship with the true and living God.

Your priorities are indicative of your sanity! During my studies of addiction, I discovered that there are degrees of sanity. Two factors determine our sanity. One is time (or experience) and the other is our relationship with God (specifically our reverence for God.)

You can be free of whatever addiction has bothered you and still not be sane. The soundest approach to addiction is to first bridge the gap between us and God. The ultimate answer to addiction is to choose God over everything else. We come to our senses as we choose what is of the greatest value. Can you name anything of greater value than being in one accord with God?

Fortunately, unnumberable undocumented people have looked to Christ for the eradication of addiction. But, if you look at the methods currently being used by the masses you will note that they have rejected Christ. The sad thing is that most people do not know the difference.

1. Anti-Christ means of dealing with addictions don't care if God is dishonored through our engagement with addictions.

2. Anti-Christ means of dealing with addictions don't care about your condemnation (they don't talk about people going to hell.)

3. The various methods of dealing with addictions that exclude Christ are more self-centered. (There are instances where there is a mention of Christ, however, through close observation, it can be noted that the focus is given more to individuals; it is almost as though we worship ourselves rather than Christ.)

June 7

Choose sides! (part 4)

For from him and through him and to him are all things. To him be glory forever. Amen. Romans 11:36

Many of the theories that the world has contrived about addiction are contrary to the Word of God. One of the main theories that contradict the Word of God is that addictions can be adequately dealt with outside of Christ. Outside of Christ, our answers can never meet God's satisfaction.

> "Let us never forget that 'fruits' from a corrupt tree can also be doctrinal, as well as ethical and moral. A person may be ethically and morally 'good' by human standards, but if he sets his face against Jesus Christ as Lord and Savior, and rejects Him, his fruit is corrupt and he is to be rejected as counterfeit." -*The Kingdom of the Cults*, Walter Martin

I was once intrigued by the thought that a movie character named Jason Borne was much like Jesus Christ in his response to his circumstances. It seemed as though Jason Bourne knew just what to do, at a moment's notice, in every circumstance. And if we are to become more like Jesus, then we are to know how to respond to our circumstances as well as the circumstances of others.

> "Now if a sailor has skill he does not say, 'If it were any other wind but this, if the wind blew in any direction but this, I could manage my ship, I could show skill in other directions but not in this.' Would not sailors laugh at such a one? It would be a shame for a Christian to say that he has skill in any other affliction but this. A Christian should be able to manage his ship, if the wind blows any way; to guide his soul any way." -*The Rare Jewel of Christian Contentment*, Jeremiah Burroughs

Being human qualifies us as someone who can understand addiction (to a degree.) One of the fallacies of *Narcotics Anonymous* is the belief that an addict can best understand and help another addict (unless it is agreed that as humans we all are drawn to something outside of God thereby making everyone addicts unless our lives are given to Christ.)

Jesus was not an addict and yet Hebrews 4:15 says "we do not have a high priest who is unable to sympathize with our weaknesses, but one who in every respect has been tempted as we are, yet without sin."

June 8

Generators (part 1)

> He put a new song in my mouth, a song of praise to our God. Many will see and fear, and put their trust in the LORD. Psalms 40:3

Your song and your reverence are related as well as your sobriety and your reverence. Productivity can also be related to your song. One of the blessings that we inherited by being created in the image, of God is productivity.

One of the liabilities of addiction is not only how they are destructive, but also how they are non-productive. I had to learn that in my addictive behavior that although at most times, I was not directly hurting anyone, I was hurting others *by not helping the*m. It has been said that "you are either part of the problem or part of the solution." Addiction, in all its varieties, can be called the greatest challenge to the human race.

> "Drunkenness also interferes with our God-given task of subduing the earth. Drunkenness leads to dereliction of duty in the marketplace. Industrial accidents, lateness, and absenteeism are commonplace for the heavy drinker. Unemployment is too familiar. As Proverbs indicates, the norm for drunkenness is poverty (21:17, 23:21). Relationships are disrupted too. 'Wine is a mocker, and beer is a brawler' (Prov. 20:1). All heavy drinkers leave a wake of broken relationships and victims. In fact, studies of alcohol abuse estimate that each heavy drinker leaves a wake of pain for at least ten people. The pain does not always come by way of fistfights, but through car accidents, harsh words, neglect, broken promises, and unwise decisions. Heavy drinkers inevitably hurt others deeply."
> -*Addictions: A Banquet in the Grave,* Welch

All of creation is found in Christ. Without Christ, we would have nothing. So it is that the Lord can put a new song in our mouths to replace the taste of addiction. On many occasions, I have stated that "**the highest form of sobriety known unto mankind is in Jesus Christ and anything that poses itself as sobriety outside of Him is only a façade.**" God generates song just as everything else He created.

> For by him all things were created, in heaven and on earth, visible and invisible, whether thrones or dominions or rulers or authorities—all things were created through him and for him. And he is before all things, and in him all things hold together. Colossians 1:16-17

June 9

Generators (part 2)

He put a new song in my mouth, a song of praise to our God. Many will see and fear, and put their trust in the LORD. Psalms 40:3

Quality sobriety longs for the power of God to flow through us!

The same power that raised Christ from the dead is in every believer. The power of God is demonstrated as He carries us from the pit of destruction and sets our feet on a rock while making our steps secure (establishing our goings.) The power of God gives you a new song. Finally, that same power causes many others to find awe in God, and put their trust in Him as well.

> *"Many shall see it, and fear, and shall trust in the Lord.* First of all they see. Their eyes are opened; and their opened eyes see and survey *what* they are, *where* they are, and *whence* they came, and *whither* they are going ... When the attention of sinners is really and decisively arrested by the propitiation of Jesus, not only are their eyes opened to their various moral relations, not only do they 'see' but they *fear* too. They 'see' and 'fear.' ... Conviction follows illumination...But while the sinner only sees and fears, he is but in the initial stage of conversion, only in a state of readiness to flee from the city of destruction. He may have set out on his pilgrimage, but he has not yet reached his Father to receive the kiss of welcome and forgiveness. The consummating step has not yet been taken. He has seen indeed; he has feared too; but he still requires to *trust,* to trust in the Lord, and banish all his fears." *-James Frame*

Quality sobriety thinks so highly of God that it is productive. Quality sobriety recognizes that God deserves your allegiance as well as the allegiance of others. Quality sobriety causes you to be a generator along with God while in tune with His guidance and cheer.

You were not only created to praise God but also to allow the power of God to flow through you. Generators are known for power. They not only have the power within but they transmit power without. An awe-factory is a generator that produces light in a darkened world. You were created to be a reflection of God. ***When we fulfill the purposes of God then it becomes a source of joy that conquerors the cravings of addiction.***

> that you may be blameless and innocent, children of God without blemish in the midst of a crooked and twisted generation, **among whom you shine as lights in the world.** Philippians 2:15

June 10

Unrepentant (part 1)

> God will give ear and humble them, he who is enthroned from of old, Selah because they do not change and do not fear God. Psalms 55:19

> God will hear and humiliate them—the One enthroned for the ages—Selah because they do not change and they have no fear of God. *Berean Study Bible*

On several occasions, I have asked if God has the right to judge! Some people don't like to acknowledge God as a judge who punishes evil. Some don't believe that a good God would condemn people to Hell.

If you look closely, you will find that the Scriptures teach us that Hell is a choice that people make just as people choose the hell of addiction. Reverence has a part in our *salvation* as well as our sanctification. The way that we respond to God determines our fate.

> Then they will call upon me, but I will not answer; they will seek me diligently but will not find me. Because they hated knowledge and did not choose the fear of the LORD, would have none of my counsel and despised all my reproof, therefore they shall eat the fruit of their way, and have their fill of their own devices. Proverbs 1:28-31

Although we would all like to be free from the consequences of our actions and the general suffering of life, apart from God we are without hope. "God is good" is an expression that even a child can understand. On the contrary, whatever is absent of God (or not of God) is evil.

Whatever or whoever does not glorify God (reflecting His image) is not of God and is subject to judgment. The judgment that people suffer by turning from God is a choice. It has been said that if you don't want Christ in this life then God is not going to force you to spend eternity with Him.

> And this is the judgment: the light has come into the world, and people loved the darkness rather than the light because their works were evil. For everyone who does wicked things hates the light and does not come to the light, lest his works should be exposed. But whoever does what is true comes to the light, so that it may be clearly seen that his works have been carried out in God. John 3:19-21

A preacher once asked a man what he thought were the main problems in the world. When the man answered that he didn't know and he didn't care. The preacher said, "You're right, ignorance and apathy."

June 11

Unrepentant (part 2)

God will hear and humiliate them—the One enthroned for the ages—Selah because they do not change and they have no fear of God. Psalms 55:19 *Berean Study Bible*

Reverence for God changes us in ways that we could never imagine. Reverence is the vehicle that God uses to take us where He wants us. True sobriety can be defined as agreeing with God. There is no agreement with God until our sin has been dealt with through the blood of Christ.

Ignorance harbors pride leading to a hard heart and estrangement from God as well as from others. Ignorance keeps us from understanding the nature of addictions, God, and ourselves. Whenever you turn to addiction, you are leaning on your own understanding. *To lean on your own understanding could be the most basic definition of insanity.*

Dudley J. Delffs says that "to repent is to come to your senses. It is not so much something you do as something that happens." Those in Psalms 55:19 are unrepentant because they refuse to revere God. It seems as though they are living comfortably.

> "It is a very manifest fact that long continued ease and pleasure are sure to produce the worst influences upon graceless men: though troubles do not convert them, yet the absence of them makes their corrupt nature more readily develop itself. Stagnant water becomes putrid. Summer heat breeds noxious insects. He who is without trouble is often without God. It is a forcible proof of human depravity that man turns the mercy of God into nutriment for sin: the Lord save us from this." *-C. H. Spurgeon*

Addictions are thought to offer comfort. We are all looking for comfort in one form or another, and if that comfort is not God (or from God) then it is a façade. Spurgeon said that comfort often causes corruption. Proverbs Chapter One refers to those who find calamity in their refusal to reverence God. God is a God of order and apart from Him, the world lies in chaos and confusion. Some Old Testament translators have said that before God created the world there was only chaos.

> "Belief in Jesus as Lord is not merely intellectual acceptance; it changes what we do, who we are and who we become." *-Called to Be a Soldier,* The General of The Salvation Army

June 12

The value of vows

For you, O God, have heard my vows; you have given me the heritage of those who fear your name. Psalms 61:5

Awe makes vows! If it is an awe of what you fear, you vow to stay away from it! If it is an awe of attraction, you vow to cherish it! If it is an awe of reverence, you vow to worship it. That's because awe has priorities. So it is with the awe of addiction and the awe of God.

The vows that you make are expressed in your priorities. A vow is something that you give yourself to in one degree or another. In many cases, you give your all. We are all in awe over what we vow!

Many passages in the Bible associate vows with reverence. Vows may be either private or public. Every vow is a commitment. Addiction is a commitment as well.

Vows should not be taken lightly. The result of a vow can be life-changing for the individual as well as families, communities, and even nations. For instance, a passage from Isaiah 28 was a vow that the nation of Israel made. Just like some addictions, it was an irreverent vow with life-threatening consequences.

> You boast, "We have entered into a covenant with death, with the grave we have made an agreement. When a overwhelming scourge sweeps by, it cannot touch us, for we have made a lie our refuge and falsehood our hiding place. Isaiah 28:15

Vows can be seriously sobering. One of the definitions for sobriety is the word ***serious***. I have watched *To Sir with Love* many times. I purchased the movie years ago because of the line about marriage spoken by the main character. He said something like this: "Marriage is not for the weak, the selfish, nor the fainthearted." The same can be said for those who war against addictions.

Vows are a sign of determination. God wants to make us like Christ as He did not turn from the vow that He made to pay for the sins of the world no matter what the cost. Hebrews 12:3 says to "consider him who endured from sinners such hostility against himself, so that you may not grow weary or fainthearted." ***Vows lead to consistency. And consistency is essential to long-termed sobriety.***

> And going a little farther he fell on his face and prayed, saying, "My Father, if it be possible, let this cup pass from me; nevertheless, not as I will, but as you will." Matthew 26:39

June 13

Getting your attention (part 1)

Then all mankind fears; they tell what God has brought about and ponder what he has done. Psalms 64:9

And all men shall fear, and shall declare the work of God; for they shall wisely consider of his doing. *KJV*

I am eternally grateful that God knows how to get our attention or I would still be lost in sin. Pondering and considering are valuable in our war on addiction. I'm often amazed at how God gets our attention.

The process of transformation begins with God gaining our attention. God uses people and circumstances to confirm His Word. It has been said that a coincidence is God's way of remaining anonymous.

For some of us, it doesn't take much for God to get our attention. For others, it takes a lot. Regardless of who we are, I have often said that God speaks everyone's language. The judgment of God gets our attention. He desires to draw us closer to Himself and away from the things that would lead us to dereliction and destruction.

> "The judgments of God are frequently so clear and manifest that men cannot misread them, and if they have any thought at all, they must extract the true teaching from them. Some of the divine judgments are a great deep, but in the case of malicious persecutors the matter is plain enough, and the most illiterate can understand."
> -*The Treasury of David*, Spurgeon

While I have been blessed with many situations that God used to capture *my* attention, I want to share a miraculous story told by Dr. David Jeremiah. Dr. Jeremiah said that one day a young man who was bandaged, bruised, and hardly able to walk because of his injuries came to visit him because of the method that God used to get his attention.

The man lived about 300 miles away from Dr. Jeremiah and had his mother drive him. He had recently been in a serious accident in his truck that could have killed him if it were not for the grace of God. The man told Dr. Jeremiah how his truck flipped over and was dangerously leaning over him. Without help, he could have been crushed.

During the accident, the radio dial was shifted to a station with a message from Dr. Jeremiah. Just at that moment in the sermon, Dr. Jeremiah was saying that God was saying, "Don't worry, everything is going to be all right." The man was rescued before the truck turned over. I can only hope that something like this would get someone's attention. Unfortunately, not everyone is impressed with God.

June 14

Getting your attention (part 2)

And all men shall fear, and shall declare the work of God; for they shall wisely consider of his doing. *KJV*

As God gets your attention, you ponder and consider. Consideration may become amazement. One of the adequate definitions of reverence is amazement. So long as you are amazed at God, addiction is not an option. It has been said that the best way to get the air out of a glass is to fill it with water. God wants to empty the addictions in your life by filling you with Himself

It also took some consideration for me to choose cocaine as a means of enjoyment from the beginning of my 23 intermittent years of addiction. I had to consider whenever I relapsed after being clean for a while.

> "If God's wonderful presence alone does not capture their devotion, how will they ever be satisfied with anything else? Such a sense of dissatisfaction leads people to seek other ways of satisfying perceived needs. It is a dangerous spirit to be in, for if God's wonderful provisions aren't enough to hold a person's attention, what will it take?" –Steve Gallagher

Reasoning is the first part of addiction intervention for any program. Unfortunately, *shallow* reasoning will never get us where God wants us. The problem lies in our understanding. Appendix A of *Turning to God from Idols* outlines the Scriptures that explain God's understanding, our lack of understanding, how to seek understanding, the source of understanding, and the results of understanding.

Psalms 64:9 tells us that an understanding of what God has done leads to amazement. We can go from the beginning of time and think of all that God has done. Or we can look over our lives and consider the intervention of God. But the greatest act of God was in sending His Son. The book of Hebrews starts by explaining how God got Man's attention throughout the annuals of time and how He has chosen to get our attention in the last days.

> Long ago, at many times and in many ways, God spoke to our fathers by the prophets, but in these last days he has spoken to us by his Son, whom he appointed the heir of all things, through whom also he created the world. He is the radiance of the glory of God and the exact imprint of his nature, and he upholds the universe by the word of his power. After making purification for sins, he sat down at the right hand of the Majesty on high. Hebrews 1:1-3

June 15

Abiding desire (part 1)

God shall bless us; let all the ends of the earth fear him! Psalms 67:7

Psalms 67:7 expresses a desire of the psalmist. Addictions express desires that are often hidden and/or unattainable through the addiction. We all have our reasons for practicing addiction.

Sometimes I tell people that drugs could not get me high enough. Addictions can never fill our souls the way that God can. God never intended for us to seek our fulfillment in His creation apart from Him.

Psalms 67:7 is an unselfish, noble desire. It reflects how unselfish Christ was when He delighted over the Father's will above His as *we* should. It is irreverent to leave Jesus out of the discussion of addiction.

The desire of the psalmist will not be complete until Christ rules over the entire earth. ***So long as Jesus is denied the world and our very lives will always be dysfunctional.*** Colossians 1:16 says "by him all things were created, in heaven and on earth, visible and invisible, whether thrones or dominions or rulers or authorities—all things were created through him and for him."

> "The far off shall fear. The ends of the earth shall end their idolatry, and adore their God. All tribes, without exception, shall feel a sacred awe of the God of Israel. Ignorance shall be removed, insolence subdued, injustice banished, idolatry abhorred, and the Lord's love, light, life, and liberty, shall be over all, the Lord himself being King of kings and Lord of lords. *Amen, and Amen."*
> *-The Treasury of David,* C. H. Spurgeon

Deep and lasting sobriety is built and maintained by such a desire to see Christ that we abide in Him. We want to see Jesus so much that we allow Him to live through us! We want to see Jesus so much that we long for others to see Him as well. ***An abiding desire prevents you from relapsing.***

> And now, little children, abide in him, so that when he appears we may have confidence and not shrink from him in shame at his coming. 1 John 2:28

June 16

Abiding desire (part 2)

God shall bless us; let all the ends of the earth fear him! Psalms 67:7

Yearning Over Addiction and *The Highest Yearning* elaborate on the desire for addiction and the desire for God. Both explain that we may have healthy or unhealthy desires. The highest yearning wants God to be exalted. ***Any program that promises freedom from addiction without a yearning for God to be exalted is incomplete.***

God will be highly exalted at the return of Jesus Christ. One of the soberest issues relating to addiction that you will seldom hear is how Jesus will see you when he returns. Ironically, this is probably the most important issue surrounding addiction. In my 23 years of jumping back and forth to addiction, God would remind me of the relevancy of Christ's return through a passage.

> And now, little children, abide in him, so that when he appears we may have confidence and not shrink from him in shame at his coming. 1 John 2:28

Jesus explained the importance of abiding in Him in John 15. I like to call it perpetual reverence. Perpetual reverence gives us the consistency that is needed to form the integrity of a godly life.

> Abide in me, and I in you. As the branch cannot bear fruit by itself, unless it abides in the vine, neither can you, unless you abide in me. I am the vine; you are the branches. Whoever abides in me and I in him, he it is that bears much fruit, for apart from me you can do nothing. John 15:4-5

Abiding in Christ expresses your love and reverence for God. Jesus gave a parable of what it means to abide in Himself and to be ready for His return in the story of the ten virgins (Matthew 25:1-12). Just like addiction and sobriety, the parable is a contrast between wisdom and folly.

From apathy to awe is as darkness to light!

June 17

Abiding desire (part 3)

> May they fear you while the sun endures, and as long as the moon, throughout all generations! Psalms 72:5

The desire for the rule of Christ is continued in Psalms 72:5. By contrast, Psalms 2 is a *protest* against the rule of Christ. The desire for the rule of Christ in the previous passage was a command to all people (Psalms 67:7).

The desire for the rule of Christ in Psalms 72:5 is a plea to God just as the plea at the end of Revelation is for the Lord to come (Revelation 22:20b). The same desire is expressed as we pray "thy kingdom come, thy will be done in earth as it is in heaven" (Matthew 5:10 *KJV*).

The real question concerning addictions is whether Jesus Christ is more worthy of my life than addiction.

Love, joy, and peace are found in the rule of Christ. Wherever addiction rules there is selfishness, strife, deception, confusion, and chaos. Desires express themselves in many ways *along with variations of intensity*. Perhaps, you have heard of "an overwhelming desire." Could this not describe the addictions that plague mankind?

The Hebrew word that is translated as desire in the Bible is sometimes translated as **besought, inquisition, seek, request, demand, to strive after, acceptable, to like, a valued thing, favorable, to beg, to pant after, breath heavily, self-will,** as well as, **making one's mark, prone,** or **inclined towards** according to *Strong's Bible Dictionary*.

> "The word 'desire' covers a wide range of human wants, emotions, and cravings. It can describe natural desires, which include hunger for food, sexual longings, and desire for God. It can also describe unnatural desires or cravings, which include such things as greed and lust. On a few occasions desires are ascribed to God. Most of the time they are ascribed to man, and these desires come under the scrutiny of God. How do we know if a desire is good or bad? The answer lies in the object or reason for the desire. If the desire is self-centered then it is bad, because the essence of sin is the determination to have one's own way. ***It is an act of idolatry in that one has put self in the place of God***. Good desire is simply the opposite. It is putting the desire for God's will first. ***When the Lord is our greatest desire, all other desires find their proper expression***." -*Baker's Evangelical Dictionary of Biblical Theology*, Daniel L. Akin

June 18

Abiding desire (part 4)

> May they fear you while the sun endures, and as long as the moon, throughout all generations! Psalms 72:5

I once said that the two issues that have confronted Man from the beginning of creation are whether God is worthy of ruling and whether God is capable of ruling. Christ has proved both His worthiness and His capability by the life that He lived and the death that He died. And if that is not enough, He will yet prove Himself upon His return.

While addictions leave us in despair, Christ is called *"The Desire of all nations"* (Haggai 2:7). All that Christ gives is what man is seeking. Addictions deceive us into thinking that they can give us what we want. G.K. Chesterton said, "The man who rings the bell at the brothel, unconsciously does so seeking God"

> "Man finds it hard to get what he wants because he does not want the best, God finds it hard to give, because He would give the best, and man will not take it." -George MacDonald

> "The word *desire* can be given as 'hope' ... Alas! Today the Messiah is not desired by all nations for to the vast majority of men He is as 'a root out of a dry ground' have no beauty that they should desire Him (Isaiah 53:2). While the nations do not presently desire Him, yet He is the only One who can satisfy the yearning desires within the heart of man." -*All the Divine Names and Titles in the Bible,* Hebert Lockyer

Jesus said that those who hunger and thirst after righteousness will be filled (Matthew 5:6). Hunger and thirst are desires. Do we just hunger and thirst once? No, hunger and thirst abide with us. And so it is that God wants our desire for Him to abide. He is our Righteousness and as we hunger and thirst for Him we are filled.

The kingdom of Christ shall never end. This is a source of security that addictions are not able to offer. The everlasting kingdom of Christ is a source of joy and contentment that can not be found anywhere else.

By regularly considering His love we are motivated to remain faithful to Him in the hours of temptation. In 1 John 4:19, John said that "we love Him because He first loved us." Someone has said that we should preach the Gospel to ourselves every day (i.e. how Christ died for our sins out of His love for the Father and us and rose again.)

June 19

Abiding desire (part 5)

> May they fear you while the sun endures, and as long as the moon, throughout all generations! Psalms 72:5

Yesterday, I mentioned how valuable it is for us to remember the love of God as we are tempted by addictions. I explained how it relates to abiding in Christ. The Apostle John has been nicknamed *The Love Disciple* because of his close relationship with Christ. In First John Chapter Three, John wants his readers to be amazed by God's love.

> And now, little children, abide in him, so that when he appears we may have confidence and not shrink from him in shame at his coming. See what kind of love the Father has given to us, that we should be called children of God; and so we are. The reason why the world does not know us is that it did not know him. Beloved, we are God's children now, and what we will be has not yet appeared; but we know that when he appears we shall be like him, because we shall see him as he is. And everyone who thus hopes in him purifies himself as he is pure. 1 John 2:28-3:1-3

John tells us that God loves us so much that in Christ we have the honor of the greatest privilege that there ever could be. That privilege is to be as pure as God when Christ returns. John tells us that the process has already begun. In light of this, the quality of our reverence gives us an abiding desire for the complete change that will occur at the return of Christ.

Salvation has three phases. After accepting Christ as your Savior you are saved from the penalty of sin. As you trust Christ each day, you are saved from the power of sin. And when you finally see Christ face to face you will be saved from the presence of sin. The Apostle Paul confirms the process of our total transformation that John spoke of in his letter to the Romans.

> For I consider that the sufferings of this present time are not worth comparing with the glory that is to be revealed to us. For the creation waits with eager longing for the revealing of the sons of God. ... For we know that the whole creation has been groaning together in the pains of childbirth until now. And not only the creation, but we ourselves, who have the firstfruits of the Spirit, groan inwardly as we wait eagerly for adoption as sons, the redemption of our bodies. Romans 8:18,19, 22-23

Every addiction has its longing!

June 20

Stronghold

Then they will call to me but I will not answer; they will look for me but will not find me, since they hated knowledge and did not choose to fear the Lord. Since they would not accept my advice and spurned my rebuke. Proverbs 1:28-30

Addiction is a stronghold! Where do we ever get the idea that we are smarter than God? What makes you think that you are more powerful than God? How could we be so irreverent?

Blessed is the one who fears the Lord always, but whoever hardens his heart will fall into calamity. Proverbs 28:14

The hardening of our hearts is a deliberate act. When we harden our hearts the wisdom of God is not only rejected but also disdained. This is what is referred to in 2 Corinthians 10:4 as a "stronghold." As the individual chooses to harden their heart, their heart becomes callous.

We see this in the case of Pharaoh. The first words of Pharaoh in response to God's command to let His people go were, "Who is the Lord that I should obey Him?" (Exodus 5:2). And so, from there, we see the hardening of Pharaoh's heart. In Exodus 7-14 we are told 16 times that Pharaoh's heart was hardened.

A stronghold is portrayed in John Bunyan's *Holy War*. *The Holy War Made by King Shaddai Upon Diabolus, to Regain the Metropolis of the World, Or, The Losing and Taking Again of the Town of Mansoul* is a 1682 novel by John Bunyan. This novel, written in the form of an allegory, tells the story of the town "Mansoul" (Man's soul).

Though this town is perfect and bears the image of Shaddai (Almighty), it is deceived to rebel and throw off his gracious rule, replacing it instead with the rule of Diabolus. Though Mansoul has rejected the Kingship of Shaddai, he sends his son Emmanuel to reclaim it.

In the city, there were three esteemed men, who, by admitting Diabolus to the city, lost their previous authority. The eyes of "Understanding", the mayor, are hidden from the light. "Conscience", the recorder, has become a madman, at times sinning, and at other times condemning the sin of the city.

But worst of all is "Lord Willbewill," whose desire has been completely changed from serving his true Lord to serving Diabolus. With the fall of these three, for Mansoul to turn back to Shaddai of their own will, is impossible. Salvation can come only through the victory of Emmanuel. (A summary from *Wikipedia*.)

June 21

The destruction of the third world of the United States of America (part 1)

> Surely his salvation is near to those who fear him, that glory may dwell in our land. Psalms 85:9

Let me first state that I am in no way anti-America. Do you know what I mean by the Third World of the *United States of America*? Where is it located? Who are its citizens? Is there really such a place?

The media no longer speaks of underdeveloped nations. Instead, they refer to *developing* nations. Yet, the truth is that some nations are not developing. Some nations are either stagnant or decaying. The same can be said of individuals.

Underdeveloped nations are known as the third world. Conversely, that which is not of the third world is often referred to as "the civilized world." I first began to refer to the Third World of the *United States* during my years as a homeless drug addict.

During my years of addiction and homelessness, I was exposed to environments that were quite uncivilized and underdeveloped. The media could not refer to those environments as developing. They were rotting as much as my life so long as I was systematically committed to ignoring God.

The third world of the *United States of America* not only resides in drug-infested environments but also resides in corporate America as well. The third world exists wherever addictions prevail. You must be aware that addictions take on all sorts of forms and may be socially acceptable while still being offensive to God and do not reflect His glory!

We've all seen hideous pictures of war-torn nations where genocide rules out of hatred, prejudice, and greed. We've seen pictures of starving nations that have no one to rescue them. Where is the dignity? Where is the grace? Addictions, whether socially acceptable or not, are devoid of dignity and grace because they do not reflect the glory of God.

The glory of God is the most magnificent thing there is. Since addictions are devoid of the glory of God then they are hideous. Some only see the hideousness of addiction because of their fruit.

Fruit is another word that measures the productivity of a nation or individual. Addictions not only produce bad fruit but they are hideous at the very root. The root of addiction is found in the irreverence of ignoring God.

June 22

The destruction of the third world of the United States of America (part 2)

> Surely his salvation is near to those who fear him, that glory may dwell in our land. Psalms 85:9

So long as ancient Israel listened to God, all was well. The verse before Psalms 85:9 says, "Let me hear what God the LORD will speak, for he will speak peace to his people, to his saints; but let them not turn back to folly." A civilized environment is described in Psalms 89:9, "where glory dwells." Such an environment was found in the order of King Solomon's rule so long as he revered the Lord.

> And she said to the king, "The report was true that I heard in my own land of your words and of your wisdom, but I did not believe the reports until I came and my own eyes had seen it. And behold, the half was not told me. Your wisdom and prosperity surpass the report that I heard. Happy are your men! Happy are your servants, who continually stand before you and hear your wisdom" 1 Kings 10:6-8

One of the things that I learned while watching and playing the game of chess is that your game is not going to be very successful unless your pieces become developed. A friend once compared his chess pieces to employees and said that it would be foolish for him to pay them and not assign them to work. God is not foolish! He has plenty of work for you to do. His first words to Man were to "be fruitful and multiply and replenish the earth" (Genesis 1:28).

Psalms 85:8-9 is a formula for relapse prevention. Relapse is the return to addiction that can be defined biblically as backsliding for those who are united with God. It can be said that relapse begins when you start believing the lies of the devil.

Whatever you hear has your attention. This is one of the elements of worship. We give our attention to what we worship. How much attention is given to addiction? Giving God your attention is a sign of reverence. Everyone knows that lies are combatted with the truth. To abide in the truth of God, we overcome.

> We destroy arguments and every lofty opinion raised against the knowledge of God, and take every thought captive to obey Christ. 2 Corinthians 10:5

June 23

An undivided heart (part 1)

Teach me your way, O LORD, that I may walk in your truth; unite my heart to fear your name. Psalms 86:11

Sobriety is supported by truth, Psalms 86:11 provides the relation of truth and reverence as well. Just as walking and abiding in the truth of God exemplify reverence, it also provides clarity and sobriety.

Walking and abiding by the truth of God is based on our devotion to God. How devoted you are to God determines the devotion that you have for the things of the world. The most relevant question in your struggle with addiction is how much you love God.

No one can serve two masters, for either he will hate the one and love the other, or he will be devoted to the one and despise the other. Matthew 6:24a

He is a double-minded man, unstable in all his ways. James 1:8

How many times have you thought or said, "I should have followed my first mind?" If you are anything like me then you have broken many vows with a double mind. A double mind is a weak mind. A double mind turns its attention away from God to addiction. A double mind is like Peter sinking in the water after taking his eyes off the Lord (Matthew 14:28-30).

The mind of Christ can conquer a double mind.

Jesus told his disciples that if they continued in His word, they "*would know the truth and the truth would make them free.*" This is what it means to walk in the truth. It is as much of a practice as addiction. As you grow in truth, you gain the freedom that God wants for you.

> "*I will walk in thy truth. Walking,* in the Scripture, takes in the whole of our conversation or conduct: and to walk *in* anything, intends a fulness of it. For a man to *walk in* pride, is something more than to be proud: it says, that pride is his way, his element; that he is wholly under the influence of it." -*William Jay.*

We are either influenced by the truth of God or the lies of the devil in so many ways. Many times, the devil will try to tell you that God is wrong as he did with Adam and Eve in the *Garden of Eden*. The devil and our pride are God's greatest enemies (as well as *ours.*)

June 24

An undivided heart (part 2)

Teach me your way, O LORD, that I may walk in your truth; unite my heart to fear your name. Psalms 86:11

It takes humility to deny ourselves and embrace the Word of God. There are so many things that we do not understand and it has been proven that we cannot always trust our senses. While there are so many things that scream for your attention, you must decide that God will come first. But, just like the children of Israel, some of us must be humbled until we give God the honor that He deserves.

So He humbled you, allowed you to hunger, and fed you with manna which you did not know nor did your fathers know, that He might make you know that man shall not live by bread alone; but man lives by every word that proceeds from the mouth of the LORD. Deuteronomy 8:3

"*Teach me thy way, O LORD.* Instruct me thus at all times, let me live in thy school; but teach me now especially since I am in trouble and perplexity. Be pleased to shew me the way which thy wisdom and mercy have prepared for my escape; behold I lay aside all wilfulness, and only desire to be informed as to thy holy and gracious mind. Not *my* way give me, but *thy* way teach me, I would follow thee and not be wilful. I will walk in thy truth. When taught I will practise what I know, truth shall not be a mere doctrine or sentiment to me, but a matter of daily life." -Spurgeon

The psalmist wanted to be single-minded. The quality of your sobriety is determined by how single-minded you are. The Apostle Paul and Jesus were single-minded. Many other Bible characters were single-minded as well. You have to be single-minded to accomplish the purposes of God for your life.

And now, behold, I go bound in the spirit unto Jerusalem, not knowing the things that shall befall me there: Save that the Holy Ghost witnesseth in every city, saying that bonds and afflictions abide me. But none of these things move me, neither count I my life dear unto myself, so that I might finish my course with joy, and the ministry, which I have received of the Lord Jesus, to testify the gospel of the grace of God. Acts 20:22-24 *KJV*

June 25

An undivided heart (part 3)

Now when the time was approaching for Him to be taken up [to heaven], He was determined to go to Jerusalem [to fulfill His purpose]. Luke 9:51 *Amplified Bible*

Determination is another word for a united heart. How determined can we be to practice addiction! Many have risked their lives as well as the lives of others for things that are not worthy of allegiance. Many have given up wealth and opportunity untold to addiction with the determination that only God deserves.

"Unite my heart to fear thy name. Having taught me one way, give me one heart to walk therein, for too often I feel a heart and a heart, two natures contending, two principles struggling for sovereignty. Our minds are apt to be divided between a variety of objects, like trickling streamlets which waste their force in a hundred runnels; our great desire should be to have all our life floods poured into one channel and to have that channel directed towards the Lord alone. A man of divided heart is weak, the man of one object is *the* man. God who created the bands of our nature can draw them together, tighten, strengthen, and fasten them, and so braced and inwardly knit by his uniting grace, we shall be powerful for good, but not otherwise. To fear God is both the beginning, the growth, and the maturity of wisdom, therefore should we be undividedly given up to it, heart, and soul." -Spurgeon

The greatest benefit of having a united heart for God is that God is pleased and we find true joy. A sound mind seeks to please God first. While you may encounter rewards in your abstinence, this is not to be the primary reason for remaining sober. Yet and still, there is so much joy in the sobriety that Christ brings that you will have no desire for addiction.

You must be aware of what you feed your mind. Spiritual nourishment comes through your mind. You must train your mind so that it will be conditioned to the atmosphere where God can be found.

Just as the preacher in the movie *The Sunset Limited* (played by Samuel L. Jackson) said, "If it doesn't have the lingering scent of divinity, I don't want anything to do with it", so should it be for us all (with anything ungodly, including the use and recommendation of non-biblical approaches for addictions.)

I'm grateful for an illustration by Jim Berg, in *Changed into His Image*, of how someone full from a complete Thanksgiving meal can't be tempted with a baloney sandwich any more than those who savor the things of God with the things of the world.

June 26

Inconceivable (part 1)

> For who in the skies can be compared to the LORD? Who among the heavenly beings is like the LORD, God greatly to be feared in the council of the holy ones, and awesome above all who are around him? Psalms 89:6-7

The psalmist shares how God is incomparable. Addictions don't agree. Addictions claim to be greater than God and more worthy of your affection. Do you think that you have God figured? That's probably where much of the insanity of addiction begins.
One of the thoughts that gripped my mind early in my sobriety was that God will always, always, always ... be greater than I imagine. I had belittled God with my drug use and loose living. If the quality and degree of your sobriety are based on your reverence then you are never as sober as when you comprehend the greatness of God. One of the characteristics of addiction is an inaccurate understanding of God.

A God that is not incomprehensive could never fill your immortal souls. First, addictions have you believe that you know more than God. Then, addictions have you believe they can offer you more than God.

> These things you have done, and I have been silent; you thought that I was one like yourself. But now I rebuke you and lay the charge before you. Psalms 50:21

> "**Why do I get high?** I get high because it is a stronghold! Where do we ever get the idea that we are smarter than God? What makes you think that you are more powerful than God? How could we be so irreverent? Blessed is the one who fears the Lord always, but whoever hardens his heart will fall into calamity (Proverbs 28:14)."
> *Why Not Get High*, Gregory L. Madison

Disillusionment defines the insanity of beholding addictions in awe. God desires our awe, but if we do not recognize the majesty that He possesses then we will *find* a god. Awe is related to sanity as well as insanity. The awe that we possess may be a distortion (or not.) Awe that is distorted is sometimes referred to as denial. The awe of addiction draws allegiance.

> "Every addiction comes with kingdom allegiances, We indulge in addictive habits because we've committed ourselves to certain visions of the good life and, as a result, will serve whatever master most enables those visions to become realities." –*Addictive Habits,* David R. Dunham

June 27

Inconceivable (part 2)

> For who in the skies can be compared to the LORD? Who among the heavenly beings is like the LORD, God greatly to be feared in the council of the holy ones, and awesome above all who are around him? Psalms 89:6-7

God is not to be trifled with. But, God can be trusted. One of the safeguards against temptation is to develop the same type of reverence that Joseph had when approached by Potiphar's wife. Joseph said, "How then can I do this great wickedness and sin against God?" (Genesis 39:9). ***Quality sobriety is unto the Lord.***

Psalms 89:6-7 is just one of the many passages that refer to the incomprehensiveness of God and how nothing and no one can compare with Him. Thomas Goodwin said the Dutch translated *"Who can be compared?"* as *"Who can be shadowed with him?"* The Dutch were saying that they are not worthy to be accounted shadows unto such a comparison with God.

Let's look at some of the passages that mention how no one can compare with God! The first few passages of how no one is like God are found in Exodus. Just as the Israelites were to discover the greatness of God in their emancipation from Egypt, we must recognize the greatness of God as we find our exodus from addiction.

> Who is like you, O LORD, among the gods? Who is like you, majestic in holiness, awesome in glorious deeds, doing wonders? Exodus 15:11

Deuteronomy contains several passages that refer to no one as God also. Deuteronomy was written to establish order in the new nation of Israel that had come out of the slavery of Egypt. The reverence of acknowledging God, beyond anything else, brings order. For in recognizing Him as above all, we cease to rely on our *own* understanding.

> O Lord GOD, you have only begun to show your servant your greatness and your mighty hand. For what god is there in heaven or on earth who can do such works and mighty acts as yours? Deuteronomy 3:24

The song of true sobriety is the greatness of God over all else. It is this reverence for God that produces such love and attraction for Him that every soul longs for (though some will not admit it to be the one thing that mankind cannot do without.)

June 28

Reason to repent (part 1)

For all the gods of the peoples are worthless idols, but the LORD made the heavens. Splendor and majesty are before him; strength and beauty are in his sanctuary. Ascribe to the LORD, O families of the peoples, ascribe to the LORD glory and strength! Ascribe to the LORD the glory due his name; bring an offering, and come into his courts! Worship the LORD in the splendor of holiness; tremble before him, all the earth! Psalm 96:5-9

Tremble is a word that expresses the deepest awe. *Quakers* were ridiculed for their outward trembling but it is the inward trembling that is recognized by God because that's where worship begins. The outward expressions of our worship are only a manifestation that we have comprehended the majesty of the Almighty (to some degree.) They are generated by an overwhelming love for God that produces action.

True repentance from addiction requires that you conceive the majesty of God. It has been said that instead of dwelling on how big or small our sin is, it would be wiser for us to dwell on the enormity of the God that we sin against. And while we may not outwardly tremble in our repentance, there are visible signs of our love for God over addictions.

The fear of the Lord is displayed with trembling. It is an indication of excitement. Just as two objects cannot occupy the same space at one time, you cannot tremble over God and cling to the idols of addiction. Either God holds your attention or addiction.

In his book *The Forgotten Fear: Where Have All the God-fearers Gone*, Pastor Albert N. Martin illustrates the fear that a nine-year-old boy has before a fourteen-year-old bully is different from the fear that the boy would have if he stood before the president of the *United States*.

> "There is a sacred trembling which is quite consistent with joy, the heart may even quiver with an awful excess of delight. The sight of the King in his beauty caused no alarm to John in Patmos, and yet it made him fall at his feet as dead. Oh, to behold him and worship him with prostrate awe and sacred fear!" -Spurgeon

Although the word **quake** is only used in Scripture once as Moses witnessed the power of God on Mount Sinai as God instructed Israel (Hebrews 12:21 *KJV*), why should we refuse to quake or tremble in reverence towards the Almighty?

Who will not fear, O Lord, and glorify your name? Revelation 15:4a

June 29

Reason to repent (part 2)

For all the gods of the peoples are worthless idols, but the LORD made the heavens. Splendor and majesty are before him; strength and beauty are in his sanctuary. Ascribe to the LORD, O families of the peoples, ascribe to the LORD glory and strength! Ascribe to the LORD the glory due his name; bring an offering, and come into his courts! Worship the LORD in the splendor of holiness; tremble before him, all the earth! Psalm 96:5-9

In *Addictions: A Tug of War*, I explained how many have subtly chosen to remove God from the process of overcoming addiction. They see no need for biblical repentance. They are not primarily concerned with the magnificence of God. In *My Beloved Addiction*, Pastor Jeff Mullins said, "Many self-help groups, including 12-step programs, focus on the addiction rather than restoring a right relationship with God. This is treating the symptom rather than the problem."

"There is a vital sense in which 'the natural man discerneth not the things of the Spirit of God; and in which all the realities of Christian experience are utterly hid from his perceptions. To speak to him of communion with God, of the sense of pardon, of the lively expectation of heaven, of the witness of the Holy Ghost, of the struggles of the spiritual life, would be like reasoning with a blind man about colours, or with one deaf about musical harmony." -John Morison

Pastor A. N. Martin uses the illustration of a man unconcerned about an approaching locomotive to explain the insanity of irrepentance.

"It is only ignorance of the character of God or spiritual insanity that would keep a man from this type of fear of God if he were in the path that leads to God's judgment. ... He is a man either completely oblivious or insane who does not perceive nor react in an appropriate way to the facts that are obvious to everyone else. He is out of touch with reality. Hence, he has no fear. In the same way, the only reason any unconverted person does not find himself gripped with a constant terror and dread of God is that he is either spiritually blind or spiritually insane. He is blind to the character of the God of the Bible, or, having been made acquainted with that character, he is so filled with spiritual insanity that he can make no connection between the fury of God's wrath and his own certain reception of that wrath in judgment." -*The Forgotten Fear: Where have all the God-fearers gone*, A.N. Martin

June 30

Who wants to be holy? (part 1)

Worship the LORD in the splendor of holiness; tremble before him, all the earth! Psalm 96:9

Holiness is highly relative to reverence and sobriety. Being holy not only unites you with God so that you may see the evils of addiction clearly but being holy also gives you a hunger for God that nullifies the cravings of addiction. Perhaps this is one reason why Psalms 96:9 refers to the *splendor* of holiness.

Rather than ***splendor,*** the *King James Version* translates the Hebrew word as ***beauty***. And it is a beautiful thing for men and women to be holy in the sight of God. It is the right and responsibility of every human being to be holy as we have been created in the image of God. Being holy makes us more human. There was never anyone more human than Christ.

There was never anyone as holy as Christ. He had such a longing for the Father that there was never anything that tore Him from His communion with the Father except for the sins of man.

Jesus not only found delight in revering the Father but possessed the contentment that every addict longs for. Isaiah 11:3 says that He delights in the fear of the Lord and Isaiah 33:6 says that the fear of the Lord is His treasure. Jesus is the soberest man that ever lives.

> "There was never any man or woman so contented as a self-denying man or woman. No-one ever denied himself as much as Jesus Christ did: he gave his cheeks to the smiters, he opened not his mouth, he was as a lamb when he was led to the slaughter, he made no noise in the street. He denied himself above all, and was willing to empty himself, and so he was the most contented that ever any was in the world; and the nearer we come to learning to deny ourselves as Christ did, the more contented shall we be, and by knowing much of our own vileness we shall learn to justify God." -*The Rare Jewel of Christian Contentment*, Jeremiah Burrough

To partake of God's holiness is the greatest gift that is available to all mankind. Hebrews 12:14 says *"without holiness no one will see the Lord."* While holiness is essential to reverence as well as sobriety, it is not likely that you will hear it used in a regular group for addictions. Who in their right mind does not want to be holy? **Without holiness, we find no satisfaction!**

As there is nothing that surpasses the beauty of Christ.
Splendor is indicative of the preeminence of Christ!

July 1

Who wants to be holy? (part 2)

> Worship the LORD in the splendor of holiness; tremble before him, all the earth! Psalm 96:9

Being holy is a supernatural experience that only the Holy Spirit of God can supply. What we see in addiction is natural, but what we see in God is supernatural. Being holy allows us to see God as different than us. You won't be any different if you do not see God as different.

God wants us to become more and more set apart; more like Him and less like ourselves. If you don't see God as set apart, neither will you be! G.K. Beale's book *We Become What We Worship* indicates our growth. **Reducing God is one of the most horrific traits of addiction!** It reduces us as well! Oswald Chambers said, "Holiness, not happiness, is the chief end of man."

> "Holiness is the habit of being of one mind with God, according as we find His mind described in Scripture. It is the habit of agreeing in God's judgment, hating what He hates, loving what He loves, and measuring everything in this world by the standard of His Word." -*J.C. Ryle*

Holiness is the highest state that is attainable. It is filled with humility in its purity and love. If addictions create and exacerbate our incompletion, then holiness causes us to be whole. The *Salvation Army's Soldiership Class Manual* says, "Holiness is perfect love, not just the removal of sin, but the provision of love. It is loving the Lord your God with all your heart, soul, and strength, and loving others as yourself. It is attainable only through the Holy Spirit's power and life in us. ... Holiness is living without sinning. That's the negative side. It is fullness of love. That's the positive side."

The natural inclination to worship ourselves with the pursuit of addiction can only be destroyed by the supernatural intervention of the Holy Spirit applying the holy Word of God to our hearts causing us to worship God instead. This is what makes us holy. Holy is simply defined as different or set apart to God. The key to sobriety is what pleases God.

> But you are a chosen race, a royal priesthood, a holy nation, a people for his own possession, that you may proclaim the excellencies of him who called you out of darkness into his marvelous light. 1 Peter 2:9

The fruit of holiness is the greatest privilege that is borne in a life that is lived in harmony with God. Jesus said, "Truly, truly, I say to you, whoever believes in me will also do the works that I do; and greater works than these will he do, because I am going to the Father" (John 14:12).

July 2

The fulness of times

> Nations will fear the name of the LORD, and all the kings of the earth will fear your glory. Psalms 102:15

Psalms 102:15 describes us at our best. It describes why we were created and how we find fulfillment beyond all that the world has to offer.

Unless you long for the glory of God greater than addiction then you will never be free. His glory must be your greatest pleasure that you vigilantly guard and treasure. John Piper said that "The chief end of man is to glorify God by enjoying Him forever." He also said that "God is most glorified when Man is most satisfied in Him."

The name of the Lord is significantly relevant to addictions. If those who are held captive to addiction and those who desire to minister to them do not see the significance of the name of the Lord, then they will never devise a plan that will bring freedom to the lives of addicts.

One of the greatest questions is whether God is worthy of the glory that He could receive from your life. But, this is not the primary concern for many. Who would deny God's glory?

If there is one thing that you can count on is that when Christ returns, those who are His will instantly become just as He is. I love how the Son of God became the Son of Man so that the sons of men could become the sons of God.

> For the creation waits with eager longing for the revealing of the sons of God. Romans 8:19

A glimpse of the revelation in Psalm 102:15 and Romans 8:19 are beneficial to those who long for a sober life. They both are centered on the return of Christ. They both prophesy a time when everyone will bow to Jesus. That's why they can be referred to as "the fulness of times."

The return of Christ is an important issue for us to consider while remaining sober. When a believer in Christ struggles with an addiction, the thought of Christ's return has motivating potential.

> "As the battle is waged, the focus becomes our own heart more than the external barriers we have erected. We commit ourselves to be ruthless with our covetous imaginations. As we do, the things that were once affections gradually feel more like afflictions. That is, we still notice our heart's desire for the past idols, but these desires feel like a nagging salesperson more than an object of great love. We wish the desire would disappear, but it still occasionally shows up. When we encounter it, we groan, anticipating the day when we will be fully perfected." -Edward T. Welch

July 3

Security

> For as high as the heavens are above the earth so great is his steadfast love toward those who fear him. Psalms 103:11

Who has not looked for security in addiction? One of the biggest problems with addiction is that we look to them for things that we can only find in God. That's one reason why faith in Christ is called an anchor to the soul.

Anchors give security. While we may be deceived into looking for security in addictions, we discover that they only lead to chaos as one of the definitions for an idol in Hebrew is ***chaos***.

> *"'Like the height of the heavens'* is the original language, which implies other points of comparison besides extent, and suggests sublimity, grandeur, and glory. As the lofty heavens canopy the earth, water it with dews and rains, enlighten it with sun, moon, and stars, and look down upon it with unceasing watchfulness, even so the Lord's mercy from above covers all his chosen, enriches them, embraces them, and stands for ever as their dwellingplace."
> -Spurgeon

> We have this as a sure and steadfast anchor of the soul. Hebrews 6:19a

The *Strong's Bible Dictionary* says that the soul is the inner being and that it involves the heart, mind, passion, desires, and appetite of every individual. It involves your will because you choose the condition of your soul based on your response to Christ.

> "An anchor is outside the ship; and that which steadies us cannot be a part of ourselves, must be something external to us, on which our fluttering and mutable emotions can repose and be still. ... A sure anchor is one which does not drag. It is not too light for the ship that rides by it. It has found firm ground, its flukes are all right, and it belch. It does not deceive. The ship's crew may trust it. An anchor which is steadfast, or, as the original word might be rendered, 'firm,' is one that will not break, but is strong in its own substance, made of good tough iron, so that there is no fear of the shank snapping, whatever strain may be put upon it." -*Maclaren's Exposition of the Bible*

First Peter 2:11 tells us that passions of the flesh wage war against the soul. Our souls are too valuable and fragile to leave in the care of anyone besides the Good Shepherd.

July 4

God's compassion (part 1)

As a father shows compassion to his children, so the LORD shows compassion to those who fear him. For he knows our frame he remembers that we are dust. Psalms 103:13-14

As a father pities his children, So the LORD pities those who fear Him. For He knows our frame; He remembers that we are dust. *New King James Version*

Have you ever looked for pity? Have you ever pitied yourself? After years of feeling sorry for myself because of a wide range of events, I vowed to cancel my "pity parties." I also vowed to keep my distance from the pity parties of others. I learned two valuable lessons in all of my years of self-pity.

One of the lessons that I learned through all of the pain of self-pity is that I am a poor judge of when, how, and why I need to be pitied. There are times when I should be reprimanded rather than pitied. There are times self-pity prevents you from acting.

Pity is not always the appropriate response to a situation. It takes maturity for us to know the difference. Hebrews 5:14 says that those who are mature *"have their senses exercised to discern both good and evil."*

Another reason that I refrain from self-pity is that I came to realize that I cannot pity myself enough. I'm just not capable of giving myself the comfort and consolation that is necessary when it is appropriate. Only God knows when, why, and how to perfectly pity.

> "Frustration and sadness cause pity parties which lead to relapse. They sometimes begin with the declaration that 'life isn't fair.' When I used to say that, my sponsor would accurately point out, 'And you are lucky it isn't because if you reaped what you sowed when you were using, you might not be alive.' Bottom line: each day we need to recognize as early as possible when we are exercising selfish pity. It is less important why we are feeling sorry for ourselves, than substituting it with gratitude and perspective." -*Sobertool.com*

How often have we turned to addictions while pursuing pity? The old saying is "poor me turns into pour me another drink!" In a song called *Whiskey Glasses*, Morgan Wallen sings, "Poor me, pour me another drink. 'Cause I don't wanna feel a thing. No more, hell nah. I just wanna sip 'til the pain wears off. Poor me, pour me another round. Line 'em up and knock 'em down. Two more let's go. 'Cause I ain't never hurt like this before." And what kind of compassion do we find in addiction? None!

July 5

God's compassion (part 2)

As a father shows compassion to his children, so the LORD shows compassion to those who fear him. For he knows our frame he remembers that we are dust. Psalms 103:13-14

As a father pities his children, So the LORD pities those who fear Him. For He knows our frame; He remembers that we are dust. *New King James Version*

Since God is holy, He has holy compassion. That means that it is pure and just. *Our* compassion or pity can be impure and unjust. Just as God has compassion for those who reverence Him, He does not have compassion for those who do not. Such was the case when Israel turned to idols. No one in their right mind wants to be in this situation. I once said that if the hand of the Lord is not upon you, then the hand of the Lord is against you!

And I will dash them one against another, fathers and sons together, declares the LORD. I will not pity or spare or have compassion, that I should not destroy them. Jeremiah 13:14

Therefore, as I live, declares the Lord GOD, surely, because you have defiled my sanctuary with all your detestable things and with all your abominations, therefore I will withdraw. My eye will not spare, and I will have no pity. Ezekiel 5:11

And my eye will not spare you, nor will I have pity, but I will punish you for your ways, while your abominations are in your midst. Then you will know that I am the LORD. Ezekiel 7:4

"Like as a father pitieth his children, so the Lord pitieth them that fear him. To those who truly reverence his holy name, the Lord is a father and acts as such. These he pities, for in the very best of men the Lord sees much to pity, and when they are at their best state they still need his compassion. This should check every propensity to pride, though at the same time it should yield us the richest comfort. Fathers feel for their children, especially when they are in pain, they would like to suffer in their stead, their sighs and groans cut them to the quick: thus sensitive towards us is our heavenly Father. We do not adore a god of stone, but the living God, who is tenderness itself. He is at this moment compassionating us, for the word is in the present tense; his pity never fails to flow, and we never cease to need it." -Spurgeon

July 6

God's compassion (part 3)

As a father pities his children, So the LORD pities those who fear Him. For He knows our frame; He remembers that we are dust. Psalms 103:13-14 *New King James Version*

Who will have pity on you, O Jerusalem, or who will grieve for you? Who will turn aside to ask about your welfare? You have rejected me, declares the LORD; you keep going backward. Jeremiah 15:5-6a

Alas, numerous passages refer to the compassion of God in the Old Testament and no less than twelve passages refer to the compassion of Christ in the New Testament. Some translations of the Bible use the word *mercy* to express the compassion of God. The passages reveal the depth as well as the extent of God's compassion. That's why Lamentations 3:22 says that His compassions never fail!

And he passed in front of Moses, proclaiming, "The LORD, the LORD, the compassionate and gracious God, slow to anger, abounding in love and faithfulness. Exodus 34:6 *NIV*

The LORD, the God of their fathers, sent persistently to them by his messengers, because he had compassion on his people and on his dwelling place. 2 Chronicles 36:15

Yet the LORD longs to be gracious to you; therefore he will rise up to show you compassion. For the LORD is a God of justice. Blessed are all who wait for him! Isaiah 30:18 *NIV*

In all their affliction he was afflicted, and the angel of his presence saved them; in his love and in his pity he redeemed them; he lifted them up and carried them all the days of old. Isaiah 63:9

When he saw the crowds, he had compassion for them, because they were harassed and helpless, like sheep without a shepherd. Matthew 9:36

Behold, we consider those blessed who remained steadfast. You have heard of the steadfastness of Job, and you have seen the purpose of the Lord, how the Lord is compassionate and merciful. James 5:11

July 7

Excel!

> His divine power has granted to us all things that pertain to life and godliness, through the knowledge of Him who called us to His own glory and excellence, by which He has granted to us His precious and very great promises, so that through them you may become partakers of the divine nature, having escaped from the corruption that is in the world because of sinful desire. 2 Peter 1:3-4

One of the questions that people ask while striving to overcome addiction is how to become normal. Yet **being normal is not all that God desires**. God wants you to excel. I was once a member of a Men's Bible program whose goal was for every member "to become a mature, contributing member of a Christian community."

Second Peter Chapter One offers some great insight on not just maintaining but excelling as well. It shares how to overcome addictions and become more like the children that God longs for.

The most fully functional people on the planet are little children. How wise it was for Jesus to say that if we are to enter the Kingdom of Heaven we must become as little children! Ironically, we mature spiritually by becoming more childlike before God!

Peter addresses those who have the capacity to function fully because they have been **made whole by the blood of Christ**. Through your intimacy with God, you conquer the lures of addiction and become a reflection of the light that comes from God in a dark and troubled world.

Don't let anyone fool you! *The joy and delight that is found in God exceed whatever pleasure that you might find in addiction.* Two of the most beautiful pictures that I hold in my memory are of children.

One was the joyful fellowship of a father and a daughter at church. The girl thoroughly enjoyed the father's company (as we may enjoy our *heavenly* Father.) It was most amusing when the girl told her father that she was going across the room for a while only to quickly return stating that she had changed her mind and that she preferred to be with him. Don't you prefer to be with your heavenly Father rather than the idols of addictions?

The other picture that I hold dear is that of a child at another church many years ago who strained to share a piece of candy with her daddy. Oh, how we should strain to give to our heavenly Father! Did not He strain while giving Himself to us through Christ? Don't we strain after addictions? The sweetest thing that you have for God is you! The two children in my illustrations were highly functional (they are awe-factories.) They certainly made an impression on *me*!

July 8

Practice (part 1)

> For if these qualities are yours and are increasing, they keep you from being ineffective or unfruitful in the knowledge of our Lord Jesus Christ. For whoever lacks these qualities is so nearsighted that he is blind, having forgotten that he was cleansed from his former sins. Therefore, brothers, be all the more diligent to confirm your calling and election, for if you practice these qualities you will never fall. For in this way there will be richly provided for you an entrance into the eternal kingdom of our Lord and Savior Jesus Christ. 2 Peter 1:8-11

The question of how to be normal while overcoming your addictions remains on the table as well as how to excel! Yet, another question that you may ask is what will prevent you from returning to addiction. Second Peter Chapter One gives us sound answers to combat the return to addiction (or relapse.) Just look at the list of issues that are covered in the verses above!

- Ineffective/effective
- Unfruitful/fruitful
- The knowledge of our Lord Jesus Christ
- Blind/sight
- Never fall
- Practice
- A rich entrance into the Kingdom

Though we will not be able to comment on each issue at this time, why don't you pause and think of how each applies to your war against addiction? Peter says that it is something that you **practice**. We don't become highly functional overnight. It requires practice! Mark Shaw says, "the fact that you can learn bad habits proves that you can learn good habits too."

> "Active addiction is like a spiral staircase. When you give in to your addiction just one time, you begin to spiral downward and separate from God and His power...To give you hope, the same spiral staircase that goes down also goes up with acts of obedience! In other words, by acting obediently to God and choosing to act righteously, you begin to be led by the Holy Spirit back up the spiral staircase and into intimate fellowship with your Creator, the Lord Jesus Christ. Just as your disobedient and rebellious addictive choices led you down the spiral staircase, your obedient and God-centered choices will lead you up that same spiral staircase." -*The Heart of Addiction,* Mark Shaw

July 9

Practice (part 2)

Therefore, brothers, be all the more diligent to confirm your calling and election, for if you practice these qualities you will never fall. For in this way there will be richly provided for you an entrance into the eternal kingdom of our Lord and Savior Jesus Christ.
2 Peter 1:8-11

Peter says to believers that if they possess the qualities contained in the practices that he recommends then they would never fall. Isn't that something that people need who struggle with addictions? Most certainly! But, before we look at the practices that Peter recommends, I think that we should first look at the source.

Up to 60% of the human adult body is water. According to H.H. Mitchell, *Journal of Biological Chemistry*, the brain and heart are composed of 73% water, and the lungs are about 83% water. The skin contains 64% water, muscles, and kidneys are 79%, and even the bones are watery: 31%.

It is common knowledge that we need water to survive. It is not commonly known that we need the Word of God to thrive. You don't wait until you get weak from thirst to drink water, you make a practice of drinking water! You need to practice drinking from the Word of God daily or you will thirst for the things of the world!

The greatest source Peter mentions to prevent a fall is being a "partaker in the divine nature." This is where sanctification begins. Sanctification means to be set apart from sin. Sin is selfish in every way!

Over the last few days, I asked about becoming normal. The question is deceptive because **God doesn't want you to be normal. God wants you to be different!** He wants you to be like Himself. In a word- unselfish. Who would argue that addiction is a selfish practice? *Your degree of sobriety reflects how much you are like Christ.*

Becoming more like Christ is more than a ritual; it's a relationship. It involves abiding in Christ while allowing His power to flow through you. It is closely associated with the peace of God that passes all understanding (Philippians 4:7).

"Christlikeness is not the same as following a moral or ethical ideal. It is not simply possessing more knowledge of Bible content or Bible principles. It is not merely replacing old habits with new ones or being and doing good. Furthermore, it is not becoming well-adjusted or recovering from some life-dominating sin. Christlikeness is the manifestation of the fruit of God's Spirit in the life of a believer beholding the glory of God." –*Changed into His Image,* Jim Berg

July 10

Confidence (part 1)

> As for man, his days are like grass; he flourishes like a flower of the field; for the wind passes over it, and it is gone, and its place knows it no more. But the steadfast love of the LORD is from everlasting to everlasting on those who fear him, and his righteousness to children's children, to those who keep his covenant and remember to do his commandments. Psalms 103:15-18

Confidence is an important issue for us (whether we have a problem with addiction or not.) Confidence is related to sanity. Insanity lacks confidence (or at least the right type of confidence.) Psalms 103:15 makes it clear that we cannot have confidence in ourselves. At best, you can have confidence *about* yourself based on what you have in God.

Verse fourteen says that God knows our frame. Unfortunately, *we* don't know our frame as well as we should. This becomes evident when we start believing that we can endure the effects of addiction unscathed. Proverbs 6:27 can be applied to both sexual and spiritual adultery.

> Can a man carry fire next to his chest and his clothes not be burned? Proverbs 6:27

A lack of confidence can be frightful. I remember all the fearful moments that I had while turning my back on God as the Israelites would as be described in Deuteronomy 28. As a result of their unfaithfulness, they would be in fear. Psalms 103:16-18 builds our confidence in the Lord. Deuteronomy shares a vivid description of the lack of confidence Israel would experience.

> And among these nations you shall find no respite, and there shall be no resting place for the sole of your foot, but the LORD will give you there a trembling heart and failing eyes and a languishing soul. Your life shall hang in doubt before you. Night and day you shall be in dread and have no assurance of your life. In the morning you shall say, "If only it were evening!" and at evening you shall say, "If only it were morning!" because of the dread that your heart shall feel, and the sights that your eyes shall see. Deuteronomy 28: 65-67

The only way that we can develop the confidence that we need is through humility. Psalm 103:15-18 gives us a glimpse of the connection between reverence and humility. It begins by explaining why we should be humble. It then gives us the reward of humility and how to *maintain* it. If Jesus Christ was the soberest person then His humility was the source of His sobriety.

July 11

Confidence (part 2)

As for man, his days are like grass; he flourishes like a flower of the field; for the wind passes over it, and it is gone, and its place knows it no more. But the steadfast love of the LORD is from everlasting to everlasting on those who fear him, and his righteousness to children's children, to those who keep his covenant and remember to do his commandments. Psalms 103:15-18

Yesterday, I closed with the humility of Christ as the source of His sobriety. The humility of Christ was His reliance on the Father. When we engage in things that are outside of God's will, such as addictions, then we are taking our lives into our own hands. We become our worst critics by overestimating ourselves. And in doing so, we insult God by *underestimating Him*.

"Humility is one of the chief and the highest graces; one of the most difficult of attainment; one to which our first and chiefest efforts ought to be directed; one that only comes in power, when the fullness of the Spirit makes us partakers of the indwelling Christ, and He lives within us." -*Humility*, Andrew Murray

"Without this there can be no true abiding in God's presence, or experience of His favor and the power of His Spirit; without this no abiding faith, or love or joy or strength. Humility is the only soil in which the graces root; the lack of humility is the sufficient explanation of every defect and failure. Humility is not so much a grace or virtue along with others; it is the root of all, because it alone takes the right attitude before God, and allows Him as God to do all." -*ibid*

No one finds confidence while walking in a dark place. Perhaps, you have heard of groping through life as someone does in a dark place. ***Among the darkest places on earth is addiction.*** If darkness lacks confidence then light gives us hope. The Scriptures provide the contrast between darkness and light. Some examples are Matthew 4:16; Luke 1:79; John 8:12; Acts 28:18; 2 Corinthians 4:6; 1 Peter 2:9.

Humility leads to commitment. Psalm 103:17-18 assures us of the confidence to be found in God as we keep His covenant. A covenant is a commitment. How unfortunate that we make a covenant with death when pursuing addiction as Israel did as described in Isaiah 28:15. None of us are strangers to covenants. We live by our covenants and we die for our covenants. The covenants that we make reveal what we value.

July 12

Confidence (part 3)

As for man, his days are like grass; he flourishes like a flower of the field; for the wind passes over it, and it is gone, and its place knows it no more. But the steadfast love of the LORD is from everlasting to everlasting on those who fear him, and his righteousness to children's children, to those who keep his covenant and remember to do his commandments. Psalms 103:15-18

It takes humility to deny ourselves and embrace the Word of God. Humility is the way to holiness. Holiness is the highest state. It is filled with humility in its purity and love. Our only other option is to place ourselves above God and to seek a god that appears to be more powerful and attractive than Him. And this is the dilemma that we all face. That's why addictions take on all kinds of forms.

"*Idolatry is huge in the Bible, dominant in our personal lives, and irrelevant in our mistaken estimations.*" –Os Guiness

How frail and fragile we are! Our pride would not admit it. Addiction is filled with pride. Here is another proof that addiction is not a disease. No disease can produce pride. The contrast is made clear when Jesus said that everyone that hears His words and does them would be like a house on a rock and everyone who hears His words and does not do them would be like a house built on sand (Matthew 7:24-27).

When pride comes, then comes disgrace, but with the humble is wisdom. Proverbs 11:2

"It all lies in the strife between pride and humility: pride and humility are the two master powers, the two kingdoms in strife for the eternal possession of man. There never was, nor ever will be, but one humility, and that is the one humility of Christ. Pride and self have the all of man, till man has his all from Christ. He therefore only fights the good fight whose strife is that the self-idolatrous nature which he has from Adam may be brought to death by the supernatural humility of Christ brought to life in him." -*Humility*, Andrew Murray

The great confidence that you have in following Christ is that you will become more like Him. He is full of life. Addictions offer death on many levels. You can have the same confidence as the Apostle Paul that "he who began a good work in you will bring it to completion at the day of Jesus Christ (Philippians 1:6).

July 13

Perpetuate! (part 1)

> The fear of the LORD is the beginning of wisdom; all those who practice it have a good understanding. His praise endures forever!
> Psalms 111:10

It doesn't matter who you ask, all will agree that wisdom is needed to combat addiction. Wisdom is essential to sobriety as flour is needed to make bread or cake. Psalm 111:10 refers to reverence as a practice that leads to wisdom. It's what I call ***perpetual reverence***.

> *"The fear of the LORD is the beginning of wisdom.* It is its first principle, but it is also its head and chief attainment. The word 'beginning' in Scripture sometimes means the chief; and true religion is at once the first element of wisdom, and its chief fruit. To know God so as to walk aright before him is the greatest of all the applied sciences. Holy reverence of God leads us to praise him, and this is the point which the psalm drives at, for it is a wise act on the part of a creature towards his Creator. A good understanding have all they that do his commandments. Obedience to God proves that our judgment is sound. Why should he not be obeyed? Does not reason itself claim obedience for the Lord of all? Only a man void of understanding will ever justify rebellion against the holy God. Practical godliness is the test of wisdom." -Spurgeon

Addiction: A Tug of War explains perpetual reverence as conditioning. Addiction can be known as a heart attack. It attacks our hearts from cleaving to the Lord. The major weapon against addiction is a fortified heart that has been conditioned. A conditioned heart is both pure and strong. Since addiction is a spiritual issue, then we need to acquire and develop the highest degree of reverence to overcome addiction!

Physical conditioning will change the shape and size of your muscles. Physical conditioning can make you stronger. Spiritual conditioning will change the shape, size, and strength of your heart. The condition of our hearts causes us to delight in the Lord. A conditioned heart provides redemption. One reason why redemption is imperative is so that our yearning for what is not of God may desist!

> "Certainly our contentment does not consist in getting the thing we desire, but in God's fashioning our spirits to our condition."
> Jeremiah Burroughs

July 14

Perpetuate! (part 2)

The fear of the LORD is the beginning of wisdom; all those who practice it have a good understanding. His praise endures forever! Psalms 111:10

Addiction reveals a lack of communication with God. Addiction accuses God of being unreasonable and foolish. Jim Berg said, "In our wickedness, we believe that God is the biggest evil we could encounter and that it is our resistance to Him that keeps life from charging headlong into misery!" Psalm 34:9 says not to be *"as the horse or the mule which have no understanding."* Your perpetual reverence is based on the understanding that God gives you.

That the God of our Lord Jesus Christ, the Father of glory, may give to you the spirit of wisdom and revelation in the knowledge of Him, the eyes of your understanding being enlightened; that you may know what is the hope of His calling, what are the riches of the glory of His inheritance in the saints. Ephesians 1:17-18

"If you have learned to estimate things in some measure as God estimates them, to desire what he offers, to relinquish what he forbids, and to recognize the duties that he has appointed you, you are in the path of wisdom, and the great men we have been speaking about are far behind you—far from the narrow gate which you have entered. He only is wise, who can call Christ the wisdom of God." -*George Bowen.*

Breaking free of addiction is not just about abstinence, it's about understanding that God is more worthy and more satisfying than the idols of addiction. Without an understanding of the superiority of God, you are subject to either return to your former addiction or turn to some other idolatrous addiction.

I will always remember a phrase that I would hear from some people who were seeking to remain drug-free that relates to perpetual reverence. They would say that they were going to let nothing or no one take them off of their square. Perpetual reverence means to take a stand.

Englishbaby.com says to take a stand is "to have a strong opinion about something and not change it." *Idioms.thefreedictionary.com* says taking a stand is "to take a position in opposition to someone or something; to oppose or resist someone or something." That's perpetual reverence!

July 15

Perpetuate! (part 3)

> The fear of the LORD is the beginning of wisdom; all those who practice it have a good understanding. His praise endures forever!
> Psalms 111:10

Meditation, stillness, and awe are all relative to the quality of sobriety that is rooted in reverence. Quality sobriety is a continual reverence for God because reverence is the epitome of becoming more like Christ. Perpetual reverence is nothing more and nothing less than abiding in Christ.

Perpetual reverence brings glory and pleasure to God, satisfies your soul, and prevents you from relapsing. 1 John 2:28 says to "abide in Him, so that when He appears we may have confidence and not shrink from Him in shame at his coming." ***A soul that is not given to God is vulnerable to every evil imaginable and unimaginable.***

> Little children (believers, dear ones), guard yourselves from idols—[false teachings, moral compromises, and anything that would take God's place in your heart]. 1 John 5:21 *Amplified Bible*

Lastly, perpetual reverence is not just a stand; it's a walk. Walking consists of steps. Perpetual reverence is faithful. Every step that you take in life must be approved by God. Walking is designed to take you from one place to another. The fear of the Lord takes you where God wants you. As Psalm 37:23 says that "the steps of a good man or ordered by the Lord," reverence gives you the understanding to walk uprightly.

> *"The fear of the LORD is the beginning of wisdom.* It is not only the beginning of wisdom, but the middle and the end. It is indeed the Alpha and Omega, the essence, the body and the soul, the sum and substance. He that hath the fear of God is truly wise...It is surely wisdom to love that which is most lovable, and to occupy our hearts with that which is most worthy of our attachment, and the most capable of satisfying us." *-From the French of Daniel de Superville,* 1700

In a series called *Fearing God*, Dr. Tony Evans said that the fear of God keeps our spiritual heart pumping just as blood keeps our physical heart pumping. Reverence for God occurs in stages. Its degrees vary among individuals as well as communities and programs that deal with addiction. Just as with anything else, its stability relies on your consistency.

July 16

Perpetuate! (part 4)

> The fear of the LORD is the beginning of wisdom; all those who practice it have a good understanding. His praise endures forever! Psalms 111:10

For three days, I defined perpetual reverence while listing the ingredients or components. Now, I want to share with you the results of perpetual reverence in association with addictions because it defines relapse prevention. Perpetual reverence provides both growth and stability because of God's approval.

Is there such a thing as sobriety without God's approval? Who doesn't want God's approval? But if we refuse to obtain God's approval in the way that He has prescribed then we display irreverence and dwell in a state of insanity.

That's why sobriety goes beyond being free of toxins. There are hordes of people that are drunk on other influences besides the love of God.

The most exciting and rewarding result of perpetual reverence is that it is recognized by God. For God to take notice of us as He did Enoch, Job, and Jesus, is the most delightful experience there is. It's like being kissed by God.

God's approval is the greatest compliment there is. While you may get compliments from your fellow man, to get a compliment from God is supreme. Just look at the compliments that Enoch, Job, and Jesus received from God and you will see the magnificence of being honored by God!

> And Enoch walked with God: and he was not; for God took him. Genesis 5:24

> By faith Enoch was taken up so that he should not see death, and he was not found, because God had taken him. Now before he was taken he was commended as having pleased God. Hebrews 11:5

> And the LORD said to Satan, "Have you considered my servant Job, that there is none like him on the earth, a blameless and upright man, who fears God and turns away from evil? He still holds fast his integrity, although you incited me against him to destroy him without reason." Job 2:3

> And behold, a voice from heaven said, "This is my beloved Son, with whom I am well pleased." Matthew 3:17

July 17

Perpetuate! (part 5)

The fear of the LORD is the beginning of wisdom; all those who practice it have a good understanding. His praise endures forever! Psalms 111:10

Awe-induced reverence perseveres as the examples from yesterday. That's why Psalm 111:10 ends with the phrase that the praise of the Lord endures forever. Awe-induced reverence initiates the perpetual reverence of abstaining from anything outside of God's will <u>because of His worthiness</u>. In the case of Jesus, we see how His reverence for the Father gave Him the determination to fulfill the purposes He was given.

When the days drew near for him to be taken up, he set his face to go to Jerusalem. Luke 9:51

Perpetual reverence is marked by the same determination that Jesus displayed at the *Garden of Gethsemane* as He sweats drops of blood and cried, "*Abba, Father, for you all things are possible; remove this cup from me; yet, not what I want, but what you want*" (Luke 22:44; Mark 14:36).

"Did you know that flint when struck by steel sparks? It is hard. Harder than the other rock that makes up the Negev we traveled through. Jesus set his face like the flint in the walls of the Negev. So **resolute and unshakable to get to Jerusalem to complete His true mission on earth**." -*Stonegableblog.com*

I gave my back to those who strike, and my cheeks to those who pull out the beard; I hid not my face from disgrace and spitting. But the Lord GOD helps me; therefore I have not been disgraced; therefore I have set my face like a flint, and I know that I shall not be put to shame. Isaiah 50:6-7

This was the account of how Jesus lived out the passage in Hebrews that explains how He grew in His reverence as a man in the same way that you must if you are to maintain a life of sobriety and fulfill the purposes that God has for your life (see Hebrews 5:7-8). That's why quality sobriety abides in Christ and looks like Christ and *the only answer to addiction that is approved by God is for Him to make us more like Jesus.* It's only natural for any one of us to drift from the things of God (since the Fall.) Perpetual reverence is *supernatural*.

July 18

Perpetuate! (part 6)

In the days of his flesh, Jesus offered up prayers and supplications, with loud cries and tears, to him who was able to save him from death, and he was heard because of his reverence. Although he was a son, he learned obedience through what he suffered. And being made perfect, he became the source of eternal salvation to all who obey him. Hebrews 5:7-9

Consider him who endured from sinners such hostility against himself, so that you may not grow weary or fainthearted.
Hebrews 12:3

Perpetual reverence can also be defined as abiding in Christ. Abiding in Christ means to remain or continue in Him. Abiding in Christ keeps us sober. Abiding in Christ can also be described as walking with Him or being yoked with Him.
In *Yearning Over Addiction* and *The Highest Yearning,* I said that we may embrace healthy yearning or unhealthy yearning. I also explained how we may practice good habits or bad habits. We meditate on things that are either godly or ungodly. We are either in awe of God or in awe of the things that God has made. Just as addiction can be defined as a fixation, perpetual reverence is a fixation.
Perpetual reverence secures your soul. Perpetual reverence is implied when the Apostle Paul said to the Philippians to rejoice in the Lord always" (Philippians 4:4). Philippians 3:1 says that rejoicing in the Lord is a safeguard. Why? Because "the name of the Lord is a strong tower, the righteous run into it and is safe" (Proverbs 18:10).
Every once and a while, as I frequented the downtown area of Cleveland, Ohio, I would encounter a brother in Christ who was blind. I asked him once if he was walking with the Lord. His response was, "I've got my eyes set on Him!" That's perpetual reverence!

"Habitual SUBMISSION to the Divine authority brings its own reward in this life—part of which is a spiritual discretion which preserves from impostures. When the understanding is DOMINATED by the Word the whole soul is 'full of light,' so that all its faculties are under its beneficent influence: the conscience being informed, the affections turned to their legitimate object, the will moved in the right direction."
- A.W. PINK (1886-1952) From "An Exposition of the Sermon on the Mount, Chapter 55: False Prophets (Matthew 7:15-20), Concluded"

July 19

The supremacy of reverence

> Wisdom is the principal thing; therefore get wisdom: and with all thy getting get understanding. Proverbs 4:7 *KJV*

The relevancy of reverence/irreverence is essential to exposing and disposing of addictions. Reverence is the most significant issue because it reveals the condition of your soul as well as determines the course of your actions. Reverence is pleasing to God as it seeks God's pleasure.

Quality sobriety is the reverence that recognizes the magnificence of God. It shows you how small you are. Reverencing God means that you are obliged to give your attention to Him above all in grateful, loving obedience. Reverence is an awareness of His presence for support as well as accountability.

Reverence involves consideration, pondering, and understanding. Reverence helps you to understand the insanity of addiction that rejects the truth that God has established and devises something false (hence the idols of addiction.) Insanity involves withholding from God with determination.

Quality sobriety is based on the truth of God. The contrast between addiction and sobriety is marked by a degraded, depraved distortion, disillusion, dysfunction, deformity, and deficiency compared to the confidence, comfort, stability, security, and satisfaction that are found in the anchor of our souls (Christ.)

The mind of Christ is the epitome of reverential sobriety. Regeneration (being born again) through the blood of Christ breaks the bonds of pride, selfishness, and ignorance. The mind of Christ is practiced by recognizing every situation as either godly or ungodly, foolish or wise. Your decisions become based on God's approval rather than personal preference.

Sobriety involves acknowledging the worthiness of God. Addictions ignore the majesty of God. A reverence that leads to quality sobriety longs to be a partaker of the holiness of God and delight in what Peter calls "joy that is inexpressible and filled with glory" (1 Peter 1:8).

Quality sobriety gives to God. It bears fruit in many ways. It has purpose and direction. Quality sobriety produces the fruit of our hands as well as the fruit of our lips (praise.) One of the strengths of reverence that creates quality sobriety is praise and worship. Fulfillment can only be found in the quality of sobriety that begins and continues with reverence for God.

The consistency of perpetual reverence is essential to quality sobriety and relapse prevention. It is practiced by loving God and others as well as maintaining a delight in the Lord expressing His value over addictions. Perpetual reverence recognizes the rule of Christ and longs for His return. That's because quality sobriety does not just rejoice in the blessings but more so in the Blesser.

July 20

The war of truth (part 1)

You have set up a banner for those who fear you, that they may flee to it from the bow. Selah Psalms 60:4

It is no mystery that addiction is warfare. When referring to Satan, Jesus said "the thief comes only to steal and kill and destroy. I came that they may have life and have it abundantly" (John 10:10). The Apostle Peter said, "Beloved, I urge you as sojourners and exiles to abstain from the passions of the flesh, which wage war against your soul" (1 Peter 2:11).

Psalms 60:4 promises a refuge for all who fear God. Psalms 60:4 also promises victory over addiction. It is easier for us to understand the victory of Psalms 60:4 from the *New King James Version*.

You have given a banner to those who fear You, That it may be displayed because of the truth. Selah Psalms 60:4 *NKJV*

The MacArthur Study Bible says, "God and His truth serve as a rallying point for the perplexed people." Are you perplexed by addiction? What is it that can free you from perplexion? The truth!

Territories and boundaries were established by God before we were created. God designed the world and sectioned or separated one part from another. For instance, God separated the waters from the dry land. God made a distinction between night and day.

When you start to mature in the Lord, God gives you the ability to distinguish good from evil (Hebrews 5:14). God knows how to separate one thing from another. God wants you to be separate from addiction.

Little children (believers, dear ones), guard yourselves from idols—[false teachings, moral compromises, and anything that would take God's place in your heart]. 1 John 5:21

In *Turning to God from Idols*, I explained how addictions are better defined as idols rather than a disease. I mentioned how my approach has been used since the beginning of time. But, to address addictions without the use of the Bible (per se), many have devised other methods to explain and combat addictions. Some of these methods give out false information mixed with *some* truth.

Insanity is the rejection of the truth while manufacturing false perceptions.

July 21

The war of truth (part 2)

You have set up a banner for those who fear you, that they may flee to it from the bow. Selah Psalms 60:4

Truth is one of our most valuable commodities. Think of what would happen if some of the things that you see every day were not true. What if it was not true that you were walking on solid ground? What if your next bite of food was poisonous? *Life is dangerous without the truth.* Think of how it is important for those you are close with to be honest and truthful! How important is it for companies to be truthful about their products?

One of the greatest weapons against addiction is truth. Jesus said that He is the Truth (John 14:6). God described Himself to Moses as *"abundant in goodness and **truth**"* (Exodus 34:6). Exodus 18:21 refers to "men of truth." Proverbs 23:23 says to "buy the truth and do not sell it." Last but not least, the Scriptures refer to *walking* in the truth.

Teach me your way, O LORD, that I may **walk in your truth**; unite my heart to fear your name. Psalms 86:11

I rejoiced greatly to find some of your children **walking in the truth**, just as we were commanded by the Father. 2 John 4

The idols of addiction are based on lies. The Hebrew word for an idol (awen) denotes a vain, false, wicked thing and expresses at once the essential nature of idols and the consequences of their worth." Truth is both reverent and sober! The insanity of idolatry that Isaiah describes is relative to addiction and the way that it is dealt with.

You boast, "We have entered into a covenant with death, with the grave we have made an agreement. When a overwhelming scourge sweeps by, it cannot touch us, for we have made a lie our refuge and falsehood our hiding place. Isaiah 28:15

Matthew Henry said, "these scornful men lulled themselves asleep in carnal security, and even challenged God Almighty to do his worst." *Apart from Jesus Christ, programs that offer help with addiction are only carnal.* They may claim to be spiritual, but anything that does not include Christ is *not* spiritual.

Since addiction is primarily a spiritual issue, then you need spiritual help. Jesus said, "It is the Spirit who gives life; the flesh is no help at all. The words that I have spoken to you are spirit and life" (John 6:63). The Spirit of God is also referred to as the Spirit of truth (John 16:13).

July 22

Equipped

He provides food for those who fear him; he remembers his covenant forever. Psalms 111:5

The rewards of reverencing God are vast. Psalm 111:5 is listed as one of the rewards of reverencing God. How many times have we insulted God by questioning His ability and willingness to provide? Every time we seek addiction!

Everyone knows that food is a necessity. We cannot live without food. But, God has said that *"man shall not live by bread alone, but man lives by every word that comes from the mouth of the LORD."* (Deuteronomy 8:3; Matthew 4:5) If only we were all as concerned about the Word of God as much as we are with food!

Fasting is a good exercise when developing a life free from addiction. Biblical fasting is a way for you to show God how much He is worth to you. The old English word for **worship** was **worthship**.

Since food is a necessity, then we consider it to be important. What matters most is the theme of our lives. One of the characteristics of addiction is that they become our priority

One of the elements of worship is trust. You put your trust in what you worship. Just as some people see *God* as being trustworthy, others believe that addiction is worthy of their trust. By using it for some advantage (to boost their ego, relieve stress, loosen their inhibitions, etc.) they consider addictions as trustworthy.

How important it is for us to know how well God provides for those who reverence Him! It is directly related to our sanity. Years ago, my wife bought me a copy of *All the Questions in the Bible* by Jimmie L. Hancock. As I read through the questions in the Bible, I discovered that our *sanity* is questioned. Although there are probably hundreds of references that question our sanity, I'll just give you a few.

They spoke against God, saying, "Can God spread a table in the wilderness? Psalm 78:19

But he was in the stern, asleep on the cushion. And they woke him and said to him, "Teacher, do you not care that we are perishing?" Mark 4:38

Do you not know? Do you not hear? Has it not been told you from the beginning? Have you not understood from the foundations of the earth? Isaiah 40:21

July 23

Live on! (part 1)

> On the third day Joseph said to them, "Do this and you will live, for I fear God." Genesis 42:18

Can't you hear the sobriety in Joseph's voice? Both Joseph and his brothers knew that the situation was serious. Often, we do not see how serious addictions are.

Apart from God's Word, you will never know the severity of addiction. As I stated in *Turning to God from Idols,* "I have spent a lot of time explaining the nature, origin, and effects of addiction to reveal how severe of a problem we face. If the Word of God had nothing to say about addictions then He would not have created us!"

> Did that which is good, then, bring death to me? By no means! It was sin, producing death in me through what is good, in order that sin might be shown to be sin, and through the commandment might become sinful beyond measure. Romans 7:13

The instruction that Joseph gave his brothers seemed bizarre. At this point, they did not know that it was Joseph who spoke to them (they had not seen him for many years.)

Joseph was a stranger to them. God is a stranger to us outside of Jesus Christ. Joseph was as Jesus with the Samaritan woman at the well (John 4). Jesus explained to the woman how to find life as did the Apostle John to his readers.

> Jesus answered her, "If you knew the gift of God, and who it is that is saying to you, 'Give me a drink,' you would have asked him, and he would have given you living water." John 4:10

> Now Jesus did many other signs in the presence of the disciples, which are not written in this book; but these are written so that you may believe that Jesus is the Christ, the Son of God, and that by believing you may have life in his name. John 20:30-31

Just as Joseph, Jesus, and John offer assurance! All who wage war against addiction need assurance. Assurance is based on confidence.

> In the fear of the LORD one has strong confidence, and his children will have a refuge. Proverbs 14:25

July 24

Live on! (part 2)

> On the third day Joseph said to them, "Do this and you will live, for I fear God." Genesis 42:18

Joseph's reverence made him responsible. Addictions have a reputation for making us irresponsible. Wherever God places you, you have the privilege and responsibility of reverencing Him. ***Those who revere God the most are the most responsible of all.***

Joseph was responsible for the welfare of his family and the entire land of Egypt. Joseph declared his innocence out of clear conscience to his brothers in declaring that he feared God.

The most impressive proof of Joseph's reverence for God was when he rejected the advances of Potiphar's wife. It was because of his reverence for God that Joseph was given discernment.

> How then could I do such a wicked thing and sin against God? Genesis 39:9b

Joseph's brothers had to be cautious with their answers to Joseph. We must likewise be careful how we respond to godly advice. Do you look for those who have a discernment that is brought by the knowledge and obedience of the Word of God (Hebrews 5:14)? Is your first concern whether someone's advice will benefit you or whether it is pleasing to God?

Sometimes they are both the same, at other times the result may not be pleasing to you (in fact, it may be painful.) God has not called us to a pain-free life. Addictions claim to be pain-free. Peter says that every follower of Christ is called to suffer (1 Peter 2:21).

Addiction is one of the methods we practice to circumvent suffering though it may be the will of God for us to suffer. Joseph's reverence for God was perpetual. Even while suffering in prison, Joseph acknowledged God.

The fear of the Lord gave Joseph purpose, prosperity, and discernment. Where do you go for advice? Joseph was trained by God. Through his training, Joseph gained understanding. Understanding is essential to overcoming addictions.

> For though by this time you ought to be teachers, you need someone to teach you again the basic principles of the oracles of God. You need milk, not solid food, for everyone who lives on milk is unskilled in the word of righteousness, since he is a child. But solid food is for the mature, **for those who have their powers of discernment trained by constant practice to distinguish good from evil.** Hebrews 5:12-14

July 25

The reward of resistance

But the midwives feared God and did not do as the king of Egypt commanded them, but let the male children live. Exodus 1:17

And because the midwives feared God, he gave them families. Exodus 1:21

Addictions make demands on our lives as the king of Egypt did the midwives. The midwives could have responded with terror, just as we do when our addiction is withheld. Instead, the midwives' response to the king's commands was to fear God.

Think about how the midwives saw God in comparison to the king and how we see God compared to addictions! **Do you have an addiction that seems to be greater than God?**

The midwives were used by God to troth the king's plans. **Divine reverence *sometimes* opposes human decisions; reverence <u>always</u> opposes demonic decisions.** What the king wanted the midwives to do was ungodly. Do you look at addictions as ungodly? Do you stand against addictions the way that the midwives stood against the king? Resist what seems to be irresistible!

> "Is your method of waging war against your addiction pretty tame? If so, it is because you think you are fighting with a friend. You don't have the heart for it. Are you afraid to fight the way Jesus teaches you for fear that you will no longer have addictions as an insurance policy?" -*Addictions: A Banquet in the Grave,* Edward T. Welch

The midwives had no concern about suffering because of their decisions. Comfort was not the issue for the midwives. Addictions are always seeking comfort (even at the risk of others.)

> "The Scriptures list so many rewards for reverencing God, we need to examine them in four basic categories. First, we will look at the protection that reverencing affords. Second, the prosperity that the fear of the Lord initiates deserves examination. Third, we will review passages that reveal the inner strength rewarded by our reverence for God. Fourth, we will explore how reverencing God is rewarded by our intimacy with God. What a comfort to truly realize that God Himself knows our reverence and rewards us accordingly! The rewards of reverencing God could just as well be called promises. Rest assured; God never breaks His promises!" –*The Fear of the Almighty,* Madison

July 26

Sober Praise (part 1)

Who is like you, O Lord, among the gods? Who is like you, majestic in holiness, awesome in glorious deeds, doing wonders? Exodus 15:11

Who is like unto thee, O Lord, among the gods? who is like thee, glorious in holiness, fearful in praises, doing wonders? *KJV*

For great is the Lord, and greatly to be praised, and he is to be feared above all gods. 1 Chronicles 16:25

The verses above express verbal praise. But, praise begins in your heart. Just as worship and praise are inseparable, reverence is relative to praise as well. Praise is a component of reverence that produces quality sobriety. Why? Because to offer praise is to express solid worth.

Praise is first etched in your mind, deposited into your spirit, and then translated into words and actions. A sober mind does not have a disproportionate appraisal of earthly things. Simply stated—***what you think of God will affect your actions.***

Praise is a valuable combatant against addiction in many ways. Initially, praise unto God counteracts the praise that we secretly give to ourselves in deserving the honor that we wish to bestow upon ourselves by partaking in whatever it is that God has forbidden.

Praise has a humbling element that we cannot live without. Praise also breaks the chains of addictions as you turn your attention to God more than the source of your addiction. Besides, praise relates to self-control.

Would you not agree that addictions are the object of praise for many? Who doesn't praise something that they find value and delight in? As we praise externally, we endorse our object of worship. Praise is usually recognized by the words that we express.

External praise begins internally. As you praise internally, you embrace your object of worship, and it fills your thoughts. **Addictions tell us that God is lacking. Praise exalts the sufficiency of God.** Praise recognizes Who God is and what He does. To praise God is to concur with God. **Addiction does not concur with God's plans for our lives.**

Passion and awe produce praise. When in awe of addictions, we say "Who is like you?" In Exodus 15:11, Moses is telling God that He is holy. To be holy means to be different. Addiction is natural, but God is supernatural. If we do not see God as different, neither will we be. **Reducing God is one of the most horrific traits of addiction**! It reduces *us* as well!

July 27

Sober Praise (part 2)

Who is like you, O Lord, among the gods? Who is like you, majestic in holiness, awesome in glorious deeds, doing wonders? Exodus 15:11

Who is like unto thee, O Lord, among the gods? who is like thee, glorious in holiness, fearful in praises, doing wonders? *KJV*

For great is the Lord, and greatly to be praised, and he is to be feared above all gods. 1 Chronicles 16:25

When turning to God from the idols of addiction praise is produced as you grow in the knowledge of Christ and spend time with God. As you grow in your understanding of God through His Word and watch Him at work, praise is stimulated.

The psalmist made praise a practice (it was a habit.) **Habits get a bad name because they are usually associated with selfish acts that lack control while damaging lives.** Whenever we master a habit or habit masters us, our actions become spontaneous (some say second nature.)

Seven times a day I praise you for Your righteous rules. Psalms 119:164

***We* master good habits; bad habits master *us*.** I once heard it said that you know that you are growing in the Lord when doing the right thing is almost "natural." Habits are either desirable or undesirable, godly or ungodly, productive or non-productive.

"Rituals, unlike habits, are done with deliberate intention and concentration. When we choose our habits and repeat them, they become rituals. By making something into a ritual we give it focus. Everyone has habits, now we should make a mindful choice to make those habits into positive rituals." *–Circuelle Foundation*

Praise sets things in order. Primarily it sets your *mind* in order. Isn't this the definition of sobriety? God is given His proper place with praise. It is a testimony and a witness. Out of praise unto the Lord emerges integrity, thanksgiving, and contentment. The addictive heart is never content. Praise depends on our integrity as we find satisfaction in God. Who doesn't need integrity while struggling with addictions?

July 28

Sober Praise (part 3)

Who is like you, O Lord, among the gods? Who is like you, majestic in holiness, awesome in glorious deeds, doing wonders? Exodus 15:11

Who is like unto thee, O Lord, among the gods? who is like thee, glorious in holiness, fearful in praises, doing wonders? KJV

For great is the Lord, and greatly to be praised, and he is to be feared above all gods. 1 Chronicles 16:25

Confession is a powerful element of praise. Praise is a confession as you say the same thing about God that He says. Addictions never render praise to God. *Addictions are ever discontent and accusing God of being unfair, unwise, not all-powerful, not all-knowing, and uncaring ...* Praise dwells in the truth. Addictions dwell in falsity.

One of the most valuable assets of praise is joy. I believe that every method of tackling addictions involves three elements in some form or another. Those elements are reasoning, repenting, and rejoicing (true joy is lacking in any program that excludes the peace of God that is found in Christ.)

"Rejoicing and repentance must go together. Repentance without rejoicing will lead to despair. Rejoicing without repentance is shallow and will only provide passing inspiration instead of deep change. ... When we repent out of fear of consequences, we are not really sorry for the sin, but for ourselves... In fear-based repentance, we don't learn to hate the sin for itself, and it doesn't lose its attractive power. We learn only to refrain from it for our own sake... Fear-based repentance makes us hate ourselves. Joy-based repentance makes us hate the sin." -*Counterfeit gods,* Tim Keller

True reverence is always, always, always accompanied by praise. A lack of praise is an indication of discontent, ingratitude, and even greed. Neither is sober! True sobriety does not exist without praise. If sobriety is equal to sanity, then it is not sound-minded to withhold from God the praise that He is due. If we fail to give God recognition then we are not thinking soundly.

Thou shalt fear the LORD thy God; Him shalt thou serve, and to Him shalt thou cleave, and swear by His name. **He is thy praise**, and he is thy God, that hath done for thee these great and terrible things, which thine eyes have seen. Deuteronomy 10:20-21 *KJV*

July 29

Productivity (part 1)

> But select capable men from all the people—men who fear God, trustworthy men who hate dishonest gain—and appoint them as officials over thousands, hundreds, fifties and tens. Exodus 18:21 *NIV*

Nonproduction can be listed as one of the liabilities of addictions in the workplace, at school, in government, at home, and in every other phase of life or institution. The statistics prove the cost that addictions have on society.

If third-world countries are defined as undeveloped, then addictions create third-world citizens of people residing in developing nations. The fear of the Lord can mold and shape us into being useful members of society (as the men that Moses was to look for.)

Before I knew anything about drug addiction, I was asked to counsel at a Christian summer camp. I was caught off guard when asked to lead a class about drugs and alcohol. My research from the Scriptures led to a passage in Deuteronomy 21. My study addressed our responsibilities and our usefulness to society.

> If a man has a stubborn and rebellious son who will not obey the voice of his father or the voice of his mother, and, though they discipline him, will not listen to them, then his father and his mother shall take hold of him and bring him out to the elders of his city at the gate of the place where he lives, and they shall say to the elders of his city, "This our son is stubborn and rebellious; he will not obey our voice; he is a glutton and a drunkard" Then all the men of the city shall stone him to death with stones. So you shall purge the evil from your midst, and all Israel shall hear, and fear. Deuteronomy 21:18-21

One of the first questions that came to mind after reading the passage above is why the son was given such a severe sentence. I had to remember that Israel was in a crude environment (they were in the desert.) Everyone was needed for the survival of others. Men were especially needed to bear their load and assist others.

The son in the passage had no desire to help and was, in fact, a burden. While pursuing addictions, we are inclined to withhold our talents and resources. We may even find ourselves useless. I did not say worthless; these are often mistaken. I have come to view everyone as having infinite worth but not always useful and productive.

July 30

Productivity (part 2)

But select capable men from all the people—men who fear God, trustworthy men who hate dishonest gain—and appoint them as officials over thousands, hundreds, fifties and tens. Exodus 18:21 *NIV*

During one of my very first drug treatments, one of the counselors asked if I had ever stolen from my parents. When I, proudly, said that I had never stolen from my parents, he immediately insisted that I had.

I was angered over this since I was almost certain that he had not talked with my parents, and this was the very first conversation that he and I had ever had. I just sat there speechless, wondering how he was going to get himself out of what I thought to be a mistake. Then, he asked me, "Do you know what you stole from your parents, Greg?" "You stole you", he said.

This I could not deny. And such it is with an addiction. We steal from everyone (in actuality, all mankind.) More importantly, our addictions rob *God* in many ways. Here are a few!

1. The time that we could send with Him.
2. Not lending our ear to Him.
3. Failing to give Him glory (internally.)
4. Failing to give Him glory (externally.)
a. by not reflecting Him
b. by not conforming to the image of His Son
c. by not allowing Him access to our finances
our abilities, opportunities …

We are all called to mature and be fruitful. I was cheating everyone out of the leader that God wanted me to be. Some are called to lead in various capacities. And as we grow older, we all have a responsibility to lead.

Those who do not reverence God are not fit to lead because they are more likely to be selfish, unjust, or partial in their decisions. Integrity is at the heart of godliness.

Addictions are subject to selfish decision-making. Quite often we read in Scripture that there is a link between reverence for God and how we treat others. One example is found with the unjust judge who would not help the widow (Luke 18:1-6).

Your reverence is your response to the privilege of bearing His image by being a fruitful blessing to others. To deny yourself of God is to deny God and others of yourself. If you are a disciple of Christ then you have been appointed and equipped for productivity. ***Productivity defines the quality of your sobriety!***

July 31

Productivity (part 3)

> But select capable men from all the people—men who fear God, trustworthy men who hate dishonest gain—and appoint them as officials over thousands, hundreds, fifties and tens. Exodus 18:21 *NIV*

Reverence for God has been a requirement for leaders since the days of Moses. Although this was the advice given to Moses by his father-in-law, we see this same requirement for leaders in other portions of Scripture as well. One example is found in 2 Chronicles 18:4-6. A word concerning the reverential leaders is also recorded in King David's final words from 2 Samuel 23.

> Jehoshaphat ... appointed judges in the land, in each of the fortified cities of Judah. He told them, "Consider carefully what you do, because you are not judging for man but for the LORD, who is with you whenever you give a verdict. Now let the fear of the LORD be upon you. Judge carefully, for with the LORD our God there is no injustice or partiality or bribery." 2 Chronicles 18:4-6 *NIV*

> The God of Israel has spoken; the Rock of Israel has said to me: When one rules justly over men, ruling in the fear of God, he dawns on them like the morning light, like the sun shining forth on a cloudless morning, like rain that makes grass to sprout from the earth. 2 Samuel 23:3-4

Those who do not reverence God are not fit to lead because they are not approved of God. In 1 Samuel 2:30, the Lord God said, "Those who honor Me I will honor, but those who despise me will be disdained." It is no wonder that the apostle Paul told Timothy to study (be diligent) to show himself **approved of God** (2 Timothy 2:15).

Though people usually emphasize how the passage above shares the importance of studying the Scriptures, I understand how it mostly emphasizes our accountability to God. **Reverential sobriety doesn't just cry for abstinence, it has the desire to please God.**

I have learned to take great pleasure in working beside God. The Gospel of Mark is referred to as "the action gospel." The last verse describes action and productivity. We have the same privileges as the early followers of Christ.

> And they went forth, and preached everywhere, *the Lord working with them*, and confirming the word by the signs that followed. Amen. Mark 16:20

August 1

A strong defense (part 1)

> Moses said to the people, "Do not fear, for God has come to test you, that the fear of him may be before you, that you may not sin." Exodus 20:20 *KJV*

As God made Himself known to the Israelites, their response was fear and confusion. Just as many need others to clear the confusion of addictions, the Israelites needed Moses to give them clarification. As a godly leader, Moses was able to tell the Israelites about the things that were happening from God's perspective.

Moses provided guidance and encouragement. God blesses us with leaders who exemplify and encourage reverence. Rather than being afraid of the *situation,* the Israelites were told to fear (reverence) the Lord. The story was told again in Hebrews Chapter Twelve for the followers of Christ as encouragement with a warning.

> For you have not come to what may be touched, a blazing fire and darkness and gloom and a tempest and the sound of a trumpet and a voice whose words made the hearers beg that no further messages be spoken to them. For they could not endure the order that was given, "If even a beast touches the mountain, it shall be stoned." Indeed, so terrifying was the sight that Moses said, "I tremble with fear." But you have come to Mount Zion and to the city of the living God, the heavenly Jerusalem, and to innumerable angels in festal gathering, and to the assembly of the firstborn who are enrolled in heaven, and to God, the judge of all, and to the spirits of the righteous made perfect, and to Jesus, the mediator of a new covenant, and to the sprinkled blood that speaks a better word than the blood of Abel. See that you do not refuse him who is speaking. For if they did not escape when they refused him who warned them on earth, much less will we escape if we reject him who warns from heaven. Therefore let us be grateful for receiving a kingdom that cannot be shaken, and thus let us offer to God acceptable worship, with reverence and awe, for our God is a consuming fire.
> Hebrews 12:18-25, 28-29

The Israelites' response to God is similar to the secular approach to addiction. The difference between a secular approach to addiction and a biblical approach is that the Bible emphasizes the majesty of God over the enormity of our shortcomings. Secular programs insanely attempt to rob God of displaying His majesty.

August 2

A strong defense (part 2)

Moses said to the people, "Do not fear, for God has come to test you, that the fear of him may be before you, that you may not sin." Exodus 20:20 *KJV*

Just as Moses, the author of Hebrews was cautioning his readers to be sober-minded and not panic. When faced with addiction, the Scriptures teach us not to panic but to be sober-minded.

The Scriptures along with the Holy Spirit teach us to accurately evaluate every situation from the eyes of the Lord. **God does not want us to fear the situations we encounter as if He does not exist.** He wants us to reverentially fear Him (pay attention to Him.)

For God gave us a spirit not of fear but of power and love and self-control. 2 Timothy 1:7

God proves (tests) us so that we may reverence Him. Life is filled with opportunities for reverence. It is harder to reverence God in some situations than in others. We must be able to see beyond the circumstances. Vision comes with maturity.

For everyone who lives on milk is unskilled in the word of righteousness, since he is a child. But solid food is for the mature, for those who have their powers of discernment trained by constant practice to distinguish good from evil. Hebrews 5:13-14

As we look not to the things that are seen but to the things that are unseen. For the things that are seen are transient, but the things that are unseen are eternal. 2 Corinthians 4:18

The Lord used Moses to help the Israelites to see beyond their circumstances. The text says that "when all the people saw the thunder and the flashes of lightning and the sound of the trumpet and the mountain smoking, the people were afraid and trembled, and they stood far off" (Exodus 20:18).

God wants to know that we will love and honor Him no matter what happens. God knows when, where, and how to test each of us. Reverence is always tested. It is the way that you become more like Christ as well as declaring the majesty of God.

August 3

A strong defense (part 3)

> Moses said to the people, "Do not fear, for God has come to test you, that the fear of him may be before you, that you may not sin." Exodus 20:20 *KJV*

I closed yesterday with the thought that reverence is always tested. It is the process that God uses to make you more like Christ in your maturity. Every trial and temptation is an opportunity to increase your love for God.

> Count it all joy, my brothers, when you meet trials of various kinds, for you know that the testing of your faith produces steadfastness. And let steadfastness have its full effect, that you may be perfect and complete, lacking in nothing. James 1:2-4

Moses told the people that the fear of God would keep them from sinning. This was nothing new. Had Satan reverenced God, he would not have sought to dethrone God, as we do in our sins. Had Adam and Eve reverenced God, they would have been in awe of His Word, as much as in awe of His person.

Sin begins with irreverence. **Addiction is an attempt to dethrone God.** Sin is by far the worst enemy that we have. And the only remedy for sin is a reverence for God that leads to a cross.

1. The cross of Christ
2. The cross that *we* must bear each day

The fear of the Lord prevents people from sinning. Our actions are governed by our thoughts. The fear of the Lord gives us the right kind of mentality to disdain sin.

Reverence produces self-control. The fear of the Lord is a choice. Psalms 4:4 says to "stand in awe and sin not" (*KJV*). The answer to temptation and sin is contemplative reverence.

In a book titled *The Sinfulness of Sin*, which was originally published in 1669, Ralph Venning said, "sin being a transgression of God's law, which was made for man's good, the sinfulness of sin must needs lie in this, that it is contrary (1) to God, (2) to man."

> "On both accounts, it is justly obnoxious to, deservedly worthy of the hatred of God and man. And I heartily wish that the outcome will be that man may hate it as God does, who hates it, and nothing else but it; or (to be sure) he hates none but for it." –*The Sinfulness of Sin,* Ralph Venning

August 4

State of affairs (part 1)

> I will send my terror before you and will throw into confusion all the people against whom you shall come, and I will make all your enemies turn their backs to you. Exodus 23:27

While most of the other passages that we are studying lean toward a delightful, reverential, fear of adoration, Exodus 23:27 speaks of a scary, dreadful fear. The fear of the Lord is different than all other fear as God is different.

The Israelites were given an advantage over others because of God's intervention. Israel was to influence all the other nations. Their advantage would depend on their response to God's Word.

Israel would not be able to withstand the lies that other nations embraced because of their alienation from the true and living God without relying on the truth of God's Word. (Some examples of the lies that the other nations embraced involved their idolatry just like people today.) We who offer the Bible as the supreme weapon against addictions oppose those who would make light of God's answers.

Presuming that they are against addiction, some oppose the Cross of Christ and deny the basic truths that the Bible has to say about addictions. **Rather than acknowledging what can already be understood about addictions from the Scriptures, they are looking for some other answer.**

Ultimately, they seek to dethrone God. We who know that the answer to addiction is found in Christ must be willing and able to persuade them that they are not only promoting confusion with issues that are not scriptural but they are making themselves enemies of God (by not revering Him.)

> Knowing therefore the terror of the Lord, we persuade men.
> 2 Corinthians 5:11a

It is because of pride that man seeks to find answers apart from God. A proud man avoids acknowledging God. It is much like someone who asks you for directions and once you tell them then they dispute your answer.

One of the things that some fail to realize is that addictions are primarily worship disorders. Who knows more about worship than God? Who knows more about everything but God? In *Mere Christianity,* C.S. Lewis said that "in God, you come up against something which is in every respect immeasurably superior to yourself. Unless you know God as that—and, therefore, know yourself as nothing in comparison—you do not know God at all."

August 5

State of affairs (part 2)

> I will send my terror before you and will throw into confusion all the people against whom you shall come, and I will make all your enemies turn their backs to you. Exodus 23:27

I could never overemphasize how joy and peace are two tremendous aids to our abstinence from the things that are unpleasing to God. Jesus provides peace beyond understanding because it is not of this world (Philippians 4:7; John 14:27).

Those who follow Christ possess an inexpressible joy (1 Peter 1:8). There is no joy or peace in terror. Terror is promised to those who oppose God. While man explores biological answers to resolve spiritual issues, joy and peace have no place in his diabolical formula. Therefore there is no true sobriety outside of a reverence for God founded upon His Word!

> On this rock I will build my church, and the gates of hell shall not prevail against it. Matthew 16:18b

> Because they hated knowledge and did not choose the fear of the LORD, would have none of my counsel and despised all my reproof. Proverbs 1:29-30

What you think of Jesus will always determine what you think of addiction. The terror that the enemies of Israel had is no different than the terror that unbiblical programs for addiction have. It is the terror of facing God. It is the insanity that either there is no judgment we must face for our actions or there is no God to comfort and confront us.

> The fool says in his heart, "There is no God." Psalms 14:1a

"No man likes to live in dread and terror. Every son of Adam, prior to a work of God's grace in his heart, tries to rid himself of that terror. What does he do? He tries to convince himself that the locomotive is only a papier-mâché plaything, and he attempts to tamper with the character of God. He will try to convince himself that God loves His creatures too much to inflict eternal destruction on them." *The Forgotten Fear: Where Have all the God-fearers Gone?*, A.N. Martin

The state of affairs is that Calvary is the only answer!

August 6

Cleaving

You shall fear the Lord your God. You shall serve him and hold fast to him, and by his name you shall swear. Deuteronomy 10:20

You shall walk after the Lord your God and fear him and keep his commandments and obey his voice, and you shall serve him and hold fast to him. Deuteronomy 13:4

The word "cleave" is used in some translations instead of "holding fast." **Unfortunately, many cleave to addictions while looking for something that only God can give.** And while I do not recommend that people only seek God for what He can do for them, I will not deny that God rewards genuine faith.

How tightly do you hold on to addictions? I remember a commercial that used to illustrate how committed someone may become toward addictions. There was a voice that asked a person, "Would you steal for me?" The person would then answer yes. Another person would appear. The same voice would ask, "Would you desert your family for me?" The person would hesitate and then say yes.

There were perhaps several other questions of that nature until the voice would finally ask, "Would you die for me?" And the person would answer (with hesitation) yes. Then the narrator would tell us that this was the voice of addiction.

The Hebrew word for "cleave" (dabaq) is used over fifty times in the Bible. Eleven times 'dabaq' refers to cleaving to God. The word 'dabaq' means to be attached to anyone, to be lovingly devoted.

Cleaving to God is more than just an interest. When you cleave to God you give your entire being to Him. *Addictions may capture our entire being.* Cleaving to God is a matter of giving to God what He deserves. It involves transparency, sincerity, and perseverance.

Cleaving to the Lord is a day by day, sometimes moment by moment activity. Jesus said that if any man would come after Him (cleave to Him) he must take up his cross <u>daily</u> and follow Him.

Cleaving is seen in Proverbs. In Proverbs 2:2 we are admonished to *incline* our ear to wisdom. Proverbs 3:21 says to *not let it depart* from our eyes. Proverbs 4:7-8 says that "wisdom is the principal thing…exalt her, and she will promote you, she will bring you honor, when you *embrace* her." Proverbs 8:34 says that there is a blessing for the one who *watches daily* at wisdom's gates, *waiting at the post of wisdom's doors*. Christ is the wisdom of God that you must cleave to (1 Corinthians 1:18, 24).

August 7

Renewal vs. recovery

> You were taught, with regard to your former way of life, to put off your old self, which is being corrupted by its deceitful desires; to be made new in the attitude of your minds; and to put on the new self, created to be like God in true righteousness and holiness.
> Ephesians 4:22-24

If I had things my way the word "recovery" would be eliminated from the discussion on addictions. Recovery does not accurately describe what God wants to do in our lives. Recovery indicates that you are seeking to regain something.

The word was used early in *Alcoholics Anonymous* among those who had once lived what would be considered a normal life and had drifted into dysfunctional living. For those who are dominated by addictions and have never lived a normal life, there is nothing to recover.

Alcoholics Anonymous was formed by those who professed to be Christians and embraced the Bible to give us an accurate view of the issues of life. Over time, many of their words were misconstrued. Not everyone who joins *Alcoholics Anonymous* looks to the Word of God for answers. Over the years much of what was said became tainted.

Another thing that I don't like about using recovery to describe the process of sobriety is that it does not coincide with the Scriptures. God calls people out of darkness into light. If we are seeking recovery we want to go back into darkness.

In Ephesians 4:22-24, Paul explains to believers in Christ how they become new persons. He does not encourage them to recover something, he teaches them that they must be made new.

After Paul tells the Ephesians that they were being made new, he explains how God wants to make them more like Himself. This is new rather than recovered. You were not born like God and you have never been as much like God as you can become.

Being made new in Christ initially occurs as you first put your faith in Him and then go on as you grow. Even "growing" would be a more accurate word for the process of sobriety than "recovery".

I love the explanation of putting off the old and putting on the new. Some of the Greek words used in the passage had to do with changing clothes. Back in the Biblical days, the average person would rarely obtain a new set of clothing. By the time they did get a change of clothing, their old clothes were usually pretty raggedy and soiled. As it was a joy and a delight for them to put off their old clothes and put on new ones. I don't want to recover my old clothes. I don't want to recover my old self.

August 8

A sense of fear

And all Israel shall hear and fear and never again do any such wickedness as this among you. Deuteronomy 13:11

And all the people shall hear and fear and not act presumptuously again. Deuteronomy 17:13

And the rest shall hear and fear, and shall never again commit any such evil among you. Deuteronomy 19:20

All the passages above describe the judgment of God. His judgment is sometimes administered by the officials. We may also find ourselves held accountable for addictions by law enforcement in certain instances. God may also administer judgment through parents, spouses, or employers.

I would be the last to deny that God is love because of the grace that He has bestowed on me! By the same token, love will do whatever is necessary for the greatest good. Hebrews 12:4-10 gives us a good understanding of how we can be afraid of God while recognizing that He loves us.

There are two things that we must remember as we contemplate the fear or terror of the Lord. One is that Jesus is not to be trifled with. Two is that Jesus can be trusted. Both characteristics are expressed in my most favorite line from C. S. Lewis' *Chronicles of Narnia* as the Beavers describe Aslan (who represents Christ in the story.)

> "Lucy and Susan's thoughts go to what Aslan is actually like. If he is a king who is safe, they reason, that will certainly be of great comfort in light of the battle being all but lost. 'Is—is he a man?' asked Lucy. 'Aslan a man!' said Mr. Beaver sternly. 'Certainly not. I tell you he is the King of the wood and the son of the great Emperor-Beyond-the-Sea. Don't you know who is the King of Beasts? Aslan is a lion—the lion, the great Lion.' 'Ooh!' said Susan, 'I'd thought he was a man. Is he—quite safe? I shall feel rather nervous about meeting a lion.' 'That you will, dearie, and no mistake,' said Mrs. Beaver; 'if there's anyone who can appear before Aslan without their knees knocking, they're either braver than most or else just silly.' 'Then he isn't safe?' said Lucy. 'Safe?' said Mr. Beaver; 'don't you hear what Mrs. Beaver tells you? Who said anything about safe? 'Course he isn't safe. But he's good. He's the King, I tell you.'" - *The Lion, the Witch, and the Wardrobe*, C.S Lewis

August 9

The judgment of God (part 1)

All the wicked of the earth You discard like dross, therefore I love Your testimonies. My flesh trembles for fear of You, and I am afraid of Your judgments. Psalms 119:119-120

Who wants to be known as wicked? Probably few! Wicked people often try to justify themselves as being good. The wicked and the righteous are characterized as wheat and tare by Jesus in Matthew 13.

The tares in Jesus' parable symbolize the wicked. (By the way, tares are poisonous.) By the judgment of God, the wicked are banished from His sight! The psalmist took delight in this aspect of God's judgment. He says "therefore I love Your testimonies."

Equal rights have been a major theme in the United States for more than 100 years. ***Does God have rights?*** What are those rights? ***Do the rights of God include permission to judge? Does He need our permission to judge? Is it wrong for God to become angry over our actions?*** What happens when we take the judgment of God lightly?

The most severe judgment that God will ever issue was laid upon His Son. The severity of the judgment is seen as Jesus was stripped of all His glory. Before being sent to earth and being judged for our sins, He reflected the glory of God with perfection for all eternity.

The glory that we may possess is only found in our reflection of God (as we were created in His image.) The judgment that was passed down by Adam is that we would no longer bear the image of God.

As quiet as it is kept, outside of Christ, we bear the image of Satan (children of wrath, Ephesians 2:3.) If left to ourselves, we think and act just like the Evil One himself. We possess within us a clone of Satan's nature, and it violently opposes God and is subject to judgment.

> "When we begin to see the human heart as God has been seeing it all along, we are stunned that He would want to redeem the likes of us. We all are truly deserving of nothing but His wrath and judgment." –*Changed into His Image,* Jim Berg

The judgment of God concerning addictions is revealed through various means. God often judges by letting people go on with their addiction (which never truly satisfies and leads to Hell.) Someone once said that if you don't want Jesus now, then God is not going to force you to spend eternity with Him. Addiction is just one of the ways that we choose to reject Christ (who is personified as wisdom, while addictions are foolish.)

August 10

The judgment of God (part 2)

> All the wicked of the earth You discard like dross, therefore I love Your testimonies. My flesh trembles for fear of You, and I am afraid of Your judgments. Psalms 119:119-120

The wrath of God is an expression that signifies the intensity of the judgment of God because of His anger. The severity of God's judgment can be seen in the consequences of our actions. You can trust God to judge (whether directly or indirectly.)

When you take Christ as your Savior, you are saved from the judgment of hell. But that does not mean that you will not suffer judgment before reaching heaven. Though God is forgiving, offending God should not be as lightly considered as it is with most programs for addictions. **It has become so horrific that many times the issue of offending God is never mentioned as though we should not sin simply because it does us harm**.

The judgment that Israel received as a result of her idolatry is much like the consequences of addiction. We often see the severity of God's judgment as Israel was judged for their idolatry. Yet, the judgment of God is not without warning. The judgment of God has led many to change. Only God can say that someone is "at the point of no return."

> The Lord, the God of their fathers, sent persistently to them by His messengers, because He had compassion on His people and on His dwelling place. But they kept mocking the messengers of God, despising His words and scoffing at His prophets, until the wrath of the Lord rose against His people, until there was no remedy. 2 Chronicles 36:15-16

Gentle and Lowly: The Heart of Christ for Sinners and Sufferers, expresses how God is more compassionate than we can imagine. Isaiah 20:18 says "the LORD waits to be gracious to you, and therefore he exalts himself to show mercy to you."

> "Not once are we told that God is provoked to love or provoked to mercy. His anger requires provocation; His mercy is pent up, ready to gush forth. We tend to think: divine anger is pent up, spring-loaded; divine mercy is slow to build. It's just the opposite. Divine mercy is ready to burst forth at the slightest prick. ... the Bible is one long attempt to deconstruct our natural vision of who God actually is." -*Gentle and Lowly,* Dane Ortlund

August 11

Revelation (part 1)

> If you are not careful to do all the words of this law that are written in this book, that you may fear this glorious and awesome name, the Lord your God. Deuteronomy 28:58

Deuteronomy 28:58 reveals the magnificence of God in stating that His name is glorious and awesome. The revelation of God is incomprehensively magnificent. **If we could understand the magnificence of God it would take an eternity to explain it.**

One of the atrocities of addiction is an evil misconception of God. Addictions claim to know God as weak and senseless, uninvolved, and uncaring. Deuteronomy 28:58 is a warning. The way that you judge God determines the way that God judges *you*. As Moses warned the Israelites, and Paul warned Athens, there is a warning for us who would belittle God and look to the idolatry of addiction.

> Being then God's offspring, we ought not to think that the divine being is like gold or silver or stone, an image formed by the art and imagination of man. The times of ignorance God overlooked, but now he commands all people everywhere to repent, because he has fixed a day on which he will judge the world in righteousness by a man whom he has appointed; and of this he has given assurance to all by raising him from the dead. Acts 17:29-31

The revelation of God is essential to the quality of your sobriety because it gives you a greater understanding of God. Once you have a greater understanding of God, then you get greater reverence for God. **Revelation and reverence precede revival.**

Isaiah spoke against Israel's idolatry. A greater understanding of idolatry gives us a greater understanding of addictions. In *Turning to God from Idols,* while offering a very brief list of the marks of idolatry found in the Bible, I mentioned that "In my studies on idolatry, I have found that the phrases of this nature could conservatively reach six to eight hundred phrases."

Isaiah contrasts the greatness of God with the idols of the nations in the same way that we need to recognize the greatness of God over addictions. God questions our sobriety as well as our reverence for God with a long list of questions from Isaiah that are listed for the next two days!

August 12

Revelation (part 2)

Why will you still be struck down? Why will you continue to rebel? Isaiah 1:5a

What more was there to do for my vineyard, that I have not done in it? When I looked for it to yield grapes, why did it yield wild grapes? 5:4

And when they say to you, "Inquire of the mediums and the necromancers who chirp and mutter," should not a people inquire of their God? Should they inquire of the dead on behalf of the living? 8:19

For the Lord of hosts has purposed, and who will annul it? His hand is stretched out, and who will turn it back? 14:27

Ah, you who hide deep from the Lord your counsel, whose deeds are in the dark, and who say, "Who sees us? Who knows us?" 29:15

You turn things upside down! Shall the potter be regarded as the clay, that the thing made should say of its maker, "He did not make me"; or the thing formed say of him who formed it, "He has no understanding?" 29:16

Whom have you mocked and reviled? Against whom have you raised your voice and lifted your eyes to the heights? Against the Holy One of Israel! 37:23

Who has measured the waters in the hollow of his hand and marked off the heavens with a span, enclosed the dust of the earth in a measure and weighed the mountains in scales and the hills in a balance? Who has measured the Spirit of the Lord, or what man shows him his counsel? Whom did he consult, and who made him understand? Who taught him the path of justice, and taught him knowledge, and showed him the way of understanding? 40:12-14

To whom then will you liken God, or what likeness compare with him? 40:18

Do you not know? Do you not hear? Has it not been told you from the beginning? Have you not understood from the foundations of the earth? 40:21

August 13

Revelation (part 3)

To whom then will you compare me, that I should be like him? says the Holy One. Lift up your eyes on high and see: who created these? Isaiah 40:25-26a

Why do you say, O Jacob, and speak, O Israel, "My way is hidden from the Lord, and my right is disregarded by my God?" 40:27

Who has performed and done this, calling the generations from the beginning? I, the Lord, the first, and with the last; I am he. 41:4

Who among you will give ear to this, will attend and listen for the time to come? 42:23

Who is like me? 44:7a

Is there a God besides me? 44:8

Does the clay say to him who forms it, "What are you making?" or "Your work has no handles?" 45:9b

To whom will you liken me and make me equal, and compare me, that we may be alike? 46:5

Why, when I came, was there no man; why, when I called, was there no one to answer? Is my hand shortened, that it cannot redeem? Or have I no power to deliver? 50:2a

Who has believed what he has heard from us? And to whom has the arm of the Lord been revealed? 53:1

Why do you spend your money for that which is not bread, and your labor for that which does not satisfy? 55:2

Whom did you dread and fear, so that you lied, and did not remember me, did not lay it to heart? Have I not held my peace, even for a long time, and you do not fear me? 57:11

August 14

Vision and purpose

> In the year that King Uzziah died I saw the Lord sitting upon a throne, high and lifted up; and the train of his robe filled the temple. Above him stood the seraphim. Each had six wings: with two he covered his face, and with two he covered his feet, and with two he flew. And one called to another and said: "Holy, holy, holy is the Lord of hosts; the whole earth is full of his glory!" And the foundations of the thresholds shook at the voice of him who called, and the house was filled with smoke. And I said: "Woe is me! For I am lost; for I am a man of unclean lips, and I dwell in the midst of a people of unclean lips; for my eyes have seen the King, the Lord of hosts!" Then one of the seraphim flew to me, having in his hand a burning coal that he had taken with tongs from the altar. And he touched my mouth and said: "Behold, this has touched your lips; your guilt is taken away, and your sin atoned for." And I heard the voice of the Lord saying, "Whom shall I send, and who will go for us?" Then I said, "Here I am! Send me." Isaiah 6:1-8

Isaiah's reverence for God was found in his vision of God. Isaiah saw the Lord "sitting on a throne, high and lifted up." Isaiah also recognized the Lord as holy. Addictions are sure to cloud your vision of God. Because of his vision of God, Isaiah recognized his need for cleansing. And it was after his cleansing that Isaiah recognized his purpose.

You will never be all God wants you to be without comprehensive reverence. The reverence that God is worthy of goes beyond abstaining from addictions. God is longing for us to join Him in the delight of being holy. **Perhaps the most generous invitation that God has made to mankind is for us to be partakers of His holiness (Hebrews 12:10).**

When you revere God, He reveals more of Himself to you and you have the privilege of becoming more like Him. This joy can sustain you amid trouble or success, heartache, and failure, trials and temptations, and even pleasure and prosperity.

> In the days of his flesh, Jesus offered up prayers and supplications, with loud cries and tears, to him who was able to save him from death, and he was heard because of his reverence. Although he was a son, he learned obedience through what he suffered. Hebrews 5:7-8

> And we all, with unveiled face, beholding the glory of the Lord are being transformed into the same image from one degree of glory to another. For this comes from the Lord who is the Spirit.
> 2 Corinthians 3:18

August 15

Reverence is relevant!

> Do you not fear me? declares the LORD. Do you not tremble before me? Jeremiah 5:22

How important is God's approval? That's a really important question we must all face! Reverence cries for severity. The severity of the addiction is not the loss of employment or possession, it is not broken homes or loss of friends. The severity of addictions is how it affects God.

We can never imagine how hurt and angry God is over addictions. There is a greater issue at stake in our war against addictions than the welfare of ourselves and others (in our care.) Addictions are unbecoming of God. The image of God that we are called to bear rests upon our reverence.

The greatest motivation for abstaining from addiction is love and reverence for God. Reverencing God has been the secret to sobriety since the beginning of time. The very nature of reverence gives a personal awareness of God's presence and creates a sense of obligation to God. Reverence for God is, also, supported by a proper understanding of who God is. One thing that you can be sure of is that what you think of God will affect your actions.

Reverence is the chief component of Bible-based sobriety. The power of reverence for conquering addiction is undeniable. Somewhere along the way, that vision was lost as people strayed from looking to the Word of God for the answers to the most complex issues (as though God is insufficient to meet the demands that addictions place on our souls.)

But, the Bible has not changed. Nor has our nature changed (so long as we are captivated by anything outside of God.) **Just as the insult of irreverent idolatry defines addictions, our reverence for God defines sobriety.**

Addictions insult God by telling us that we can find answers in them that can only be found in God. One of the greatest characteristics of reverencing God that helps us to overcome addictions is to admit that we are dealing with something that goes beyond our understanding. Self-denial lies in the heart of reverence. Revering God also involves seeking advice from God-fearing people.

Addictions can be called a priority that we put into practice. All of our priorities are based on our reverence for God (or the lack thereof.) Reverence produces the transformation that makes us responsible to God and others. One of the greatest blessings of reverencing God is to be recognized by God. God wants us to make a priority of progressively practicing reverence for Himself that produces a perpetually predisposed reverence!

August 16

The awe-factory (part 1)

Or do you despise the riches of His goodness, forbearance, and longsuffering, not knowing that the goodness of God leads you to repentance? Romans 2:4 *NKJV*

If you know anything about anatomy, then you are familiar with the olfactory nerve. The olfactory nerve transmits special sensory information, allowing us to have a sense of smell. I would like to suggest the ***awe-factory*** of our souls is the aroma of God's goodness and kindness.

I once discussed with a friend how God leads us to repentance. My friend said, "the fear of the LORD may be the beginning of wisdom, but God's normal MO is to overwhelm us with his goodness and kindness." My response was, "I love the passage in Romans 2 that you used. As I have studied and written about the fear of the Lord for years, I do not think that the passage excludes the fear of the Lord. I think that it presents the awe factor of repentance."

The fact of the matter is that the fear of the Lord and recognition and display of His goodness coexist in true repentance. In terms of turning to God from the idols of addictions, you must be so overwhelmed, so in awe of God (in His Majesty) that addictions just don't appeal to you anymore.

I am ashamed to admit that there were times in my drug addiction when I had made a conscious decision that whenever I would dine at a place where a free meal was served that I would no longer practice giving thanks to God before the meal. I was humbled every time I went to a place and they would present us with a feast.

All I could do was cry out to God about how foolish I had been to treat Him in this manner and how kind He was to bless me despite my irreverence. I cannot say that just one of these occurrences led to what is now a perpetual life of repentance in response to the truth of God that becomes more and more evident, but it sure helped.

The idols of addiction are merciless and demanding. They enslave everyone who is captivated by their vain promises. The idols of addiction brutally demand your attention and never bring fulfillment.

> "Our Lord finds our desires not too strong, but too weak. We are half-hearted creatures, fooling about with drink and sex and ambition when infinite joy is offered us, like an ignorant child who wants to go on making mud pies in a slum because he cannot imagine what is meant by the offer of a holiday at the sea. We are far too easily pleased." -*The Weight of Glory*, C.S. Lewis

August 17

The awe-factory (part 2)

For I delivered to you as of first importance what I also received: that Christ died for our sins in accordance with the Scriptures, that He was buried, that He was raised on the third day in accordance with the Scriptures. 1 Corinthians 15:3-4

What is of first importance to you? Is it related to Christ? Or is it an addiction? Is it something outside of God? Or is it something within the will of God? Just what is it that has your attention the most? This can be described as an awe factor.

The awe of addictions held me captive for many years! The awe of Christ is more worthy! The awe of Jesus will keep you from the awe of addictions in many ways.

> "There are two ways in which a practical moralist may attempt to displace from the human heart its love of the world—either by a demonstration of the world's vanity, so as that the heart shall be prevailed upon simply to withdraw its regards from an object that is not worthy of it; or, by setting forth another object, even God, as more worthy of its attachment, so as that the heart shall be prevailed upon not to resign an old affection, which shall have nothing to succeed it, but to exchange an old affection for a new one." -*The Expulsive Power of a New Affection,* Thomas Chalmers (1780-1847)

Once again, we see the relevance of the fear of the Lord in conquering addiction. One of the definitions for reverence is "to be in awe of." Children are most often found to be in awe of their senses. And, maybe, that's why Jesus said for His followers to be like children.

John Calvin is quoted as saying that the heart of man is an idol factory. We are an "awe factory" by default. Here is the big question- Where is your awe? Have you not found Christ to be worthy of your awe?

> "There is something even higher and better than being kept from sin,--that is but the restraining from evil: there is the positive and larger blessing of being now a vessel purified and cleansed, of being filled with His fullness, and made the channel of showing forth His power, His blessing, and His glory." -*Gospel Treason: Betraying the Gospel with Hidden Idols,* Brad Bigney

God is worthy of awe!

August 18

The awe-factory (part 3)

> Truly, truly, I say to you, you will weep and lament, but the world will rejoice. You will be sorrowful, but your sorrow will turn into joy. When a woman is giving birth, she has sorrow because her hour has come, but when she has delivered the baby, she no longer remembers the anguish, for joy that a human being has been born into the world. So also you have sorrow now, but I will see you again, and your hearts will rejoice, and no one will take your joy from you. John 16:20-22

Jesus was explaining the joyful awe that His disciples would experience resulting from His resurrection. Because of His intimacy with God the Spirit, Jesus knew that His disciples would have a greater understanding of Himself resulting in a tighter bond after His death and resurrection. Awful reverence describes the joy experienced by the women at the tomb of the resurrected Christ.

> So they departed quickly from the tomb with fear and great joy, and ran to tell his disciples. Matthew 28:8

I don't think that the fear the women experienced was frightful. I believe that it was a reverential experience for them. Reverence draws us to a higher plane. There is nothing heavenly about an addiction. The humdrum of addiction outweighs its fleeting pleasures. Jesus promises a joy that will last. You will never find the joy that Jesus gives in an addiction.

> By faith Moses, when he was grown up, refused to be called the son of Pharaoh's daughter, choosing rather to be mistreated with the people of God than to enjoy the fleeting pleasures of sin. He considered the reproach of Christ greater wealth than the treasures of Egypt, for he was looking to the reward. Hebrews 11:24-26

I dare anyone to tell me what is more awesome and longed for than intimacy with the Almighty

You have the opportunity, each day, every waking moment, to enjoy the intimacy with the Almighty that is afforded as a result of the death and resurrection of Christ. You have the privilege and responsibility of challenging others to not settle for anything less.

Be an awe factory!

August 19

The awe-factory (part 4)

> They said to each other, "Did not our hearts burn within us while He talked to us on the road, while He opened to us the Scriptures?"
> Luke 24:32

My love for Luke 24:13-35 began early in my relationship with Jesus Christ. I think that it was because of the same intimacy that I discovered as the disciples on the *Road to Emmaus* that caused my heart to burn as well. Awe is on display throughout the passage.

That which awes us can be overwhelming. It's good to be overwhelmed by Jesus. It creates a burning in your heart (as with the disciples on the *Road to Emmaus*.)

Addictions overwhelm us, causing further corruption in our hearts (note that the heart is deceitful outside of Christ's command, Jeremiah 17:9.) The awe that we experience in life is either based on what is real or what is an illusion.

John Piper unknowingly describes the illusion of addiction in his book on fasting titled *A Hunger for God*. Piper says, "Disillusionment often follows naïve admiration." Jesus wanted those two disciples, as well as you and I, to know that He is real.

Many of our fears are illusions. It is an undesirable emotion. On the other hand, the awe of addictions can be desirable. When you are in awe of what you desire, you respond with affection; creating a tighter bond. Such was the case with the disciples on the *Road to Emmaus*! The same is true when you are captured by the snares of addiction!

One of the biggest problems that we have with embracing the awe of God is that we cannot fully see it! The disciples on the *Road to Emmaus* told Jesus about the things that they saw. Jesus told them what they could not see.

There is no awe with no vision! Where there is no vision, the people perish (Proverbs 29:18).

> So we fix our eyes not on what is seen, but on what is unseen, since what is seen is temporary, but what is unseen is eternal.
> 2 Corinthians 4:18 *NIV*

> If ye then be risen with Christ, seek those things which are above, where Christ sitteth on the right hand of God. Set your affection on things above, not on things on the earth. For ye are dead, and your life is hid with Christ in God. Colossians 3:1-3 *KJV*

August 20

The awe-factory (part 5)

> And we all, with unveiled face, beholding the glory of the Lord, are being transformed into the same image from one degree of glory to another. For this comes from the Lord who is the Spirit.
> 2 Corinthians 3:18

We Become What We Worship is a book by G.K. Beale that God used to reinforce my convictions concerning the nature of addictions and the transforming power of Christ. Beale describes how lifeless we become when we are in awe of lifeless idols.

Likewise, Beale explains the vitality of worshipping the true and living God. This becomes the most powerful reason for a Christ-centered approach to addictions. To His disciples, Jesus said, "because I live, you too shall live" (John 14:19).

Who would deny that Jesus is close to God the Father? There is no one closer to the Father! Who would deny that anyone was more pleasing to the Father than Jesus? Who would deny that there is anyone more like God than Jesus?

To omit Jesus from the equation of addressing addictions is insulting to God the Father, God the Son, and God the Holy Spirit! Why? Because He deserves to be recognized! Yet another reason why Christ should be included while addressing addictions is explained by Dr. Edward T. Welch in his book *Addictions: A Banquet in the Grave*.

> "This might sound strange, but you don't have to turn to the true God to stop your addiction! I'm sure you've met people who kicked addictions without turning to Christ in repentance and faith. You could probably find strategies that are not Christ-centered that would nevertheless keep you away from alcohol for the rest of your life. But God wants more. He wants us to know Him, serve Him, fear Him, and love Him. Somehow, God must be bigger than our own desires- so big that we worship Him alone." -Dr. Edward T. Welch

The ultimate answer to addictions is to be made like Christ. Who doesn't want to be like Christ? It begins by being born-again. 2 Corinthians 5: 21 says God "has made Him Who knew no sin (Jesus) to be sin for us, that we might be made the righteousness of God in Him."

Unless your righteousness is found in Christ, you are incomplete. Isn't it great to know that God has made us in His image? That's just one of the components of an awe-factory that demolishes every addiction that competes with God!

August 21

The awe-factory (part 6)

And we all, with unveiled face, beholding the glory of the Lord, are being transformed into the same image from one degree of glory to another. For this comes from the Lord who is the Spirit.
2 Corinthians 3:18

Of course, though some are opposed to God, they like the idea of being made in the image of God! Do you resemble God while being selfishly involved in the idolatry of addictions? Are you intimate with the Father as Jesus so long as you live a self-indulgent life?

Jesus "went about doing good" (Acts 10:38). Of what use are you to others while being mesmerized by addictions? The *Westminster Catechism* says that the chief end of man is to glorify God and enjoy Him forever!

I am, also, grateful for the wisdom of Jay Adams in *How to Help People Change* in noting the difference between change that comes short of the glory of God and change that gives God glory.

"When we talk about changing people, what do we mean? Because counselors do not all have the same kind of change in mind, it is not strictly correct to say that they agree on the need for changing counselees. Just as the word *automobile* conveys strikingly different images to owners of new BMWs than to owners of third-hand Toyotas, so also counselors, who agree on the need for modification in counselees, many have vastly different ideas and attitudes concerning that change." -*How to Help People Change,* Jay Adams

"All counseling change is a matter of greater or lesser love toward Him." -*ibid.*

"So, the change we are talking about is *substantial* change of a person's life. Brought about by the ministry of the Word, and blessed by the Spirit of God, it brings the counselee closer to the likeness of Christ. In short, it is significant change because it glorifies God." -*ibid.*

"Change affected by non-Christian counselors is not neutral either. In one way or another, it dishonors God, either by adopting attitudes or actions contrary to His will or by outwardly, hypocritically confirming to His law without a changed heart (a form of godliness that denies the power thereof.)" -*ibid.*

August 22

The awe-factory (part 7)

Teach me Your way, LORD, that I may rely on Your faithfulness; give me an undivided heart, that I may fear Your name.
Psalms 86:11 *NIV*

Awe this! Awe that! We are so much in awe of the world around us! There are so many things that seem to grab our attention. When we are in awe of an addiction, it becomes hard to focus on anything else. Dr. Edward T. Welch said, "temptations are like unwanted noise." There are so many things that we consider to be worthy of our affection.

> "But, alas, you say, 'I have no control over such things: they come unbidden and I am powerless to prevent them.' So the Devil would have you believe! Revert again to the analogy of your garden: do not the weeds spring up unbidden; do not the slugs and other pests seek to prey upon the plants? What, then? Do you merely bewail your helplessness? No, you resist them and take means to keep them under. Thieves enter houses uninvited, but whose fault is it if the doors and windows be left unlocked? O heed not the seductive lullabies of Satan. God says, 'purify your hearts, you double minded' (James 4:8); that is, one mind for Him, and another for self; one for holiness, and another for the pleasures of sin." -A.W. Pink

How important it is for us to remember that Jesus is most worthy of our affection! Someone once said, "We need to preach the gospel to ourselves every day." Gospel means "good news." The core of the gospel is that Christ died for our sins and rose again for our justification
(read 1 Corinthians 15:1-4.)

The implications go beyond understanding more than anything in the entire universe! The gospel gives us a greater understanding of God than anything imaginable.

What we cannot fully understand causes awe. Since there are so many things that we cannot understand, our heart is easily divided. The gospel keeps your heart undivided.

> O the depth of the riches both of the wisdom and knowledge of God! how unsearchable are His judgments, and His ways past finding out! Romans 11:33 *KJV*

August 23

Duel occupation

> And the leaders stood behind the whole house of Judah, who were building on the wall. Those who carried burdens were loaded in such a way that each labored on the work with one hand and held his weapon with the other. And each of the builders had his sword strapped at his side while he built. Nehemiah 4:16b-18a

Do you ever feel like the builders who had to build with one hand and fight with the other? One day, I had the excruciating pleasure of this experience at a more intense level than ever as I entered the final day of a month-long process of publishing my first book.

Everyone who is fighting to help those that are bound to addictions is building and fighting at the same time, as well as those who are struggling to break free of the bondage of addictions.

Building

Building a strong and lasting relationship with the Almighty.
Building relationships with others.
Building a wall of defense against addictions.
Building upon the truth that God has given.
Building ourselves and others up in the faith.
Building groups that address the issues of addictions.
Building institutions that combat addictions.
Building a data base of resources against addictions.

Fighting

Fighting against the lies of the Devil.
Fighting the lies that the world presents.
Fighting the lies that we tell ourselves
Fighting *for* others.
Fighting to tear down the walls or strongholds that addiction construct in our souls and in the souls of others.
Fighting the fatigue and weariness of our flesh.
Fighting the urges of giving in.

These are probably not the only elements that we are faced with in our dual occupation. Just like the builders in Nehemiah, we are seeking the stability of ourselves and others.

August 24

Home-court advantage (part 1)

And because of him you are in Christ Jesus, who became to us wisdom from God, righteousness and sanctification and redemption.
1 Corinthians 1:30

As I settled at my desk from a trip away from home for a week, I thought about the advantages of home. I had been home long enough to once again relax in a familiar setting, sleep better, and enjoy my wife more fully. I, also, began to appreciate how my work was more easily performed at home. I thought about the sports term called ***home-court advantage***.

When it comes to dealing with addictions, we have the home-court advantage in Christ. 1 Corinthians 1:30 gives us four reasons. Do we not need the wisdom to combat addictions? It's in Christ!

Isn't our righteousness before God a major issue in addictions? That's only available in Christ! Don't we need to be sanctified (set apart) unto God as an expression of His worthiness over everything else? It is answered by God in Jesus' prayer in John 17:17.

Isn't it time for redemption? The complete turn-around that Second Corinthians 5:17 refers to is when it says that if anyone is in Christ they are a new creation (home-court advantage as well.)

Addictions are housed in the opponent's court (the devil.) Not only that, if we go to war against addictions outside of the provisions that God has given to us in Christ, we offend the Almighty because we have rejected His wisdom, His righteousness, His sanctification, and His redemption.

The NBA and NFL have the biggest regular-season home advantages, improving a team's chance of winning by 10 and 7 percentage points, respectively. While a sports team can still lose despite its home-court advantage, you can never lose in Christ while waging war against addictions.

> "More than nineteen hundred years ago, there was a Man born contrary to the laws of life. This Man lived in poverty and was reared in obscurity. ... In infancy He startled a king; in childhood He puzzled doctors; in manhood He ruled the course of nature, walked upon the waves as pavement, and hushed the sea to sleep. ... He never marshaled an army, nor drafted a soldier, nor fired a gun; and yet no leader ever had more volunteers who have, under His orders, made more rebels stack arms and surrender without a shot fired. He never practiced psychiatry, and yet He has healed more broken hearts than all the doctors far and near." -*from The Incomparable Christ,* unknown author

August 25

Home court advantage (part 2)

Give no opportunity to the devil. Ephesians 4:27

Within the game of basketball, there is what is known as a "full-court press." "A full-court press is a basketball term for a defensive style in which the defense applies pressure to the offensive team the entire length of the court before and after the inbound pass. Pressure may be applied man-to-man, or via a zone press using a zone defense." -*Wikipedia*

The struggle we face against addictions is no game (it's war). In war, the equivalent of a full-court press is what is known as "no quarter." In war, a victor gives no quarter (or takes no prisoners) when the victor shows no clemency or mercy and refuses to spare the life of a vanquished opponent in return for their surrender at discretion (unconditional surrender.) 2 Corinthians 10:4-5 gives us a clue of what this means as we fight against addictions.

> For though we walk in the flesh, we are not waging war according to the flesh. For the weapons of our warfare are not of the flesh but have divine power to destroy strongholds. We destroy arguments and every lofty opinion raised against the knowledge of God, and take every thought captive to obey Christ. 2 Corinthians 10:3-5

Satan ever argues that we should turn from Christ, alluring us through those who subject themselves to him by the lust of the flesh, the lust of the eyes, and the pride of life. It is when we decide that we will accept no compromise that we have the home-court advantage.

Would you let someone into your house and do whatever they want? Could they persuade you to misuse or even destroy the things that are dear to you and your family? Would you let them walk away with your most cherished possessions? This is just what you do when you allow the devil to convince you to withhold from Christ the reverence and honor He deserves.

One of the things that you will hear during a sporting event is how the home team will not allow the visitor to come into 'their house' and beat them. "THIS IS MY HOUSE", they chant. Well, if you have given your life to Christ, God says, "THIS IS MY HOUSE!" He truly cares what you allow to dwell there!

> Or do you not know that your body is a temple of the Holy Spirit within you, whom you have from God? You are not your own.
> 1 Corinthians 6:19

August 26

Home court advantage (part 3)

Yet You are holy, enthroned on the praises of Israel. Psalm 22:3

But Thou art holy, O Thou that inhabitest the praises of Israel. *KJV*

God inhabits the praise of His people. If we were to translate this into what takes place at a sporting event it is the cheer of the home team (but in the Kingdom of God it goes beyond that.)

I was greatly encouraged in church this Sunday as the song *Every Praise* was sung. It had been a demanding week (just as the lure and temptations of addictions are demanding.) It is no wonder that Jesus warns us to "take heed to yourselves, lest at any time your hearts be overcharged with surfeiting, and drunkenness, and cares of this life..." in Luke 21:34.

It is our praise that keeps us ahead of the "game." Praise recognizes the greatness of God over our problems as well as anything else that robs our attention and affection.

Joy and praise go together. Joy is such a tremendous factor in our war against addictions that the third phase of our transformation listed in *Turning to God from Idols* is rejoicing. The joy of the Lord is your strength (Nehemiah 8:10).

What matters most to a sporting team? They cheer at winning. Joy expresses what matters most to you. They brag about a good record. How about the record that God has? It is most praiseworthy!

You can tell what's important to people by what they brag about. If their kids are most important, they brag about their kids. If their job is the most important thing in their life, they brag about their job. If partying or buying new clothes is what you talk about most, guess what you value most?

You brag about what you value most. God says in Jeremiah 9:23-24, *"The wise should not boast of their wisdom, nor the strong of their strength, nor the rich of their wealth. If any want to boast, they should boast that they know and understand me"* (*GNT*).

While we sometimes talk about boosting the team's morality, joy goes beyond. Joy is based on contentment, satisfaction, and gratitude (neither are found in addiction.) It is your reward as God recognizes the love and reverence that you have for Him though you are enticed by the things of the world. While basketball teams only play full-court press occasionally, God *always* plays full-court press.

For the eyes of the Lord run to and fro throughout the whole earth, to give strong support to those whose heart is blameless toward Him. 2 Chronicles 16:9a

August 27

Home court advantage (part 4)

The earth is the Lord's, and the fulness thereof; the world, and they that dwell therein. Psalms 24:1

We have been looking at the "home court advantage" over addictions through Christ. While we could extend our comments into many more entries, I will conclude with how our home court advantage is based on design. The design of the stadium or arena of a home team can provide an advantage. In Christ, the advantage over addictions is by design.

1. The Designer (Himself, is involved)

2. The place (Psalms 24:1)
(Thy Kingdom come, Thy will be done on earth as it is in heaven.)

3. The Team Captain
Since then we have a great high priest who has passed through the heavens, Jesus, the Son of God, let us hold fast our confession. For we do not have a high priest who is unable to sympathize with our weaknesses, but one who in every respect has been tempted as we are, yet without sin. Hebrew 4:14-15

4. Choice players
... raised us up with him and seated us with him in the heavenly places in Christ Jesus, Ephesians 1:8
Therefore, if anyone is in Christ, he is a new creation. The old has passed away; behold, the new has come. 2 Corinthians 5:17

5. Equipped players
And he gave the apostles, the prophets, the evangelists, the shepherds and teachers, to equip the saints for the work of ministry, for building up the body of Christ, until we all attain to the unity of the faith and of the knowledge of the Son of God, to mature manhood, to the measure of the stature of the fullness of Christ, Ephesians 4:11-13

6. Designed equipment
Blessed be the God and Father of our Lord Jesus Christ, who has blessed us in Christ with every spiritual blessing in the heavenly places. Ephesians 1:3

August 28

Turning to God from Idols (part 1)

> For they themselves shew of us what manner of entering in we had unto you, and how ye turned to God from idols to serve the living and true God. 1 Thessalonians 1:9 *KJV*

The issue of addiction can be very complicated. The reason behind this is that you are dealing with something foreign. *Turning to God from Idols* is designed as a study for exposing and disposing of the idolatry of addictions (any and every addiction.)

Down through the years, I had adopted a phrase that was used by the Apostle Paul in explaining his love and concern for the church of Ephesus. "I kept back nothing that was profitable unto you" (Acts 20:20) was the commitment that Paul made, which I now embrace.

Turning to God from idols most accurately describes the process of reverentially discarding addictions. It is for this reason that I have chosen to address addictions in the most biblical accuracy of idolatry. The title of *Turning to God from Idols* comes from 1 Thessalonians 1:9.

The ultimate alternative to addiction is Jesus. He alone is the link to the true and living God. And although we may be able to achieve some degree of sobriety outside of Christ, the <u>highest</u> form of sobriety known unto mankind is found in Jesus Christ (since He bridges the gap between God and man and gives everlasting peace to all that come to Him.)

Reasoning, repentance, and rejoicing can be found in every program from one degree to another. But the main thing that gives strength to a biblical program is the element of reverence toward God.

The common bond among Christian groups

1. We believe that addictions dishonor God
2. We recognize that addictions are useless
3. We believe that we are all vulnerable to addictions
4. We believe that true life is found in Christ alone
5. We believe that reverencing God is the key to sobriety
6. We believe in striving to please God
7. We believe that God's only answer to addiction is to make us more like Christ

> And he died for all, that those who live might no longer live for themselves but for him who for their sake died and was raised.
> 2 Corinthians 5:15

August 29

Turning to God from idols (part 2)

> For this cause left I thee in Crete, that thou shouldest set in order the things that are wanting, and ordain elders in every city, as I had appointed thee. Titus 1:5 *KJV*

Who would deny that whatever the means we use to address addictions, we are striving to set things in order? It is when we start by labeling addictions as idols that we can set things in the order in the way God wants more than any other method of dealing with addictions. Why do I say that?

When we address addictions as idols it not only gives us a more accurate definition of addictions than other sources, it provides the "reverential factor" that is necessary for our repentance. Nothing determines our character greater than the amount of reverence that we have for God. Revering God defines us and determines every action we make.

Any resource that addresses addictions and does not include the "reverential factor" to a large degree is weak. Do you remember when a lot of people were concerned about being "politically correct?" As we expose and dispose of addictions, we must do so in a manner that is biblically correct to give unto God the glory that is due His name and to establish a formula that would be towards our greatest good.

Idolatry is the most biblically accurate definition of addiction. Idolatry separates us from God. That's why it is so important to bring Christ into the equation from the very start. Only He can bridge the gap between God and man. Without Jesus, we cannot "set things in order."

Setting things in order is what we do in war as well. Who would deny that addictions are a battle? In a battle, we must have the right weapons. A tank will do you little good in a battle that is at sea. A ship will not be of great service while waging war in a desert.

Even more important than the equipment we use to war with is the personnel. Jesus is the greatest Conqueror there is. He has promised that the gates of hell would not prevail against His Kingdom. And if you are a subject of that Kingdom, you have the victory!

The aim of a Christian approach to addictions

a. Bringing people to a saving knowledge of Christ
b. To encourage repentance of all that displeases God
c. To promote the joy and peace that is found in an active relationship with Christ
d. Fellowship with other believers (on various levels)
e. Allowing God to work through us

August 30

Need a hand? (part 1)

> For the Lord your God dried up the waters of the Jordan for you until you passed over, as the Lord your God did to the Red Sea, which he dried up for us until we passed over, so that all the peoples of the earth may know that the hand of the Lord is mighty, that you may fear the Lord your God forever. Joshua 4:23-24

If you are reading this book there is a pretty good chance that you are overwhelmed by an idol that has taken the form of addiction just as Israel and all the other ancient nations were vulnerable to the irreverence of bowing down to other gods. ***One thing that I don't ever want you to forget is that God cares about your struggle with addiction more than you ever will.*** God always gives us a way to escape the temptations that would ensnare us and reap havoc in our lives.

> Now these things took place as examples for us, that we might not desire evil as they did. Do not be idolaters as some of them were; as it is written, "The people sat down to eat and drink and rose up to play." No temptation has overtaken you that is not common to man. God is faithful, and he will not let you be tempted beyond your ability, but with the temptation he will also provide the way of escape, that you may be able to endure it. 1 Corinthians 10:6-7, 13

As I have stated on multiple occasions, there are only four basic reasons that you abstain from addiction. **(Only four, although they sometimes coincide with one another or can be expressed in other words.)**

1. To better your life
2. To avoid the consequences of addiction
3. To better the lives of those around you
4. Out of reverence for God (which includes being in awe of Him)

Joshua 4:23-24 explains how God has blessed you with the gift of reverence to combat anything contrary to what He created you to be and that would distort His image. Joshua emphasizes that God had proved to His people that His hand is mighty so that they would show Him the reverence that He deserves.

How you respond to the hand of the Lord reveals the quality of your reverence. And the quality of your reverence reveals the quality of your sobriety. Your response to the hand of the Lord is found in your attitude as well as your actions. As the hand of the Lord is revealed then you can choose to either submit or rebel.

August 31

Need a hand? (part 2)

> For the Lord your God dried up the waters of the Jordan for you until you passed over, as the Lord your God did to the Red Sea, which he dried up for us until we passed over, so that all the peoples of the earth may know that the hand of the Lord is mighty, that you may fear the Lord your God forever. Joshua 4:23-24

Hardened hearts harbor addiction. I would be the first to admit that it was a hard heart that empowered my commitment to addiction despite the hand of the Lord working to tear me away from it.

It is a thing of beauty when we recognize that the hand of God is at work, we hear it speak to us, we are content with what He does, and we are invited to join Him with the work He has proposed. *Is it not most sane to agree with God?* But, addictions never consent to God. Addiction accuses God of being unfair, unjust, unloving, and evil.

An addicted heart does not realize the power of the hand of the Lord. The addicted heart needs to become convinced of the qualifications of the Most High! *So long as we insist on ruling we irreverently insult God by claiming that we are better qualified to rule than He!*

Perhaps, the questions that God asked Job may prove that we do not have the qualifications to rule. While Job was rightfully dissatisfied with the circumstances of his life, he had many questions. He, like us, needed God to reason with him for sanity to rule rather than confusion. God is not the author of confusion. Satan is!

Whenever we insist on being in command, we are allowing Satan to rule. He has no right to rule and is not qualified either. The 77 questions that God asked Job prove that no one is better qualified to rule than God. Let's look at a few! (references omitted)

> Where were you when I laid the foundation of the earth?
> Have you ever in your life commanded the morning,
> And caused the dawn to know its place,
> That it might take hold of the ends of the earth?
> Have you understood the expanse of the earth?
> Can you lift up your voice to the clouds,
> So that an abundance of water will cover you?
> Do you give the horse his might?
> Is it at your command that the eagle mounts up?
> Will the faultfinder contend with the Almighty?
> Do you have an arm like God,
> And can you thunder with a voice like His?

Sempterber 1

Need a hand? (part 3)

> For the Lord your God dried up the waters of the Jordan for you until you passed over, as the Lord your God did to the Red Sea, which he dried up for us until we passed over, so that all the peoples of the earth may know that the hand of the Lord is mighty, that you may fear the Lord your God forever. Joshua 4:23-24

The glory of God is revealed through His mighty hand. The reason why the hand of the Lord strongly combats addiction is because of the awe that it produces. Certainty lies in the hand of the Lord while addictions only offer doubt and confusion. Joshua 4:23-24 is similar to three other verses that explain reverence as the means of breaking away from all that is displeasing to God.

> Moses said to the people, "Do not fear, for God has come to test you, that the fear of him may be before you, that you may not sin." Exodus 20:20 *KJV*

> Since we have these promises, beloved, let us cleanse ourselves from every defilement of body and spirit, bringing holiness to completion in the fear of God. 2 Corinthians 7:1

> Therefore, my beloved, as you have always obeyed, so now, not only as in my presence but much more in my absence, work out your own salvation with fear and trembling, for it is God who works in you, both to will and to work for his good pleasure. Philippians 2:12-13

One of the by-products of reverential sobriety is contentment. Contentment says that the hand of the Lord is just, fair, and loving. **Addictions begin with discontentment.**

> "My brethren, the reason why you have not got contentment in the things of the world is not because you have not got enough of them- that is not the reason-but the reason is, because they are not things proportionate to that immortal soul of yours that is capable of God himself." *–The Rare Jewel of Christian Contentment*, Jeremiah Burroughs

> "I want to be a part of something that can only be explained by the hand of God!" -David Platt

Sempterber 2

Regression (part 1)

> For the Lord has made the Jordan a boundary between us and you, you people of Reuben and people of Gad. You have no portion in the Lord. So your children might make our children cease to worship the Lord. Joshua 22:25

In this verse, we read of the concern that the nation of Israel had with some of her tribes who had separated themselves from the others. There was a fear that they would influence others into abandoning their reverence for God. This was a serious issue; as addiction is serious. Two issues related to addictions are found in this verse. The first is the influence that we have on others and the second is regression.

No matter who you are, whatever gender, race, color, nationality... you have been created in the image of God. God wants you to represent Him as Christ did. It is God's desire for you to be so loving towards others that they would be able to see the love of Christ better. ***Addictions have no such intention!***

While you haven't been crucified for the sake of others as Christ was for the sins of all mankind, God wants you to be a reflection of Himself. Jesus said to His followers to let their "light so shine among men that others might see your good works and glorify your Father which is in heaven" (Matthew 5:16). When you fail to do this, you dishonor God.

It starts the moment that God is no longer special to you. The Israelites feared that God would no longer be special to their children because of the influence of the tribes who had separated from the rest of the nation. You are responsible for the influence that you have on others.

The Israelites in Joshua 22:25 told the others that their descendants would be a bad influence on their descendants. They said that they would cause their children to do the most horrendous thing (failing to give God the glory that He is due.)

I use to pretend that my drug addiction was not hurting anyone as long as I didn't steal anything, I didn't physically harm anyone, and I disassociated myself from others in a way that there was no risk of causing any emotional pain to them. Over the years, I had to admit that so long as I was living such a self-absorbed life, I was hurting others by depriving them of all that I am blessed to give to them. I had been irreverent toward God by not making use of all that He has given to me for the good of others.

> So then, as we have opportunity, let us do good to everyone, and especially to those who are of the household of faith. Galatians 6:10

Sempterber 3

Regression (part 2)

> For the Lord has made the Jordan a boundary between us and you, you people of Reuben and people of Gad. You have no portion in the Lord. So your children might make our children cease to worship the Lord. Joshua 22:25

On many occasions, I have said that addiction is a matter of national security. Jesus said that during the end times, "because iniquity shall abound, the love of many shall wax cold" (Matthew 24:12 *KJV*). I believe that part of what Jesus said is that as we withhold our love from others, or even show hatred, it creates a cycle. This causes the erosion of civilization.

We all influence others for good or for evil. We are all responsible for the progression or the regression of our society. Is there anything or anyone that can cause *you* to regress? The Apostle Paul demanded progress during his farewell to his friends at Ephesus.

> But ***none of these things move me***; nor do I count my life dear to myself, so that I may finish my race with joy, and the ministry which I received from the Lord Jesus, to testify to the gospel of the grace of God. Acts 20:24 *KJV*

Addictions have the possibility of moving us. They take us to places of regression where God doesn't want us, and eventually, where we don't want to be ourselves. I like the phrase that some of the residents used at a particular program from my years of rehab. One resident would say to another, "I'm not going to let nothing or no one take me off of my square."

Regression for those of us who once succumbed to addiction is better known as relapse. According to *Serenity at Summit,* "The definition of a drug relapse is a downward spiral into compulsive behavior and addiction. This means a drug **relapse does not occur suddenly**. There are warning signs and other identifiable factors that typically appear early on."

After just a few years of addiction, and a few times in treatment, I began to realize that I could see a relapse occur long before it happened. Sometimes, I wasn't even trying to stay true to the Lord. I was just going through the motions. Perhaps, deep inside, I did not mourn over my irreverence for God, I just sorrowed over the consequences of my addiction.

> *Revering God is the ultimate solution to addiction that is not only pleasing to God but provides the the greatest fortification that you can find.*

September 4

Regression (part 3)

For the Lord has made the Jordan a boundary between us and you, you people of Reuben and people of Gad. You have no portion in the Lord. So your children might make our children cease to worship the Lord. Joshua 22:25

The remarkable thing about Joshua 22:25 was that some were so concerned about the glory of God that they recognized what was happening. That's why it is always best to rely on the advice of God-fearing people.

Addictions can get your attention. I once read that temptations are like unwanted noise. Just as Jesus was able to silence the noise of those who would oppose His purposes while He was on earth, He can silence the noise that would oppose the purposes that He has for your life!

For those who live according to the flesh set their minds on the things of the flesh, but those who live according to the Spirit set their minds on the things of the Spirit. For to set the mind on the flesh is death, but to set the mind on the Spirit is life and peace. Romans 8:5-6

Now all has been heard; here is the conclusion of the matter: Fear God and keep His commandments, **for this is the whole duty of man**. Ecclesiastes 12:13 *NIV*

Any city, person, family, or nation that is not in awe of God is dysfunctional. Because Solomon knew a lot about life, he knew that we cannot do without the fear of the Lord. Where there is no reverence for God, there is but calamity, confusion, and disorder.

Irreverence for God is devoid of the blessing of God. Where there is no reverence for God there is no wisdom, because wisdom *comes from God.* Irreverence leaves us vulnerable to the deception of addictions because in rejecting God we reject the truth.

Paul Tripp said that our deficiency of awe towards God "lies at the core of all the horrible choices, family dysfunction, violence, idolatry, jealousy, greed, immorality, foolishness, materialism, power hunger, discontentment, and self-centeredness in our world." <u>Entire nations have been destroyed because of their irreverence for God.</u>

"God is the Ultimate Reality. Any evaluation of a situation that leaves Him out of the picture is going to result in wrong conclusions because not all the facts are being considered." –Jim Berg

Sempterber 5

Are you satisfied? (part 1)

> Now therefore fear the Lord and serve him in sincerity and in faithfulness. Put away the gods that your fathers served beyond the River and in Egypt, and serve the Lord. And if it is evil in your eyes to serve the Lord, choose this day whom you will serve, whether the gods your fathers served in the region beyond the River, or the gods of the Amorites in whose land you dwell. But as for me and my house, we will serve the Lord. Joshua 24:14-15

Joshua 24:14-15 speaks volumes concerning addictions. The question that Joshua poses is as old as the *Garden of Eden* and as relative as your next breath. Throughout the ages, two basic questions have challenged humanity. The first question is where to find contentment. The second question is why we should revere God.

At the heart of every addiction lies discontent!

In *Yearning Over Addictions*, I explained the difference between healthy yearning and unhealthy yearning. One of the attributes of unhealthy yearnings, such as addiction, is that it is never satisfied.

The first thing that I ask someone who is seeking sobriety is why they want to overcome their addiction. The second question that I ask is for them to tell me why God is worthy of their life. Joshua gave Israel some good reasons to choose God over the idols of the land (Joshua 24:3-13).

> God led your Father Abraham
> He made Abraham many offspring
> God put Jacob and His children in Egypt
> God sent Moses and Aaron
> God plagued Egypt
> God brought you out of Egypt
> God made the sea cover the Egyptians
> God brought you to the land
> God gave your enemies into your hand
> God destroyed your enemies
> God delivered you out of the hand of Balak
> God gave Jericho, the Amorites, Perizzites, Canaanites, Hittites, Girgashites, Hivites, and Jebusites into your hand.
> God gave you land on which you have not labored
> God gave you cities to dwell in that you did not build
> God gave you fruit and olives to eat that you did not plant

September 6

Are you satisfied? (part 2)

Now therefore fear the Lord and serve him in sincerity and in faithfulness. Put away the gods that your fathers served beyond the River and in Egypt, and serve the Lord. And if it is evil in your eyes to serve the Lord, choose this day whom you will serve, whether the gods your fathers served in the region beyond the River, or the gods of the Amorites in whose land you dwell. But as for me and my house, we will serve the Lord. Joshua 24:14-15

Though I often frown on people focusing on the gifts more than on the giver, I cannot deny that there is *some* value in acknowledging the blessings of God and showing reverence towards Him because of His blessings. Yet, I never want anyone to forget that the first reason that God deserves reverence is because of who He is.

Abstinence that is only motivated by the blessings of God is irreverent. Only your abstinence that is borne with a hunger for God is sound and sober.

"If God gave you not only earth but heaven, that you should rule over sun, moon, and stars, and have the rule over the highest of the sons of men, it would not be enough to satisfy you, unless you had God himself. There lies the first mystery of contentment. And truly a contented man, though he is the most contented man in the world, is the most dissatisfied man in the world, that is, those things that will satisfy the world will not satisfy him." –*The Rare Jewel of Christian Contentment*, Jeremiah Burroughs

"One of the most basic reasons for honoring and reverencing God is simply because He is worthy. All other reasons for reverencing God are secondary. God is worthy of our reverence because of His many attributes (who He is) and because of His glorious acts (what He does.) Though there are many other reasons that we should give reverence to God, if we fail to realize that He is, by nature, worthy of reverence, then our reverence of God is incomplete and unacceptable before God." –*The Fear of the Almighty*, Gregory Madison

The satisfaction that the Israelites found in the Lord would be expressed in sincerity and faithfulness. Sincerity and faithfulness are essential for continual reverence (bringing long-term sobriety.) If the Israelites were not truly satisfied, they would not be sincere or faithful no more than you.

Sempterber 7

Harden not your heart! (part 1)

> If you will fear the Lord and serve him and obey his voice and not rebel against the commandment of the Lord, and if both you and the king who reigns over you will follow the Lord your God, it will be well. But if you will not obey the voice of the Lord, but rebel against the commandment of the Lord, then the hand of the Lord will be against you and your king. 1 Samuel 12:14-15

Once again, we encounter the hand of the Lord. The hand of the Lord may be for you or against you. We saw in Joshua 4:23-24 how the hand of the Lord worked on behalf of the Israelites and how it worked against Saul in 1 Samuel 2:30. Although many other passages explain how God is either for us or against us, there is one that may explain it best.

> And as the Lord took delight in doing you good and multiplying you, so the Lord will take delight in bringing ruin upon you and destroying you. Deuteronomy 28:63a

Why was this promise of judgment made to Israel? The answer is found in the second half of the previous verse. *"Because you did not obey the voice of the Lord your God"* (Deuteronomy 28:62b). The voice of the Lord is mentioned 27 times in the book of Deuteronomy.

The book of Deuteronomy is an account of the transition made by Israel to become an established nation. God wants to establish you as well. A transition can be sobering. The voice of the Lord is even more sobering. ***The voice of the Lord is more powerful than we could ever imagine.*** Direction from God is a necessity for every transition.

Did you know that addiction is rebellion against God? Why do I say that? Does not God give us signs and warnings against addiction? This is the voice of the Lord! ***Insanity may be defined as a weak and futile attempt to stifle the voice of God.*** Insanity will not be reasoned with. Insanity makes its own reality while rebelling against the truth.

> Be sober-minded; be watchful. Your adversary the devil prowls around like a roaring lion, seeking someone to devour. Resist him, firm in your faith, knowing that the same kinds of suffering are being experienced by your brotherhood throughout the world. And after you have suffered a little while, the God of all grace, who has called you to his eternal glory in Christ, will himself restore, confirm, strengthen, and establish you. To him be the dominion forever and ever. Amen.
> 1 Peter 5:8-11

September 8

Harden not your heart! (part 2)

> If you will fear the Lord and serve him and obey his voice and not rebel against the commandment of the Lord, and if both you and the king who reigns over you will follow the Lord your God, it will be well. But if you will not obey the voice of the Lord, but rebel against the commandment of the Lord, then the hand of the Lord will be against you and your king. 1 Samuel 12:14-15

The foundation of my sobriety began by confessing that I had rebelled against God and turned to idols. *Idolatry and the Hardening of the Heart* by Edward Meadors is a book that God used to show me how rebellious I had been. Where does rebellion originate?

> **Do not harden your hearts as in the rebellion**, on the day of testing in the wilderness, where your fathers put me to the test and saw my works for forty years. Therefore I was provoked with that generation, and said, "**They always go astray in their heart**; they have not known my ways." As I swore in my wrath, "They shall not enter my rest." Hebrews 3:8-11

Only brokenness can defeat the idols of our hearts. I have heard that the greeting in one Christian community is for one to ask the other if they are still broken. Brokenness prevents us from hardening our hearts. Brokeness and humility go hand in hand. Pride is the opposite of humility. At the center of a hard heart is pride. Pride is irreverent.

Jesus' closing in the Sermon on the Mount is similar to 1 Samuel 12:14-15. It is interesting how Jesus distinguishes the wise from the foolish by their response to His Word. The voice of the Lord sounds so strongly from Jesus that He is called "the Word of God" (Revelation 19:13). Proverbs 9:10 says that "the fear of the Lord is the beginning of wisdom."

> Everyone then who hears these words of mine and does them will be like a wise man who built his house on the rock. And the rain fell, and the floods came, and the winds blew and beat on that house, but it did not fall, because it had been founded on the rock. And everyone who hears these words of mine and does not do them will be like a foolish man who built his house on the sand. And the rain fell, and the floods came, and the winds blew and beat against that house, and it fell, and great was the fall of it. Matthew 7:24-27

> Blessed is the man who always fears the LORD, but he who hardens his heart falls into trouble. Proverbs 28:1

Sempterber 9

Overwhelmed (part 1)

So Samuel called upon the Lord, and the Lord sent thunder and rain that day, and all the people **greatly** feared the Lord and Samuel.
1 Samuel 12:18 *NIV*

In the council of the holy ones God is **greatly** feared; He is more awesome than all who surround Him. Psalms. 89:7 *NIV*

And Ahab called Obadiah, who was over the household. (Now Obadiah feared the Lord **greatly**, and when Jezebel cut off the prophets of the Lord, Obadiah took a hundred prophets and hid them by fifties in a cave and fed them with bread and water.)
1 Kings18:3-4 *KJV*

If you are ever to overcome your addictions then God must be far greater than you ever imagined! In his series on fearing God, Dr. Tony Evans says that "a great God deserves great respect and a little God receives little honor and respect." Evans says that "if God is not all that great to us, then He will not get much reverence."

If you are ever to overcome your addictions then God must be revered so strongly that you yearn for Him more than anything else. That includes the addictions that cause you displeasure and are socially acceptable as well as the ones that both you and society disdain. Yearning after God conquers every addiction imaginable.

Yearning can be either good or evil. Yearning also goes by the name of lust. **Lust motivates, stimulates, either corrupts or preserves, inspires, dominates (or at least influences) our actions with passion, purpose, and awe, surpassing logic, and reason at times, and leads us from one place to the next physically, and mentally, emotionally, and spiritually.**

Whatever satisfies us, we call great! In their greatness, we become overwhelmed by addictions! How great are addictions? As great as you make them! At what point do we turn to addiction while seeking satisfaction? Is this not based on our *dissatisfaction*? And why are we not satisfied? Is there any way for our dissatisfaction to be resolved apart from addiction?

Why do you spend your money for that which is not bread, and your labor for that which does not satisfy. Listen diligently to me, and eat what is good, and delight yourselves in rich food. Isaiah 55:2

"I know of no other way to triumph over sin long-term than to gain a distaste for it because of a superior satisfaction in God."
–John Piper

September 10

Overwhelmed (part 2)

So Samuel called upon the Lord, and the Lord sent thunder and rain that day, and all the people **greatly** feared the Lord and Samuel.
1 Samuel 12:18 *NIV*

In the council of the holy ones God is **greatly** feared; He is more awesome than all who surround Him. Psalms. 89:7 *NIV*

And Ahab called Obadiah, who was over the household. (Now Obadiah feared the Lord **greatly**, and when Jezebel cut off the prophets of the Lord, Obadiah took a hundred prophets and hid them by fifties in a cave and fed them with bread and water.)
1 Kings18:3-4 *KJV*

What does our dissatisfaction say about our relationship with God? Dissatisfaction could stem from discontentment which may originate from a lack of gratitude in addition to poor communication with God. We may not be aware of the means that God has to resolve the issues that we try to solve with addiction.

Reverential sobriety means that you see things the way that God does. Quality sobriety exposes addictions as the idols that they are. Quality sobriety sees the greatness of God and His care for us. The struggle that we face is what Hebrews 3:13 calls "the deceitfulness of sin." Several days ago, I commented on hard hearts. Hebrews 3:13 says that the deceitfulness of sin produces a hard heart.

We often use the word captivated or mesmerized to describe what draws our interests, earns our trust, preoccupies our thoughts, and provokes our praises. We are overwhelmed by much! They get our attention!

God longs to have our attention. 1 Corinthians 10:11 says that "these things happened to them as an example, but they were written down for our instruction, on whom the end of the ages has come."

Call unto me, and I will answer thee, and **show thee great and mighty things, which thou knowest not**. Jeremiah 33:3 *KJV*

"What is an idol? It is anything more important to you than God, anything that absorbs your heart and imagination more than God. Anything you seek to give you what only God can give."
-*Counterfeit gods*, Tim Keller

Sempterber 11

Overwhelmed (part 3)

> They took the bull that was given them, and they prepared it and called upon the name of Baal from morning until noon, saying, "O Baal, answer us!" But there was no voice, and no one answered. And they limped around the altar that they had made. ... And they cried aloud and cut themselves after their custom with swords and lances until the blood gushed out upon them. And as midday passed, they raved on until the time of the offering of the oblation, but there was no voice. No one answered; no one paid attention. 1 Kings 18:26, 28-29 *NIV*

Today, there are those of us who chase after a false and lifeless god called addiction. After 10 years clean and sober, I can still recall shouting for my addiction, just as these Baal worshippers. Though I never slashed myself physically, I injured myself spiritually, emotionally, and mentally in many ways in the name of my addictions. And, just like the Baal worshippers I engaged in frantic behavior (an understatement.)

As we are created in the image of God, God wants to fellowship with us. To deny Him of fellowship is irreverent. Not only is idolatry irreverent towards God, but it also robs your fellow man of what you would be able to give to him as a result of the relationship that you would have with a God who wants to use you for His glory just as He was glorified in Christ.

I remember once being led by God to help a homeless man who had no shoes. After convincing him not to commit suicide and allowing him to stay with me for several days, I took him to a shelter to get help with his drug addiction. When I visited him at the shelter, he told me that he was reading about me during his devotion. I was overjoyed when he said that Jesus going about doing good reminded him of me.

> How God anointed Jesus of Nazareth with the Holy Spirit and with power. He went about doing good and healing all who were oppressed by the devil, for God was with him. Acts 10:38

The glory and greatness of God are seen most vividly in the face of Jesus Christ. My greatest joy is found in the glory of God!

> "Imagine having drug cravings subdued by the joy of knowing and obeying Christ. Imagine having temptations lose their allure because there is more pleasure in walking humbly with our God. Imagine waking up and strategizing how to please the God who loves you rather than where you will get your next drink."
> -*Addictions: A Banquet in the Grave,* Edward T. Welch

September 12

Consider! (part 1)

Only fear the Lord and serve him faithfully with all your heart. For consider what great things he has done for you. 1 Samuel 12:24

Consideration and reason go hand in hand. Reasoning is the first step to change. Reverence for God involves reasoning *and* consideration. Consideration is also a part of maturity. *Dictionary.com* says that to consider is "to think carefully about (something), typically before making a decision." It is a known fact that when someone is insane, they cannot be reasoned with.

There is also something about considering that makes us human. For instance, as human beings, we take great care in preparing food. We season it with *consideration* to our liking. We *consider* the flavors. Animals don't go around with salt and pepper shakers. Addictions make us like animals.

I can remember there were times in my addiction when God would bring Psalms 32:8 to my memory. It tells us not to be "like the horse or the mule which have no understanding." God was saying to me, "you're better than that!" Through the power of God, we don't have to be compulsive. Consideration provides restrain. But for us to possess restrain, we must have vision.

> Where there is no vision the people perish: but he that keepeth the law, happy is he. Proverbs 29:18 *KJV*

> Where there is no revelation, people cast off restraint; but blessed is the one who heeds wisdom's instruction. *NIV*

While scientists have been trying to discover the answers to addiction through physiology, I can tell you that one of the leading causes of addiction is impaired vision. Poor vision leads to poor judgment. And poor judgment leads to doing things that are not pleasing to God. The wisdom that is found through consideration prevents us from rash behavior.

What's in your head is what determines how you respond to the things that the world offers and whether you will succumb to an addiction. Years ago, in a class, I was *extremely* impressed with the fact that Jesus was more human than anyone who had ever lived.

Reverencing God makes us human. Addictions are not human. In many cases, addictions exhibit cruel, barbaric, savage, and selfish behavior. That's not what God had in mind when He created man in His image. Through Jesus, we can be human as well.

September 13

Consider! (part 2)

> Only fear the Lord and serve him faithfully with all your heart. For consider what great things he has done for you. 1 Samuel 12:24

We must rely on the blood of Christ for the forgiveness of our sins, deny ourselves, and rely on the power of Christ to change us into who God wants us to be every day. When we deny ourselves, we consider. When we consider, we humble ourselves.

Sobriety, abstinence, sanctification, transformation, or recovery (whatever word you want to use) is fueled by humility. Consideration can humble us and put us in our right minds. One of my favorite quotes is that "genius has its limits, but stupidity knows no bounds."

God is the only one whose genius is not limited. I would be the first to admit that sometimes I look at God as either crazy or stupid. Isaiah 40 was written to draw Israel to her senses, which can do the same for us.

> Lift up your eyes on high and see: who created these? He who brings out their host by number, calling them all by name; by the greatness of his might and because he is strong in power, not one is missing. Why do you say, O Jacob, and speak, O Israel, "My way is hidden from the Lord, and my right is disregarded by my God"? Have you not known? Have you not heard? The Lord is the everlasting God, the Creator of the ends of the earth. He does not faint or grow weary; his understanding is unsearchable. Isaiah 40:26-28

Among the concerns of those who are seeking a life of sobriety is consistency. When you consider, you become consistent. Understanding becomes the result of consistent consideration that is guided by God since His understanding is beyond yours.

I once confronted a man about his obsessive drinking by asking him if it was what God wanted his life to be. When he said that there is no God, I said to him, "You'd like to think that there is no God so that you can do as you please."

> Now, therefore, thus says the Lord of hosts: **Consider your ways**. You have sown much, and harvested little. You eat, but you never have enough; you drink, but you never have your fill. You clothe yourselves, but no one is warm. And he who earns wages does so to put them into a bag with holes. Haggai 1:5-6

September 14

Pleasing God (part 1)

> And David was afraid of the Lord that day, and he said, "How can the ark of the Lord come to me?" 2 Samuel 6:9

Second Samuel chapter six reveals how God angrily responds to something that He is displeased with. Uzzah was struck down "because of His error" of not doing things the way that God had commanded long before (v.7).

Did God have the right to strike Uzzah down? Does God have the right to be angry? Addictions accuse God of being unfair. Addictions seek another god.

This is how you are susceptible to relapse. If you have the wrong idea about God or insist on doing things your way then you create a god in your mind and spirit that will go along with whatever you want. Then your desire is not to please God, but to please yourself.

Verse eight says that David was angry because "the Lord had broken out against Uzzah." The situation must have been as shocking to David as some of the situations that we encountered.

Please note: The Scriptures do not say that David was angry with God; it merely states that "David was angry because the Lord had broken out against Uzzah." David may have been angry with himself or with Uzzah. But, if you dig below the surface of any addiction you will discover anger toward God in one form or another

> "Here's the reality: most people who are angry with God are angry with Him for being God. They're not angry because He has failed to deliver what He promised. They're angry because He has failed to deliver what they have craved, expected, or demanded. When awe of self replaces awe of God, God ceases to be your Lord and is reduced to being your indentured servant." -Paul Tripp

While it is tempting to get bogged down with the questions of whether we should be afraid of God or if is it right to be angry with God, the more important issue concerns pleasing God. ***The most important question for someone who is seeking a life of sobriety is to ask themselves whether they want it for themselves or God.*** Tomorrow, I will explain where the two intersect but we must first be concerned with pleasing God.

> And he died for all, that those who live might no longer live for themselves but for him who for their sake died and was raised.
> 2 Corinthians 5:15

Sempterber 15

Pleasing God (part 2)

And David was afraid of the Lord that day, and he said, "How can the ark of the Lord come to me?" 2 Samuel 6:9

Striving to please God goes beyond being abstinent from addiction. Improper motives are all centered upon the person. Improper motives could be based on trying to gain a good reputation, earn wealth, get the family back, please the boss, etc. These *lesser* motives may appear to be okay (on the surface), but let us not be deceived; they are self-centered motives just the same. Here is where people run the risk of either returning to the same addiction or running to a different one.

If your sobriety is not based on the principles of God, then you are living by your *own* standards. You determine what's right and what's wrong. Who's to say that you might not change your mind about whether it's right to drink or do drugs or view pornography? What's to keep you from doing *other* things that are not in your best interest or the interest of others (as well as displeasing to God.)

> "The concern that you have for yourself can reflect your love for God in many ways. God does not want you to abandon yourself to an addiction that makes empty promises on resolving issues that He has the solution to. God does not want to see you or others hurt by addiction. God does not want your fellowship with Him to be broken over addiction. God does not want you to miss opportunities that addictions destroy. So, while caring about yourself, you could at the same time care about God. **Self-concern can either be honoring to God or just selfish.**" –*Why Not Get High,* Gregory Madison

John Piper said that "God is most glorified in us when we are most satisfied in Him." I would be the first to admit that this does not come overnight, after 40 years of knowing Christ, with 23 of those years intermittently indulging in addictions, and 12 years clean and sober at the time of this writing. Hebrews 11:6 says that "without faith, it is impossible to please Him." The question is whether you will have faith in God in whatever situation you encounter.

> "It should be a shame for a Christian to say that he has skill in any other affliction but this. A Christian should be able to manage his ship, if the wind blows any way; to guide his soul any way."
> -*The Rare Jewel of Christian Contentment,* Jeremiah Burroughs

September 16

An intimate conversation with God (part 1)

Then hear in heaven your dwelling place and forgive and act and render to each whose heart you know, according to all his ways (for you, you only, know the hearts of all the children of mankind), that they may fear you all the days that they live in the land that you gave to our fathers. 1 Kings 8:39-40

Communication involves a conversation between two or more. Solomon is asking God to hear them according to what they say. *Much of what we say to God is spoken by what we do. God not only hears what we say, more importantly, He also hears what we do.*

Quality sobriety is synonymous with an intimate conversation with God.

I like the way actions are expressed in the *King James Version* with the use of the word "conversation" in various passages that refer to one's life or actions. As you do what God says *with the right kind of attitude*, it is a practice of worship (as you are telling God that He is worthy of your obedience.) This is what others see and hear as well. And when you don't do as He says, or do it with a poor attitude, you are telling Him, as well as others, that He is not worthy.

No one knows you like God. I remember being angry with my dad once because he said that he knew me better than I knew myself. He was probably right at that time. Though we hate to admit it, someone can know us better than we know ourselves. This is always true of God.

This is probably why some don't want God to be fully involved with their abstinence (if at all!) It allows reservations. It allows us to limit God. Just as sobriety has levels and degrees, there are degrees and levels of reverence.

Reservations indicate a lack of reverence.

Reservations take on different forms. Some have a problem with letting go of their addiction while others have a problem with letting go of things that are associated with their addiction. You must make a clean break from addiction <u>without any reservations</u>.

As long as it is being indulged, indwelling sin will expand its operation in the soul, taking over more areas of life and increasing its control and bondage. If you don't deal with everything that you know to be offensive to God then you will not hear His voice so well.

Sempterber 17

An intimate conversation with God (part 2)

> Then hear in heaven your dwelling place and forgive and act and render to each whose heart you know, according to all his ways (for you, you only, know the hearts of all the children of mankind), that they may fear you all the days that they live in the land that you gave to our fathers. 1 Kings 8:39-40

Whenever you don't hear God you become vulnerable to drifting from the safety that He affords. If you continue to engage in a certain behavior (outside of your *primary* addiction), it may eventually lead you back. I know that it won't be easy for people to give up all their addictions at once, but it's biblical and the Scriptures tell us that with God all things are possible.

> "We must run from temptation, but we must also run toward godliness. What are you running toward? If it isn't Christ, you will likely only replace one sinful habit with a different one." -*Addictive Habits,* David R. Dunham

What is your conversation with God like? How important is it? Is it pleasant or disturbing? Do you have an ongoing conversation with God or a sporadic one? Can an intimate conversation with God keep you from addiction? Jesus tells of the value of a healthy, ongoing conversation with the Father.

> I am the true vine, and my Father is the vinedresser. Every branch in me that does not bear fruit he takes away, and every branch that does bear fruit he prunes, that it may bear more fruit. Already you are clean because of the word that I have spoken to you. Abide in me, and I in you. As the branch cannot bear fruit by itself, unless it abides in the vine, neither can you, unless you abide in me. I am the vine; you are the branches. Whoever abides in me and I in him, he it is that bears much fruit, for apart from me you can do nothing. If anyone does not abide in me he is thrown away like a branch and withers; and the branches are gathered, thrown into the fire, and burned. If you abide in me, and my words abide in you, ask whatever you wish, and it will be done for you. By this my Father is glorified, that you bear much fruit and so prove to be my disciples. John 15:1-8

Abiding in Christ requires the mind of Christ. An intimate, conversation with God begins with the mind of Christ that gives us the highest degree of sobriety ever.

September 18

Development

And as soon as I have gone from you, the Spirit of the Lord will carry you I know not where. And so, when I come and tell Ahab and he cannot find you, he will kill me, although I your servant have feared the Lord from my youth. 1 Kings 18:12

As I was in the process of writing *Quality Sobriety Volume Two*, I commemorated 40 years of professing Christ as my Savior. I also commemorated 10 years of sobriety. Though I grew up in a Christian home and accepted Christ as my Savior when I was nineteen years old, unfortunately, I don't have the testimony that Obadiah did.

Since learning the game of chess when I was about twelve years old, I have picked up a few points over the years. I remember someone explaining to me the importance of development in a chess game. He said that if you don't get your pieces in play, it's like paying someone to work while they just sit around doing nothing. As a valuable instrument of God, Obadiah was developed by God.

We see the same thing with David as he grew and maintained his faith in God through all his experiences. Just as one chess piece is prepared to face the opposition as it is developed, God prepares you for the opposition. Before facing Goliath, David testified how God had prepared him for the moment that he would become a giant slayer.

> But David said to Saul, "Your servant used to keep sheep for his father. And when there came a lion, or a bear, and took a lamb from the flock, I went after him and struck him and delivered it out of his mouth. And if he arose against me, I caught him by his beard and struck him and killed him. Your servant has struck down both lions and bears, and this uncircumcised Philistine shall be like one of them, for he has defied the armies of the living God." 1 Samuel 17:34-36

Training is another way of expressing the development that God uses to make us the people that He wants us to be. Training and development are necessary for maturity.

Development and training lead to **productivity**. For years I have desired to write a book called *The Third World of the United States of America*. Third-world countries are underdeveloped. Years ago, as I was deeply involved with drugs, I noticed how underdeveloped drug-infested neighborhoods are (as well as those of us who use drugs.) Drug-infested neighborhoods can be barbaric and uncivilized.

September 19

Irreverence: inevitably dangerous (part 1)

And at the beginning of their dwelling there, they did not fear the Lord. Therefore the Lord sent lions among them, which killed some of them. 2 Kings 17:25

"Love is beautiful, but it is also terrible—terrible in its determination to allow nothing blemished or unworthy to remain in the beloved."
Hannah Hurnard

According to *biblestudyministry.com,* "2 Kings chapter 17 begins with the introduction of what would become the last king of Israel (in Samaria). His name was Hoshea. He was ruling when the king of Assyria invaded his land and forced taxes and servitude on Hoshea. Hoshea complied (with Shalmaneser, king of Assyria) for a while, then he rebelled. When he rebelled, he was arrested, and with him removed from daily administerial power, the Assyrian king invaded Israel again."

Biblestudyministry.com goes on to say that "three years later, Shalmaneser took Israel down and took the citizens into captivity to Assyria. The chapter then spun into a brief lamentation and narration of how stubborn the children of Israel were." Though much of the text reveals the judgment of God, I hope that you may see His mercy, love, and wisdom. Your sobriety depends on seeing God as He is!

"In God you come up against something which is in every respect immeasurably superior to yourself. Unless you know God as that-and, therefore, know yourself as nothing in comparison-you do not know God at all." – C. S. Lewis

In *Turning to God from Idols*, I stressed how relevant idolatry is to addiction. If we fail to categorize addictions as idols we show contempt for the judgment of God as well as His love, mercy, and power! ***To dismiss the idea of idolatry from the discussion of addictions gives us an incomplete picture of the most perplexing issue that man has faced.***

"Idolatry is huge in the Bible, dominant in our personal lives, and irrelevant in our mistaken estimations." –Os Guinness

"Two Jewish philosophers who knew the Scriptures intimately concluded: 'The central ... principle of the Bible [is] the rejection of idolatry.' The Bible is therefore filled with story after story depicting the innumerable forms and devastating effects of idol worship." -*Counterfeit gods*, Tim Keller

September 20

Irreverence: inevitably dangerous (part 2)

> And at the beginning of their dwelling there, they did not fear the Lord. Therefore the Lord sent lions among them, which killed some of them. 2 Kings 17:25

The characters in 2 Kings 17 were far removed from their homeland, just as we are far removed from what God created us to be when we practice addiction. Sometimes God allows things to happen to us as with the characters in 2 Kings 17 who got killed by lions to bring us to our senses.

> "God loves you just the way you are, but He refuses to leave you that way. He wants you to be just like Jesus." -Max Lucado

At other times God issues death when people fail to give Him glory for the sake of a community. Those who refuse to give God glory may cause their community to deteriorate. An example is found in Acts 5. This is not a subject that I have ever heard discussed relating to addictions. If we do not discuss all the issues that are involved in addictions then we do not gain the level of sobriety that God wants us to reach!

> But a man named Ananias, with his wife Sapphira, sold a piece of property, and with his wife's knowledge he kept back for himself some of the proceeds and brought only a part of it and laid it at the apostles' feet. But Peter said, "Ananias, why has Satan filled your heart to lie to the Holy Spirit and to keep back for yourself part of the proceeds of the land? While it remained unsold, did it not remain your own? And after it was sold, was it not at your disposal? Why is it that you have contrived this deed in your heart? You have not lied to man but to God." When Ananias heard these words, he fell down and breathed his last. And great fear came upon all who heard of it. The young men rose and wrapped him up and carried him out and buried him. After an interval of about three hours his wife came in, not knowing what had happened. And Peter said to her, "Tell me whether you sold the land for so much." And she said, "Yes, for so much. "But Peter said to her, "How is it that you have agreed together to test the Spirit of the Lord? Behold, the feet of those who have buried your husband are at the door, and they will carry you out." Immediately she fell down at his feet and breathed her last. When the young men came in they found her dead, and they carried her out and buried her beside her husband. Acts 5:1-10

Sempterber 21

Irreverence: inevitably dangerous (part 3)

> So one of the priests whom they had carried away from Samaria came and lived in Bethel and taught them how they should fear the Lord. 2 Kings 17:28

Yesterday, we discovered how God sent lions to kill a community of Samaritans because they failed to revere Him. They knew that the lions were the consequence of their disregard for God. Unfortunately, many who suffer the consequences of addiction do not associate them with God's displeasure.

If you ask the average person whether they fear God they will most likely tell you that they do. But the question is, "What kind of reverence are we talking about?" Tony Evans says, that there is what could be called a "general" reverence for God and then there is a "specific, intimate" reverence for God.

As I have stated before, the quality of our sobriety is determined by the quality of reverence we possess. Anyone may possess a general reverence for God. Only those who are born again and maintain an active relationship with Christ are given a specific, intimate reverence for God.

A general reverence may only be one of fear and superstition. A general reverence may be one that merely possesses a fondness for the goodness that is expressed in the principles of faith in God without a *commitment* to faith.

And so, there was a priest sent to teach the people how to fear the Lord. Do you think that they would have wanted to know how to fear the Lord if they had not suffered consequences for their idolatry?

How often do we turn from addictions when there are no consequences? In most cases, we don't! As the Samaritans were given a moment of sanity, we have the same opportunity for repentance in our afflictions that are the result of our love for addiction.

> It is good for me that I was afflicted, that I might learn your statutes. Psalms 119:71

The text also reveals how the fear of the Lord is something that is taught. Reverence for God is not something that we are born with nor is it manufactured through human efforts. Reverencing God, though often taught by others, is a supernatural phenomenon that is produced by the Holy Spirit of God. Left unto ourselves we will never give God reverence. Romans 3:18 speaks of all mankind by stating that "there is no fear of God before their eyes."

September 22

Irreverence: inevitably dangerous (part 4)

> They also feared the Lord and appointed from among themselves all sorts of people as priests of the high places, who sacrificed for them in the shrines of the high places. So they feared the Lord but also served their own gods, after the manner of the nations from among whom they had been carried away. 2 Kings 17:32-33

The people began to *willfully* progress in their estrangement from God. They appointed their own priests rather than the ones that God had ordained. It's no different than the trend of seeking help from someone who knows nothing of the true origin of addictions as described by God.

Suppose you had a vacuum cleaner that didn't work! Would you take it to a florist? Most likely not! Addiction is, first and foremost, a spiritual issue. Is there anyone more spiritual than Jesus and those who associate with Him?

Who is more spiritual than a god-fearing person that is well acquainted with the Word of God? The Word of God is better qualified to dispel addictions than any human device. (Both the written Word and the living Word, Christ)

Idols are substitute gods. We are not strangers to making substitutions. It can be said that **addictions are nothing more than substitutions for what we really want**. The priests that the Samaritans appointed, the gods that they served, and the idols of addiction were counterfeit. Anything counterfeit is made in exact imitation of something valuable or important with the intention to deceive or defraud.

> Beloved, do not believe every spirit, but test the spirits to see whether they are from God, for many false prophets have gone out into the world. 1 John 4:1

I have heard it said that behind every false teaching is a false teacher and an evil spirit that all go against God. Imagination is supported by images. Before you indulge in addiction, you behold an image in your mind of what you want from the addiction. I don't need to tell you how addiction never delivers what is promised.

Inventions come from our imaginations. It is a tremendous blessing that we are capable of inventing. An invention is something that is man-made. The problem is that our inventions do not always honor God. The idolatry of ancient Israel was called an invention (among other things.)

Addiction takes a lot of imagination!

September 23

Irreverence: inevitably dangerous (part 5)

And God saw that the wickedness of man was great in the earth, and that **every imagination of the thoughts of his heart was only evil continually.** Genesis 6:5

I imagined that crack was greater than God! I imagined that crack was worth sacrificing my health, wealth, relationships, risking my life and so much more. I imagined that crack was under my command! If you are anything like me, you have no problem imagining. Early in history, we see how Man's imagination was a problem.

But that doesn't mean that our imaginations are bad! God can use our imaginations to produce things that are worthy of His glory. Remember, God created imaginations as well as everything else! But Satan will pervert our imaginations if we do not submit to God. It has been said that "if your God lets you do whatever you want to do … then your god is really you!"

Yesterday, I referred to those who invent methods for handling addiction outside of the Word of God. It can be called an invention. It can be a subtle form of idolatry. The definitions from *Strong's Bible Dictionary* for the Hebrew words translated as "invention" are amazing!

"A plan, counsel, craftiness, the devising of snares, malice, plot, purpose, practices, actions, work, evil deeds, thought, intents, of the deeds of men (especially in a bad sense), wantonness, wicked device, mischievous device, and a warlike machine."

Thus they provoked him to anger with their inventions: and the plague brake in upon them. Psalms 106:29 *KJV*

Thus were they defiled with their own works, and went a whoring with their own inventions. Psalms 106:39 *KJV*

Lo, this only have I found, that God hath made man upright; but they have sought out many inventions. Ecclesiastes 7:29 *KJV*

Behold, I know your thoughts, and the devices which ye wrongfully imagine against me. Job 21:27 *KJV*

The wicked, through the pride of his countenance, will not seek after God: God is not in all his thoughts. Psalms 10:4 *KJV*

September 24

Irreverence: inevitably dangerous (part 6)

The Lord made a covenant with them and commanded them, "You shall not fear other gods or bow yourselves to them or serve them or sacrifice to them, but you shall fear the Lord, who brought you out of the land of Egypt with great power and with an outstretched arm. You shall bow yourselves to him, and to him you shall sacrifice." 2 Kings 17:35-36

Addiction is predetermined!
All worship is!

A covenant with God predetermines your response to everything that you encounter. I remember watching a sitcom where the main character formed a bond with three other young men and became a group. His covenant was tested when they agreed to go to a wrestling match, but the main character's girlfriend wanted to be alone with him.

Was it too much for the girl to ask for some quality time with the boy? Suppose they were married? Would that make matters different? After all, marriage is a deep covenant. Marriage is a sobering proposition. On the day that I got married, I had a brother explain to me that the covenant of marriage is only second to the covenant that we take with God.

The Bible compares the covenant that God makes with His people to marriage. Marriage requires that we think highly of someone. The predominant factor of a covenant with God is that we think of Him more highly than anything else. The dangers of being unfaithful to God are astronomical! It would take an eternity for me to explain how infidelity is unjust toward God, others, and ourselves.

> "Suppose that a firm in the East appointed an agent to represent them in the West and that every month they forwarded to him his salary. But suppose also at the end of the year his employers discovered that though the agent had been cashing the cheques they sent him, nevertheless, he had served another firm all that time. Would not that agent be a thief? Yet this is precisely the situation and state of every sinner. He has been sent into this world by God, and God has endowed him with talents and the capacity to use and improve them. God has blessed him with health and strength; he has supplied his every need and provided innumerable opportunities to serve and glorify him. But with what result? The very things God has given him have been misappropriated." -A.W. Pink (1886-1952) from "The Seven Sayings of the Saviour on the Cross, 2: The Word of Salvation"

Sempterber 25

Irreverence: inevitably dangerous (part 7)

> However, they would not listen, but they did according to their former manner. So these nations feared the Lord and also served their carved images. Their children did likewise, and their children's children—as their fathers did, so they do to this day. 2 Kings 17:40-41

For many years, I was confused about 2 Kings 17. I could not understand how *"these nations feared the Lord and also served their carved images."* Verse 33 says that *"they feared the Lord but also served their own gods."* There appeared to be a contradiction until I looked at the nature of hypocrisy. Yet and still, it all seems confusing!

I don't need to explain how confusion lies amid addiction! Confusion is the nature of idolatry as well. Try to make sense of insanity and you will exhaust yourself! Where there is no reverence for God, there is but calamity, confusion, and disorder. By the way, confusion is one of the definitions of the one Hebrew words translated as "idol."

> We lie down in our shame, and our **confusion covereth us**: for we have sinned against the Lord our God, we and our fathers, from our youth even unto this day, and have not obeyed the voice of the Lord our God. Jeremiah 3:25 *KJV*

> Behold, they are all a delusion; their works are nothing; their metal images are empty wind. Isaiah 41:29

> Behold, they are all vanity; their works are nothing: their molten images are **wind and confusion**. Isaiah 41:29 *NIV*

> All who make graven idols are **confusion, chaos, and worthlessness.** Isaiah 44:9 *Amplified Bible*

Change can be found in 2 Kings 17. The changes that happened gave no true reverence to God. No matter what your method for conquering addiction is, change is the predominant theme as well. Jay Adams' *How to Help People Change* gives us a tremendous understanding of the difference between genuinely godly repentance (change) and symbolic or partial repentance. The chief issue is the level of reverence that you have for God.

Tomorrow, I will share some of Jay Adams's statements that will give you a greater understanding of how 2 Kings 17:40-41 applies to how addictions are dealt with.

September 26

Irreverence: inevitably dangerous (part 8)

However, they would not listen, but they did according to their former manner. So these nations feared the Lord and also served their carved images. Their children did likewise, and their children's children—as their fathers did, so they do to this day. 2 Kings 17:40-41

"Given such disharmony, it might surprise you when I say that counselors of all stripes hold one point in common. No matter how divergent their dogmas, all counselors—Christians included—agree that the aim of counseling is to *change* people. ... Because change is central to counseling, and therefore vitally important, the Christian counselor must come to a scriptural understanding of change in all of its dimensions—its nature, goals, and process. Otherwise, he might as well forget about helping others change, and when comparing ideas with counselors of a humanistic bent, he will have nothing better to offer. ... When we talk about changing people, what do we mean? Because counselors do not all have the same kind of change in mind, it is not strictly correct to say that they agree on the need for changing counselees. Just as the word *automobile* conveys strikingly different images to owners of new BMWs than to owners of third-hand Toyotas, so also counselors, who agree on the need for modification in counselees, many have vastly different ideas and attitudes concerning that change. ... All counseling change is a matter of greater or lesser love toward Him. ... So, the change we are talking about is *substantial* change of a person's life. Brought about by the ministry of the Word, and blessed by the Spirit of God, it brings the counselee closer the likeness of Christ. In short, it is significant change because it glorifies God. ... Change affected by non-Christian counselors is not neutral either. In one way or another, it dishonors God, either by adopting attitudes or actions contrary to His will or by outwardly, hypocritically confirming to His law without a changed heart (a form of godliness that denies the power thereof)." –*How to Help People Change*, Jay Adams

One of the interesting dynamics of addictions is that before we put an idol before God, we *ourselves* are the first idol and then the object. It is then that the idol/addiction, which we try to control and use to our advantage, **uses and controls us instead**. And even after leaving addiction, unless our lives are controlled by God, *we* remain the first idol.

Sempterber 27

Intense reverence (part 1)

Tremble before him, all the earth; 1 Chronicles 16:30a

Our interest, delight, joy, and reverence can all be measured by their intensity! Trembling denotes the intensity of our reverence. And since it is **before God** that we tremble, addictions become more of a serious issue than we could ever imagine.

Our reverence for God is measured by its strength and potency, depth, expanse, and intensity. The dimensions of revering God are expressed in Scripture with words like "greatly," "more than most," "all the day long," and "from generation to generation."

Another word to describe our intensity is passion. The intensity of our reverence for God is determined by our passion. Passion is also known as affection. Both passion and affection are matters of the heart. Addictions are objects of passion.

Only God can accurately measure our reverence. There are, however, some indications that we can use as a gauge. One way to gauge our reverence is by our actions. God gave an accurate measurement of Job's reverence stating that he turned away from evil (Job 1:8). Both today and tomorrow, I want you to look at some of the verses that measure the intensity of reverence!

> And Ahab called Obadiah, which was the governor of his house. (Now **Obadiah feared the Lord greatly**). 1 Kings 18:3 *KJV*

> And Ahab had summoned Obadiah, his palace administrator. (**Obadiah was a devout believer in the Lord.**) *NIV*

> Now when the centurion, and they that were with him, watching Jesus, saw the earthquake, and those things that were done, **they feared greatly**, saying, Truly this was the Son of God. Matthew 27:54

> I put in charge of Jerusalem my brother Hanani, along with Hananiah the commander of the citadel, because he was a man of integrity and feared God **more than most men do**. Nehemiah 7:2

> Let not thine heart envy sinners, but be thou in fear of the Lord **all the day long**. Proverbs 23:17 *KJV*

> Do not let your heart envy sinners, but **always be zealous for the fear of the Lord**. *NIV*

September 28

Intense reverence (part 2)

Tremble before him, all the earth; 1 Chronicles 16:30a

While our reverence for God is measured by our actions, our actions are prompted by at least two other measurements of reverence. Just off the top of my head, I would say that humility and sincerity can be used to measure our reverence (as well as the origin of our actions). By now, you should know that humility is a major element of sobriety.

> "It all lies in the strife between pride and humility: pride and humility are the two master powers, the two kingdoms in strife for the eternal possession of man. There never was, nor ever will be, but one humility, and that is the one humility of Christ. Pride and self have the all of man, till man has his all from Christ. He therefore only fights the good fight whose strife is that the self-idolatrous nature which he has from Adam may be brought to death by the supernatural humility of Christ brought to life in him." -*Humility*, Andrew Murray

To be <u>devoted</u> to something is a sign of intensity as well. Your devotion proves your sincerity. Devotion describes worship, but addiction as well. It is the acquired desire of addiction that people are devoted to. Sometimes it is said that people hunger and thirst for addiction. We also may observe the devotion that the *psalmist* had for God expressed by his hunger and thirst.

> You, God, are my God, **earnestly I seek** You; **I thirst for You, my whole being longs for You,** in a dry and parched land where there is no water. Psalm 63:1 *NIV*

> My soul **thirsts** for God, for the living God. When can I go and meet with God? Psalm 42:2 *NIV*

You are devoted to quenching your thirst? If you are thirsty for water, it becomes the only thing that you focus on. If you thirst enough then all of your thoughts and efforts become focused on getting a drink or you will die. So, it is in your reverence for God that you thirst for Him. To be devoted is a sign of loyalty and faithfulness. The more intensely you revere God, the more you will be committed to godly sobriety.

Sempterber 29

Intense reverence (part 3)

Tremble before him, all the earth; 1 Chronicles 16:30a

Nothing determines your character greater than the amount of reverence that you have for God. Revering God defines you and determines your every action. To fear the Lord with a perfect heart is yet another way that the intensity of your reverence is defined (2 Chronicles 19:9). Some of the other passages that refer to the intensity of reverence are listed below!

> His mercy extends to those who fear him, **from generation to generation.** Luke 1:50 *NIV*

> Remember the day you stood before the LORD your God at Horeb, when he said to me, "Assemble the people before me to hear my words so that they may learn to revere me **as long as they live in the land and may teach them to their children.**" Deuteronomy 4:10 *NIV*

> Oh, that their hearts would be inclined to fear me and keep all my commands **always**, so that it might go well with them and their children forever! Deuteronomy 5:29 *NIV*

> So that you, your children and their children after them may fear the LORD your God **as long as you live** by keeping all his decrees and commands that I give you, and so that you may enjoy long life. Deuteronomy 6:2

The intensity of your reverence is determined by the condition of your heart. There was a charge given by Jehoshaphat to those who administered the law to fear God with a **"perfect heart"** (2 Chronicles 19:9, *KJV*). The *NIV* to fear the Lord **"wholeheartedly."**

The degree of your intimacy and the quality of your reverence are very closely related. The degree of your intimacy measures the intensity at which you cleave to the Lord. It is impossible to cleave to God and addiction at the same time.

> "As there are degrees of wisdom, so of the fear of the Lord; but there is no degree of this fear so inferior or low, but it is a beginning, at least, of wisdom; and there is no degree of wisdom so high or perfect, but it hath its root in, or beginning, from this fear."
> -Joseph Caryl

September 30

The name of God

Hear from heaven your dwelling place and do according to all for which the foreigner calls to you, in order that all the peoples of the earth may know your name and fear you, as do your people Israel, and that they may know that this house that I have built is called by your name. 2 Chronicles 6:33

"What's in a name?" That's a question that I can remember hearing from a very young age! Since then, I have learned that a name is something that you can rely on. 2 Chronicles 6:33 stressed the importance of knowing God's name. When people know the name of God, they revere Him. The health and wealth of everyone depends on knowing the name of God. The name of God is also relative to the quality of our sobriety.

I am told that the word "name" occurs in the Scriptures about 1500 times (mostly as references to Deity or the name of Deity.) If it is used that many times then it must be important. The name of God is the authority of God, as well as His fame, honor, character, essence, identity, reputation, and glory.

"In biblical thought a name is not a mere label of identification; it is an expresion of the essensital nature of its bearer. A man's name reveals his character. Adam was able to give names to beast and birds (Gen. 2:20) because, as Milton says, he understood their nature. This was a concept shared by the peoples of the ancient world. Hence to know the name of God is to know God as he has revealed himself. The full disclosure of his nature and character is given in Jesus Christ, who has manifested his name (John 17:6, 26)." -*Interpreter's Dictionary of the Bible*

Do we not place great value on a name? Just think of some of the name brands that have become so well known that when someone mentioned the brand then we automatically recall the product! For instance; if I say "*Tide*" then most people in the United States will say detergent. Or if I say, "*Quaker*", they will say oatmeal. In doing so, we are saying that the products are the best at what they do!

It bothers me to see the name of the Lord consciously eliminated from the discussion of addictions. God has been known for transforming things since the beginning of time. He spoke everything into being. The name of the LORD is a strong tower; the righteous man runs into it and is safe (Proverbs 18:10). People not only need to know that the Lord can resolve the issues of addiction but that He is worthy of the highest reverence.

October 1

The high order of reverence

> Therefore, my beloved, as you have always obeyed, so now, not only as in my presence but much more in my absence, work out your own salvation with fear and trembling, for it is God who works in you, both to will and to work for his good pleasure. Philippians 2:12-13

The relevance that reverence has for sobriety is seen in many ways. One of the reasons that reverence is such a pertinent issue for addictions is because of the spiritual implications of addiction.

The issue of idolatry is undeniably related to addiction. Here you will discover addiction to be more of a spiritual issue than a physiological one. The answers to addiction are not found in man but in God. To deny that God has anything to say about addictions is insulting. If addiction is idolatry then it is a rejection of the true and living God.

The reverential factor proves that there is a lot at stake when you exchange the true and living God for a false god. God proves Himself time and time again. And yet, it is our hardheartedness that draws us to rebel insanely against the gracious reasoning that God has given us to be as loving, caring, and useful as He.

The reverential factor explains how the glory of God is at stake with every addiction that would distort His image (as every addiction does.) As His image is distorted, we become less human. When G.K. Beale said that "we become what we worship", he went on to mention how Man becomes as lifeless as the idols that he worships.

And if it isn't enough to have the glory of God at stake, addiction, and idolatry jeopardize our welfare as well as those among us. There is a contrast that is made between reverence and irreverence. Reverence for God is surrounded by serenity, solitude, peace, hope, love, and joy. Agony, confusion, disorder, and unrest are found in irreverence as well as addiction.

It is no mystery that in the Scriptures you will learn about God. It is also no mystery that idols are counterfeit gods. Do you know how the *Secret Service of the United States of America* trains its officers to recognize counterfeit money? They are taught to recognize fake bills by studying the real ones. The reverential factor warns against relapsing into a life that is led by addiction rather than God.

The Bible depicts the transition of Israel with revering God. The central issue of sobriety is the reverential transition of turning to God from the idols of addiction. Israel was in transition like you. Your whole life is transitory. Transition requires reflection. And your transition must be full of reverence.

October 2

Becoming/unbecoming (part 1)

> The former governors who were before me laid heavy burdens on the people and took from them for their daily ration forty shekels of silver. Even their servants lorded it over the people. But I did not do so, because of the fear of God. Nehemiah 5:15

When Jesus Christ was asked to name the greatest command, His answer was, *"You shall love the Lord your God with all your heart and with all your soul and with all your mind. This is the great and first commandment. And a second is like it: You shall love your neighbor as yourself"* (Matthew 22:36-39).

Nehemiah's reverence for God affected his relationship with others. This is the quality of sobriety that he possessed. Early in history, it was proven that our reverence for God is shown by the way that we treat others as Abraham interacted with Abimeleceh.

> "The very first mention of the fear of God in the Bible is when Abram told Abimelech that because he thought that there was no fear of God in Gerar they would kill him for his wife (Genesis 20:11). One of the main characteristics of reverence is that it is civil. There would be no civilization without reverence for God."
> –*The Fear of the Almighty*, Gregory Madison

Addictions are not civil. ***Addictions unchecked become barbaric.*** We all know that addictions affect our relationships. Addictions have been responsible for damaging friendships, families, neighborhoods, churches, businesses, governments, cities, states, and countries. Addictions have torn relationships in the most horrible ways imaginable. Addictions tend to be selfish and self-centered. That is one of the reasons why addictions can be defined as unhealthy yearning.

> "One of the ironies of sin is that when human beings try to become more than human beings, to be as gods, they fall to become lower than human beings. To be your own God and live for your own glory and power leads to the most bestial and cruel behavior. Pride makes you a predator, not a person" –*Counterfeit gods*, Tim Keller

> Let each of you look not only to his own interests, but also to the interests of others. Have this mind among yourselves, which is yours in Christ Jesus, who, though he was in the form of God, did not count equality with God a thing to be grasped, but emptied himself, by taking the form of a servant. Philippians 2:4-7a

October 3

Becoming/unbecoming (part 2)

> The former governors who were before me laid heavy burdens on the people and took from them for their daily ration forty shekels of silver. Even their servants lorded it over the people. But I did not do so, because of the fear of God. Nehemiah 5:15

Nehemiah proves that because of their lack of reverence for God, the former governors withheld their love for others. We expect someone in their position to show care and concern. The former governors were not what the people were looking for. Never in my wildest dreams would I have imagined that addictions would cause me to become as callous as the governors described by Nehemiah.

Documentation proves that a large percentage of crimes have been related to addiction. Addiction has been responsible for spouse and child neglect and abuse. Addiction has prevented us from contributing to our communities. Addiction causes many to isolate themselves. When we do not love others as God has prescribed, we show irreverence toward God.

Who knows how many could be helped by placing what we have in the hands of God which would otherwise have been sacrificed to the idols of addictions? Think of the loss that our communities suffer because of the blessings that are withheld from those who withhold their abilities for the sake of their addiction! If we were all like that, there would be no advancement. One of the phrases that I use in outreach is, "*You owe me!*"

Godliness is the by-product of reverence. Nehemiah took care of people as did other godly characters in the Bible. Nehemiah was sent by God to build. God has placed you where you are mentally, physically, and spiritually to build. Just as God placed this desire in the heart of Nehemiah, He can remove the unhealthy desires of addiction from your heart and give you noble desires.

> Therefore, my beloved, as you have always obeyed, so now, not only as in my presence but much more in my absence, work out your own salvation with fear and trembling, **for it is God who works in you, both to will and to work for his good pleasure.** Philippians 2:12-13

The goal of addiction is self-serving. Becoming like Christ leads us to serve others. ***The depth of Nehemiah's reverence made him a servant.*** The deficiency of reverence in the former governors' reverence caused them to use and mistreat others. Pastor A.N. Martin says, "The absence of the fear of God is the unholy soil in which is produced the ungodly life."

October 4

Becoming/unbecoming (part 3)

> The former governors who were before me laid heavy burdens on the people and took from them for their daily ration forty shekels of silver. Even their servants lorded it over the people. But I did not do so, because of the fear of God. Nehemiah 5:15

Service requires self-denial. Self-denial is the ultimate sign of reverence. Need I tell you how sane it is to reverence God? Quality sobriety depends on self-denial. ***Self-denying service is Christ-like. This should be the aim and emphasis for every program battling addiction!***
One of the greatest problems with many programs is that people are encouraged to focus on themselves too much. This same fuel empowers addiction. Nehemiah was a reflection of Christ in his true concern for the welfare of others above his comfort. This contradicts the very nature of every addiction.

> "Putting off and putting on are biblical concepts essential to the transformation process from addict to servant of God" –*The Heart of Addiction,* Mark Shaw

Again, I insist that there was never anyone as sober as Jesus Christ! Jesus taught his disciples that it was the will of God for them to be different just as Nehemiah was different than the former governors. Once again, the phrase "recovery" does not fit the changes that God wants to make in your life because if you recover something, nothing is different. God deserves much more! You must be different than your old self (that's not recovery.) Jesus taught His disciples that they were to be different than the world (just as He was.)

> But Jesus called them to him and said, "You know that the rulers of the Gentiles lord it over them, and their great ones exercise authority over them. **It shall not be so among you. But whoever would be great among you must be your servant, and whoever would be first among you must be your slave,** even as the Son of Man came not to be served but to serve, and to give his life as a ransom for many." Matthew 20:25-28

Every addiction contrived by man seeks comfort. Service often requires sacrifice. Suffering is as essential to sobriety as it is to service. A sober approach to life tells us that things will not always be to our liking and that it should never be our goal to configure everything to please us with little thought of pleasing God

October 5

Called to order (part 1)

I gave my brother Hanani and Hananiah the governor of the castle charge over Jerusalem, for he was a more faithful and God-fearing man than many. Nehemiah 7:2

The book of Nehemiah is an account of the rebuilding of the walls of Jerusalem, and the re-establishing of the sacred ordinances. God assigned men like Nehemiah and Hanani to establish order in Jerusalem.

Nehemiah was sent by God after the Babylonian captivity of Israel which was foretold by Jeremiah and recognized by Daniel. The walls of Jerusalem were as much in shambles because of Israel's idolatry as our lives become in shambles because of addictions.

Chaos is one of the predominant characteristics of addiction as well as idolatry. Though the events in Judges occurred long before Nehemiah, we can see the pattern of idolatry emerge.

"Judges portrays all humanity as corrupt and disoriented. 'In those days there was no king in Israel; everyone did what was right in his own eyes' (Judges 21:25). In view of the preceding books of the OT, we should understand the chaos of Judges as resulting from the fact that Israel did not revere Yahweh as king during this period of her history. And in anticipation of the historical books that follow, Judges sets the precedent for the kings of Israel, many of whom similarly experience chaos and disaster when they forsake God to pursue idols and foreign support." -*Idolatry and the Hardening of the Heart*, Edward P. Meador

If there were ever to be order and justice in Israel, it would have to be administered through god-fearing people. In the past, I have emphasized that addiction is a threat to national security as well as the security of the family and individuals.

"Nonproduction can be listed as one of the liabilities of addictions in the workplace, at school, in government, at home, and in every other phase of life or institution. The statistics prove the cost that addictions have on society. **If third-world countries are defined as undeveloped, then addictions create third-world citizens of some who reside in developing nations.**" *Quality Sobriety Volume One*, Gregory Madison

It has been said that you are either part of the problem or part of the solution.

October 6

Called to order (part 2)

> I gave my brother Hanani and Hananiah the governor of the castle charge over Jerusalem, for he was a more faithful and God-fearing man than many. Nehemiah 7:2

If we are ever to have a program that best destroys the roots of addiction and honors God first rather than emphasizing the pain that people experience before and as a result of addiction, we must adequately emphasize reverence. Reverence is made to order as Nehemiah and Hanani were. Reverence is made to order against all our concerns because it <u>produces</u> order.

Just as Nehemiah had proved himself as different than the former governors, Hanini was different because he *"was a more faithful and God-fearing man than many."* Is there anyone alive who can claim that they reverence God perfectly? Outside of Christ, of course not! Jesus was different! Outside of Christ, we are all very vulnerable to succumbing to things that are displeasing to God (including addictions.) ***Jesus was the only one who ever lived who never once bowed down to an idol!***

To destroy the idols of addiction and make the glory of God your chief concern, you must have a passion for the reverence that is found in Christ. The state of a nation, neighborhood, family, and individual is governed by their state of mind.

It was the humility of Christ that produced His reverence for God. This was the state of mind *(sobriety, if you will)* that Jesus had! We must have the mind of Christ to conquer the enemies of our souls. This is a process that is known as sanctification. It means to be set apart unto God.

I cannot overemphasize a Christ-centered approach to addictions. There is so much that can be seen and heard through the eyes and ears of Christ concerning addictions! The Apostle Paul said that *"eye has not seen, nor ear heard, nor have entered into the heart of man, the things which God has prepared for those who love Him"* (1 Corinthians 2:9). The wonderful thing is that God teaches us how to love Him as He opens our eyes to how much He loves us.

The epitome of reverencing God is the mind of Christ. The quality of our sobriety rests with the mind of Christ. The beauty of being transformed into the image of Christ through being in awe of Him is like the butterfly who travels far beyond her ability as a caterpillar.

> Since we have these promises, beloved, let us cleanse ourselves from every defilement of body and spirit, bringing holiness to completion in the fear of God. 2 Corinthians 7:1

October 7

Called to order (part 3)

> I gave my brother Hanani and Hananiah the governor of the castle charge over Jerusalem, for he was a more faithful and God-fearing man than many. Nehemiah 7:2

Hanani was to Nehemiah what Titus was to the Apostle Paul. Paul said to Titus, *"This is why I left you in Crete, so **that you might put what remained into order** and appoint elders in every town as I directed you."* (Titus 1:5) Over the last 20 years, we have been tremendously blessed with the resources on addictions that I prayed for many years ago. ***Since God wants us to be thoroughly equipped, there is so much to learn about addictions in the Word of God that my job will never be done.***

It brings me joy that I am not the only one who explains addictions biblically. Just as Crete was called to order by God through Titus and Jerusalem was called to order by God through Nehemiah and Hanani, God calls to order our understanding of addiction through those who are guided by His Word with the quality of reverence that matches His supremacy.

I have often said that "if the Word of God had nothing to say about addictions then God would not have created us!" On being thoroughly and adequately equipped, Jay Adams wrote:

> "...before a ship was to sail, all contingencies on the journey would be considered, and supplies to meet each would be stowed on board (e.g., extra canvas from which to make new sails should the original sails be damaged); the ship would be 'thoroughly rigged out.' Mere men, of course, cannot foresee every possibility, and so their best plans often end in shipwreck. But God; the omniscient One, Who knows the end from the beginning, controls every contingency of history. When, therefore, He rigged out His 'men of God' for their work. He neglected nothing. In the pages of Scripture are stowed every principle they might ever need to perform their tasks." - *How to Help People Change*, Jay Adams

The way that things are called into order requires distinction. ***Unless addiction is properly distinguished then it cannot be properly dealt with.*** Unfortunately, many believe themselves to be wiser than God and do not take into account the things the Word of God has to say concerning addiction.

Those who reverence God, look for answers from the Word of God. *Quality Christian Resources on Addictions* is a *Facebook* page that is dedicated to providing the soundest answers to addiction. Look under the guides for quotes, articles, videos, and websites!

October 8

Called to order (part 4)

I gave my brother Hanani and Hananiah the governor of the castle charge over Jerusalem, for he was a more faithful and God-fearing man than many. Nehemiah 7:2

Last but not least, Hanani was called to order and able to call things into order because he had integrity. ReverencingGod is essential to our integrity. Integrity, in turn, is vital to sobriety. Integrity is defined as 1. the quality of being honest and having strong moral principles that you refuse to change. 2. an unimpaired condition: soundness. 3. the quality or state of being complete or undivided: completeness.

During Job's trials, God rejoiced over his integrity as his wife asked him if he was still maintaining his integrity (Job 2:3, 9). Addictions cause us to be unreliable. Again, we see how we become what we worship because just as the objects of our addictions are untrustworthy; as we give ourselves to them, we become untrustworthy.

One of the principles for change that every program can agree on is honesty. There is a need for honesty as you determine what you desire in addiction and whether you may obtain the desire in a healthy, godly manner or even do without what is desired. There is the honesty that your friends, loved ones, and acquaintances deserve. You must also be honest with those who want to help you to overcome your addiction.

Wholeness is a characteristic of integrity as well. If you lack integrity then you are dysfunctional. Dysfunction lacks wholeness.Wholeness lacks nothing, it is complete and unimpaired. Integrity is built on a sound mind. Would you trust someonewho doesn't have a sound mind? Nehemiah would not risk the fate of Jerusalem with anyone who did not possess integrity.

Proverbs 11:3 says, *"The integrity of the upright guides them, but the unfaithful are destroyed by their duplicity."* Are you guided by integrity or the lust for an addiction? A lack of integritycauses us to be double-minded. The lack of integrity disrupts the order of our society.

Perhaps the most notable characteristic of integrity is faithfulness. A life that is in order, a family that is in order, and a nation that has order, all depend on faithfulness to God! ***Addiction is primarily a worship disorder!***

> "The message is remarkably simple. Israel's life should be totally devoted to faithful, sincere exclusive worship of Yahweh. Existentially, nothing else matters. When worship of Yahweh is pure and undefiled, every other aspect of national security is safe and strong. On the other hand, when worship is divided and fraudulent, every dimension of Israel's life suffers confusion, dysfunction, and utter breakdown." -*Idolatry and the Hardening of the Heart*, Edward P. Meadors

October 9

Consistency (part 1)

> And the Lord said to Satan, "Have you considered my servant Job, that there is none like him on the earth, a blameless and upright man, who fears God and turns away from evil" Job 1:8

Yesterday, I mentioned how integrity is related to faithfulness. The trials and sufferings of Job are the subjects of many studies. How did Job respond to his trials? Faithfully! The patience/perseverance of Job is mentioned in the book of James (5:11).

The English Standard Version uses the word **steadfastness** rather than patience. And what was it that caused Job to be steadfast? It was his faithfulness. Faithfulness matches the integrity that is produced by reverence. Faithfulness is displayed by consistency. **One of the characteristics of quality sobriety is consistency.**

Faithfulness is a goal that is sought by everyone who wants to develop a life of sobriety. Just as insanity, sobriety, and reverence, faithfulness can be measured. Who in their right mind wants to be *partially* faithful? This is better known as having reservations.

How far does your reverence for God go? What would you do (or not do) in reverence of God? Would you show the love to others that Christ has shown to you? Would you cling to the Word of God and allow it the priority it deserves? Would you make your conversation with God a primary activity?

Would you sacrifice all your possessions for God's sake? Would you sacrifice your very life? Psalm 15:4 describes the one who fears God *"keeps his oath even when it hurts."* Is there anything or anyone that can draw you from reverencing God?

Our consistency reveals our values. It is with consistency that we worship God or the idols of addiction. Does God deserve our consistency? The level of our reverence is revealed by our consistency or inconsistency.

Richard G. Scott said, "We become what we want to be by consistently becoming what we want to be each day." The same can be said concerning the person that we don't want to be or the person that God does not want us to be.

Job was examined by God. God tells Satan to consider Job. God puts Job on display. **It is one thing for us to tell others that we have a deep reverence for God, and it is another thing for God to say that we revere Him.** It is rewarding to know that God sees our reverence. 2 Chronicles 16:9 tells us that *"the eyes of the Lord run to and fro throughout the whole earth, to give strong support to those whose heart is blameless toward him."*

October 10

Consistency (part 2)

And the Lord said to Satan, "Have you considered my servant Job, that there is none like him on the earth, a blameless and upright man, who fears God and turns away from evil" Job 1:8

Job is an example as we may find examples in our communities of those who remain clean and sober because of their reverence for God. Job's experiences let us know that despite whatever circumstances we may encounter, God is worthy of our trust.

As Job was different, God wants us to be different! The practices of Job are worth noting. His practices reveal how consistent he was with his reverence for God. Consistency leads to stability. Once someone has been abstinent for a little while then it's easier to just stay that way. Job made a habit of reverencing God.

"Habit is an important factor and deserves more attention in theology and Christian counseling. In the Bible, it plays the same important part it does in everyday living. A large share of what we do day by day is by habit. The Bible recognizes that and gives habit its rightful place. Habit is a blessing from God that enables us to do things unconsciously, automatically, skillfully, and comfortably (its four characteristics) so that we can do other things at the same time. But as sinners we have perverted this blessing and, like other God-given capacities (e.g. sex), we have often turned it into a curse. Counselors must learn the power of habit, the importance of habit, how to eliminate sinful habits, and how to establish new righteous ones." - *How to Help People Change*, Jay Adams

"If you, the Christian addict, have established sinful habit patterns in the flesh, then you must replace them with godly habits. You have made small decisions in the beginning of your usage of the substance that has now led you to a *seemingly* hopeless situation in which you feel as if you have no choice.... Some of the habits you have learned are not just physical habits but are habitual patterns of ***thinking and responding*** to life's hardships. Your responsibility as a Christian is to cultivate godly ways of habitually thinking, speaking, behaving, and feeling." – *The Heart of Addiction*, Mark Shaw

Habits require devotion. The practices of Job reveal the predetermination of his reverence for God during the most unpleasant experiences that he had to endure. Job's consistency was fueled by his reverence for God resulting in patterns that became habits. ***Habits are either godly or ungodly in one form or another!***

October 11

Who's on the throne? (part 1)

> Now therefore, O kings, be wise; be warned, O rulers of the earth.
> Serve the LORD with fear, and rejoice with trembling. Psalms 2:11

Who's on the throne? That's the question that determines the fate of a nation. Who's on the throne also determines the quality of our lives and the quality of our sobriety. Who's on the throne determines whether we fall prey to addictions. Who's on the throne determines if we become devoted to addictions. Who is on the throne also determines how addictions are dealt with.

As the second Psalm reveals the magnificence of Christ, so should we! This is one of our least concerns when we are committed to an addictive life. Why should the magnificence of Christ be a priority? First, because He is worthy.

Second, when we do not strive to reveal Christ's magnificence, we forfeit our divine purpose. We were created to reflect God's image. **I challenge anyone to tell me how addictions reflect God's image!** God is love, but addictions are purely self-seeking. Jesus was the most *selfless* person who ever lived.

> Why do the nations rage and the peoples plot in vain? The kings of the earth set themselves, and the rulers take counsel together, against the LORD and against his Anointed, saying, "Let us burst their bonds apart and cast away their cords from us." Psalms 2:1-3

The idolatry of addiction seeks self-worship. Our natural inclination to worship ourselves originates in our thoughts and manifests in our actions. We don't need anyone to teach us how to love ourselves. Even when someone wants to commit suicide it is because they love themselves so much that they do not want to go on living the life that they possess.

> "[Sin] strives with and fights against God, and if its power were as great as its will is wicked, it would not suffer God to be. God is a troublesome thing to the sinner, and therefore they say to him, Depart from us (Job 21.14), and of Christ Jesus, Let us break his bands in sunder, and cast his cords far from us (Psalms 2.3). And when the Holy Ghost comes to woo and entreat them to be reconciled, they resist and make war with the spirit of peace (Acts 7:51). ... Can you find it in your heart to hug and embrace such a monster as this? Will you love that which hates God, and which God hates? God forbid! Will you join yourself to that which is nothing but contrariety to God, and all that is good?" -*The Sinfulness of Sin,* Ralph Venning

October 12

Who's on the throne? (part 2)

At the end of twelve months he was walking on the roof of the royal palace of Babylon, and the king answered and said, "Is not this great Babylon, which I have built by my mighty power as a royal residence and for the glory of my majesty?" Daniel 4:29-30

Does the last part of the verses sound familiar? It's the voice of addiction that refuses to acknowledge God and be ruled by Him! Later we see how King Nebuchadnezzar was humiliated just as we are with addictions.

Later, King Nebuchadnezzar's sanity was restored as his situation produced the clarity that we all need. Unfortunately, many of us who drift into the insanity of addiction don't take advantage of the opportunity to change as Nebuchadnezzar did. (By the way, Daniel advised Nebuchadnezzar to change v. 27.)

> While the words were still in the king's mouth, there fell a voice from heaven, "O King Nebuchadnezzar, to you it is spoken: The kingdom has departed from you, and you shall be driven from among men, and your dwelling shall be with the beasts of the field. And you shall be made to eat grass like an ox, and seven periods of time shall pass over you, until you know that the Most High rules the kingdom of men and gives it to whom he will." Immediately the word was fulfilled against Nebuchadnezzar. He was driven from among men and ate grass like an ox, and his body was wet with the dew of heaven till his hair grew as long as eagles' feathers, and his nails were like birds' claws. At the end of the days I, Nebuchadnezzar, lifted my eyes to heaven, and my reason returned to me, and I blessed the Most High, and praised and honored him who lives forever. Daniel 4:31-34

"Yet so subtle is self that scarcely anyone is conscious of its presence. Because man is born a rebel, he is unaware that he is one. His constant assertion of self, as far as he thinks of it at all, appears to him a perfectly normal thing. He is willing to share himself, sometimes even to sacrifice himself for a desired end, but never to dethrone himself. No matter how far down the scale of social acceptance he may slide, he is still in his own eyes a king on a throne, and no one, not even God, can take that throne from him. Sin has many manifestations but its essence is one. A moral being, created to worship before the throne of God, sits on the throne of his own selfhood and from that elevated position declare, 'I AM.' That is sin in its concentrated essence: yet because it is natural it appears to be good." -*The Knowledge of the Holy,* Tozer

October 13

Your heart is His throne! (part 1)

Be angry, and do not sin; ponder in your own hearts on your beds, and be silent. Selah Psalms 4:4

Tremble and do not sin; when you are on your beds, search your hearts and be silent. *NIV*

Stand in awe, and sin not: commune with your own heart upon your bed, and be still. Selah. Psalms 4:4 *KJV*

In keeping with yesterday's theme, let's look at where addictions originate and rule! Is it not from our hearts that addictions materialize? It is no wonder that Proverb 4:23 says to *"watch over your heart with all diligence, For from it flow the springs of life"* (*Amplified Bible*). **Your heart is the throne of your life that God alone is worthy of ruling!**

Little children (believers, dear ones), guard yourselves from idols—[false teachings, moral compromises, and anything that would take God's place in your heart]. 1 John 5:21 *Amplified Bible*

I have taken the liberty of listing three translations of Psalms 4:4 so that you may appreciate the various aspects relative to addiction. I want to emphasize the principles of meditation, stillness, and awe. Each of these reverence components is essential to the quality of our sobriety.

Neither sobriety nor active addiction can exist without meditation. To meditate is to ponder or to think deeply. How much do people ponder addictions? How deep are our thoughts about addiction? Narcotics Anonymous says, "Our whole life and thinking was centered in drugs in one form or another—the getting and using and finding ways and means to get more." Is not our obsession with addiction expressed by meditation?

As with every other area of our lives, we must consider whether God is pleased with our meditation. The psalmist longed for his meditation to be acceptable in God's sight (Psalms 19:14). God is unpleased with our obsession with addictions. In most cases, it competes with the meditation He wants for us.

The yearning for addiction is supported and strengthened by your meditation. **Meditation is the breath of yearning.** I guarantee that whatever it is that you long for, you meditate on it as well. You think about it! You think about it a lot! Meditation is usually talked about in a positive sense. **The meditation of addiction is what places you under its influence, not just indulgence. You are under the influence before indulging.**

October 14

Your heart is His throne! (part 2)

> Tremble and do not sin; when you are on your beds, search your hearts and be silent. *NIV*
>
> Stand in awe, and sin not: commune with your own heart upon your bed, and be still. Selah. Psalms 4:4 *KJV*

Pslams 4:4 is similar to Exodus 20:20 as a deterrent against sin. To stand in awe requires mediation. So as the flames of addiction are fed by the mediation of their lying promises they are distinguished by meditating on the truth of God.

> "Meditation is the activity of calling to mind, and thinking over, and dwelling on, and applying to oneself, the various things that one knows about the works and ways and purposes and promises of God. It is an activity of holy thought, consciously performed in the presence of God, under the eye of God, by the help of God, as a means of communion with God. Its purpose is to clear one's mental and spiritual vision of God, and to let His truth make its full and proper impact on one's mind and heart. It is a matter of talking to oneself, reasoning oneself out of moods of doubt and unbelief in to a clear apprehension of God's power and grace. Its effect is ever to humble us, as we contemplate God's greatness and glory, and our own littleness and sinfulness, and to encourage and reassure us—'comfort' us, in the old, strong, Bible sense of the word—as we contemplate the unsearchable riches of divine mercy displayed in the Lord Jesus Christ." -*Knowing God*, J. I. Packer

Temptation often seems to call to our souls. Some people will tell you that they hear their addiction speaking to them. Psalms 4:4 encourages us to direct our thoughts to the greatness of God in response to our temptations. Psalms 46:10 quiets the soul and reminds us that God has power over everything (including addiction.)

> Be still, and know that I am God. I will be exalted among the nations, I will be exalted in the earth! Psalms 46:10

The Highest Yearning describes mediation as savoring. Savoring is an expression of yearning. Who or what we love, we savor! The highest yearning not only strives to learn of God but the highest yearning savors God as well. Meditation is a form of reverence. **To allow God to control your soul is an act of reverence!**

October 15

Your heart is His throne! (part 3)

Tremble and do not sin; when you are on your beds, search your hearts and be silent. *NIV*

Stand in awe, and sin not: commune with your own heart upon your bed, and be still. Selah. Psalms 4:4 *KJV*

Stillness and tranquility are envied by those who are hounded by addiction. It is ironic that in our addiction we are in search of some sort of tranquility only to find turmoil, chaos, and confusion.

Stillness and tranquility are emotions. Emotions reveal the condition of our souls. Stillness is a matter of the soul. Desire, passion, and lust can destroy our tranquility. Addictions are at war with your soul. 1 Peter 2:11 says, *"as sojourners and exiles to abstain from the passions of the flesh, which wage war against your soul."*

Since Jesus is the Prince of Peace, we cannot experience stillness and tranquility unless we allow Him to take His rightful place. That place is the throne of our hearts.

Hebrews 6:19 says that the hope found in Christ is *"a sure and steadfast anchor of the soul."* ***A soul that is not given to God is vulnerable to every evil imaginable and unimaginable.*** When God is on the throne, He has your full attention.

The awe factor of addiction cannot be denied! Addictions capture our attention. Standing in awe gives God our attention. As the psalmist beckons the reader to stand in awe, he proclaims that God is worthy of awe. The greatest response to addiction is to turn your attention from addiction to God.

> **"Why do I get high?** I get high because it has me in awe! If I owned a racehorse, I would be sure to name it *Awe in Awe*. *Awe in Awe* would beat every other horse on the track just like the wild camel that described Israel while chasing idols. Awe has great potential! In *Turning to God from Idols*, I defined addiction as 'the frenzy and barbarism of idolatry which stems from a commitment to an erroneous, improper, and irreverent view of the living and true God." – *Why Not Get High!*, Gregory L. Madison

Awe involves wonder, amazement, astonishment, and admiration. It can sometimes be filled with fear or dread. We sometimes become afraid of the things that we see as overpowering, overwhelming, and grand. Awe leads to passion, which can also take the form of lust and thereby have the potential to rule. Awe is an emotion that rules and ruins many lives when given precedence over God.

October 16

Your heart is His throne! (part 3)

Tremble and do not sin; when you are on your beds, search your hearts and be silent. *NIV*

Stand in awe, and sin not: commune with your own heart upon your bed, and be still. Selah. Psalms 4:4 *KJV*

We must see the beauty of the Lord as more attractive than addiction to overcome our lust for addiction. I never knew the beauty of an *Azalea* until visiting my grandmother's house. The funny thing is that I had seen the bush many times while living in Memphis for 8 ½ years.

It was only after I moved to Atlanta and arrived at my grandmother's house at night did I notice the beauty of her *Azalea* bush as the white flowers glowed in the darkness of the evening.

If you never see the beauty of the *Azalea*, it's not going to be of much harm. But, if you never recognize, acknowledge, and embrace the beauty of Christ, the results are eternal damnation and you not only lie against the Spirit of God, you also lie to yourself.

Why? Because what is found in Christ is the answer to life. He alone is the Light that can lead you from the darkness of sin and degradation.

And the Word became flesh and dwelt among us, and we have seen his glory, glory as of the only Son from the Father, full of grace and truth. John 1:14

"[No war] rises to the level of significance of another war that has determined the course of human history and the lives of every individual who has ever lived. What is that war? It's the war of awe, the war that is fought on the turf of every human being's heart."
-*Awe: Why It Matters for Everything We Think, Say, and Do,* Paul Tripp

Jesus said that the greatest commandment is to love the Lord God with all your heart, soul, and mind (Matthew 22:37). It is a love for God that creates stillness. Our souls desire stillness. Our hearts are captured by what we are in awe of. Psalms 4:4 is a reflection of the greatest commandment.

> *God desires your awe!*
> *Give God your heart!*
> *Give God your mind!*
> *Give God your soul!*
> *Give God your love!*

October 17

Elements of Joy

> Repent ye therefore, and be converted, that your sins may be blotted out, when the times of refreshing shall come from the presence of the Lord. Acts 3:19 *KJV*

The times of refreshing in Acts 3:19 is joy. It can't be anything but joy since it comes from the presence of the Lord! Joy has power over all that would oppose God.

Webster's Dictionary defines joy as "a strong feeling of great happiness, delight, a state or source of contentment or satisfaction." *Dictionary.com* defines joy as the emotion of great delight or happiness caused by something exceptionally good or satisfying; keen pleasure; elation."

One of the elements of joy is **contentment**. Contentment allows those who have chased after the idols of addiction to rest. Joy produces satisfaction with what God has given us. Very closely related to contentment is the element of **gratitude** or thanksgiving. We are not just satisfied with what God has provided, we are thankful.

> "The addicted heart is greedy for more: more alcohol, more shoes, more money, more attention, more sex, more food. The very nature of greed is that it can't see beyond what it covets. It's so preoccupied with what it wants that it's blind to what God has already given. Thankfulness is the opposite of greed. It is so overcome with gratitude for God's goodness that it can't help but thank Him. Thankfulness then becomes a weapon for our warfare."
> – *Addictive Habits*, Dunham

God created us to be completely satisfied with Himself. To grow in the Lord is like trying to bribe someone with a piece of Spam after he has just backed away from a five-star meal with all that he could eat at the finest restaurant. He is just too full to eat anything else.

You rejoice in what you value. That's why your reverence for God is a key ingredient in the practice of sobriety. To rejoice in something is to find delight in it. Of all the things in the universe, the fear of the Lord is the thing Jesus chooses as His delight. Isaiah 33:6 says "The fear of the Lord is His treasure."

What is it that you find delight in? What is it that you value most? What is your treasure? Make no mistake! We choose the things that we delight in. And if we choose those things over God then they become our idols.

If you never experience the joy of the Lord in your repentance, then I doubt if you have repented. Repentance does not only mean that you turn <u>from</u> sin, but that you turn <u>to</u> Jesus! In Jesus Christ there is joy.

October 18

The joy of the Lord (part 1)

Rejoice in the Lord always; again I will say, rejoice. Philippians 4:4

Many years ago, while attending an *Alcoholics Anonymous* meeting, I listened to a speaker who had such broken English that I thought that I heard him say that he was "merciful." During the many times that he had stopped drinking, he would go back to drinking time and time again.

Over and over, the speaker said that he was "very merciful" when he stopped drinking. Towards the end of his speech, I finally realized that the speaker had been telling us that he had been "miserable" during those times of abstinence (without true fellowship with God.)

While God wants us to be merciful in our walk with Him, He does not want us to be miserable. George Muller said, "The first great and primary business to which I ought to attend every day is to have my soul happy in the Lord." Muller said, "Our first duty as Christians is to get ourselves happy in God." Nehemiah 8:10 says "**The joy of the Lord is your strength.**"

What good is repentance if it does not lead to joy? Deliverance is not complete without joy. Joy is what makes the formula of sanctification complete. More than anything else, turning to God from idols is all about intimate fellowship with the Father through Jesus Christ while recognizing God's glory.

One of Jesus' closest disciples (John) said, "That which we have seen and heard declare we unto you, that ye also may have fellowship with us: and truly our fellowship is with the Father, and with His Son Jesus Christ. And these things write we unto you, **that your joy may be full**." (1 John 1:3-4, *KJV*) Our joy is focused on what we find to be of value.

Jesus Christ provides the only means of God's forgiveness. The blood of Christ supplies the greatest level of intimacy with a God who is infinitely beyond all there is (including the idols we would embrace.) This is priceless. The joy that God gives in Christ is measureless.

The greatest manifestation of God is seen at the Cross of Calvary! At the Cross, we can see how God is worthy of our praise. What a delight it is to know that our soul may be secure for eternity through the sacrificial payment of our sins that would otherwise damn us! Whatever else we may encounter is beyond compare.

The joy of the Lord can sustain you through the darkest night. In a world of darkness, you need the joy of the Lord supported by His Word.

> And we have the prophetic word more fully confirmed, to which you will do well to pay attention as to a lamp shining in a dark place, until the day dawns and the morning star rises in your hearts, 2 Peter 1:19

October 19

The joy of the Lord (part 2)

Looking unto Jesus the author and finisher of our faith. Hebrews 12:2a.

At times, I am shocked, really shocked over my wife's attitude towards me. Just yesterday, she and I had a casual discussion about how blinding the lights are at our church in the choir loft, as she sings.

She said that every once and a while a friend will ask if she saw them in the audience while she was in the choir loft. My wife then said to me, "The only one that I look for is you."

The lights of the world (addictions included) have the potential of blinding us with artificial joy. We must determine that our focus will be upon He alone who is worthy of our complete attention and adoration! Repentance refocuses your attention. Joy is attentive!

Another time that I was shocked by my wife's attitude towards me, came during the conversion of a mutual friend (in my wife's absence.) As I encountered an acquaintance that I had not seen in a long time, I mentioned my wife.

Though he and my wife had been close for years, he did not know that she and I were related to one another (in any shape, form, or fashion.) And so, when I said something about Joanna, he asked, "Joanna who?"

After I told him who I was talking about, I was shocked by his response. "Oh, you're *the husband*! She speaks very highly of you," he said. I am ever grateful for a wife who respects me as the Church should respect its Head.

Addictions are very highly spoken of. They are given much respect. Praise is one of the expressions of worship. To render unto Jesus the honor and reverence that He deserves and to think and speak very highly of Him is the soberest response to addiction.

Make no mistake! Although the joy that I have been describing is a practice, it is not self-manufactured. The joy of the Lord is the fruit of the Spirit (therefore supernatural.)

For one thing, the joy of the Lord is not based on circumstances. Herbert Lockyer said, "An evident sign that we are living in harmony with the mind and will of the Holy Spirit is the way in which He can make us joyful – even when it seems there is nothing to sing about – joyful in *all* our tribulation" (2 Corinthians 7:4).

When all is said and done, we can define sobriety as being in sync with God. And the strongest indication of being in sync with God is finding delight in Him. Within finding delight in God, you find delight in His Word. This is the fruit of true repentance as you turn to God from the idols of addiction.

October 20

More Delight (part 1)

In the way of Your testimonies I delight as much as in all riches. Psalms 119:14

Have you noticed how delight has been a major topic in our discussion about addiction and Christ? **One of the elements of worship is finding delight in whoever or whatever we make our god.** The old English word for worship was "worthship." It meant that we express the worth of whatever or whoever we worship.

It is only natural that we delight in the things that are of worth to us. I have heard people say that their addiction talks to them. This can be very annoying for someone who wants to remain abstinent. It is to the degree that you delight in God's voice that the voice of addiction will no longer influence you.

Not only do we find delight in what we worship. We find delight in others. We give our attention to those we love. One of the ways that I know how much my wife loves me is the way that she listens to me. She values what I have to say. Sometimes, it is as if she clings to every word that I say. And so, I aim to speak words of delight to my wife.

God has words of delight for us. The psalmist said that he valued the Word of God as much as all riches. The chains of addiction are broken as you delight in the Word of God more than all addictions. This "delight" is otherwise known as joy.

The Apostle Paul's letter to the Philippians is called "the letter of joy." In Chapter Three, the Apostle Paul says, "Finally, my brethren, rejoice in the Lord. To write the same things to you, to me indeed is not grievous, but for you it is safe." I believe that Paul was expressing the security that is found in choosing our delight in the things of God. Sobriety is not complete without joy.

Today as well as tomorrow, I want you to read some passages about delight, from the *King James Version*. You will notice that delight can be found in what is good as well as what is evil!

Negative (ungodly)

They only consult to cast him down from his excellency: they **delight** in lies: they bless with their mouth, but they curse inwardly. Selah. Psalm 62:4

How long, ye simple ones, will ye love simplicity? and the scorners **delight** in their scorning, and fools hate knowledge? Proverbs 1:22

October 21

More Delight (part 2)

Who rejoice to do evil, and **delight** in the frowardness of the wicked. Proverbs 2:14

Folly **delights** a man who lacks judgment, but a man of understanding keeps a straight course. Proverbs 15:21 (*NIV*)

A fool hath no **delight** in understanding, but that his heart may discover itself. Proverbs 18:4

To whom shall I speak, and give warning, that they may hear? behold, their ear is uncircumcised, and they cannot hearken : behold, the Word of the LORD is unto them a reproach; they have no **delight** in it. Jeremiah 6:10

Positive

For then shalt thou have thy **delight** in the Almighty, and shalt lift up thy face unto God. Job 22:26

But his **delight** is in the law of the LORD; and in his law doth he meditate day and night. Psalm 1:2

Delight thyself also in the LORD; and he shall give thee the desires of thine heart. Psalm 37:4

I **delight** to do Thy will, O my God: yea, Thy law is within my heart. Psalm 40:8

I will **delight** myself in Thy statutes: I will not forget Thy word. Psalm 119:16

Thy testimonies also are my **delight** and my counsellors. Psalm 119:24

Then shalt thou **delight** thyself in the LORD; and I will cause thee to ride upon the high places of the earth, and feed thee with the heritage of Jacob thy father: for the mouth of the LORD hath spoken it. Isaiah 58:14

"Biblical change leads to a passionate relationship with the God of heaven that makes every other love pale in comparison." –Jim Berg

October 22

Awe is forsaken (part 1)

He who withholds kindness from a friend forsakes the fear of the Almighty. Job 6:14

It seems Job could not find the kindness he thought he would find in his friends. The kindest people in the world should be godly. And what makes people godly? The answer is reverence for God. It is no mystery that godly people strive to be more like God. With God as the kindest of all, people who reverence Him are naturally kind.

In his book, *We Become What We Worship*, G.K. Beale sets out to prove that if we bow down to idols, then we become as cold, inhumane, and lifeless as they are. The opposite is true as we worship God. We become more alive, as we worship Him; since He is the Author of Life.

We become more kind and loving as we give our attention to the God who is love. The Apostle John says, *"he who does not love his brother whom he has seen cannot love God whom he has not seen"* (John 4:20).
Irreverence has certain characteristics and consequences. Jeremiah 44:10 equates irreverence with a lack of humility. **Our reverence for God is proportionate to our humility.** Irreverence seeks to put God on the same level as ourselves. "I" is in the middle of pride and in sin.

Wherever there is a deficiency of awe for God, we are vulnerable to addiction or relapse. Paul Tripp said, "I know that in ministry I will be preaching, teaching, and encouraging people who are awe forgetful, awe discouraged, awe empty, awe deceived, awe seduced, awe kidnapped, and awe weary."

Irreverence can also be called a deformity of the soul! The deficiency of awe causes a deformity that leads to dysfunction! That's why Job said, *"He who withholds kindness from a friend forsakes the fear of the Almighty."* His friends were dysfunctional.

Irreverence is a serious matter. At a conference on fearing God, a speaker said, "Christian counseling is nothing more than convincing people to fear God." There would be no end of books that could be written on irreverence as an eternal God deserves eternal homage. In *Evil of Evils*, Jeremiah Burroughs said, "sin has a kind of infiniteness in it." Irreverence begets sin.

Idolatry can very well be called the epitome of irreverence (in whatever form it may present itself, whether it is sociably acceptable or not.) Where there is no genuine reverence for God, then God is belittled, not very highly commended, and ultimately cursed. ***Every sin is (in effect) a curse against God in that we are belittling Him, we are not expressing His worth, His wisdom, His wealth…***

October 23

Awe is forsaken (part 2)

Transgression speaks to the wicked deep in his heart; **there is no fear of God before his eyes.** For he flatters himself in his own eyes that his iniquity cannot be found out and hated. The words of his mouth are trouble and deceit; he has ceased to act wisely and do good. He plots trouble while on his bed; he sets himself in a way that is not good; he does not reject evil. Psalms 36:1-4

It has been said that action speaks louder than words. Transgression is a hideous proclamation of what is in our hearts. Wickedness is the fruit of an irreverent disposition. The *Thompson Chain Reference Study Bible* gives us an even greater understanding as the margin for Psalm 36 speaks of atheism and godlessness. This is the breeding ground of addiction.

1. v. 1 no fear of God
2. v. 2 He flatters himself in his own eyes (pride)
3. Narcism
4. v. 2b. his iniquity is found to be hateful
5. v. 3a. the words of his mouth are iniquity and deceit
6. v. 3b. He has left off to be wise and do good
7. v. 4a. He devises mischief upon his bed
8. v. 4b. He sets himself in a way that is not good
9. v. 4c. He does not abhor evil.
10. *Thompson-Chain* also mentions self-righteousness and self-deception.

"The arts, motives, assistances, results, and punishments of self-flattery, and the discovery which concludes it. In his own eyes- He had not God before his eyes in holy awe, therefore he puts himself there in unholy admiration. ***He who makes little of God makes much of himself.*** They who forget adoration fall into adulation. The eyes must see something, and if they admire not God, they will flatter self." -Spurgeon

When Romans 3:18 says that "there is no fear of God before their eyes", we discover that we are all born with the natural ability of irreverence or disregard for God. The ability is further enhanced and intensified as we put it into practice. There comes a time when irreverence becomes a stronghold. Tomorrow you will discover how the characteristics of irreverence are revealed in Jeremiah 2:19.

October 24

Awe is forsaken (part 3)

Your evil will chastise you, and your apostasy will reprove you. Know and see that it is evil and bitter for you to forsake the Lord your God; the fear of me is not in you, declares the Lord God of hosts. Jeremiah 2:19

Your wickedness will punish you; your backsliding will rebuke you. Consider then and realize how evil and bitter it is for you when you forsake the Lord your God and have no awe of me, declares the Lord, the Lord Almighty. *NIV*

1. It is exemplified through wickedness
2. It is exemplified through backslidings
3. It is an evil thing
4. It is a bitter thing
5. It is to forsake the Lord

Wickedness and evil are closely related. *Strong's Bible Dictionary* says that evil in this case "refers to **that which is evil in appearance to the point of deformity.**" Do we not have souls that are deformed causing us to forsake the true and living God who is the source of all that is good while turning to the idols of addiction? The definitions for wickedness found in *Strong's Bible Dictionary* reveal the devastation of wickedness.

"Adversity, calamity, displeasure, exceedingly evil, great and heavy grief, a hurtful thing. It is also associated with mischief, misery, naughty, noisome, notpleasing, sorrow, trouble, vexation, and wretchedness."

Perhaps, the most hideous thing in all the universe is a lack of reverence for God. It is what led to Satan's prideful rebellion against God as expressed in Isaiah 14:12-15.

How you have fallen from heaven, morning star, son ofthe dawn! You have been cast down to the earth, you who once laid low the nations! You said in yourheart, "I will ascend to the heavens; I will raise my throne above the stars of God; I will sit enthroned on the mount of assembly, on the utmost heights of Mount Zaphon. I will ascend above the tops of the clouds; I will make myself like the Most High." Butyou are brought down to the realm of the dead, to the depths of the pit. Isaiah 14:12-15

October 25

Awe is forsaken (part 4)

And I saw, when for all the causes whereby backsliding Israel committed adultery I had put her away, and given her a bill of divorce; yet her treacherous sister Judah feared not, but went and played the harlot also. Jeremiah 3:8 *KJV*

Backsliding is irreverent. Backsliding, also known as falling away or committing apostasy, is a term used within Christianity to describe a process by which an individual who has converted to Christianity reverts to pre-conversion habits and/or lapses or falls into sin. This occurs when a person turns from God to pursue their own desire. Jeremiah 3:8 not only equates backsliding with irreverence but also compares it to adultery.

Verse thirteen of Jeremiah 3 goes on to explain how Israel rebelled against God and ignored His voice with irreverence. Addiction is no different. *Insanity may be defined as a weak and futile attempt to stifle the voice of God.*

Insanity willnot be reasoned with. Insanity makes its own reality while rebelling against the truth. One of my pet peeves is when someone is looking for answers and proceeds to tell me the answer to what they are asking. *One of thesobering questions is whether you want to hear what God has to say or do you want Him to give you the answers that you want to hear.*

If you are looking for God to give you the answers that you are looking for with no regard to His, then you are seeking another god. Author Os Guiness says that *"Idolatry is huge in the Bible, dominant in our personal lives, andirrelevant in our mistaken estimations."*

I mentioned in earlier entries that the fear of the Lord isa matter of national defense. Addictions tear at the fabric ofsociety in ways that are far too numerous to mention. Third-world countries have no defense; they are underdeveloped. Addictions produce a third-world environment (even in developing nations.) Three basic issues relate to irreverence,addiction, and underdevelopment.

1. Wherever there has been a deficiency of reverence for God civility is endangered.
2. Wherever there is a deficiency of reverence for God the vision that is necessary for advancement is stagnated.
3. Wherever there is no reverence for God then our standard of living becomes compromised.

October 26

Abiding love (part 1)

"Teacher, which is the great commandment in the Law?" And he said to him, "You shall love the Lord your God with all your heart and with all your soul and with all your mind. This is the great and first commandment. And a second is like it: You shall love your neighbor as yourself. Matthew 22:36-39

Why Not Get High? The highest motive for abstaining from addiction is a love for God because *loving God is the soberest thing that you will ever do.* A love for God and an appreciation for His blessings will ever remain the highest and strongest deterrent against addictions.

Loving God goes beyond all else. Loving God goes beyond giving up an addiction, it involves putting aside *anything* that displeases Him while doing the things that bring Him joy. God deserves our love because of the love that He has for us.

We have no problem loving ourselves. We do have a problem loving God! We love ourselves to death! That's why many people become suicidal while under the influence of an addiction. If they cannot find a way to continue feeding their addiction and still function normally, or if they are unhappy about the consequences of the addiction and cannot see a way out, then out of self-love, they contemplate suicide. They are willing to die for themselves. Who would die for God? That's sober!

I used to ask myself whether I would be willing to die for Christ until God showed me that I needed to ask myself if I am willing to live for Christ. Surely, if we are willing to live for Him then we would be willing to die for Him! On the day that I married my wife, I told her that as Christ laid down His life for me, I would lay my life down for her (every day.)

Loving God and reverencing God go hand in hand. Loving God and sobriety go together as well as loving God and revering Him. **The soberest thing ever was for Jesus to love us enough to pay the price for our sins. The soberest thing that we can do is love God.**

If sobriety and sanity are descriptive of being sound-minded, then there is no sobriety without a love for God. The Word of God presents the choice of either loving God or loving the things of the world in 1 John 2:15. Loving God puts us on a different level.

It takes a sober mind to love God! Is there anyone who loved the Father more than Jesus? So, once again we can understand why there was no one soberer than Jesus Christ. *We all know that Christ died for us because He loves us. But, more importantly, Jesus died for us because of His love for the Father.*

October 27

Abiding love (part 2)

> But you, beloved, building yourselves up in your most holy faith and praying in the Holy Spirit, keep yourselves in the love of God, waiting for the mercy of our Lord Jesus Christ that leads to eternal life. Jude 20-21

Among other things, loving God is concerned about His glory. Addictions draw us away from God's glory. They draw your attention away from God. It is only natural that what we love steals our attention. So it is with our love for God! Jesus said that He always did the things that were pleasing to the Father (John 8:29.) **The simplest solution to addictions is to strive to live a life that is pleasing to God.**

Strong's Bible Dictionary says, "When used of love to a master, God or Christ, the word involves the idea of affectionate reverence, prompt obedience, grateful recognition of benefits received." *Strong's Bible Dictionary* also says "The love of a thing is "to take pleasure in the thing, prize it above other things, be unwilling to abandon it or do without it." It is no wonder that we can define addictions as idols! Some of the definitions found in *Strong's Dictionary of the Bible* for love in the Old Testament are "to desire, to breathe after, to delight in, and to be intimate with.

Loving God is synonymous with abiding in Christ. Abiding in Christ means to remain or continue in Him. Abiding in Christ keeps us sober. Abiding in Christ can also be described as walking with Him or being yoked with Him. Jesus extends the same invitation today for us to take His yoke and learn of Him so that we may find rest in our souls as He did to all while on earth. (Matthew 11:28-30) Jesus said that we would find joy by abiding in Him. (John 15:11)

> Whoever says he abides in him ought to walk in the same way in which he walked. 1 John 2:6

"Christ-centered counseling involves understanding the nature and courses of our human difficulties, understanding the ways we are unlike Christ in our values, aspirations, desires, thoughts, feelings, choices, attitudes, actions, and responses. Resolving those sin-related difficulties includes being redeemed and justified through Christ, receiving God's forgiveness through Christ, and acquiring from Christ the enabling power to replace unChristlike (sinful) patterns of life with Christlike, godly ones." -*The Distinguishing Feature of Christian Counseling*, Dr. Wayne A. Mack

October 28

You can't get any higher!

> Since then we have a great high priest who has passed through the heavens, Jesus, the Son of God, let us hold fast our confession. For we do not have a high priest who is unable to sympathize with our weaknesses, but one who in every respect has been tempted as we are, yet without sin. Let us then with confidence draw near to the throne of grace, that we may receive mercy and find grace to help in time of need. Hebrews 4:14-16

I often tell people that one of the reasons that I stopped drinking and using drugs is because I couldn't get high enough. The word **high** is used 20 times in the book of Hebrews. God wants you to get high! But, isn't this writing about abstaining from fleshly lusts which wage war against the soul? (see 1 Peter 2:11) Yes, but I'm not inviting you to that kind of high.

I am inviting you to view the majesty of Christ, which gives you victory over all that oppose God (especially addictions). The key word in the book of Hebrews is "better." If you have the 20/20 vision to escape the corruption in the world through lust, then you must see Christ as He is.

The central character of Hebrews is Christ. Unfortunately, Christ is not the central character in our treatment of addictions (as in the past.) This is something that we need to repent of. One of the ways that I rate a resource for addictions when stocking my library and posting on my Facebook group *Quality Christian Resources on Addictions* is by noting how much of the source refers to Christ. Unfortunately, much of what is presented today is self-centered (sometimes subtly.)

The *Thompson Chain Reference Study Bible* says that the epistle Hebrews "was apparently written primarily to Hebrew Christians. These converts were in constant danger of relapsing into Judaism, or at least of attaching too much importance to ceremonial observances." They were not much different than us who are susceptible to addictions and need to be reminded of the awe of the true and living God.

Ever since the late 1980s, I have been exposed to all kinds of methods of dealing with addictions. In 1994, I began writing about addictions from the Scriptures. Some programs address addictions well, others better, and one is best. The more Christ-centered a program is, the better.

1. Without Christ, there is no remission of sin
2. We need the wisdom that is found in Christ to conquer addictions
3. We need the power that is in Christ to conquer addictions
4. Through Christ, we have the Holy Spirit

October 29

Let the Church say amen!

Long ago, at many times and in many ways, God spoke to our fathers by the prophets, but in these last days He has spoken to us by His Son, whom He appointed the heir of all things, through whom also He created the world. Hebrews 1:1-2

Let the Church Say Amen is the title of a song written by Andraé Crouch. "God has spoken. Let the Church Say Amen" are the lyrics to the song. How you handle addictions depends largely on how you agree with God.

The word "amen" means to agree. The truth of the matter is that every time you indulge in whatever is displeasing to God, you are calling Him a liar. Doesn't sound pretty, does it? Well, addictions aren't pretty.

After this, the Word of the Lord came to Abram in a vision: "Do not be afraid, Abram. I am your shield, your very great reward." Genesis 15:1

I became so fascinated by the phrase "the Word of the Lord came" once that I did a study. The phrase is used 92 times in the Word of God. In the past, I thought the soberest thing in all the universe was to be "before the Lord" (yet another interesting study of phrases.) Now, I wonder if this "Word of the Lord came" is even more sobering.

When the Word of the Lord comes, it is sobering and refreshing. The Word of the Lord breaks the bonds of addictions and unites us with God. There is no other "vehicle" that will take us there.

One of the scariest things I have ever experienced was the erroneous thought that since I had forsaken God for the idolatry of addiction so many times He would never speak to me again. Thank God, I was wrong! And it is so very gracious of Him to bring His Word to us.

We all get high for various reasons. One of the reasons that I got high was because I found it to be exciting. The Word of God is by far, the most exciting thing that I have ever found!

God has manifested Himself most vividly in Christ. Hebrews 1:2 says that God has spoken through His Son. The cross of Christ is the most vivid proof of God's love for you. The question is whether it means anything to you!

This is just one reason why a Christ-centered approach to addictions is essential. Without Jesus we do not have a complete view of God nor can we be friends with Him. Addictions don't want to be friends with God.

October 30

How special?

And a cloud overshadowed them, and a voice came out of the cloud, "This is My beloved Son; listen to Him." And suddenly, looking around, they no longer saw anyone with them but Jesus only. Mark 9:7-8

Are not addictions considered to be special to many? Desire involves what we hunger, thirst, yearn, long for, hanker, want, yen, need, crave, lust for, will, and love. It is a known fact that the things we desire we set apart. They are special to us. How true this is for addictions!

The same is true with God! One of the definitions for sanctify is "to set apart." That is what Peter meant when he told his readers to "sanctify the Lord" in their hearts (1 Peter 3:15). How special is God to you? This is what it means to reverence Him!

God is only as special to us as we realize how special we are to Him. 1 John 4:19 says that "we love Him because He first loved us." He first loved us by sending His Son to die for us. That's why programs that exclude Jesus Christ are not only insufficient but insulting to God.

Our interest and ability to reverence God are based on a personal relationship with Him. God wants to speak to us. Hebrew Chapter One tells us our conversation with God begins with Jesus.

I love how Edward T. Welch wrote his workbook (*Crossroads*) with listening as a priority. God commanded the disciples of Christ to listen to His beloved Son. He commands us as well. Oh, that we were overshadowed by His love and would no longer fooled by the counterfeit glories of addictions longing to see Jesus only!

Because I have learned that the idols of addictions can speak loudly to our souls, I was able to appreciate Welch's approach to addictions as I overcame my addiction to crack cocaine. I believe that our reverence for God should fuel and strengthen our abstinence from addictions. We must listen to God.

- God initiates communication
- We begin an honest investigation
- God provides confirmation
- We begin a deeper relationship
- God provides transformation
- We delight in sanctification

October 31

What do you trust? (part 1)

You who fear the LORD, trust in the LORD! He is their help and their shield. Psalm 115:11

Do you trust the Lord to stand between you and everything else as a shield? Addiction will always stand between us and God (as the idols we make them). God offers safety for all who would humble themselves to Him. Trust is either based on ourselves or God.

A shield is something apart from ourselves. We cannot shield ourselves. Addictions deceptively promise to help and shield us through the difficulties of life. If we believe the lies of addiction, we are trusting in ourselves. Many think that they can find comfort in addictions. God longs to give you what addictions cannot.

Reverence and trust go hand in hand. Refusing to trust God is irreverent not to trust God. If you don't trust God then you are saying He is either incapable or uncaring. That's an insult. Anything less is self-reliant. We either trust God or ourselves. Anyone who wants to overcome addiction must learn they cannot trust themselves. The alternative is to deny reality (giving root to insanity.)

Shields are made to protect from things that cause harm. Our greatest harm comes from ourselves. William Spurstowe said, "Satan can convey himself and his suggestions to both the understanding and the will in a more intimate and efficacious manner than any human agent possibly can." That is why many believe that Satan is our greatest enemy. But he can do nothing without the cooperation of our fleshly nature.

> "Satan only by moral persuasions, which may be powerful to solicit, but not to constrain. And in this respect he is (as Jerome truly calls him) a feeble and weak enemy, who can only overcome him who yields, not him who resists; and hurts him who puts his weapons into his hand, not him who keeps them in his own." -*The Wiles of Satan,* Spurstowe (1605-1666)

There are at least six variables of worship. Trust is one of those elements. The other elements are awe, dominion, sacrifice, love, and praise. Worship was originally spelled "worthship". It means acknowledging the worth of the object worshipped. The reverential factor of addiction asks whether God is worth trusting or whether you will put your trust in the things of this world.

November 1

What do you trust? (part 2)

> Do not love the world or the things in the world. If anyone loves the world, the love of the Father is not in him. For all that is in the world—the desires of the flesh and the desires of the eyes and pride of life—is not from the Father but is from the world. And the world is passing away along with its desires, but whoever does the will of God abides forever.
> 1 John 2:15-17

Perhaps the question of the day is who you love! Our trust in addiction is built on our senses. That's why it is only natural for us to get wrapped up in addictions. It takes the supernatural power of God to reverentially turn from every idol that would separate us.

Euphoria can be good or evil. God gave us euphoria just like all our senses. Satan desires to pervert euphoria just as He does everything else that God has made.

To "get high" is to achieve a state of mental euphoria. Euphoria is defined as a state of intense happiness and self-confidence. I call it "the desired effect." Words related to euphoria are jubilation, joy, elation, exhilaration, frenzy, relaxation, madness, ecstasy, intoxication, and bliss.

Notice that some of the definitions of euphoria are undesirable! That's because euphoria does not always reflect reality! *"The man who's falling, he thinks he's flying"* is one of my favorite lyrics from a Christian rapper named *Phanatik*.

Shields are designed to protect. A shield is one of the names that God is given to describe how He protects and secures His own. In *All the Divine Names and Titles in the Bible,* Herbert Lockyer said, "Scripture furnishes us with a rich variety of impressive names and graphic pictures to reveal who and what our Lord actually is in regard to the protective safety and positive security of His redeem children."

> "What wonderful assurance is derived from knowing that in all circumstances and under all conditions we have a Protector, a Provider, and a Preserver, an ever present Shield and Defender, the ancient of days, environment and grandeur, exalted and honor, and enthroned in Glory. All power resides in the hand of this Potentate … David portrays Deity as the basis of his defense in a score of ways … my Strength, my Rock, my Fortress, my Deliverer, my Buckler, my Salvation, my High Tower, my Defense, my Habitation, my Refuge, my Shepherd." -Dr. C.J. Rolls

November 2

What do you trust? (part 3)

You who fear the LORD, trust in the LORD! He is their help and their shield. Psalm 115:11

1 Peter 2:11 says that lust wages war against your soul. Fleshly lusts wage war against the soul because they do not fulfill. Ephesians 4:22 refers to them as deceitful lusts. Fleshly lusts draw us away from God (where there is peace, wholeness, strength, soundness, and reward).

Fleshly lust wage war against the soul by robbing you of the affection that you should have for God and others. When you indulge in fleshly lusts then you are not able to function as God intended and so it destructively affects your soul.

1. you repine
2. you become less human
3. you make poor choices
4. you allow your passions to dominate you
5. it is not safe
6. ruins your integrity

Jesus' answer to addiction in a new life. Colossians 3:10 refers to clothing "yourselves with the new [spiritual self], which is [ever in the process of being] renewed and remolded into [fuller and more perfect knowledge upon] knowledge after the image (the likeness) of Him Who created it." (*Amplified Version, Classic Edition*) 2 Peter 1:3-4 explains how Jesus shields His followers from deceitful lusts.

His divine power has granted to us all things that pertain to life and godliness, through the knowledge of Him who called us to His own glory and excellence, by which He has granted to us His precious and very great promises, so that through them you may become partakers of the divine nature, having escaped from the corruption that is in the world because of sinful desire. 2 Peter 1:3-4

"In Roman times, a perfectly plain shield was given to a young warrior in his maiden campaign, and was known as 'The Shield of Expectation.' As he achieved glory, his deeds were recorded or symbolized on it. God is ever 'The Shield of Expectation' of His warriors, who fight the good fight of faith, and their names are inscribed upon His heart, just as the high priest in Israel bore the names of the tribes on his breast." -*All the Divine Names and Titles in the Bible,* Herbert Lockyer

November 3

Blindness

For whoever lacks these qualities is so nearsighted that he is blind, having forgotten that he was cleansed from his former sins.
2 Peter 1:9

While physical blindness can hinder us from being highly functional physically, it cannot prevent us from being highly functional spiritually. I will always remember greeting a blind brother in the Lord by asking him if he was walking with the Lord. His response was, "I've got my eyes set on Him!"

The Greek word that is used for "blind" in the verse above means "to raise a smoke or darkened by smoke!" Anyone who knows anything about addiction knows the relevance. ***While some are permanently blind physically, no one has to remain permanently blind spiritually.***

The irony is that no one in their right mind would choose to be physically blind, but some prefer spiritual blindness. **Blindness is perhaps the leading cause of addictions.** The blindness of addiction is that I cannot see the goodness of God (along with His reasoning.)

The blindness of addictions is that I cannot see how offensive it is to God. The blindness of addictions is that I cannot see how my time, energy, and resources would be better spent on others. **While physical blindness may not always be preventable or treatable, spiritual blindness can always be prevented or treated.**

A smokescreen is defined as something designed to obscure, confuse, or mislead. Since Satan does not want God to receive the glory that He is due, he does everything he can to obscure our vision while confusing and misleading us concerning our priorities.

The blindness that Peter speaks of may be prevented or treated with the light that is in Christ. There are initially two dangers caused by blindness. One is the danger of misdirection. The other danger of blindness is stumbling.

The cure for the blindness that Peter speaks of is not found in our eyes but in our hearts. Jesus said that the "pure in heart shall see God" (Matthew 5:8). Our hearts are made pure through the blood of Christ which takes away the sins of the world.

Sin is the only thing that can keep you from God. Here is yet another argument against the "disease concept" because **there is no disease that can keep you from God** (addiction does.)

So long as we can see clearly, we have direction. Addiction is misdirection. Clear vision also prevents us from stumbling or falling. A lack of appreciation for my physical sight may not cause blindness, but a lack of appreciation for my spiritual sight is disastrous.

November 4

Don't forget! (part 1)

> For whoever lacks these qualities is so nearsighted that he is blind, having forgotten that he was cleansed from his former sins.
> 2 Peter 1:9

July 21, 2014, was unforgettable! I have the ring to remind me. Better yet, I have my wife to remind me! Since I did not get married until I was 53, for the first six months, I would often think "I'm married, I'm *really* married!"

Many of my friends and relatives were shocked as well! No one ever has to remind themselves that they are married (at least I hope not.) When someone forgets that they are married, problems are bound to occur.

The most memorable day in my life was in February 1981. On that day I became united with the God of heaven for all eternity because I accepted the payment for all my sins (past, present, and future) made by His Son. Just as when someone forgets they are married, I run into problems whenever I forget that I have been cleansed of my sins.

One thing that we need to remember concerning addictions is that God loves us just as we are *and that He loves us too much to let us stay as we are.* We must be reminded of the love of God that is in Christ to break the spell of addiction. We must, also, remember that God has a greater purpose for us than addiction (which is, also, more fulfilling.)

Forgetfulness was a major theme for Israel (as it should be with us who are susceptible to the idols of addiction.) **The Hebrew word for forgetting often used in Scripture is not just a lapse of memory but to ignore, cease to care, or give attention to.** There are warnings and consequences of forgetting God throughout the Old Testament.

Among the eight occurrences in Deuteronomy

> Only take care, and keep your soul diligently, **lest you forget** the things that your eyes have seen, and lest they depart from your heart all the days of your life. 4:9

> Take care, **lest you forget** the covenant of the Lord your God, which He made with you, and make a carved image, the form of anything that the Lord your God has forbidden you. 4:23

Forgetting can be as much of a practice as remembering!

November 5

Don't forget! (part 2)

Then take care **lest you forget the Lord**, who brought you out of the land of Egypt, out of the house of slavery. It is the Lord your God you shall fear. Him you shall serve and by His name you shall swear. You shall not go after other gods, the gods of the peoples who are around you— for the Lord your God in your midst is a jealous God— lest the anger of the Lord your God be kindled against you, and He destroy you from off the face of the earth. 6:12-15

Then your heart be lifted up, and **you forget the Lord your God**, who brought you out of the land of Egypt, out of the house of slavery, Who led you through the great and terrifying wilderness, with its fiery serpents and scorpions and thirsty ground where there was no water, who brought you water out of the flinty rock, who fed you in the wilderness with manna that your fathers did not know, that He might humble you and test you, to do you good in the end. Beware lest you say in your heart, 'My power and the might of my hand have gotten me this wealth.' 8:14-17

And if **you forget the Lord your God** and go after other gods and serve them and worship them, I solemnly warn you today that you shall surely perish. 8:19

Moses said that he "*solemnly*" warned the Israelites. Solemn is one of the definitions for sobriety that is not often mentioned. Peter places great emphasis on forgetting and remembering in Second Peter Chapter One. Of the many subjects I have encountered while writing on addictions, forgetting is not a subject that we can take lightly.

I don't apologize for pausing to explore the issue of forgetting at length. **If we forget the things God wants us to remember, we make ourselves vulnerable to the lies of the devil once again!** As lies of the devil lead to addiction, the Word of God is the solution to our puzzled lives.

Forget ⇒ Fall ⇒ Misfunction.

As I mentioned, the Hebrew word for forgetting that is often used refers to not just a lapse of memory ***but to ignore, cease to care, or give attention to.*** Throughout the Old and New Testaments, there are warnings and consequences of forgetting God.

November 6

Don't forget! (part 3)

For whoever lacks these qualities is so nearsighted that he is blind, having forgotten that he was cleansed from his former sins.
2 Peter 1:9

And he took bread, and when he had given thanks, he broke it and gave it to them, saying, "This is my body, which is given for you. Do this in remembrance of me." And likewise the cup after they had eaten, saying, "This cup that is poured out for you is the new covenant in my blood. Luke 22:19-20

When Jesus took the Passover with His disciples for the last time, He commanded His followers to do so in remembrance of Him. This is commonly known as "The Lord's Supper or Communion." **The war against addictions must begin with a union with Christ to have God's approval. (Though you may remain abstinent, without Christ there is no peace with God.)**

The Lord's Supper is a time to reflect upon the sacrifice that Christ made for our sins (which includes the sin of addiction.) It is a time to remember that sin is so displeasing to God that He sacrificed His Son out of His love for us.

What we forget has less value. If there is nothing of more value, addictions await. The most valuable thing we may own is the redemption of our souls. Jesus asked, "What does it profit for a man to gain the whole world and lose his soul?" (Matthew 16:26)

While studying Ezekiel 16, I noticed that God began reminding Israel of how He adorned them as His Bride with silver, gold, and fine clothing as well as prestige among the nations. While Israel could see the love that God had for them through the silver, gold, and prestige that He blessed her with, *after the sacrifice of Christ we have been blessed with the most vivid display of God's love.*

Since you call on a Father Who judges each person's work impartially, live out your time as foreigners here in reverent fear. **For you know that it was not with perishable things such as silver or gold that you were redeemed** from the empty way of life handed down to you from your ancestors, but with the precious blood of Christ, a lamb without blemish or defect. 1 Peter 1:17-19

Peter began <u>reminding</u> others in his first recorded letter. Many essentials are covered in the passage above that relate to a Christ-centered view of addictions. Tomorrow, I'll show you the significance of the passage above!

November 7

Don't forget! (part 4)

For whoever lacks these qualities is so nearsighted that he is blind, having forgotten that he was cleansed from his former sins.
2 Peter 1:9

Since you call on a Father Who judges each person's work impartially, live out your time as foreigners here in reverent fear. **For you know that it was not with perishable things such as silver or gold that you were redeemed** from the empty way of life handed down to you from your ancestors, but with the precious blood of Christ, a lamb without blemish or defect. 1 Peter 1:17-19

Yesterday, I said Peter began <u>reminding</u> his reader of some essentials in his first recorded letter. The passage above covers many essentials related to a Christ-centered view of addictions. While some of the themes are commonly mentioned among various Christian resources, ironically I have rarely seen the last two discussed.

1. Don't forget Who God is!
2. Don't forget who you are!
3. Don't forget your worth!
4. Consider the judgment of God!
5. Revere the Lord!

While we recognize that God offers forgiveness in Christ, we must not forget the judgment of God. God offers forgiveness so that we may escape judgment. The judgment of God is real.

If we ignore the judgment of God, the level of our sobriety is shallow!

If one of the definitions of sobriety has to do with being serious, then why do so many programs overlook the judgment of God? The answer is that some programs and writings on addictions are more Christ-centered than others. Alas, as I have mentioned, there are levels and degrees of sobriety and reverence.

Whatever the program or resource for addictions, one of the common goals is for people to be different. The most significant difference anyone can experience is being cleansed of their sins. The only thing that separates us from God is sin. And so, the cleansing of our sins provides unity with God.

November 8

Don't forget! (part 5)

For **you have forgotten the God of your salvation and have not remembered the Rock of your refuge**; therefore, though you plant pleasant plants and sow the vine-branch of a stranger, though you make them grow on the day that you plant them and make them blossom in the morning that you sow, yet the harvest will flee away in a day of grief and incurable pain. Isaiah 17:10-11

Can a virgin forget her ornaments, or a bride her attire? Yet **My people have forgotten Me days without number**. Jeremiah 2:32

Surely, as a treacherous wife leaves her husband, so have you been treacherous to Me, O house of Israel, declares the Lord. A voice on the bare heights is heard, the weeping and pleading of Israel's sons because they have perverted their way; **they have forgotten the Lord their God**. Jeremiah 3:20-21

I will scatter you like chaff driven by the wind from the desert. This is your lot, the portion I have measured out to you, declares the Lord, because **you have forgotten Me** and trusted in lies. Jeremiah 13:24-25

But My people **have forgotten Me**; they make offerings to false gods; they made them stumble in their ways, in the ancient roads, and to walk into side roads, not the highway, making their land a horror, a thing to be hissed at forever. Everyone who passes by it is horrified and shakes his head. Like the east wind I will scatter them before the enemy. I will show them My back, not My face, in the day of their calamity." Jeremiah 18:15-17

Have you forgotten the evil of your fathers, the evil of the kings of Judah, the evil of their wives, your own evil, and the evil of your wives, which they committed in the land of Judah and in the streets of Jerusalem? They have not humbled themselves even to this day, nor have they feared, nor walked in My law and My statutes that I set before you and before your fathers. Jeremiah 44:9-10

From the Old Testament, we see how Israel suffered dire consequences by forgetting her unity with God. Remembrance counteracts forgetting. You cannot function as God intends without remembering. As a result, we lack stability. **Remembrance is needed to function as God intends spiritually.** (Passages are from the *NIV*.)

November 9

At home with God (part 1)

> Dominion and fear are with God; he makes peace in his high heaven. Job 25:2
>
> Dominion and awe belong to God; he establishes order in the heights of heaven. *NIV*

God is quite comfortable with dominion, awe, order, and peace. **Quality sobriety depends on how comfortable *you* are with God's dominion, awe, order, and peace!** It is to the degree that you are not comfortable with God's dominion, awe, order, and peace that you will attempt to manufacture your own in some form or another (even in the guise of Christianity.)

God is so distinctly different, so uniquely set apart in His greatness that He *owns* dominion and awe. We can only grasp a very small degree of what we think to be dominion and awe while never really owning it (and that only at the permission of God.) Awe and dominion are naturally God's. This is a reality!

Nature reveals reality. Throughout history, man has never been able to change the course of nature. It is not the nature of addictions to give us what we are truly in need of. *To give ourselves to addiction is an attempt to defy nature and alter reality.*

This is the insanity of addiction. Ultimately, if we don't like the way that God is doing things and we don't want to abide by His conditions for change, then we manufacture our own devices. This is how idolatrous addictions are produced!

The atrocity is that we are trying to perform the impossible by attempting to steal from God what rightly belongs to Him (dominion and awe.) The irony is that we are not capable of stealing the dominion and awe that we are seeking. It is not in our power.

Jesus taught his disciples to acknowledge the awe and dominion of God in their regular prayers (Matthew 6:9-10, 13 *KJV*)! In our pride, we think our addictions to be ingenious. *Name one genius that has gone outside the realm of reality.* Although it has been said that there is a fine line between genius and insanity, you will never meet a true genius who lives in a make-believe world.

Addiction is a make-believe world. Addiction tells you that you are in command. Addiction tells you that you are a genius to come up with a formula for producing all that you long for. **Addiction will tell you that you are smarter than God.** Our reverence for God must be more intense than we ever imagined to overcome addiction.

November 10

At home with God (part 2)

Dominion and fear are with God; he makes peace in his high heaven. Job 25:2

Dominion and awe belong to God; he establishes order in the heights of heaven. *NIV*

I remember my brother-in-law, Ellis, waiting on two brothers in their '90's. When he asked Chalie if he wanted some ice-water, Charlie sharply and hastily replied "Naw, I don't want no water." Ellis came back five minutes later with the same glasses of water announcing how water was good for them. He said, "Don't you guys want some *ice-water?*" Charlie cheerfully sang, "Oh, I'll take some *ice-water!*"

The quality of water that Chalie was seeking was different than what he believed Ellis was offering. Charlie didn't know that Ellis had what he was looking for all along. We may respond to God as starkly as Charlie responded to Ellis when God offers us what we are looking for instead of addictions.

Our degree of reverence must be sound and strong enough for us to distinguish the will of God and to desire His rule. Our reverence must be based on the understanding of our frailty and foolishness. Our frailty and foolishness are our dominions. Proverbs 2:6 says, "the Lord gives wisdom; from his mouth come knowledge and understanding." That is His dominion.

> "[Bildad], in a few words shows the infinite distance there is between God and man, teaching us, I. To think highly and honourably of God II. To think meanly of ourselves. These, however misapplied to Job, are two good lessons for us all to learn."
> –Matthew Henry's Commentary on the Whole Bible

Dominion can also be viewed as a place where someone dwells. Do we not dominate our own houses? If not, there is chaos and confusion. We don't do a very good job of dominating the things that God has placed in our hands without His dominion over us. This is better known as dysfunction.

I was once honored to attend a mayor's conference in Chicago with a priest as the keynote speaker who told all the mayors that "they could not master anything unless they know *the* Master." God's dominion has boundaries that we need to adhere to lest we forfeit our peace and order. It is a corrupt view that comes from a corrupt soul that produces corrupt actions.

November 11

The value of reverence (part 1)

And he said to man, "Behold, the fear of the Lord, that is wisdom, and to turn away from evil is understanding." Job 28:28

Behold is a word that captured my attention early in sobriety. I studied all the times it is used in Scripture. When someone beckons us to behold, they say this is worthy of our attention. ***We behold that which interests us.***
That which we behold causes us to stop and pause. Addictions are beheld by many. I would drop everything for the sake of my addictions. On the contrary, that which is of Christ is infinitely worthy of our interests, our attentions, and, yes, even our affections.

Jesus asked, *"What does it profit a man to gain the whole world and lose his soul?"* (Mark 8:36) We may ask, "What value do addictions have over wisdom?" Or, "How do I attain true sobriety apart from the fear of the Lord?" It is with perversion that addictions take precedence over wisdom and truth as well as love and understanding. Sobriety teaches you what is important.

Job emphasizes what is most important. The courtroom is designed to capture our attention while emphasizing important issues. The Book of Job often reads like a court case. It is no wonder since Job's faith is on trial. Every trial has its pleas and defenses. Trials are designed to uncover the truth. One would wonder if Job were on trial or if God is on trial in the book of Job. What happens when we put addictions on trial?

Our corrupt natures are deficient in beholding the magnificence of God (they are not even interested.) In a trial, facts must be stated and proven true or false. Addiction is not concerned with the facts. Addictions don't care about the truth. Addictions have no sense of fairness.

> "Desire does not want to be told that it can be satisfied only by changing. Desire wants satisfaction, not a morality lesson." -*Loving God with all My Heart*, Julie Ackerman Link

> "What gets you high? What do you get a kick out of? What turns you on? What are the things that give you great pleasure? Is there anything in your life that you are so thrilled that you would risk your life for it? What are the things that you are willing to defend? Anyone holding on to addiction is ready and willing to offer a defense of the addiction's <u>usefulness</u>. You may have noticed that I said that they were 'ready and willing to offer a defense,' but I did not say that they were **able** to offer a defense." –*Why <u>Not</u> Get High*, Gregory Madison

November 12

The value of reverence (part 2)

And he said to man, "Behold, the fear of the Lord, that is wisdom, and to turn away from evil is understanding." Job 28:28

Wisdom is the capacity to see things from God's perspective and respond according to scriptural principles. In *Duel Occupation*, on August 21st, I emphasized that we are called to build. Building requires a foundation.

Proverbs 3:19 says, *"By wisdom the LORD laid the earth's foundations, by understanding he set the heavens in place."* If the wisdom of God created everything, how much more can it recreate our lives (not just recover.)

Where there is reverence, there is wisdom, knowledge, and understanding. Where there is wisdom, knowledge, and understanding, there is confidence. This then becomes a fountain of life. The Hebrew word in Proverbs 14:26 translated as *confidence* means security, a refuge, assurance, or a sure and firm hope. The word *fountain* in Proverbs 14:27 speaks of the source of life, joy, wisdom, happiness, welfare, and purification.

> The fear of the Lord is the beginning of wisdom, and the knowledge of the Holy One is insight. Proverbs 9:10

> The fear of the LORD is the beginning of wisdom, and the knowledge of the Holy One is understanding. NIV

> In the fear of the Lord one has strong confidence, Proverbs 14:26a

> The fear of the Lord is a fountain of life, that one may turn away from the snares of death. Proverbs 14:27

Would you agree that the value that we have for wisdom determines the quality of our sobriety? When someone does not have the right motives for abstaining from addiction, then he lives by his own standards (he makes the rules.) Proverb 3:7 says, *"Be not wise in your own eyes; fear the LORD, and turn away from evil."*

The nature of reverence gives us a personal awareness of God's presence, an understanding of the magnificence of God, and creates a sense of obligation to God. Each of these is necessary for our maturity.

We owe it to God to remain free of addictions so that He will get the most use of our lives. In Ephesians 4:1 Paul encourages Christians to walk worthy of God's calling. Beyond an obsession over the consequences of addiction; beyond striving to recapture all that we have forfeited.

November 13

Significance

And Elkanah, her husband, said to her, "Hannah, why do you weep? And why do you not eat? And why is your heart sad? Am I not more to you than ten sons?" 1 Samuel 1:8

Hannah's husband asked her four questions. It is a privilege to have someone close enough to us to ask probing questions. If you are not perfect, why not have people who can help you grow by aiding you to improve? Yet, Hannah's growth may not have been Elkanah's chief concern.

Some would say that Hannah's actions made Elkanah uncomfortable. When Elkanah asked Hannah if he were more to her than ten sons, some say that Elkanah was concerned about his <u>significance</u>. In my twenties, I began to hear people ask about "significant others." <u>Addictions challenge the significance of others.</u>

What is significant to you has your time, attention, and care ... You are often preoccupied with what is significant to you. What is significant is set apart. You choose the things that are significant over other things.

You neglect or reject things that are less significant to you for more significant things. It has been said that two objects can not occupy the same space at the same time. So it is with who or what is significant to you.

Elkanah asked Hannah why her heart was sad. Hannah's sadness was comparable to the discontentment of addiction. Hannah had an unfulfilled desire. I have learned that with addiction we look for the desired effect. **The desired effect that is sought becomes more important than loving God and others.** The problem comes when you have to face the disappointment that addictions breed.

In *gods at war*, Pastor Kyle Idleman said, "When something good becomes a god, the pleasure it brings dies in the process. Pleasure has this unique trait: the more intensely you chase it, the less likely you are to catch it. Philosophers call this the 'hedonistic paradox.' The idea is that pleasure, pursued for its own sake, evaporates before our eyes."

> Hope deferred makes the heart sick, but a desire fulfilled is a tree of life. Proverbs 13:12

Hannah was seeking hope just as people seek in addiction. Hannah's hope was not in a lifeless idol but in a true and living God. God offers you hope in the living Christ in exchange for the idols of addiction. It is the nature of addiction to want more and more. This causes our souls to be driven and tossed.

> We have this as a sure and steadfast anchor of the soul. Hebrews 6:19

November 14

Fasting (part 1)

> And Elkanah, her husband, said to her, "Hannah, why do you weep? And why do you not eat? And why is your heart sad? Am I not more to you than ten sons?" 1 Samuel 1:8

Elkanah also asked Hannah why she did not eat. Eating is something that people cherish all over the world. Food is a delight except when you are preoccupied with something more worthy of your attention. Hannah's attention was drawn to her desire to mother a child. Fasting is a good practice when you want to give yourself more to God.

I recommend a book called *A Hunger for God* by John Piper to all readers who are serious about developing a practice of fasting. One of the statements that Piper makes is that **"Christian fasting is a test to see what desires control us."** Piper says that "our fast unto God is telling God that we want Him more than anything (even food and water.)" Fasting and repentance often go together in Scripture.

Hannah's fast was guided by her intense passion to contribute to the Lord and His people. Hannah's appetite was as spiritual as when Jesus told His disciples that He had meat that they knew nothing of (John 4:32). Addiction reveals an insatiable appetite.

Am I saying that people *have to* fast to develop a life of sobriety? It sure wouldn't hurt. Since fasting is a practice of denying ourselves, then it can be of great benefit to those who were previously engaged in the self-absorbing life of addiction.

It is very important for those who are turning from addictions to replace bad habits with good habits. Fasting is an act of self-denial. Such a practice must be done unto God as an expression of His worthiness.

By fasting, I am referring to abstaining from food and/or water for a certain time. Fasting can be done as a group or by a single individual. Your fasting may be something that you decide on your own, led by another believer (usually a leader,) or solely led by the Spirit of God.

There are all kinds of variations to fasting as well. It can be said that fasting is the abstinence from anything legitimate in and of itself, for some spiritual purpose. You may choose the amount of time you intend on fasting in advance or decide as you go.

You can decide on a partial fast or a strict fast. A partial fast is one in which you decide to abstain from various foods (usually the participant abstains from meats for a while.) A strict fast is a practice of abstaining from all foods (and drinking only water.)

I would advise those who have health conditions to consult their physician before fasting. The main thing is that a fast is meant to be God-centered rather than self-centered.

November 15

Fasting (part 2)

> Though He were a Son, yet learned He obedience by the things which He suffered Hebrews 5:8

No matter what kind of fast you engage in, <u>it is something different from the ordinary. That's the life that God is calling you to have (different). You might say that a fast can be a statement or</u> agreement with God that you are going to do things differently and that you are giving yourself completely to Him.

Fasting also allows you to shut out the distractions of earthly things. Many of them are not evil (in and of themselves), yet they can lure your attention away from God. Jesus said, "Be careful, or your hearts will be weighed down with dissipation, drunkenness, and the anxieties of life, and that day will close on you unexpectedly like a trap" (Luke 20:34). Fasting makes us more alert (watchful).

Another important advantage of fasting is that it teaches you to suffer. Suffering is important to our spiritual growth. It allows us to become more like Christ, who himself grew through suffering.

Mark Bertrand says that "most of what many [not just addicts] do is either to avoid pain, discomfort, and awkwardness or to achieve happiness, excitement, or pleasures."

> "There are times when virtue demands that we experience pain. There are times when doing right means forgoing pleasure. Christian wisdom differs from that of the world in that it treats as a means what others seek as ends. The end, for a Christian, is neither pain nor pleasure, but Christ. If to serve him we must suffer, it is good. If in serving him we find pleasure, it is good. But pain or pleasure aside, our lives are dedicated to service." *-(Re)Thinking Worldview*, Mark Bertrand

<u>Suffering teaches us things that we would not learn otherwise</u>. For the person repenting from an addiction, suffering must become more of a reality. Whenever someone indulges in an addiction (of any kind) he or she is attempting to avoid suffering (in one form or another.)

Fasting helps the believer to abide in Christ (to stay in fellowship with the Lord.) This is not only the key to sobriety, but it also is essential to the life of every believer.

Fasting also provides rest. While fasting your organs do not have to function as they normally do. You don't have to concern yourself with the acquisition, preparation, and disposal of food when fasting. Fasting allows you the opportunity to slow down. And, fasting allows your body to detoxify.

November 16

The fear that draws you near (part 1)

> But I, through the abundance of your steadfast love, will enter your house. I will bow down toward your holy temple in the fear of you. Psalms 5:7

The theme of God's rule prevails. In my earlier entries, I emphasized the importance of having God on the throne. In Psalms 5:7 the rulership of God is expressed as bowing.

> "As the sculpture is on the seal, so will the print on the wax be; if the fear of God be deeply engraven on thy heart, there is no doubt but it will make a suitable impression on the duty thou performest."
> -William Gurnall

Around 1996 the Lord started showing me the connection between idolatry and addictions. This has been the theme for much of my writing. Os Guiness said, "Idolatry is huge in the Bible, dominant in our personal lives, and irrelevant in our mistaken estimations." Ligon Duncan said, "The whole Bible is written as a full-scale assault on idolatry." Many bow to God, and more bow to idols.

Joshua told Israel to choose between God and idols out of reverence as did Elijah (Joshua 24:14; 1 Kings 18:21). It's always a matter of reverence. And until we are fully redeemed we will always be tempted to manufacture idols that compete with God.

> Enter by the narrow gate. For the gate is wide and the way is easy that leads to destruction, and those who enter by it are many. For the gate is narrow and the way is hard that leads to life, and those who find it are few. Matthew 7:13-14

Bowing to God not only places us where we belong, but it also places God where He belongs. The *King James Version* uses the word **worship** instead of the word **bow**. Many of my fellow authors agree that addiction is a worship disorder.

Addiction prevents us from bowing to God to the degree that He is worthy (if we bow to Him at all.) Addiction causes us to bow to something besides God. The most complete and liberating solution to addiction is found in bowing down to the true and living God.

Bowing is a sign of humility. Humility is essential to the quality of our sobriety. It is impossible to reverence God without humility. By the same token, **true sobriety is not possible without reverence toward God.**

November 17

The fear that draws you near (part 2)

> But I, through the abundance of your steadfast love, will enter your house. I will bow down toward your holy temple in the fear of you. Psalms 5:7

The humility of a servant causes him to bow. To bow is to surrender. As Jesus became a servant, we are allowed the opportunity to become like Him as we die to ourselves. Jesus said that if anyone was to come after Him, they must take up their cross and follow Him (Luke 9:23). The *Strong's Bible Dictionary* says that bowing means "to sink down."

1. He is worthy
2. His strength (comfort and care)
3. His wisdom and truth
4. His joy (contentment as well)
5. For this, we were created

No matter what you say about addictions, you cannot deny that **addictions do not bow to anyone**. Addictions are determined to get what they want. Bowing is a sign of surrender. The greatest thing about bowing is that it brings you close to God. ***The only thing that can separate us from God is sin.*** And since addiction is the sin of idolatry that seeks to dethrone God, then it separates us from God. It makes us enemies with God.

> You adulteresses [disloyal sinners—flirting with the world and breaking your vow to God]! Do you not know that being the world's friend [that is, loving the things of the world] is being God's enemy? So whoever chooses to be a friend of the world makes himself an enemy of God. James 4:4 (*Amplified Bible*)

Our intimacy with God begins with the cross of Christ. As we revere God through the sacrifice that was made by sending Jesus, we are joined with Christ. The fear of the Lord is different than all other fears as God is different. It is a fear that draws you near.

Drawing near to God needs to be the goal of our sobriety. Addictions destroy our intimacy with God. ***Whether you are interested in God or not, God is tremendously interested in you.*** To deny an earthly monarch can bring dire consequences. Would you dare deny God what He wants? ***Self-denial allows us the greatest intimacy with the Almighty that is humanly possible.*** It is expressed as we bow in reverence to God. ***I know of no other sobriety than one that reverences God!***

November 18

Unmoveable (part 1)

> O LORD, who shall sojourn in your tent? Who shall dwell on your holy hill? He who walks blamelessly and does what is right and speaks truth in his heart; who does not slander with his tongue and does no evil to his neighbor, nor takes up a reproach against his friend; in whose eyes a vile person is despised, but who honors those who fear the LORD; who swears to his own hurt and does not change; who does not put out his money at interest and does not take a bribe against the innocent. He who does these things shall never be moved. Psalms 15:1-5

Those who want long-term quality sobriety want to be unmoveable. Psalms 15 could be labeled "Relapse Prevention." The characteristics found in Psalms 15 are found in those who are stable in a mature relationship with Christ.

Servanthood is a central theme of sobriety. In Psalms 15, we see a person who moves beyond servanthood to becoming a friend of Christ just as Jesus' disciples had become. If you look closely, you will see a description of Christ in Psalms 15.

> No longer do I call you servants, for the servant does not know what his master is doing; but I have called you friends, for all that I have heard from my Father I have made known to you. John 15:15

Psalms 15 starts with two questions that determine our fate. They are questions that are most solemn and sobering. One of the things that I remember when entering the many rehabs that I attended during my struggle with drugs is what seemed like an endless number of questions about the frequency of my drug and alcohol use, how it affected my health, employment, relationships, etc. Psalm 15:1 asks two questions.

1. Who shall dwell in God's tent?
2. Who shall dwell on God's holy hill?

Quality sobriety involves much more than abstinence. Concerning Psalms 15, the *Ryrie Study Bible* says, "Here David describes the character of the person who qualifies to be a guest of God." Rather than the word ***soujourn***, other translations use the words ***dwell*** and ***abide***. To dwell or abide indicates closeness and consistency. Rather than the word ***tent***, some translations use the word ***sanctuary***. A sanctuary is a specific place that is set apart for a person who is set apart (unto God).

November 19

Unmoveable (part 2)

> O LORD, who shall sojourn in your tent? Who shall dwell on your holy hill? He who walks blamelessly and does what is right and speaks truth in his heart; who does not slander with his tongue and does no evil to his neighbor, nor takes up a reproach against his friend; in whose eyes a vile person is despised, but who honors those who fear the LORD; who swears to his own hurt and does not change; who does not put out his money at interest and does not take a bribe against the innocent. He who does these things shall never be moved. Psalms 15:1-5

The synonymous, parallel questions of verse one are answered in the following verses by an eleven-fold description of the righteous man upright in deed, word, attitude, and finances. These qualities, not natural to men, are imparted by God.

One of the many traits of someone who has drawn near to God according to Psalms 15 is that they honor those who fear the Lord. That's because they also fear God! They share a common bond. Both see the Lord as special. Malachi 3:16 says, "Then they that feared the LORD spake one with another: and the LORD hearkened, and heard, and a book of remembrance was written before him, for them that feared the LORD, and that thought upon his name."

They know the value of what belongs to God. Isaiah 33:6 says, "He will be the sure foundation for your times, a rich store of salvation and wisdom and knowledge; the fear of the LORD is the key to this treasure." The unmoveable one communes with and rejoices beside those who fear the Lord.

> "A sinner in a gold chain and silken robes is no more to be compared with a saint in rags than a rushlight in a silver candlestick with the sun behind a cloud." –Spurgeon

Psalms 15:2 says the unmoveable person **walks blamelessly**. Some translations say that they walk uprightly. The text refers to someone who walks; not those who crawl. Walking involves <u>consistency</u>. Isn't that what people are looking for as they break free of addiction?

Jesus gives us a new walk. My friend John Carlson says, "We don't work on sobriety but a New Creation- then sobriety naturally follows!" Again, quality sobriety is not just concerned about remaining abstinent. Lots of people have been abstinent for years but not any soberer or reverent.

Psalms 15:2 also says that the person who cannot be moved **speaks the truth in his heart**. How often do we lie to ourselves in the pursuit of addiction? We lie about why we indulge. We lie about having control. We lie about the dangers. We lie about the remedy.

November 20

Unmoveable (part 3)

O LORD, who shall sojourn in your tent? Who shall dwell on your holy hill? He who walks blamelessly and does what is right and speaks truth in his heart; who does not slander with his tongue and does no evil to his neighbor, nor takes up a reproach against his friend; in whose eyes a vile person is despised, but who honors those who fear the LORD; who swears to his own hurt and does not change; who does not put out his money at interest and does not take a bribe against the innocent. He who does these things shall never be moved. Psalms 15:1-5

Denial is a lie (which breeds and feeds on insanity.) Reverence for God prevents us from lying because we want our thoughts to be pleasing to Him. Lies are not only destructive, they are displeasing to God.

Let the words of my mouth and the meditation of my heart be acceptable in your sight, O LORD, my rock and my redeemer. Psalms 19:14

According to Psalms 15:4, those who **swear to their own hurt and do not change** are unmoveable. This is what I refer to as predetermined or perpetual reverence. The quality of sobriety in Psalms 15:4 involves suffering. In *The Highest Yearning*, I said "The only way for us to experience the full effect of healthy yearning is to grow into the likeness of Christ. The only way that we grow into the likeness of Christ is to suffer."

Psalms 15:5 says that those who are not moved **won't take a bribe**. Are not addictions bribes against our faithfulness to God? The root word addict comes from the Latin word addictus (past tense addicere, which means "to devote, sacrifice, **sell out**, betray or abandon." **Commitment and devotion may be used to describe addiction and our relationship with God.**

Resolving the perplexity of addictions begins with answers from God. Hebrews 2:1 says, "We must pay much closer attention to what we have heard, lest we drift away from it." Drifting lacks direction, purpose, and meaning. And there is a certain emptiness in drifting. Drifting is no fun. But more importantly, God does not want us to drift through life.

"He that doeth these things shall never be moved." No storm shall tear him from his foundations, drag him from his anchorage, or uproot him from his place. Like the Lord Jesus, whose dominion is everlasting, the true Christian shall never lose his crown. He shall not only be on Zion, but like Zion, fixed and firm. He shall dwell in the tabernacle of the Most High, and neither death nor judgment shall remove him from his place of privilege and blessedness." -Spurgeon

November 21

Fables (fantasy, part 1)

> For we did not follow cleverly devised myths when we made known to you the power and coming of our Lord Jesus Christ, but we were eyewitnesses of His majesty. 2 Peter 1:16 (cunningly devised fables, *KJV*)

Would you like to hear a lie? How would you like it if you could not believe a word that someone had to say? Would you put your life in that person's hands? This is what we do with addictions! Cleverly devised myths and fables are not real.

I remember how aggravated I would become when trying to figure out how to get more crack after all my money was gone. I kept thinking that I had some money somewhere. I would just have to figure out where it was. Alas, it was just my imagination. Imagination can be a powerful thing.

Our imaginations can be either constructive or destructive, godly, or evil. In the hands of God, imagination is productive. Genesis 6:5 gives us an ugly view of our imaginations.

> And God saw that the wickedness of man was great in the earth, and that **every imagination of the thoughts of his heart was only evil continually**. Genesis 6:5 KJV

Such is the nature of insanity. Have you ever been insane or encountered someone in this state? When someone is insane there is a lack of communication somewhere along the way. Have you ever noticed how someone insane makes things up? Insane people distort the truth. We have a warped imagination when insane.

Addictions feed on our imaginations. To be more accurate, **addictions feed on <u>distorted</u> imaginations.** Mike Cleveland explains the illusions of pornographic addiction.

> "Pornography, in its essential allurement, promises to quench our thirst. In other words, it promises satisfaction. And honestly, it does satisfy—but only for a time. Pretty soon we discover that we are 'thirsty' again, and as the years go by, we find that we are really never genuinely satisfied. Right? That is because sin never truly satisfies! It does not fulfill us; it depletes us... I thought if I could just see that perfect picture, or have that perfect sexual experience, my life would be full and satisfied. This is the nature of sin."
> -*Pure Freedom Breaking the Addiction to Pornography,* Mike Cleveland

November 22

Fables (fantasy, part 2)

> For we did not follow cleverly devised myths when we made known to you the power and coming of our Lord Jesus Christ, but we were eyewitnesses of His majesty. 2 Peter 1:16 (cunningly devised fables, *KJV*)

God has many ways of showing us the truth if we are willing to listen. The problem is that we sometimes harden our hearts. It is from here that these fantasies, myths, and fables originate.

Such was the case before the flood (as cited earlier), throughout the history of Israel, and to this present day, with mankind. Peter says that this was not the case with Christ. Addiction cannot be trusted; Jesus can!

Cunning and clever are sometimes admirable, but with addiction, they are to be disdained. Addiction is a nightmare. Peter informs his readers that his message is not based on something cunning.

Alcoholics Anonymous describes alcohol as *cunning,* baffling, and powerful. *Google's Dictionary* describes cunning as "having or showing skill in achieving one's ends by deceit or evasion." Other words that describe cunning are "wily, sly, and crafty."

In Genesis 3:1, we are told that "the serpent was more crafty than any of the wild animals the Lord God had made." And of course, we know that the serpent was used and empowered by Satan to communicate the lies that caused Adam and Eve to turn from God.

While many are spending their efforts in trying to figure out addictions from a medical view, we have enough answers that are already provided in the Word of God. The cunning, craftiness of addictions, woven by the Devil, cannot be uncovered by human logic. One of the quotes that I have memorized over the years describing our dilemma is that "genius has its limits, but stupidity knows no bounds."

I love the definition for "the Word" in the *Ryrie Study Bible* footnote to John 1:1 explaining that when Jesus is called the "Word" it is stating that He is "the Logical One." **Jesus is not just a man, He is a genius without limits.**

The credulity of the message that can be found in Scripture about addiction is matched with the supremacy of Christ. A few verses later, Peter says *"you will do well to pay attention as to a lamp shining in a dark place."* Darkness is not just found in addiction, it is also found in the absence of Christ.

> Any formula for resolving addiction that excludes Christ
> should be held under scrutiny.

November 23

Armed with truth

For we did not follow cleverly devised myths when we made known to you the power and coming of our Lord Jesus Christ, but we were eyewitnesses of His majesty. 2 Peter 1:16

Cleverly devised myths are an enemy to our souls because they are unreal. Addictions thrive on myth. The myth of addictions is the empty promises that they claim.

The myths that Peter was speaking of were the stories that people made about the nature of God, of man, and even of Christ. Peter testified to the majesty of Christ. The disgrace of addiction is outlined in the Word of God and the experiences of many witnesses. Truth is a weapon against the lies of addiction.

As I have mentioned on many occasions, addictions are most accurately defined as idols. One of the Hebrew words translated as "idol" literally means "a lie." An idol is a false god. The claims that are made concerning these false gods are just as false as the claims of the cleverly devised myths in the days of the Apostle Peter.

To embrace Christ is to embrace truth. If you are looking for comfort in addiction, then you will never find it. Jesus said to His followers that when the Comforter came (the Holy Spirit), then He would guide them into all truth. Truth is a valuable, yes, a priceless commodity.

Buy the truth, and sell it not, also, wisdom, and instruction, and understanding. Proverbs 23:23 *KJV*

Let not mercy and truth forsake thee: bind them about thy neck; write them upon the table of thine heart: So shalt thou find favour and good understanding in the sight of God and man. Proverbs 3:3-4 *KJV*

Now the Lord descended in the cloud and stood with him there, and proclaimed the name of the Lord. And the Lord passed before him and proclaimed, "The Lord, the Lord God, merciful and gracious, longsuffering, and **abounding in goodness and truth.** Exodus 34:5-6

As quiet as it is kept, *the real issue concerning addictions is whether we want Jesus.* Why do I say that? John 1:14b tells us that Jesus is full of grace and truth. Stability relies on truth. There is a parallel between truth and vision; clarity and focus as well. The cleverly devised myths that Peter spoke of can be called "fuzzy." Perhaps, that is one of the reasons that the Spirit of Truth is called the Comforter as well. **Uncertainty is by no means comfortable.**

November 24

Supernatural (part 1)

And we have the prophetic word **more fully confirmed**. 2 Peter 1:19a

We also have the prophetic message as something **completely reliable**. *NIV*

We have also **a more sure word** of prophecy. *KJV*

I love telling the story of when I got shot. Here I was, the victim of an attempted robbery, rolling around on the ground after the perpetrator had fled, and the first person to come to my aid asked me what happened. "What's wrong," he said. When I replied that I had been shot, his response was, "Are you sure?" That is one of the strangest questions anyone has ever asked me!

Turning to God from the idols of addiction requires ***convictions***. Conviction is defined as *a settled persuasion*, the state of being convinced. You have no reason to change unless you are thoroughly convinced that your actions are wrong.

Peter anticipates his readers' asking, " Are you sure?" He affirms that what has been spoken can be trusted. Affirmation is important for forming the stability that God desires. The Scriptures are so full of affirmations that Peter says that you do well to pay attention to them, like a light shining in a dark place.

Have ye not known? have ye not heard? hath it not been told you from the beginning? have ye not understood from the foundations of the earth? Isaiah 40:21 *KJV*

Since my assistant did not witness the incident and there were no visible wounds, his convictions were not very strong. At that point, I wondered just what I had to do to convince this guy that what I said was true.

I thank God that He has given us His Holy Spirit to convince us that Jesus loves us and can deal with any and every situation we encounter. "Are you sure?", you ask. That might be an even stranger question than my assistant asked the day I was shot. Yes, I'm sure!

While I do not fully embrace the philosophies of *Alcoholics Anonymous,* I agree, as they say, that alcohol is cunning, baffling, and powerful. The response from the Word of God is "the testimony of the Lord is ***sure***, making wise the simple" (Psalms 19:7b).

November 25

Supernatural (part 2)

And we have the prophetic word **more fully confirmed**. 2 Peter 1:19a

We also have the prophetic message as something **completely reliable**. *NIV*

We have also **a more sure word** of prophecy. *KJV*

According to *Strong's Bible Dictionary,* the Greek word that Peter uses that is interpreted as "sure" in the *King James Version* means "**stable, firm, of force, steadfast, and trusty**." Not only do we find these qualities in the Word of God, but these are the qualities in the *Person of God*. Have you found any of these qualities in addictions?

Peter assures his readers that the supernatural conditions by which the Word of God was transmitted are reliable and certain. He then says his readers would do well to "pay attention" (take heed, *KJV*). Peter knew from experience the dangers of allowing His attention to be drawn from Christ.

> And in the fourth watch of the night He came to them, walking on the sea. But when the disciples saw Him walking on the sea, they were terrified, and said, "It is a ghost!" and they cried out in fear. But immediately Jesus spoke to them, saying, "Take heart; it is I. Do not be afraid." And Peter answered Him, "Lord, if it is You, command me to come to You on the water." He said, "Come." So Peter got out of the boat and walked on the water and came to Jesus. But **when he saw the wind, he was afraid, and beginning to sink he cried out, "Lord, save me."** Jesus immediately reached out His hand and took hold of him, saying to him, "O you of little faith, why did you doubt?" Matt. 14:25-31

Jesus told His listeners to take heed on at least 14 different occasions as recorded in the Gospels. It is no mystery that the things that we are addicted to own our attention. The definitions for the word translated "heed" from the *Strong's Bible Dictionary* are relative to addictions.

> "to bring near, to turn the mind to, to given attention to, apply one's self to, hold or cleave to a person or thing, to devote thought and effort to, to be given to or addicted to."

The lights of the world (addictions included) have the potential to capture our attention. *We must determine that our focus will be upon He alone who is worthy of our complete attention and adoration!*

November 26

Be Fruitful! (part 1)

> From you comes my praise in the great congregation; my vows
> I will perform before those who fear him. Psalms 22:25

It seems like yesterday, over 40 years ago, I gave myself to Christ so that He could rescue me from the sin I had committed in the past and the sin I would either be tempted with or commit in the future.

After an intense conversation with God, I saw what my dad had to say. I will always remember that he said that I would have to work out what God had worked in. We get a glimpse of this in Psalms 22:25

> Therefore, my beloved, as you have always obeyed, so now, not only as in my presence but much more in my absence, work out your own salvation with fear and trembling, for it is God who works in you, both to will and to work for his good pleasure. Philippians 2:12-13

> And I am sure of this, that he who began a good work in you will bring it to completion at the day of Jesus Christ. Philippians 1:6

While the Apostle Paul wrote these verses to the followers of Christ in Philippi, the words pertain to *everyone* who is in Christ. **The insanity of addictions tells us that we don't need God (unless He is under our control just like we try to control addictions.)** The psalmist said, "*My praise comes from you.*" The Apostle Paul said, "*It is God who works in you*" and that it is God who begins a good work in the believer.

Hebrews 13:15 calls praise "*the fruit of our lips.*" What kind of fruit does addiction produce? Romans 6:21 asks, "*What fruit were you getting at that time from the things of which you are now ashamed?*" Fruit takes time to produce. We make commitments to producing fruit. We watch over the fruit. We water and fertilize it. God has committed Himself to our growth.

How fruitful are you? **One of the greatest questions we face is the contributions that we make.** This is a question that confronts every living being. It doesn't matter whether we struggle with addiction or not, we all have a responsibility to contribute. Addictions are self-seeking. They not only fail to contribute, but they also steal and/or withhold.

A vow is another word for a commitment. The psalmist said that he would perform his vows before others. **Addiction is a vow.** Many times, we read of people making vows in the Bible.

If we are not fruitful, are we not *fruitless*? No one is fruitless. **We either bear good fruit or bad fruit.** Our fruit is either of God or of the flesh (originating from the devil.)

November 27

Be Fruitful! (part 2)

> For if these qualities are yours and are increasing, they keep you from being ineffective or unfruitful in the knowledge of our Lord Jesus Christ. 2 Peter 1:8

Fruit has been cherished since the beginning of creation. God commanded Adam, Eve, and Noah to be fruitful (Genesis 1:22, 28: 8:17; 9:1, 7). In Genesis 17:6 the Lord told Abraham He would make him <u>exceeding</u> fruitful. What kind of fruit does addiction produce? Certainly not the fruit that God wants! *Strong's Bible Dictionary* defines the "unfruitful" as "**not yielding what should be yielded.**"

Go to any grocery and you will find fruit in the produce section. Fruit is what you produce. To be unfruitful is to be non-productive. If you are not productive then there is a good chance you are destructive!

I once had a landlord who told me if he had known I was on a fixed income he would not have rented to me. When I asked him why, he said, "I like for my renters to be out and about because when people sit around the house all of the time things tend to happen." One of the verses Dr. David Jeremiah uses in his series from Second Peter Chapter One speaks of fruitfulness.

> And so, from the day we heard, we have not ceased to pray for you, asking that you may be filled with the knowledge of His will in all spiritual wisdom and understanding, so as to walk in a manner worthy of the Lord, fully pleasing to Him**: bearing fruit in every good work** and increasing in the knowledge of God. Colossians 1:9-10

The fruit that is most pleasing to God and most beneficial to others is not just a life free of addiction; it is found by abiding in Christ. In John 15, Jesus explained how impossible it is to be fruitful apart from Him and how abiding in Him produces an abundance of fruit.

> Abide in Me, and I in you. As **the branch cannot bear fruit by itself, unless it abides in the vine, neither can you, unless you abide in Me**. I am the vine; you are the branches. Whoever abides in Me and I in him, he it is that bears much fruit, for apart from Me you can do nothing. John 15:4-5

By abiding in Christ you will discover the snares of the Devil, discard everything that is not of God, and begin to function as God intends. It begins with "breaking up the fallow ground."

November 28

Like God

His divine power has granted to us all things that pertain to life and godliness, through the knowledge of Him who called us to His own glory and excellence. 2 Peter 1:3

There seem to be a lot of people talking about striving to be their "best self" these days. A lot of people want to maximize their potential. They are seeking to be highly functional. God is the *most* highly functional. No one functions as well as God.

Do you think that you can function as well as God? ***Perhaps, this is the source of all our problems (not just addiction.)*** And so, if you are to be at your best then you need to be like God.

No one would argue that addictions pertain to life. Addictions are a part of life. For some, addictions become a *way* of life. And, many lives are destroyed by addictions. But, what do addictions have to do with godliness?

Our answer is found in the love God has for all. Addictions are most concerned with loving ourselves. Yet, addictions offer a twisted type of love. We strive to love ourselves by indulging (as a treat) but the outcome is usually harmful.

Addiction is full of self-interest. **To be godly is to be unselfish and thereby to function as God does.** This breaks the chains of addiction like nothing else.

Jesus Christ was the most un*selfish* person that ever lived. ***If we were all like Christ, we would be so focused on loving God the Father and our brothers and sisters that addictions would never be an issue.*** If we were all like Christ, we would lay down our lives for one another.

> Let each of you look not only to his own interests, but also to the interests of others. Have this mind among yourselves, **which is yours in Christ Jesus**, Who, though He was in the form of God, did not count equality with God a thing to be grasped, but emptied Himself, by taking the form of a servant, being born in the likeness of men. And being found in human form, He humbled Himself by becoming obedient to the point of death, even death on a cross. Philippians 2:4-8

To be highly functional, you must possess the right resources. Would riches make you functional? If you are a joint heir with Christ then you are rich! The wealth of love that is in Christ is yours to share. My late great-mother-in-law would exclaim; she didn't have a lot of money but she was rich in love.

November 29

Destitution (part 1)

> Transgression speaks to the wicked deep in his heart; there is no fear of God before his eyes. For he flatters himself in his own eyes that his iniquity cannot be found out and hated. The words of his mouth are trouble and deceit; he has ceased to act wisely and do good. He plots trouble while on his bed; he sets himself in a way that is not good; he does not reject evil. Psalms 36:1-4

Alienation from God is tragic. It is a pattern that becomes a lifestyle leading to an eternal destiny if we don't change.

I dare you to name anyone who wants to be destitute! Perhaps no one wants to be physically destitute, but it doesn't matter for some of us to be spiritually destitute.

Many have falsely taught that people participate in addiction because they hate themselves. Ephesians 5:29 says *"no one ever hated his own flesh, but nourishes and cherishes it."* Why <u>Not</u> Get High explains that no one is looking for the destitution found in addiction in a subtitle called ***I love me some me!***

> ***"Why do I get high?*** I get high because I love myself to death! While many believe that addictions express self-hatred, I see addiction as being an expression of *self-love*. Do you think that people indulge so that they can experience the negative consequences of addictions? No. They wish that they could have an addiction without negative consequences. They don't participate in addiction to experience negative consequences. (Even people who are addicted to harming themselves think that it is going to make them feel good.)" -*Why Not Get High,* Gregory L. Madison

Psalms 36:1-4 refers to people who oppose loving God. **Though very seldom mentioned this is the real issue behind every addiction.** The Scriptures give an account of people who refused to revere and honor God. Among them are Pharaoh, Amalek, and backslidden Israel.

<u>Irreverence is a choice that we make</u>. Proverbs 1:29 says that the simple ones, scorners, fools, and those who hated knowledge did not <u>choose</u> the fear of the Lord.

To reverence God means to love Him. We prove our love for Him by allowing Him to rule, just as our love for addictions is proven by allowing them to rule. Matthew 6:24 contrasts our love for God and our love for the things of the world.

November 30

Destitution (part 2)

> Transgression speaks to the wicked deep in his heart; there is no fear of God before his eyes. For he flatters himself in his own eyes that his iniquity cannot be found out and hated. The words of his mouth are trouble and deceit; he has ceased to act wisely and do good. He plots trouble while on his bed; he sets himself in a way that is not good; he does not reject evil. Psalms 36:1-4

Why not get high? The highest motive for abstaining from addiction is a love for God because ***loving God is the soberest thing that you will ever do.*** A love for God and an appreciation for His blessings will ever remain the highest and strongest deterrent against addictions.

Loving God goes beyond mere abstinence. Loving God involves putting aside *anything* that displeases Him while doing the things that bring Him joy. God deserves our love because of the love that He has for us. Jesus said that the greatest command is to love the Lord your God with all your heart, with all your soul, with all your strength, and with all your mind (Luke 10:27).

As I stated previously, **we have no problem loving ourselves. We do have a problem loving God!** We love ourselves to death! That's why many people become suicidal while under the influence of an addiction. If they cannot find a way to continue feeding their addiction and still function normally, or if they are unhappy about the consequences of the addiction and cannot see a way out, then out of self-love, they contemplate suicide.

Irreverence is as much of a component of addiction as reverence is to deliverance. Pastor A. N. Martin said, "the absence of the fear of God is the unholy soil that produces an ungodly life." If we reject what is good are we not searching for evil?

Romans chapter one reveals the progression of irreverence. Just as we may grow in our reverence, we may grow to become more irreverent. I've always been fascinated by the extent of King Ahab's irreverence. Look at the passages below and meditate on the significance of their irreverence toward God!

> For although they knew God, they did not honor him as God or give thanks to him, but they became futile in their thinking, and their foolish hearts were darkened. Claiming to be wise, they became fools, and exchanged the glory of the immortal God for images resembling mortal man and birds and animals and creeping things. Romans 1:21-23

> And Ahab the son of Omri did evil in the sight of the LORD, more than all who were before him. And as if it had been a light thing for him to walk in the sins of Jeroboam the son of Nebat. 1 Kings 16:30-31a

December 1

Destitution (part 3)

For although they knew God, they did not honor him as God or give thanks to him, but they became futile in their thinking, and their foolish hearts were darkened. Claiming to be wise, they became fools, and exchanged the glory of the immortal God for images resembling mortal man and birds and animals and creeping things. Romans 1:21-23

And Ahab the son of Omri did evil in the sight of the LORD, more than all who were before him. And as if it had been a light thing for him to walk in the sins of Jeroboam the son of Nebat. 1 Kings 16:30-31a

Romans 1:21-23 and 1 Kings 16:30-31a reveals a lot about addiction. Both passages share the characteristics of irreverent idolatry that are relative to addiction. Each of the phrases are marked by destitution.

1. Irreverence rejects God
2. Irreverence rejects the knowledge of God
3. Irreverence rejects the authority of God
4. Irreverence rejects the truth of God
5. Irreverence rejects the wisdom of God
6. Irreverence rejects the will of God
7. Irreverence rejects the Word of God
8. Irreverence rejects the people of God
9. Irreverence chooses another god
10. Irreverence rejects the love of God

Who would argue that addictions exhibit poor judgment? I warned my readers in *Turing to God from Idols* not to think too highly of themselves. It can lead to self-righteousness rather than the righteousness of Christ. Self-righteousness sees nothing wrong with a life of addiction.

Self-righteousness makes its own rules. If my sobriety is not based on the principles of God, then I am living by my own standards. This is why many seek sobriety outside of Christ. But if I determine what's right and what's wrong, who's to say that I might not change my mind about whether addiction is an option.

Just as we were designed to breathe air, we were designed to revere God. To deny God the reverence that He is due is to deny ourselves of a delight that goes far beyond any addiction. While it may not be natural to reverence God because of our sinful nature, God gives us supernatural power to reverence Him if we choose.

December 2

What's your secret? (part 1)

The friendship of the LORD is for those who fear him, and he makes known to them his covenant. Psalms 25:14

The secret of the LORD is with them that fear him; and he will shew them his covenant. *KJV*

Is there sobriety without intimacy with God? Would it be safe to say that friends have a general agreement? Yes, for the most part, friends agree! That's what makes them friends!

They may not agree on everything, but they reason with one another when there is a disagreement or lack of understanding. Enemies tend to be unreasonable. On many occasions, I have explained how unreasonable addictions are.

Suppose God wanted to reason with you! Suppose He wanted to show you things you would have **never dreamed of!** *The highest degree of sobriety comes* from having intimacy with God. And where there is no reverence there is no intimacy with God.

Our intimacy with God is proportionate to our reverence for God.

Friends not only agree with one another but, they also share. The closer you become to someone, the more you share. Where would we all be if God did not share with us?

Some things God shares with everyone and some He only shares with His friends. Becoming close friends with God opens our minds to the things of God. That includes the secret of remaining joyfully sober in a way that is pleasing to God!

What no eye has seen, nor ear heard, nor the heart of man imagined, what God has prepared for those who love him. 1 Corinthians 2:9

In the Bible, there are several examples of people called the friend of God. Michael Jermin said being a friend involves "a living familiarity." That reminds me of marriage. Marriage should be a friendship! I once found a hundred dollar bill. I thought that it would only be right, *as a friend*, to give my wife half.

Just a month before, my wife expressed her friendship by helping me to purchase a new pair of shoes. Friends are mutual. There is no mutuality in addiction. It only seeks to please the individual. Friendship enjoys the other person. Good friends exclude anything that would jeopardize the friendship.

December 3

What's your secret? (part 2)

> The friendship of the LORD is for those who fear him, and he makes known to them his covenant. Psalms 25:14

We enjoy addictions, but do we enjoy God's enjoyment? The enjoyment that friends have is found in fellowship. Where there is fellowship, there is also communication. Some friends communicate poorly. Why would anybody in their right mind want their communication with God deficient?

Friendship even enjoys the other person's enjoyment!

Addiction limits our communication with God. Because Abraham believed God, he listened to God and was called a friend of God. As a friend, God confided in Abraham. Abraham strengthened his friendship with God by reverencing Him.

> And the Scripture was fulfilled that says, "Abraham believed God, and it was counted to him as righteousness"—and he was called a friend of God. James 2:23

> The LORD said, "Shall I hide from Abraham what I am about to do?" Genesis 18:17

> He said, "Do not lay your hand on the boy or do anything to him, for now I know that you fear God, seeing you have not withheld your son, your only son, from me." Genesis 22:12

Being close friends with God is an honor and a privilege! Not everyone can say that they are close friends with God. James 4:4 says, "Friendship with the world is enmity with God. *Therefore whoever wishes to be a friend of the world makes himself an enemy of God.*"

Jesus said that there is no greater love than for a man to lay down his life for his friends (John 15:13). While Jesus was speaking about His love for us, I think that *we* may show our love for God by laying down our lives for Him. Our friendship with God is with the mind of Christ.

First Corinthians 1:9 says God has called believers "*into the fellowship of his Son, Jesus Christ our Lord.*" There is enough joy to be found in our fellowship with God for addiction to lose its appeal. That's why in Psalms 25:15 the psalmist said, "*My eyes are ever toward Him.*"

December 4

Slacking leaves you lacking (part 1)

> Oh, fear the LORD, you his saints, for those who fear him have no lack! Psalms 34:9

Is there a reason why people get addicted? Do you think that someone can get addicted without a reason or excuse? There is an infinite contrast between the insufficiency of addiction and the adequacy of God.

Would it be safe to say that we become addicted to things because there is something we are lacking? Ironically addictions cause greater deficiencies. Addictions not only reveal our deficiencies, but they also multiply our deficiencies when they are given authority. Sanity is based on knowing the inadequacy of addiction and the sufficiency of God.

Empty is the cry of addiction. It is always lacking and never satisfied. Addiction is a life of yearning. *One of the dilemmas of addiction is that while yearning for something legitimate, we become insanely deceived into thinking that the addiction will fill our longing.*

> "Men are in a restless pursuit after satisfaction in earthly things. They will exhaust themselves in the deceitful delights of sin, and, finding them all to be vanity and emptiness, they will become very perplexed and disappointed. But they will continue their fruitless search. Though wearied, they still stagger forward under the influence of spiritual madness, and though there is no result to be reached except that of everlasting disappointment, yet they press forward. They have no forethought for their eternal state; the present hour absorbs them. They turn to another and another of earth's broken cisterns, hoping to find water where not a drop was ever discovered yet." -*Spurgeon*

What can addiction do for you that God cannot? The disappointment of addiction begins with the fixation on an image that addiction is supposed to fulfill. In our imagination, we lack the vision to see that addictions cannot provide what they promise and that God can do so either directly and/or indirectly. Proverbs 29:18 says "where there is no vision, the people perish." (*KJV*)

The teaching of the psalmist gives vision. First, he teaches how big God is. The *New International Version* of Proverbs 29:14 says, *"Where there is no revelation, people cast off restraint; but blessed is the one who heeds wisdom's instruction."* The fixation on addiction becomes an obsession. The psalmist wants our fixation to be on God.

December 5

Slacking leaves you lacking (part 2)

Oh, fear the LORD, you his saints, for those who fear him have no lack! Psalms 34:9

Psalm 34:9 is something to consider. Becoming addicted takes consideration. Our ability to consider is a blessing from God that is to be used wisely. The book of Ecclesiastes is the consideration that King Solomon gave to his experiences. At the end he said, *"The end of the matter; all has been heard. Fear God and keep his commandments, for this is the whole duty of man."* (Ecclesiastes 12:13)

"Nothing more becomes a man than deliberation and consideration. This is his pre-eminence above the beasts; they act but do not consider. And herein is a great part of man's foolishness, that he does not consider the end of his actions. 'O that they were wise, that they understood this, that they would consider their latter end! (Deuteronomy 32.29).'" -*The Sinfulness of Sin,* Ralph Venning

The Highest Yearning states that addictions are better defined as a desire rather than a disease. When desires gather strength, we yearn or crave after them. *The Highest Yearning* is an explanation of how we all practice healthy yearning and unhealthy yearning. The highest yearning is the healthiest yearning.

"If God's wonderful presence alone does not capture their devotion, how will they ever be satisfied with anything else? Such a sense of dissatisfaction leads people to seek other ways of satisfying perceived needs. It is a dangerous spirit to be in, for if God's wonderful provisions are not enough to hold a person's attention, what will it take?" *At the Altar of Sexual Idolatry,* Steve Gallagher

"We all have different strategies that we use to deceive ourselves, but there is one deception that we all experience. It is perhaps the deepest of all. Deep in our hearts, we question God's goodness. We think he is holding out on us.... One of the deepest deceptions is the lie that there is something good out there and it is better than what God gives. Satan's lie is 'God is not good.' Coupled with that is 'Sin is good.' He suggests to us that there are greater pleasures outside the kingdom of God." Edward "T. Welch

December 6

Slacking leaves you lacking (part 3)

Oh, fear the LORD, you his saints, for those who fear him have no lack! Psalms 34:9

Wisdom is from God. And it certainly takes wisdom to navigate our way through life. Proverbs 19:10 says that the wisdom of God is *"more to be desired are they than gold, yea, than much fine gold: sweeter also than honey and the honeycomb."* What about addictions? Are they more valuable than the wisdom of God?

Gold has been valued throughout the ages. Unfortunately, many have valued gold over things that are of greater worth. What would you trade for your relationship with God? What would you trade for your soul?

For what does it profit a man to gain the whole world and forfeit his soul? Mark 8:36

Many people find enjoyment in the taste of honey as do others in addiction. In verse nine of Psalms 34, the psalmist appeals to our taste. He says, *"taste and see that the Lord is good."* Our tastes become refined as we grow. A two-year-old is not able to distinguish or enjoy the taste of a dish as much as a fifty-year-old experienced diner.

The two-year-old's senses must be trained to appreciate what is good. Not only must he be taught what is enjoyable, but he must also be taught what could be unhealthy (even deadly.) A young child may be easily lured to eat an attractive laundry pod just as we are attracted to addiction because of their tastes.

> "In the first stage of addiction, we are **acquainted** with the taste. When the taste gets our **attention**, we **acknowledge** it as important or valuable. If we consider it of value, it doesn't take long for the addiction to gain our **affections.** *Addictions quickly capture our affections because they usually appeal to the pleasure center of our brains.* Once the addiction captures our affections, they gain our **allegiance**." -*The Highest Yearning*, Gregory L. Madison

The psalmist says that what God has for us is sweeter than honey. This has been the question that has plagued mankind since the *Garden of Eden* and proven at *Calvary*. When we turn to addictions, we are wondering if what God has is sweeter than anything.

Calvary is the best thing there is. Calvary provides spiritual birth having the divine nature of Christ allowing you to be able to taste the goodness of the Lord more fully.

December 7

Slacking leaves you lacking (part 4)

> Oh, fear the LORD, you his saints, for those who fear him have no lack! Psalms 34:9

The Psalmist says that those who fear the Lord don't lack anything. Quality sobriety not only recognizes the impotence of the idols of addiction but is also sane enough to recognize the power and mercy of God. One of the chief concerns of those who want to overcome an addiction is whether they will lack what is needed. C. S. Lewis confirms that God is so thorough that He often goes beyond our expectations!

> "Dozens of people go to Him to be cured of some one particular sin which they are ashamed of (like masturbation or physical cowardice) or which is obviously spoiling daily life (like bad temper or drunkenness.) Well, He will cure it all right: but He will not stop there. That may be all you asked; but if once you call Him in, He will give you the full." C. S. Lewis

The sufficiency of God has been questioned since the beginning of time. God provided me with an understanding of Himself through a study of His names in *All the Divine Names and Titles in the Bible* by Herbert Lockyer for the foundation of my sobriety. Nothing silences addictions like the solemn reality of who God is! The name El Shaddai expresses the sufficiency of God. It means the all-sufficient God.

> "*El* set forth God's almightiness, and *Shaddai* His exhaustless bounty, so that together the double name expresses *The All-Bountiful One*. What a stimulus to faith it is to know that we serve a God who is all-sufficient, and who is strong enough to overpower, able to overcome all obstacles, and equal to every occasion! 'Is there anything too hard for the Lord?' He can remove mountains even 'when the order of nature offers no prospect of it and the powers of nature are inadequate to it. God is not fettered by the laws of nature; He is supreme over them, and free to intervene upon them,' as many of His miracles prove. -*All the Divine Names and Titles in the Bible,* Herbert Lockyer

I often tell people that if God wants something for them then the only one that can keep them from getting it is themselves. Do you believe that God wants everyone to be free from addiction?

December 8

Slacking leaves you lacking (part 5)

Oh, fear the LORD, you his saints, for those who fear him have no lack! Psalms 34:9

The entire life of Christ, as well as His death and resurrection, are a testimony of the sufficiency of God. Everything of Christ is flawlessly perfect. In Revelation 19:11, He is called *Faithful and True*. Throughout His life, we read how Jesus did things that were timely and beneficial.

> "...never made anything shoddy, but put the very best into necessary making and mending of tools and utensils. The shop was renowned around the countryside for its good and honest work. ... A world, so badly broken by its sin, violence, crime, and wars, needs to find its way also to the same Carpenter whose pierced hands can alone make it whole again. For the most of His life, Jesus was accustomed to wood and nails, and cruel men saw that He had them when He died. But it is only through those nail-torn hands of the Carpenter that lives, broken by sin, and be reshaped, and a shattered world remade into a thing of beauty. To right its wrongs and woe, a distracted age like ours does not need a commander of uncanny ability – only this once lowly Carpenter of Nazareth." -*All the Divine Names and Titles in the Bible,* Herbert Lockyer

While the life of Jesus revealed the sufficiency of God, His death and resurrection give greater proof. Calvary is the best that God has to offer. ***If God is our greatest need, then our greatest deficiency is being separated from Him.*** Only Jesus can bridge the gap between us and God. My favorite book in the Bible starts by confirming the sufficiency of God.

> Long ago, at many times and in many ways, God spoke to our fathers by the prophets, but in these last days he has spoken to us by his Son, whom he appointed the heir of all things, through whom also he created the world. He is the radiance of the glory of God and the exact imprint of his nature, and he upholds the universe by the word of his power. After making purification for sins, he sat down at the right hand of the Majesty on high. Hebrews 1:1-3

It is an insult to God for us to omit Calvary from our discussion of addictions. When we omit Calvary from our war on addictions, we are telling God that His methods are not sufficient. When we omit Calvary from our war on addictions we are either not seeking God or seeking God by our own efforts. Our own efforts lead to addiction.

December 9

Learning to listen (part 1)

> Come, O children, listen to me; I will teach you the fear of the LORD. Psalms 34:11

Psalms 34:11 is an invitation. It is an invitation from God through David just as in Isaiah 55 God uses Isaiah to invite others to come (Isaiah 55:1). ***How do you respond to God's invitations?*** It is sure to affect the quality of your sobriety!

The only good thing about addiction is that it warns us of our deficiencies! Psalms 34:11 directs us towards the greatest deficiency of man. The fear of the Lord!

> "Man finds it hard to get what he wants because he does not want the best, God finds it hard to give, because He would give the best, and man will not take it." -George MacDonald

Who we associate with largely affects our actions. The psalmist calls for associates. Who has not heard the proverb "Birds of a feather flock together?" It means that there is a common interest. That's why the Bible commands the people of God not to marry those who have no interest in God. It's not a good idea to go back to our old environments once we leave addiction either.

David calls out to the children. He probably is not just addressing those who are young (but all who are not as experienced as he in the ways of God.) It has been said that when a person is dominated by addiction then their maturity is affected. Studies have found that people who participate in addiction do not have the coping skills or the mental capacities that they should have for someone their age. Addiction often causes grownups to act like children.

The psalmist's cry to children also expresses his affection for the readers. God has affection for us is even greater than the psalmist's for his children. It is immeasurably beyond compare.

If there is one thing that you can be sure of it is that no matter how far you have fallen into addiction, God cares. But, God is no fool! He knows that He must create a distance between us and the things that compete for His affection as we would be wise to do with our children.

There is no reverence for God without the Spirit of God showing us just who God is and why He is worthy of our reverence. There is no reverence for God without the Spirit of God giving us spiritual life (by being born again, born into Christ.) There is no reverence for God without the Spirit of God giving us the will to do so.

December 10

Learning to listen (part 2)

> Come, O children, listen to me; I will teach you the fear of the LORD. Psalms 34:11

S. Chrysostom called the fear of the Lord "the school of the mind." I like to think of the fear of the Lord as a vehicle that God uses to take us where He wants us in our walk with Him. God uses people to give us the directions that we need. The fear of the Lord is demonstrated by our attitude toward those who can teach us the things of God.

> "You can learn to follow Jesus by following the example of someone who is following Jesus, regardless of whether that person has been an addict or not. Only someone who is following Jesus can teach you to follow Jesus. The person who knows God and the truth of God is able to understand the addict's problem and God's solution without ever having been an addict. The follower of God knows about sin, slavery to sin, the deceptiveness of sin, and the idolatry of sin because he also is a sinner." -*My Beloved Addiction*, Jeff Mullins

The fear of the Lord is a skill that God produces in those who have been given the new nature in Christ. Apart from a new nature, we are not capable or interested in reverencing God as He deserves. We need to be born again. Being born again saves us! If you are reading this book then you have been physically born. That does not mean that you have been spiritually born.

After being born of the Spirit we are children. Just as every child, we can value the guidance of someone older, more mature, and more experienced. I once had a bodybuilding trainer I got mad with when he kept calling me "son." Looking back, I understand his logic.

When it came to bodybuilding, I was like a child compared to this man who had won multiple bodybuilding contests. He got angry when I called him "son" because I had been explaining spiritual matters to him.

The Word of God provides the harmony needed for communities to grow. Addictions often produce disharmony. **Addiction may cause us to be less concerned about others unless they can do something for us. Reverence for God causes us to be like God in His kindness and love.**

Just as God had David teach others the fear of the Lord, He has people who can teach you. That's one reason Hebrews 10:25 says don't stop meeting together "as is the habit of some, but encouraging one another, and all the more as you see the Day drawing near."

December 11

Learning to listen (part 3)

> Come, O children, listen to me; I will teach you the fear of the LORD. Psalms 34:11

I still remember the first time I read about Ezra's teaching. As the years go by, I have learned to appreciate it more and more. Ezra was a scribe that helped Israel to rebuild. You need people like Ezra to help build a fortress against addictions and to build a life that honors God. The books of Ezra and Nehemiah refer to the abilities of Ezra and his contributions.

> This Ezra went up from Babylonia. He was a scribe skilled in the Law of Moses that the LORD, the God of Israel, had given, and the king granted him all that he asked, for the hand of the LORD his God was on him. Ezra 7:6

> For on the first day of the first month he began to go up from Babylonia, and on the first day of the fifth month he came to Jerusalem, for the good hand of his God was on him. For Ezra had set his heart to study the Law of the LORD, and to do it and to teach his statutes and rules in Israel.. Ezra 7:9-10

> On the first of the first month he started out from Babylon, and on the first of the fifth month he arrived in Jerusalem, for upon him was the good hand of his God. For Ezra had prepared and set his heart to seek the Law of the Lord [to inquire for it and of it, to require and yearn for it], and to do and teach in Israel its statutes and its ordinances. *APMC*

> So they read from the Book of the Law of God distinctly, faithfully amplifying and giving the sense so that [the people] understood the reading. Nehemiah 8:8 *AMPC*

Leviticus 19:32 emphasizes the reverence that is shown to God by honoring elders. Your reverence is displayed by recognizing how the Lord works and speaks through elders. Elders have much to say about addiction. Those who have not experienced addiction have lived long enough to witness the results others have.

Your reverence determines the value you place on the advice of elders. Reverence is an appreciation of the wisdom that our elders have. Proverbs 1:5 says that "a wise man will hear, and will increase learning; and a man of understanding will attain unto wise counsels."

December 12

Reasons to reverence God (part 1)

> Let all the earth fear the LORD; let all the inhabitants of the world stand in awe of him! Psalms 33:8

There's a reason for everything! So long as you have multiple reasons to revere God, your sobriety will be strong.

The lyrics of *Joy to the World* are as futuristic as Psalms 33:8. The song refers to the events that take place at the return of Christ. By the way, a good reason for abstaining from addiction is the return of Christ.

> And now, little children, abide in him, so that when he appears we may have confidence and not shrink from him in shame at his coming. 1 John 2:28

The quality of your sobriety relies on the quality of your reverence. Many verses in Psalms 33 give adequate reasons to revere God. Are we not all willing to defend a cause? As you search within your soul, I will bet that you cannot *honestly* find a reason for addiction. The reasons for reverencing God are as infinite as God Himself.

Years ago, a friend told me that before someone relapses, they must first tell a lie. We might say that the reason that we are addicted to pornography is that we are lonely, but pornography does not cure loneliness. We may say that the reason that we are addicted to painkillers is to relieve pain. But there are other ways to relieve pain

You may be able to produce a list of excuses for addiction, but they will never match the reasons we should revere God. Psalms 33 gives us many reasons. Notice how many of these contradict addictions! (The phrases are taken from the *New International Version*.)

1. The word of the Lord is right
2. He is faithful in all He does
3. The Lord loves righteousness and justice
4. The earth is full of His unfailing love
5. By the word of the Lord were the heavens made
6. The starry host by the breathe of His mouth
7. He gathers the waters of the sea into jars
8. He put the deep into storehouses
9. He spoke and it came to be
10. He commanded and it stood firm
11. The Lord foils the plans of the nations

To be continued ...

December 13

Reasons to reverence God (part 2)

> Let all the earth fear the LORD; let all the inhabitants of the world stand in awe of him! Psalms 33:8

I'm listing reasons for reverencing God. So long as you have multiple reasons to revere God, your sobriety will be strong. The list below is a continuation of reasons for reverencing God from Psalms 33.

12. He thwarts the purposes of the people
13. The plans of the Lord stand firm forever
14. The purposes of His heart throughout all generations
15. The nation whose God is the Lord is blessed
16. The people He chooses for His inheritance is blessed
17. The Lord looks down from heaven
18. He sees all
19. He watches and considers everything they do
20. The eyes of the Lord are on those who fear Him

The third chapter of *The Fear of the Almighty* addresses the basis of our reverence. Just as with anything we do, if it is not done for the right reason, then it is not acceptable to God. When it comes to reverence for God, if it is not done for the right reasons, it is not true, genuine biblical reverence.

> Though self-centered programs may disagree, an approach to addiction that has no reverence for God is not acceptable to God (it's merely tolerated.)

If we do not revere the Lord for the right reasons, then our relationship with Him becomes shallow and void of substance. There is a multitude of reasons why we should revere the Lord. One of the most basic reasons for honoring and reverencing God is simply because He is worthy. All other reasons for reverencing God are secondary.

Reverencing God has no self-seeking motives. The two main reasons God is to be revered are because of who is He and what He does. The attributes of God tell us who is He. What He does cannot be numbered.

Many scholars have offered a list of the attributes of God. Neither of which will ever be adequate in fully describing God. God is unlike anything or anyone we could ever know or imagine. He is one of a kind, unique, and without comparison. Over the next few days, I will list why God is worthy of reverence based on His attributes.

December 14

Reasons to reverence God (part 3)

> Let all the earth fear the LORD; let all the inhabitants of the world stand in awe of him! Psalms 33:8

Psalms 33:8 gives us the awe-factor of sobriety. **The awe factor of addiction cannot be denied!** Addictions capture our attention. Standing in awe gives God our attention. As the psalmist beckons the reader to stand in awe, he proclaims that God is worthy of awe. The greatest response to addiction is to turn your attention from addiction to God.

Though seldom mentioned, awe is the component that most often rules and governs our lives, our homes, our neighborhoods, our nation, our world, and ultimately our destiny. Awe can build or destroy.

Awe is related to reverence. Awe is related to sanity as well as insanity. Only awe of God can give you the right mind. A sober mind begins with your perspective. To be in awe of anything more than God is to think of it as greater than God.

God is worthy of our reverence because He is eternal.

God is worthy of our reverence because He is faithful.

God is worthy of our reverence because He foreknows.

God is worthy of our reverence because He is good.

God is worthy of our reverence because He is holy.

God is worthy of our reverence because He is immutable.

God is worthy of our reverence because He is impartial.

God is worthy of our reverence because He is incomprehensible.

God is worthy of our reverence because He is infinite.

God is worthy of our reverence because He is jealous.

God is worthy of our reverence because He is just.

God is worthy of our reverence because He is longsuffering.

God is worthy of our reverence because He is love.

December 15

Reasons to reverence God (part 4)

Let all the earth fear the LORD; let all the inhabitants of the world stand in awe of him! Psalms 33:8

The first words of Pharaoh to Moses were *"Who is the Lord that I should obey Him?"* Addictions ask the same question! You would think that after God began to reveal Himself then Pharaoh would reverence Him. But Pharaoh was no different than us as we ignore God with our addictions.

God is worthy of our reverence because He is merciful.

God is worthy of our reverence because He is omnipotent.

God is worthy of our reverence because He is omnipresent.

God is worthy of our reverence because He is omniscient.

God is worthy of our reverence because He is righteous.

God is worthy of our reverence because He is self-existent.

God is worthy of our reverence because He is self-sufficient.

God is worthy of our reverence because He is sovereign.

God is worthy of our reverence because He is transcendent.

God is worthy of our reverence because He is truth.

God is worthy of our reverence because He is wise.

God is worthy of our reverence because of His wrath

And so, we have every reason to reverence God for all He's worth. It is worth His dignity. It is worth your duty. It is worth your sobriety. It is worth everything. If you don't have a reason to reverence God, the reason for your abstinence becomes just an excuse for pleasing yourself. And while God is not against pleasing ourselves within the boundaries of His will, it is not to be absent of reverence.

December 16

The joy of the fear of the Lord

The law of the LORD is perfect, converting the soul: the testimony of the LORD is sure, making wise the simple. The statues of the LORD are right, rejoicing the heart: the commandment of the LORD is pure, enlightening the eyes. The fear of the LORD is clean, enduring forever: the judgments of the LORD are true and righteous altogether. *More to be desired are they than gold*, yea, than much fine gold: sweeter also than honey and the honeycomb. Moreover by them is Thy servant warned: and in keeping of them there is great reward. Psalms 19:7-11

The greatest joy forfeited with the fall of Man was bearing the image of His marvelous Creator. The more you reverence God, the more you desire to bear His image while disdaining all else.

To reverence God, you must deny yourself. That's how you bear His image. The more you bear His image, the more you will reverence and enjoy Him. The more you bear His image, the more you are led by Him. The more you are led by Him, the more you love Him and love others.

On the contrary—the less you revere God; the less you will bear His image. The less you bear His image; the less you will reverence Him and enjoy Him. The less you bear His image; the less you are led by Him. The less you are led by Him; the less you will love Him and others.

"[Sin] strives with and fights against God, and if its power were as great as its will is wicked, it would not suffer God to be. God is a troublesome thing to the sinner, and therefore they say to him, Depart from us (Job 21.14), and of Christ Jesus, Let us break his bands in sunder, and cast his cords far from us (Psalms 2.3). And when the Holy Ghost comes to woo and entreat them to be reconciled, they resist and make war with the spirit of peace (Acts 7:51). … Can you find it in your heart to hug and embrace such a monster as this? Will you love that which hates God, and which God hates? God forbid! Will you join yourself to that which is nothing but contrariety to God, and all that is good?" -*The Sinfulness of Sin,* Ralph Venning

The Word of God changes us by showing us the foolishness of addictions. The Word of God offers the wisdom of God. The Word of God is trustworthy and brings joy, whereas addictions cannot be trusted and eventually bring sorrow and grief. Whereas addictions darken, the Word of God enlightens. God's Word is sweet, addictions are bitter.

December 17

Out of sight!

> And the angel of the LORD appeared to him and said to him, "The LORD is with you, O mighty man of valor." And Gideon said to him, "Please, my lord, if the LORD is with us, why then has all this happened to us? And where are all His wonderful deeds that our fathers recounted to us, saying, 'Did not the LORD bring us up from Egypt?' But now the LORD has forsaken us and given us into the hand of Midian." Judges 6:12-13

Gideon's questions to the angel of the Lord involved what could be seen. Addiction is based on your senses as well. Unfortunately, you may be inclined to look at your surroundings when trying to overcome addictions as when Gideon was told of the victory that awaited him over his foes.

Gideon's first question was why they were being defeated. Judges 6:3-6 explains how Israel was "brought low" by the other nations. However, Gideon's question was answered in verse one. How often do you have the answers before you already? God had warned Israel much earlier.

The warnings of God are sometimes referred to as "the handwriting on the wall" based on the warning in Daniel Chapter Five. Addiction doesn't go without warning. It doesn't take most of us long to notice the negative effects of addiction. And it can seem as though there is no way out. The old saying is that trouble is easy to get into and hard to get out.

The next question that Gideon asked the angel of the Lord was where all the wondrous deeds that their fathers recounted that the Lord had done. Gideon inherited a rich history from a people that did not rely on their sight as their final assessment.

God was building their faith, just as He longs to build yours. God was building a legacy in Israel that would be passed on to His Church by not looking at what is seen.

> These all died in faith, not having received the things promised, but having seen them and greeted them from afar. ... By faith he left Egypt, not being afraid of the anger of the king, for he endured as seeing him who is invisible. Hebrews 12:13a, 27

One of the major characteristics of addiction is that it can overpower your thoughts. Addictions can consume you the way that Median consumed Israel. Romans Chapter Eight gives us a picture of the far-reaching grace that is needed to face addiction victoriously.

> If God is for us, who can be against us? He who did not spare His own Son but gave Him up for us all, how will He not also with Him graciously give us all things? Romans 8:31b-32

December 18

Groaning for Christ

Though you have not seen him, you love him. Though you do not now see him, you believe in him and rejoice with joy that is inexpressible and filled with glory. 1 Peter 1:8

Therefore, preparing your minds for action, and being sober-minded, set your hope fully on the grace that will be brought to you at the revelation of Jesus Christ. 1 Peter 1:13

Savoring God through anticipating Christ's return is a tremendous weapon against addictions. Years ago, I was returning from a physically challenging trip.

Though I was tired, the thought of going home gave me a boost. My chant from the beginning (which I shared with at least several people) was "I'm going home!"

After a six-hour bus ride, I texted my wife that I had made it safely to Memphis. When she said that it was raining hard in the area where we lived, I said "I don't care, I'm coming home!" **When a believer in Christ struggles with an addiction, the thought that we are homeward-bound is a tremendous motivation.**

"As the battle is waged, the focus becomes our own heart more than the external barriers we have erected. We commit ourselves to be ruthless with our covetous imaginations. As we do, the things that were once affections gradually feel more like afflictions. That is, we still notice our heart's desire for the past idols, but these desires feel like a nagging salesperson more than an object of great love. We wish the desire would disappear, but it still occasionally shows up. When we encounter it, we groan, anticipating the day when we will be fully perfected." (Welch)

I had a tremendous breakthrough in the final stages of *Yearning Over Addiction*. As I listened to the Christmas song *It Came Upon a Midnight Clear,* I realized that its lyrics reflected the yearning that is the source of complete satisfaction. The lyrics speak "Peace on the earth, goodwill to men from heav'n's all-gracious King." The groaning of Romans 8:23 is to be in one accord with God and others.

And not only the creation, but we ourselves, who have the firstfruits of the Spirit, **groan inwardly** as we wait eagerly for adoption as sons, the redemption of our bodies. Romans 8:23

December 19 (handwritten)

Joy to the World (part 1)

> Though you have not seen him, you love him. Though you do not now see him, you believe in him and rejoice with joy that is inexpressible and filled with glory, 1 Peter 1:8

Isaac Watts, an English hymn writer, wrote the lyrics to *Joy to the World* based on Psalm 98 in the Bible. This hymn is a "joyous" celebration of the sovereignty of God and the gift of Jesus. Some say that the hymn speaks of the second advent of Christ rather than the first (His birth or incarnation.) The most important question is not when He infiltrates the earth, but rather when He infiltrates our souls!

> Joy to the world! the Lord is come; Let earth receive her King; Let every heart prepare him room, And heaven and nature sing, And heaven and nature sing, And heaven, and heaven, and nature sing.

Where the Lord is, there is joy. Wherever addictions are found there is but sorrow and misery. Noble anticipation is our expectation of Christ. Do you want Him as your King? Is He not a more gracious ruler than addictions?

Prepare Him room! Is this not the essence of true sobriety; sobriety at its highest level? Does not heaven and nature sing under His command? We may sing as well.

What is sung begins in the heart; just as we may sing praises to an addiction. Receive Christ, receive righteousness, soundness, and sobriety. If we withhold from Him the song that He is due, we will have no song.

> Joy to the world! the Saviour reigns; Let men their songs employ; While fields and floods, rocks, hills, and plains Repeat the sounding joy, Repeat the sounding joy, Repeat, repeat the sounding joy.

Employ unto the Lord. Employment is an occupation. What is it that occupies your time? Better yet, what occupies your mind? It is this that you value. Many a song is unworthily sung to the idols that hold us in bondage.

> Oh sing to the LORD a new song, for he has done marvelous things! Make a joyful noise to the LORD, all the earth; break forth into joyous song and sing praises! Let the sea roar, and all that fills it; the world and those who dwell in it! Let the rivers clap their hands; let the hills sing for joy together before the LORD, for he comes to judge the earth. He will judge the world with righteousness, and the peoples with equity. Psalm 98:1a, 4, 7-9

December 20

Joy to the World (part 2)

> Though you have not seen him, you love him. Though you do not now see him, you believe in him and rejoice with joy that is inexpressible and filled with glory, 1 Peter 1:8

Again, some say *Joy to the World* speaks of Christ's second advent rather than the first (His birth or incarnation). The most important question is not when He infiltrates the earth but rather when He infiltrates our souls!

> No more let sins and sorrows grow, Nor thorns infest the ground; He comes to make His blessings flow Far as the curse is found, Far as the curse is found, Far as, far as, the curse is found.

Just as sin and sorrow grow, addictions often occur in stages. God has set before us life and prosperity, death and destruction (Deuteronomy 30:15 NLT). Sin cursed man. Christ nullifies the curse.

We are damned without Christ and vulnerable to every addiction that begins as an adorable false god. Addictions are but dark and lifeless idols. "In Him was life, and the life was the light of men. The light shines in the darkness, and the darkness has not overcome it" (John 1:4).

> He rules the world with truth and grace, And makes the nations prove The glories of His righteousness, And wonders of His love, And wonders of His love, And wonders, wonders, of His love.

His truth and grace reveal to us the deception of idols. It is also His truth and grace that reveals His glory by which we find Him attractive. Awe and adoration are bonded in our reverence of God. Reverence is the supreme component of true sobriety. The wonders of His love produce unending reverence. Our reverence is related to the awe that we have for God. Awe is sane!

> For the grace of God has appeared that offers salvation to all people. It teaches us to say "No" to ungodliness and worldly passions, and to live self-controlled, upright and godly lives in this present age, while we wait for the blessed hope—the appearing of the glory of our great God and Savior, Jesus Christ, Who gave Himself for us to redeem us from all wickedness and to purify for Himself a people that are His very own, eager to do what is good. Titus 2:11-14

December 21

Zeal

And it came to pass, as the angels were gone away from them into heaven, the shepherds said one to another, Let us now go even unto Bethlehem, and see this thing which is come to pass, which the Lord hath made known unto us. Luke 2:15 *KJV*

It is amazing how God made known to the shepherds the birth of Christ. Before Jesus' arrival, Israel had not heard from God for hundreds of years. Ironically, the last word that God gave to Israel, before the arrival of Christ, was "a curse" (Malachi 4:6).

The most important thing for us who have been fooled into thinking that addictions are worthy of our lives is a Word from God. The Word of God gives sanity in a world of madness and confusion.

We were created with a sound mind, but since the Fall of Man, we have become more and more insane while thinking that we are wiser than God. As quiet as it is kept, there is no one as reasonable as God. Unfortunately, we may adopt the wrong attitude about God.

"In our wickedness, we believe that God is the biggest evil we could encounter and that it is our resistance to Him that keeps life from charging headlong into misery!" *Changed into His Image*, Jim Berg

When I turned from my addiction to crack in 2011, my biggest fear was that God would never ever speak to me again. **I honestly thought that He would not!** What an exciting time it was for the shepherds to whom the blessing of Israel (and all mankind) was announced.

I cannot measure the excitement that Christ has brought into my life. When I left my life of addiction, I told God how I had found so much excitement in my drug use and that I needed Him to change me or to provide just as much excitement (if not more), as I followed Him.

I am tremendously grateful that God has honored that prayer! As He continues to reveal to me the magnificence of Christ, I can see why the shepherds were so excited upon the announcement of His birth! I have also found that awe even goes beyond excitement!

"Imagine having drug cravings subdued by the joy of knowing and obeying Christ. Imagine having temptations lose their allure because there is more pleasure in walking humbly with our God. Imagine waking up and strategizing how to please the God who loves you rather than where you will get your next drink."
-Dr. Edward T. Welch

December 22

Mary, Did You Know? (part 1 of 3)

And she gave birth to her firstborn son and wrapped him in swaddling cloths and laid him in a manger, because there was no place for them in the inn. Luke 2:7

Mary, Did You Know? is a Christmas song addressing Mary, the mother of Jesus, with lyrics written by Mark Lowry in 1984. The music was written by Buddy Greene in 1991. It was originally recorded by Michael English on his self-titled debut solo album in 1991.

The lyrics evolved from a series of questions that Lowry scripted for a Christmas program at his church. "I just tried to put into words the unfathomable. I started thinking of the questions I would have for her if I were to sit down and have coffee with Mary. You know, 'What was it like raising God?' 'What did you know?' 'What didn't you know?'", said Lowry. None of the questions are answered in the song.

While the Bible does not tell us whether Mary knew all the answers that were asked of her, the Bible does have all the answers concerning addictions. Unfortunately, so many have come up with answers (on their own) that subtly contradict the Word of God.

If the Word of God had nothing to say about addictions, then God would not have created us. When confronted with addictions there are so many sobering questions that we must ask ourselves (just as Lowry had so many questions for Mary.)

Did you know that addictions draw you from God? Did you know that little pill, that one little piece of crack, that one image of pornography can ruin your life and the life of an entire nation?

In the birth of Christ, we see many things hidden from past eternity revealed. Much of this was revealed to Mary in time. Some things have never been revealed at all.

I could not see all that was to follow my first encounter with crack. I would have never dreamed of resigning from the United States Post Office. I would have never dreamed of hurting my parents and friends so deeply. There are so many things that I would have never imagined from my addiction.

On the other hand, I could never have imagined the grace that is found in Christ. There are no words to explain the magnificence of His Majesty. As the song asks of Mary, I did not know just what Jesus could do! I'm more and more amazed as I watch how my life unfolds under His gracious command.

Oh, taste and see that the LORD is good! Blessed is the man who takes refuge in him! Psalm 34:8

December 23

Mary, Did You Know? (part 2 of 3)

> And she gave birth to her firstborn son and wrapped him in swaddling cloths and laid him in a manger, because there was no place for them in the inn. Luke 2:7

You should know that the Word of God has some comprehensive answers to addictions. Dr. Edward T. Welch in *Addictions: A Banquet in the Grave* asks "Do you have a good grasp on the wealth of biblical material that speaks precisely to the modern problems of addictions? Can you go through any book in Scripture, even if it doesn't mention alcohol, food, or sex, and see how it speaks to addictions?"

Bible Verses Addictions on *Facebook* and the printed version on *Amazon* are dedicated to a broader biblical understanding of addictions. I believe in offering the best there is to confront addictions. It doesn't get any better than the Word of God. Mary found this out as she encountered the Living Word very intimately.

Some of the lyrics lead to astounding answers to addictions. The questions asked of Mary reveal the answers to addictions. The two basic questions that Mary is asked are whether she knows Who her baby boy is and what her baby boy can do!

The first question about Jesus walking on water introduces what Christ can do. In each instance, we see how Christ can do the impossible.

Many who are enslaved by addictions want to become new people. Just as the song promises for Jesus to make Mary new, you can become new in Christ.

We may become so enthralled by addictions that we lose sight of a better life. Just as Jesus gave sight to those who were physically blind, He can give sight to us who are spiritually blind.

There is a restlessness like the roaring of the sea in addiction. Just as Jesus calmed the sea, He can calm our souls even more.

> Mary, did you know
> That your Baby Boy would one day walk on water?
> Mary, did you know
> That your Baby Boy would save our sons and daughters?
> Did you know
> That your Baby Boy has come to make you new?
> This Child that you delivered will soon deliver you
> Mary, did you know
> That your Baby Boy will give sight to a blind man?
> Mary, did you know
> That your Baby Boy will calm the storm with His hand?

December 24

Mary, Did You Know? (3 of 3)

And she gave birth to her firstborn son and wrapped him in swaddling cloths and laid him in a manger, because there was no place for them in the inn. Luke 2:7

As we discuss how "Mary Did You Know?" speaks of who Jesus is, we must consider two principles: Christ deserves our worship and is not to be trifled with. The song's lyrics accurately reveal Christ's identity as God in human flesh.

While that may seem hard to believe, it was not easy for me to believe I would be clean and sober for nearly 14 years. Stranger things have happened! Jesus Christ proves that God is foreign to us. Only God can describe God. John 1:18 says, "No one has ever seen God, but the one and only Son, who is Himself God and is in closest relationship with the Father, has made Him known" (*NIV*). The lyrics reveal the deity of Christ.

Did you know
That your Baby Boy has walked
where angels trod?
When you kiss your little Baby
you kissed the face of God?

Mary, did you know
That your Baby Boy is Lord of all creation?
Mary, did you know
That your Baby Boy
would one day rule the nations?
Did you know
That your Baby Boy is heaven's perfect Lamb?
The sleeping Child you're holding
is the great "I am"

The greatest question while confronting addictions is whether Christ is worthy of our lives. This is the worship that God deserves. Two basic components of worship are recognizing the object of worship as set apart and commit ourselves to the object of worship.

1. Maintaining a sense of awe
2. Exhibit trust
3. Allowing dominion or control
4. Sacrifice
5. Give glory and praise (internally and/or externally)

December 25

Behold the light of Christ!

> And she brought forth her firstborn son, and wrapped Him in swaddling clothes, and laid Him in a manger; because there was no room for them in the inn. And there were in the same country shepherds abiding in the field, keeping watch over their flock by night. And, lo, the angel of the Lord came upon them, and the glory of the Lord shone round about them: and they were sore afraid. Luke 2:7-9 *KJV*

Some would argue whether the birth of Christ was the most glorious moment in history, or whether the day He paid for our sins on the cross was the most magnificent. One thing that we all can pretty much agree on is **that there is no glory in an addiction**. Unfortunately, the devil wants us to believe that there is.

I still remember my very first encounter with crack cocaine, and how I felt that it was what I had been looking for all my life. I did not realize how deeply Satan and my flesh had deceived me. We are warned of this in Isaiah 5:20.

> Woe unto them that call evil good, and good evil; that put darkness for light, and light for darkness; that put bitter for sweet, and sweet for bitter! Isaiah 5:20

Praise God for the light that is in Christ! John said that Jesus was the true light (John 1:9). Praise God for showing us that light! Jesus, Himself said, *"many prophets and righteous men have desired to see those things which ye see, and have not seen them; and to hear those things which ye hear, and have not heard them"* (Luke 10:24).

> Behold, a virgin shall be with child, and shall bring forth a son, and they shall call His name Emmanuel, which being interpreted is, God with us. Matthew 1:23 *KJV*

"Behold" was the word emphasized in a recital for the Christmas concert at my church. It really got my interest because I once read and meditated on all the times that the word "behold" is used in Scripture. We see "behold" used at least nine times in the Gospels pertaining to the birth of Christ. When someone beckons us to behold, they are saying this is worthy of our attention.

December 26

In the beginning

In the beginning, God created the heavens and the earth. The earth was without form and void, and darkness was over the face of the deep. Genesis 1:1-2a

In the beginning God (*Elohim*) created [by forming from nothing] the heavens and the earth. The earth was formless and void *or* a waste and emptiness, and darkness was upon the face of the deep. *Amplified Version*

Genesis 1:2 describes the peril of addiction. Some commentators say that before the creation there was only chaos. Addictions are not only formless, void, wasteful, and empty, but dark; they are chaotic as well. God is not a God of confusion.

For God is not a God of confusion but of peace. 1 Corinthians 14:33

Are you an orderly person? God is! Jesus was the most orderly, trustworthy person that ever lived on this earth! How many of us live a life that is out of order? Addiction is a worship disorder! There must be some order in the way that we combat addictions!

"Addictions are ultimately a disorder of worship. Will we worship ourselves and our own desires or will we worship the true God?" - *Addictions a Banquet in the Grave*, Edward T. Welch

One of the goals of reverence is pleasing God. In *Turning to God from Idols*, I said that this can be summed up with the words "unto the Lord." Jesus sought to please the Father above all else. ***Your reverence for God will determine where you look for the answers to addiction and how hard you search!***

My son, if you receive my words and treasure up my commandments with you, making your ear attentive to wisdom and inclining your heart to understanding; yes, if you call out for insight and raise your voice for understanding, if you seek it like silver and search for it as for hidden treasures, then you will understand the fear of the Lord and find the knowledge of God. Proverbs 2:1-5

Why not get your order from above?

December 27

His excellence (part 1)

Oh, how abundant is your goodness, which you have stored up for those who fear you and worked for those who take refuge in you, in the sight of the children of mankind! Psalms 31:19

The quality of your sobriety relies on the goodness of God in many ways. His goodness is His excellence. Psalms 31:19 reveals the excellence of God towards those who revere Him.

It is encouraging to know that God notices our faithfulness. ***The greatest compliment you will ever receive is a compliment from God.*** When God lays up good things for those who fear Him it means that He takes notice. Do you want God's attention?

There's a pretty good chance you will get God's attention if He has yours!

Blessed is the man who walks not in the counsel of the wicked, nor stands in the way of sinners, nor sits in the seat of scoffers; but **his delight is in the law of the LORD, and on his law he meditates day and night.** He is like a tree planted by streams of water that yields its fruit in its season, and its leaf does not wither. In all that he does, he prospers. The wicked are not so, but are like chaff that the wind drives away. Therefore the wicked will not stand in the judgment, nor sinners in the congregation of the righteous; for the LORD knows the way of the righteous, but the way of the wicked will perish. Psalms 1

God is not skimpy on giving. The fact that He gave His Son for a rebellious human race is proof. Romans 5:7-8 says, *"One will scarcely die for a righteous person—though perhaps for a good person one would dare even to die— but God shows his love for us in that while we were still sinners, Christ died for us."* If God did that for His enemies, just think of what He will do for His friends!

The Holy Spirit's task, then, is to unfold the meaning of Jesus's person and work to believers in such a way that the glory of it--it's infinite importance and beauty--is brought home to the mind and heart…. The Holy Spirit's ministry is to take truths about Jesus and make them clear to our minds and real to our hearts--so that they console and empower and change us at our very center. -*The Meaning of Marriage*, Timothy and Kathy Keller

December 28

His excellence (part 2)

Oh, how abundant is your goodness, which you have stored up for those who fear you and worked for those who take refuge in you, in the sight of the children of mankind! Psalms 31:19

For the LORD is a sun and shield. God gives grace and glory. The LORD does not withhold any good thing from those who walk with integrity. Psalms 84:11

Jesus said that He came to give abundant life (John 10:10). Psalms 40:5 says that the things that God has done for us cannot be numbered in order. Spurgeon said, "He does not tell us how great was God's goodness, for he could not; there are no measures which can set forth the immeasurable goodness of Jehovah, who is goodness itself. Holy amazement uses interjections where adjectives utterly fail."

Within all this, God has given us all that we need to overcome addictions. You may be surprised by the abundance of artillery that can be found in the Scriptures to fight against addiction. I am also encouraged by the increasing number of those who are helping people to see how the Scriptures relate to addictions. The title of Psalms 31 is *The Lord a Fortress in Adversity*.

A reputable source told me years ago that the word that was used for ***excellent*** in these Psalms was related to the quality of wood that was used for combat arrows. As the Israelites would not settle for anything less than the best for their weapons against their enemies, we should not settle for anything less than the best in our war against addictions!

God's most excellent Word is the ultimate weapon against addiction. And so it is that I have sought to give you the very best ammunition to combat addictions.

Addictions question the goodness of God. After the children of Israel were delivered from the bondage of Eygpt, they began to murmur over and over that God was not good enough. They even made a golden calf to take the place of God. That's what we do with addictions whenever we look down on God.

"Oh, who dare say that he is a hard Master? Who that knows him will say that he is an unkind friend? Oh, what do poor creatures all, that they do entertain such harsh sour thoughts of God?" -James Janeway

December 29

His excellence (part 3)

Oh, how abundant is your goodness, which you have stored up for those who fear you and worked for those who take refuge in you, in the sight of the children of mankind! Psalms 31:19

"Tell me, oh sinner, what is it that you get in ways of sin that makes you want to abide there? What is it the world has to draw your heart from the strength of all these truths delivered in these sermons? Surely it must be some mighty thing when such truths as these, backed with arguments from Scripture and strength of reason, cannot restrain you. Surely it must be some wonderful things that must outweigh all these sermons and all these things. What, have you such a heart that is set upon any sinful way, any secret haunt of sin. That you find such good in? That by it all these truths are outweighed? Certainly there is no such good in the world."
-*The Evil of Evils,* Jeremiah Burroughs

The awe factor of God's goodness is truly amazing. Sadly, we may think that addictions are amazing. John Piper once said that "disillusionment often follows naïve admiration." There is no deficiency in God as there is in addictions. To mature in the Lord is to know Him better and better.

Unfortunately, it is not always easy to see God's goodness. The psalmist said that he would lose heart if he did not believe that he would see God's goodness in the land of the living (Psalms 27:13).

Addictions can disrupt our vision like that. Addictions remind us that we live in a world that is out of order. The goodness that God has stored up in Christ is beyond compare!

It has been testified somewhere, "What is man, that you are mindful of him, or the son of man, that you care for him? You made him for a little while lower than the angels; you have crowned him with glory and honor putting everything in subjection under his feet." Now in putting everything in subjection to him, he left nothing outside his control. **At present, we do not yet see everything in subjection to him.** But we see him who for a little while was made lower than the angels, namely Jesus, crowned with glory and honor because of the suffering of death, so that by the grace of God he might taste death for everyone. Hebrews 2:6-9

December 30

My times are in Your hands! (part 1)

My times are in your hand; rescue me from the hand of my enemies and from my persecutors! Psalms 31:1-3, 15

In Psalms 31, David was expressing his need for security. Have you found yourself in need of security throughout the year while wrestling with the issues of life? What do you look to for comfort and security?

> **"Are in thy hand,** i.e. are wholly in thy power, to dispose and order as thou seest fit, and not at all in mine enemies' power, who can do nothing against me, unless it be given them from above."
> *-Matthew Poole's Commentary*

> My times are in thy hand. "My times," **i.e.** "all the varied events, happy or sad, which make up the parti-coloured web of life" (Kay)
> *-Pulpit Commentary*

David found himself in a similar situation when at odds with his son Absalom. Though David was not perfect, he had developed the habit of calling on the Lord. That is why he was called "a man after God's own heart." Abiding in Christ is the most essential element of sobriety.

> "From the end of the earth will I cry unto thee, when my heart is overwhelmed: lead me to the rock that is higher than I. Psalm 61:2 'It is thought that David probably wrote this psalm at the time that he had been in exile as the result of the rebellion of Absalom. ... From the end of the earth (Psalms 61:2) ... In other words, 'Man, this is it. This is the end of the world. This is as far as I can go. This is as deep as I can get. This is it. ... Many things can cause our hearts to be overwhelmed: the loss of loved ones, financial problems, the loss of a job, the loss of health. So many things can cause our hearts to be overwhelmed. What do I do? When I get to the end of the proverbial rope, when I have no place else to turn, where do I turn? What do I do? Every one of us are driven by circumstances, sooner or later, to this end of the road type of an experience, where I have no place else to go, no place else to turn. And where I turn at this point is so important. Some people turn to pills, some people turn to the bottle, some people turn to a gun and just try to end it all. 'When my heart is overwhelmed,' David said, lead me to the rock that is higher than I' (v. 2)." *-Chuck Smith Bible Commentary*

December 31

My times are in Your hands! (part 2)

My times are in your hand; rescue me from the hand of my enemies and from my persecutors! Psalms 31:1-3, 15

David often found himself in danger as we are when confronted with trials and temptations. Every trial and temptation is an opportunity to grow in your love for God and become more like Christ.

For we do not have a high priest who is unable to sympathize with our weaknesses, but one who in every respect has been tempted as we are, yet without sin. Hebrews 4:15

In the days of his flesh, Jesus offered up prayers and supplications, with loud cries and tears, to him who was able to save him from death, and he was heard because of his reverence. Although he was a son, he learned obedience through what he suffered. And being made perfect, he became the source of eternal salvation to all who obey him. Hebrews 5:7-9

The fear of the Lord is the ultimate solution to the puzzle of idolatry. Becoming more and more like Jesus is the epitome of reverencing God. Abiding in Christ is equivalent to perpetual reverence.

I hope that you have found joy in Jesus this year and that in the coming new year, you will continue to find increasing joy in Him. May you savor Christ as He is worthy above all that you can imagine.

When you look to the light that is found in Christ, you will not only disdain the darkness of addiction, but you will be able to lead others. .

For you have not come to what may be touched, a blazing fire and darkness and gloom and a tempest and the sound of a trumpet and a voice whose words made the hearers beg that no further messages be spoken to them. For they could not endure the order that was given, "If even a beast touches the mountain, it shall be stoned." Indeed, so terrifying was the sight that Moses said, "I tremble with fear." But you have come to Mount Zion and to the city of the living God, the heavenly Jerusalem, and to innumerable angels in festal gathering, and to the assembly[a] of the firstborn who are enrolled in heaven, and to God, the judge of all, and to the spirits of the righteous made perfect, and to Jesus, the mediator of a new covenant, and to the sprinkled blood that speaks a better word than the blood of Abel. Hebrews 12:18-24

A simple formula

Turning to God from Idols is a simple formula for dealing with addictions biblically. As the saying goes- "easier said than done." Though you may be struggling with one addiction, you can rest assured that there may be others that you have not noticed or one that may gain your future affection.

Some addictions are accepted by society and yet hideous to God. Other addictions are neither socially acceptable nor pleasing to God. (Those are the ones that people are usually most concerned about because they yield pain.)

I urge you to be diligent in your studies and to be transparent before God, as well as others. I think that it is safe to say that you will find the elements of reason, repentance, and rejoicing within any and every program that deals with addictions, in one form or another (although it may be expressed in other words.)

A Biblical approach to addictions in its simplest form is a proclamation of Jesus Christ being worthy of the throne of our lives above all else because of the blood that He shed on the cross and the fact that He is KING OF KINGS AND LORD OF LORDS. I think that the most ingenious approach to addictions is to start by viewing them as idols. I am truly grateful for how God began to show me this fact years ago along with its implications. He showed me how we worship something or someone by allowing them/it to dominate us.

Reason

The reasoning that is needed in phase one is God's reasoning. As the Scripture says, "There is a way that appears to be right, but in the end it leads to death" (Proverbs 14:12). Without God's reasoning, you will never fully see the depth and the severity of addictions. If we do not see the depth and severity of addictions, I doubt if you would want to make any changes.

You must be in tune with the goals that God has for you. Tony Evans said that reverencing God means that "we take God seriously." You must decide that you want to change in the way that God wants you to change, for the same reasons that God wants us to change. As you stand before the Lord, you must consider your motives.

That which honors God and benefits us best is done out of reverence toward God. It is within this reasoning that you discover how addictions not only dishonor God, they have no lasting value, and that all mankind is vulnerable to addictions. And the main reason that addictions dishonor God is that they are idols.

To begin the process of change you need to be soundly convinced of the nature of addiction. In this process, you not only consider the apparent assets of our addictions but their liabilities (as well as their spiritual implications.) It is with an accurate judgment that we label addictions as idols because of the worship that is expressed toward them. Whenever you worship something or someone you make sacrifices, relinquish control, esteem praise, and you bestow trust, as well as demonstrate awe.

Our reasoning leads us to the remarkable discovery that the Scriptures have a lot to say about addictions. I believe that **if the Word of God had nothing to say about addictions then God would not have created us**. We can see the various aspects of addictions displayed in the Bible.

Repent

And so, if addiction is idolatry, then is it a sin? If addiction is a sin, then it is something that we can repent of. Repentance is to turn from self and to follow Christ. As the Spirit of God gives us conviction over addictions and concerning the truth of Jesus Christ, then we are led in repentance by the Word of God. (By the way, no one repents from a disease!)

> Let the wicked forsake his way, and the unrighteous man his thoughts: and let him return unto the Lord, and He will have mercy upon him; and to our God, for He will abundantly pardon. For My thoughts are not your thoughts, neither are your ways My ways, saith the Lord. For as the heavens are higher than the earth, so are My ways higher than your ways, and My thoughts than your thoughts. Isaiah 55:7-9 (*KJV*)

Repentance is marked and led by brokenness. The brokenness that is necessary for repentance requires that you abandon your pride and practice humbling yourself. Self-denial allows you the greatest intimacy with the Almighty that is humanly possible.

Repentance from addiction towards Christ requires action. Abstinence and communion with God and with other believers are mandatory. Fasting is very highly recommended.

Abstinence is to be done without any reservations. We avoid anything that is even remotely associated with the addictions that we once clung to as Jude says, "hating even the garments spotted by flesh." (Jude 23) Upon our repentance, we will be tempted to return to our idols. Your fasting and communion with God and with others will give us the strength that we need to remain sound-mindedly sober

Since fasting is an act of self-denial, then we can see why fasting was often done during biblical days in association with repentance. I cannot overemphasize the benefit of fasting for those of us that have once given ourselves to addiction. Whatever form of fasting that we choose, so long as we do it out of reverence for God rather than for selfish reasons, then the Lord truly will take notice!

Could it be that the aim of repentance is our fellowship with God as well as others? Did not Jesus say that the greatest commandment is to love the Lord your God with all your heart, your soul, and your mind and the second greatest is to love your neighbor as yourself? (Matthew 22:37-39). Also, the Westminster Shorter Catechism says that "**Man's chief end is to glorify God, and to enjoy him forever."**

Our fellowship with God requires that we listen to God, we talk with God, and we do what God says. We choose the people we fellowship with. We decide the degree of intimacy we have with others as well. Intimate involvement with a Bible-based support group is highly recommended for those who have been bound to addictions. Intimate involvement among all believers should be a common practice.

It is within our repentance that we put down bad habits and develop and practice good habits. The acts of repentance that I have given to you are the core essentials for pulling down the strongholds of addictions.

Rejoice

And so, after we are led by God in our reasoning and repenting, He causes us to rejoice. We rejoice that we have an unbreakable bond with God because of the forgiveness of our sins through the blood of Christ. We rejoice that we are no longer slaves to sin through Christ (that includes idolatry or whatever else displeases God.) We rejoice in the person that God has created us to be. We rejoice in the people that God has placed in our lives. We rejoice in the Lord.

The joy that we have occurs automatically as a result of our repentance. As we walk in the Spirit, God blesses us with the fruit of the Spirit (which contains joy, Galatians 5:22.) Although true joy can only be produced by the Spirit of God, it is also a practice that we are called to uphold. Joy is like every other blessing that God would have us to partake of that no one can keep us from having except us.

Have a meeting

I once talked with a woman who could not understand why people who have found a way out of addiction don't help others. While I have emphasized the reverential factor that is needed to overcome addictions, I had not mentioned the idea of reverencing God by helping others.

A reverential attitude recognizes that God is worthy of the person who is enslaved by addiction. A reverential attitude also loves others as God does and recognizes that each of us is priceless and that God has a use for us all. A reverential attitude longs for others to find the joy of an unbroken fellowship with God while delighting to reflect His glory.

Since there is a great need for Christ-centered meetings, I am giving you the format for one. Maybe you could use the readings of *Reveremtially Turning to God from Idols* for discussions.

What Matters Most

Music

This meeting is dedicated to the following proposition: There is no better answer to addiction than what we have in Jesus Christ!

> His divine power has granted to us all things that pertain to life and godliness, through the knowledge of him who called us to his own glory and excellence. 2 Peter 1:3

This group was formed to provide spiritual insight, fellowship, and support for those who desire to be cleansed of addictions and celebrate the joyful sobriety that is found in Jesus Christ. The Word of God declares that anything that we place before God is an idol.

The best reason for abstaining from addiction is to give God the glory that He deserves. When our greatest pleasure is in God, then the idols of addiction lose their power!

A biblical solution to addiction involves a higher yearning! *A love for God and an appreciation for His blessings will ever remain the highest and strongest deterrent against addiction.*

And one of them, a lawyer, asked him a question to test him. "Teacher, which is the great commandment in the Law?" And he said to him, "You shall love the Lord your God with all your heart and with all your soul and with all your mind. This is the great and first commandment. And a second is like it: You shall love your neighbor as yourself. Matthew 22:35-39

The fear of the LORD is the beginning of wisdom; all those who practice it have a good understanding. His praise endures forever! Psalm 111:10

Opening Prayer

Why do we use the Word of God?

In *Addictions: A Banquet in the Grave*, Edward T. Welch asks his readers, "Do you have a good grasp on the wealth of biblical material that speaks precisely to the modern problems of addictions? Can you go through any book in scripture, even if it doesn't mention alcohol, food, or sex, and see how it speaks to addictions?"

Using the Word of God to expose and dispose of addiction is an act of worship. When we share the Word of God to confront addiction, we see God as worthy of being heard.

Worship was originally spelled "worthship" and it means to express worth. The fear of the Lord cannot leave us indifferent to the Word of God; when we fear him, we sense the infinite weightiness of His Word.

All Scripture is breathed out by God and profitable for teaching, for reproof, for correction, and for training in righteousness, that the man of God may be complete, equipped for every good work.
2 Timothy 3:16-17

I appeal to you therefore, brothers, by the mercies of God, to present your bodies as a living sacrifice, holy and acceptable to God, which is your spiritual worship. Do not be conformed to this world, but be transformed by the renewal of your mind, that by testing you may discern what is the will of God, what is good and acceptable and perfect. Romans 12:1-2

Introduction

What Matters Most is here to strengthen your convictions over addiction, to provide fellowship and support to those who struggle, and to celebrate the freedom from addiction that is found in Jesus Christ.

We ask that all participants:

1. We ask that what is said in the group remains confidential.
2. Refrain from responding to each other's comments directly (for the sake of time.)
3. Refrain from profanity.

Getting to know you

Who are you?
Why are you here?

> "Christ-centered counseling involves understanding the nature and courses of our human difficulties, understanding the ways we are unlike Christ in our values, aspirations, desires, thoughts, feelings, choices, attitudes, actions, and responses. Resolving those sin-related difficulties includes being redeemed and justified through Christ, receiving God's forgiveness through Christ, and acquiring from Christ the enabling power to replace unChristlike (sinful) patterns of life with Christlike, godly ones." -*The Distinguishing Feature of Christian Counseling*, Dr. Wayne Mack

Discussion (one of the following)

1. A quality reading from a Christian source on addictions (from our files or other sources)
2. A message
a. in person
b. a recording or video
3. A chosen topic
4. Open discussion (everybody just shares where they're at)

Sharing
Wrap up (the moderator shares insight concerning the discussion time.)

Invitation to Christ

> Because you have said, "We have made a covenant with death, and with Sheol we have an agreement, when the overwhelming whip passes through it will not come to us, for we have made lies our refuge, and in falsehood we have taken shelter" Isaiah 28:15

Addictions are like the covenant of death that Israel made. Death separates. Jesus unites and gives life. If you have never given your life to Christ, I would like to invite you to do so at this time.

> And he died for all, that those who live might no longer live for themselves but for him who for their sake died and was raised. 2 Corinthians 5:15

Closing

"Imagine having drug cravings subdued by the joy of knowing and obeying Christ. Imagine having temptations lose their allure because there is more pleasure in walking humbly with our God. Imagine waking up and strategizing how to please the God who loves you rather than where you will get your next drink." -Dr. Edward T. Welch

Music

Prayer

Bibliography

Adams, Jay, *How to Help People Change* (Zondervan, 1986)
Adams, Thomas, quoted
Alcoholics Anonymous
Anselm, *Proslogion*
Baker Theological Dictionary of the Bible (Baker Academic, 2001)
Barrett, Michael P.V., *Union with Christ: the Ground of Sanctification*
Beale, G.K., *We Become What We Worship* (InterVarsity Press, 2008)
Berg, Jim, *Changed into His Image,* (Bob Jones University Press, 1999)
Bertrand, J., Mark, *Rethinking Worldview: Learning to Think, Live, and Speak in This World* (Crossway, October 2007)
Biblestudyministry.com 89
Bigney, Brad, *Gospel Treason* (P&R Publishing 2012)
Black Lives Matter
Bonaparte, Napoleon, quoted
Bowen, George, quoted
Bridges, Jerry, quote
Bridges, Jerry, *Discipline of Grace* (NavPress, 2006)
Bunyan, John, *Holy War* (Whitaker, 2001)
Burroughs, Jeremiah, *The Evil of Evils,* (1992, Soli Deo Gloria Publications)
Burroughs, Jeremiah, *The Rare Jewel of Christian Contentment* (public domain)
Called to be a Soldier, (Salvation Army 2020)
Calvin John, quote
Carlson, John, K., quote
Caryl Joseph, quoted
Chalmers, Thomas, *The Expulsive Power of a New Affection* Curiosmith (May 8, 2012)
Chambers, Oswald, *The Complete Works of Oswald Chambers*, (Oswald Chambers Publications Associations, Limited, 2000)
Chesterton, G. K., quoted
Cleveland, Mike, *Pure Freedom: Breaking the Addiction to Pornography* (Focus Pub. 2002)
Cleveland, Mike, *95 Theses for Pure Reformation* (FOCUS PUB Incorporated, 2003)
Circuelle Foundation
Collins Dictionary
Cool Hand Luke (Warner Brothers, 1967)
Cynthiasass.com
Dictionary.com
Delffs, Dudley J., A Repentant Heart (NavPress, 1995)
Draper Debra, *Jesus the Cornerstone of our faith,* The Woodland News
Duncan, Ligon, quote
Dunham, David R., *Addictive Habits: Changing for Good* (P & R Publishing, 2018)
Edwards, Jonathan, *Treatise on Religious Affections*
Enduringword.com

Englishbaby.com
Etymonline.com
Evans, Tony, *Fearing God*
(video sermon series, The Urban Alternative)
Frame, James, quoted
French of Daniel de Superville
Funk and Wagnalls Standard Dictionary
Gallagher, Steve, *At the Altar of Sexual Idolatry* (pure Life Ministries, 1986)
Goodwin, Thomas, quoted
Google Dictionary
gotquestions.org/prosperity-gospel.html
Guiness, Os, quote
Gurnall, William, quotation
Hancock, Jimmie, L., *All the Questions in the Bible*
Henry, Matthew, quoted
How Addiction Hijacks the Brain, A Harvard Health article
Hurnard, Hannah, *Hinds' Feet on High Places* (Tyndale House Publishers, Inc. 1975)
Idleman, Kyle, *gods at war*, (Zondervan, 2013)
Idioms.thefreedictionary.com
Incomparable Christ (author unknown)
Interpreter's Dictionary of the Bible (Abingdon Press 2009)
Janeway, James, quoted
Jay, William, quoted
Jones, Bob, Sr., Dr., quoted
Journal of Biological Chemistry
Joy to the World, Isaac Watts
Keller, Tim, *Counterfeit gods*, (Dutton, a member of Penguin Group, 2009
Keller, Timothy and Kathy, *The Meaning of Marriage* (Dutton, 2011)
Keller, W., Phillip, *A Shepherd Looks at Psalm 23* (Zondervan, 2015)
Lewis, C.S., *Mere Christianity* (HarperOne, 2015)
Lewis, C.S., *Prince Caspian* (HarperOne, 2002)
Lewis, C.S., *The Weight of Glory* (HarperOne, 2001)
Lewis, Marc, *The Biology of Desire: Why Addiction is Not a Disease,* (PublicAffairs; Reprint edition, August 23, 2016)
Link, Julie Ackerman, *Loving God with all My Heart,*
(Discovery House Publishers, 2004)
Lockyer, Herbert, *All the Divine Names and Titles in the Bible* (Zondervan, 1975)
Lucado, Max, quoted
MacArthur, John, *Hard to Believe* (2010, Thomas Nelson)
MacArthur, John, *MacArthur Study Bible* (Thomas Nelson, 1997)
MacDonald, George, quoted
Mack, Wayne A., *The Distinguishing Feature of Christian Counseling* (article)
Maclaren's Exposition of the Bible (Eerdmans's, 1959)
Madison, Gregory L., *Addiction: A Tug of War* (2021, The Awe Factory)
Madison, Gregory, *Addictions Tugging* (2022, The Awe Factory)
Madison, Gregory L., *Bible Verses Addictions: all Volumes* (2018, Awe of My Life Publications)

Madison, Gregory L., *Bible Verses Addictions: Psalms 119 Volume 1* (2019, Awe of My Life Publications)
Madison, Gregory L., Carlson, John K., *Biblical Quotes that Expose Addiction Volume One* (2021, The Awe Factory)
Madison, Gregory L., *The Fear of the Almighty* (2019, Awe of My Life Publications)
Madison, Gregory L., *The Highest Yearning* (2021, The Awe Factory)
Madison, Gregory L., *Quality Sobriety* (2021, The Awe Factory)
Madison, Gregory L., *Why Not Get High* (2020, Awe of My Life Publications)
Madison, Gregory L., *Yearning Over Addiction* (2020, The Awe Factory)
Manton, Thomas, *Exposition of the Epistle of James* (2001, Sovereign Grace Publisher's Inc)
Martin, Albert N., *The Forgotten Fear: Where have all the God-fearers gone?* (2015, Reformation Heritage Books)
Martin, Walter, *The Kingdom of the Cults* (Bethany House Publishers, Revised and Expanded Edition, 1985)
Mason, Eric, *Manhood Restored* (Lifeway Press, 2015)
Matthew Poole's Commentary
McCarthy, Cormac, *The Sunset Limited (play)*
McDowell, Josh, *Evidence Demands a Verdict* (Thomas Nelson, 2017)
Meadors, Edward P., *Idolatry and the Hardening of the Heart* (T&T Clark, 2006)
Merriam-Webster Dictionary
Morison, John, quoted
Muller, George, quoted
Mullins, Jeff, *My Beloved Addiction* (2019)
Murray, Andrew, *Abide in Christ* (Whitaker House, 2002)
Murray, Andrew, *Humility: The Journey Towards Holiness* (Bethany House Publishers, 2001)
Narcotics Anonymous
Okoh, Karleen, Elizabeth, quoted
Openbible.com/info/topics
Ortlund, Dane, *Gentle and Lowly: The Heart of Christ for Sinners and Sufferers* (2020, Crossway)
Owen, John, *The Mortification of Sin* (TradLife Press, 2013)
Oxford Dictionary
Packer, J.I., *Knowing God* (InterVarsity Press, 1973)
Patheos.com
Pascal, *Pensees*
Peterson, Eugene H., *A Long Obedience in the Same Direction* (IVP Press, 2021)
Piper, John, *Desiring God* (Multnomah, 1986)
Piper, John, *A Hunger for God* (Crossway Books, 1997)
Pink, A.W., quoted
Platt, David, quoted
Prosperity Gospel, www.hopefortheheart
PsychCheck, Phanatik, (Cross Movement Records, 2004)
Psychology Today
Pulpit Commentary
Quality Christian Resources on Addiction (Facebook page)
Rolls, C. J., quoted

Ryle, J. C., quoted
Ryrie, Charles C., *The Ryrie Study Bible* (Zondervan, 1986)
Saint Augustine, quote
Saint Jerome, quote
Salvation Army Soldiership Class Manual (Salvation Army)
Serenity at Summit
Shaw, Mark E., *Cross Talking: A Daily Gospel for Transforming Addicts* (FOCUS Publishing, 2010)
Shaw, Mark E., *The Heart of Addiction: A Biblical Perspective* (FOCUS Publishing, 2008)
Silva, Jason, quote
Sobertool.com
Spurgeon, C.H., quoted
Spurgeon, C. H., *The Treasury of David* (1988, Hendrickson Pub.)
Spurstowe, William, *The Wiles of Satan* (CreateSpace Independent Pub. Platform, 2016)
Smith, Chuck, *Chuck Smith Bible Commentary*
Smith, Randy, quote
Stonegableblog.com
Strong, James, *Strong's Exhaustive Concordance of the Bible*, (Hunt and Eaton, 1894)
Thompson-Chain Reference Bible, (HarperCollinsChristian Publishing, 2020)
To Sir with Love (Columbia Pictures, 1967)
Tozer A.W., *The Knowledge of the Holy* (New York: Harper-Collins Publishers, 1961)
Tripp, Paul, *Awe: Why It Matters for Everything We Think, Say, and Do* (Crossway, 2015)
Unger, Merrill F., Harrison, R.K., *New Unger's Bible Dictionary* (Moody Publishers, 2006)
Venning, Ralph, *The Sinfulness of Sin* (The Banner of Truth Trust, 1965, first published in 1669)
Vine's Expository Dictionary of Biblical Words
Websters Dictionary
Vocabulary.com
Wakanda Forever (Marvel Studio, 2022)
Welch, Edward T., *Addictions: A Banquet in the Grave* (P&R Publishing, 2001)
Welch, Edward T., *Crossroads: a step-by-step guide away from addiction* (New Growth Press, 2008)
Welch, Edward T., *Just One More,* (P & R Publishing, April 1, 2002)
Wesley, Susanna, quote
Westminster Catechism
Whiskey Glasses, (Morgan Wallen, 2018)
Wikipedia
Williams, Charles, *The Fundamentals*, vol. 3
Yearning Machines: Every Human is an Addict

If you or someone that you know needs constant aid, I have several Facebook pages that have frequent entries.

Bible Verses Addictions
https://www.facebook.com/groups/bibleversesaddictions

High Sobriety Society
https://www.facebook.com/groups/thebestanswer

Quality Christian Resources on Addictions
https://www.facebook.com/groups/jesusbringssobriety

Books by Gregory Madison include:

Turning to God from Idols
Turning to God from Idols Workbook
Bible Verses Addictions (series of 7)
The Fear of the Almighty
Why <u>Not</u> Get High
Yearning Over Addictions
Quality Sobriety series
The Highest Yearning
Biblical Quotes Exposing Addiction
Biblical Quotes for Addiction Disposal
Addiction: A Tug of War
Addictions Tugging (the workbook)

Go to www.turningtogodfromidols.com
for a preview of my books.

Made in the USA
Middletown, DE
17 January 2025

68763413R00215